To The Summit

TO
THE
SUMMIT

Margo Chisholm
and Ray Bruce

AVON BOOKS ◆ NEW YORK

AVON BOOKS
A division of
The Hearst Corporation
1350 Avenue of the Americas
New York, New York 10019

Library of Congress Cataloging in Publication Data:
Chisholm, Margo.
   To the summit : a woman's journey into the mountains to find her soul / Margo Chisholm and Ray Bruce.
      p.   cm.
   1. Chisholm, Margo. 2. Women mountaineers—United States—Biography. 3. Recovering addicts—United States—Biography. 4. Mountaineering—Himalaya Mountains. I. Bruce, Ray. II. Title.
GV199.92.C45A3   1997   96-45210
796.52'2'092—dc21   CIP

First Avon Books Printing: March 1997

FIRST EDITION

QM   10   9   8   7   6   5   4   3   2   1

To Jonathan, who planted the seed;
to Skip, who mentored its growth;
and to God, who made it all possible.

In memory of Rob Hall and Gary Ball,
who climbed from their hearts.

—MJC

To my spirit for willing itself to live when I'd almost
killed it; to my mother, Genevieve, for her example
of a life lived well; and to my daughters, Kimberly
and Kristin, and grandson, Michael, for the lives you
are living.

—RCB

To The Summit

CHAPTER ONE

I Can!

Saturday, April 18, 1992, Mount Everest, Camp II
Things have turned rotten. I don't want it to end
like this. Part of me wants to go home. Part
of me wants to find out how high I can go. I
just feel I can go higher than this.

The deep, wracking cough violently snaps me back into the reality of living in the shadow of the world's highest summit. The fabric of my tent protects me from the wind, but unfriendly tentacles of bitter cold reach deeply into my bones. I pull my body into a tight ball, trying to find some residual warmth in the depths of my sleeping bag, and make a futile attempt to adapt to the rock and ice under my body. Surrounded by men, mountains, and ice, I've been working, eating, and sleeping at Camp II, 21,500 feet high on the south side of Mount Everest for the past nine days: only 8,000 feet from my dream of standing on its summit. Sleep has become increasingly elusive, and I'm losing vital energy to the altitude and the cough.

As my muscles begin to relax and my mind drifts back to the memory of that peaceful place beyond the searing pain in my chest, one cough, then another, echoes of my own, ricochet like rifle shots off the walls of the Western Cwm. There's something heavy and ominous in those coughs, something more than the usual dry hacks ever present on high-altitude climbs.

Casual greetings sound out as tent flies and bulky expedition-weight jackets rustle and then are zipped closed against the biting elements.

The harsh metallic scraping of backpacks, climbing gear, and crampons being moved across rocks and ice soon follow. I surrender, turn over, and open my eyes as the first soft yellow glow of filtered light gives a false sense of brightness to the day.

Six of my climbing partners are going up to Camp III, another 2,000 feet closer to our goal. I'm not going with them. I'm too ill, too weak to exert the energy the climb will demand. Even if I were to force myself, push through the congestion in my head and chest and try to shut down the pain, I'd be too slow. My weakness would risk my safety and that of the others. Those of us remaining at Camp II make up half our expedition. The others have already returned to Base Camp to recuperate and heal.

Soon, the familiar squeak of crampons on ice is the only sound I hear as my companions make their way up the Cwm, the incredibly beautiful valley connecting the Khumbu Icefall to the face of Lhotse and the South Col on Mount Everest itself. Failure settles around me like a fog, oppressive, filling in behind the fading voices. Finally, there's nothing but silence.

I feel numb, as the increasing light picks out my backpack, parka, and other climbing gear piled close to me. They taunt me, calling me to climb, leaving me feeling helpless and abandoned like Jonah in the belly of the whale. I crave the warmth of human contact, but there's only the emptiness left by my tentmate, John Helenek, who went down to Base Camp three days ago, too sick to stay.

While John was packing his gear early that morning, Todd Burleson, our expedition leader, had stuck his head in the tent. "What do you think, Margo? You need to go down, too?"

Still in my sleeping bag, I rolled over and with more enthusiasm than I felt, said, "Nope. Not today. I'm not ready to go down yet." John was stuffing his own sleeping bag into its protective nylon cover. "I can still get to three: I got up to the fixed line at the Lhotse face yesterday. One more rest day will make the difference." That was Wednesday. Thursday and Friday I felt worse than ever.

This climb is longer and higher than any of my other major ascents, pushing me past all of my old limits. I've held up as well as most of my companions and better than some under the extreme conditions. At this altitude we're almost two-thirds of the way out of the earth's atmosphere, and the temperature swings wildly from sweltering heat in the direct sun to freezing cold in the shadows. Sunburned lips, smelly clothes, and gross hair become part of the routine of life. Then there is the joy of using pee bottles, and the strange mixture of fear and embarrassment while squatting over a narrow crevasse for a bathroom. The fact that I'm the only woman climber on the expedition hasn't seemed to affect the others. No one is making any allowances for me, and I'm not asking for any. This is Mount Everest.

Last night as I was going into the dining tent for dinner, I caught up with Skip Horner, one of the lead climbers for our expedition and my climbing mentor. "Can I talk to you for a minute? I've got a problem." I was hesitant, unsure about what I needed to say.

"Sure." Skip's voice was soothing.

"There's no way I'm going to get up there tomorrow." I was losing perspective and my words tripped over the fear and vulnerability growing inside. "Don't have the strength. Don't know what's up. Something is, and I'm just not right. I feel like a complete wimp." Disappointment swept over me, and I turned away so he wouldn't see my tears.

"Margo, you're no wimp." His arm felt solid and sure as he put it around my shoulders. "I've seen you prove that. It's good that you know your body well enough to know you can't go up tomorrow. So you go down to Base Camp, maybe even to Pheriche. It doesn't mean you're done. You'll get strong again, then you'll be back up here."

I looked up at his face, trying to see the truth behind the words, searching for a source of strength I didn't feel inside. We stood there for just a minute before I said, "Thanks," and he went into dinner. I remembered the first time I met Skip, four years ago at the airport in Nairobi. I was there to climb Mount Kenya and Mount Kilimanjaro, and he was the guide. Since then he'd been with me on seven of the twenty-three mountains I'd climbed, and I was here on Mount Everest at his invitation. He'd never lied to me before; there wasn't any reason for me to think he was lying now. He'd always been encouraging, helping me to examine my fears and to reach for dreams I didn't even know I had when we first met. I walked a little way from the mess tent to let my tears flow freely before going in.

Now, in my sleeping bag, I hold back new tears, not wanting my success or failure on this mountain to be determined by illness, not quite trusting my own ability to know what is real or imagined. Today, my mind is the only part of me working up to my old standards. Thinking, evaluating, judging, that's what it does best. I desperately fight the negative voice in my head I call Martha. She's been with me since I was a young girl, and now she tells me, "You're still eight thousand feet from the summit and at this rate you'll never make it. Whatever made you think you had the right to be here anyway? Turn this cough and weakness into a big deal, get some sympathy, and just forget about the summit."

And, no matter how many mountains I climb, she's there. Martha always finds negative images from my childhood and early adult years and says, "See, this is how you are."

I speak out loud as if she's really present. "Stop it. I'm not doing that anymore. I'm here, on Mount Everest. I may be sick, but I'm not through with this mountain and I'm sure as hell not faking this." The force of my angry reaction triggers a spasm of coughing that hurts deep inside my chest. It doesn't weaken my resolve.

The sun follows its path across the roof of my yellow cave as I spend the day reading, listening to John Denver tapes, and writing in my journal. I wait, cough, and am up and down emotionally so many times I'm nearly as worn out as the rest of the team when they return from Camp III. It takes all of the energy I can gather to pull on the three layers of clothing that protect me from the cold before I go outside to greet them. Shadows deepen across the Western Cwm in the setting sun. The black pyramid of the southwest face of Mount Everest hovers directly above me. Tears well up in my eyes and I swallow hard. I'm so grateful to be here, yet at the same time, so fearful my sickness means I will fail.

I stay as separate from the group as I can during dinner. I only answer the few questions directed my way and work hard not to make eye contact with anyone. I hardly eat any of the bland soup and rice curry prepared by the Sherpa cook. Even the mess-tent stories and laughter can't pull me out of my funk. It doesn't help to know that everyone else is coughing and some sound even worse than me. I go back to my tent, resigned to retreat to Base Camp in the morning without making it to Camp III and terrified that whatever the doctor finds might end my chances of getting to the summit.

Throughout the night nearly every tent is shaken by spasms of coughing. I sleep sporadically, coughing and thinking, anticipating tomorrow's descent through the Khumbu Icefall; it can be deadly. I see myself clipping and unclipping into the fixed line, feel the way my crampons bite into the ice and their instability while crossing the ladders. Then, Martha appears to take me back through it again, pointing out where I'm going to have trouble and why I'll fail.

"Stop it!" Like some child awakened in a nightmare, I rail against her in my half sleep. "I'm going to get down and I'm going to get healthy so I can make it to the summit. You'll see." Finally, just before dawn, I fall into a deep, dreamless sleep.

The trip down the Western Cwm from Camp II past Camp I to Base Camp should have taken four hours. This one took seven. Two thousand vertical feet of ice, the Khumbu Icefall is one of the most dangerous factors in climbing the south side of Mount Everest. Crevasses open and close seemingly overnight. Seracs, blocks of ice as big as buildings, fall over without warning. High above the Icefall avalanches break loose, sounding like artillery cannon. Ice and snow thunder past one face or another, gaining momentum, coming to rest only after they cover everything at the bottom of their slide.

Winding my way through the traverses at the base of the Cwm and into the Icefall, I begin to cough so hard it sends my breathing into spasms. I stop and double over just to keep from falling. Other climbers pass me, moving at their own pace, in their own world. It seems that any exertion or tensing of my chest muscles triggers the coughing. I work twice as hard as usual in a vain attempt to control my breathing so I won't knock myself off a ladder or fall into a crevasse. No matter how deep they are, all the crevasses look bottomless to me. Because of the constant danger, the route through the Icefall is fixed with ropes secured by a variety of ice screws, pickets, and carabiners, providing a tenuous railing of sorts and anchors in case of a fall. Eight-foot aluminum ladders are used to cross crevasses and climb the seracs. Sometimes three or four lengths are bolted or tied together to form a safe but rather unstable bridge.

Walking across a crevasse using ladder rungs for stepping stones while wearing metal crampons on plastic climbing boots and carrying a full pack is a challenge under the best of circumstances; this particular day it's almost impossible. My body is tense from the effort of not coughing, and sweat trickles from beneath the frames of the glacier glasses that both protect my eyes from the glaring sun and hide the tears that mix with the sweat. I feel sick—and scared.

I look down at the four-ladders-long bridge I am crossing, working hard to stay focused on the metal rungs rather than the dark blue of the chasm yawning below. Hook the back points of my crampon on one rung, the front points on the next and shift my weight. Breathe. Good. Now do it again. No, don't cough yet. Not yet. Shallow breaths. That's it. Now do it again. Now another step. I finally reach the other side of the ladder and realize that my hands are clenched so tightly around the carabiners clipped to the fixed lines that I have to force them open. I open the gate of each carabiner and unhook them from the thin lines. Finally a deep breath.

The resulting cough knifes through my chest, forcing me to bend over. Breathe, slowly, easily, a shallow breath—a nearly impossible task at 18,500 feet. Still bent over I reach down and clip into the next fixed line. I can see the next ladder only 50 feet away. Where is Skip? I need Skip to tell me I can do this. But he is long gone, moving at a healthier, stronger pace. This descent is mine and mine alone. Before I came to Mount Everest, other climbers told me this mountain would test everything I have. By the time I unclip myself from the fixed line for the last time and begin the long slog toward our tents, I don't have the energy or the desire to take any more tests.

Base Camp looks like a small village. Eleven expeditions representing six different countries have set up their tents on the still-active Khumbu Glacier. Canvas, nylon, and plastic of many colors create a variety of shapes and sizes, standing in stark contrast to the rock-strewn ice all around them. People from America, India, New Zealand, Spain, Russia, Holland, and Nepal work and play in multicolored clothing surrounded by climbing gear, stacks of equipment boxes, and assorted antennae, including small satellite dishes. Expedition flags and national flags join the ever-present prayer flags that fly from poles set up during the Puja, a Buddhist ceremony of blessing performed before any Sherpa will set foot on this mountain they call Sagarmatha, the Mother Goddess of the Universe.

Soon after I arrive, everyone has returned from Camp II. We're in such bad shape that Todd calls Jan, the doctor from the New Zealand expedition, to come and examine us. Ken, our own physician, was sick with pneumonia when he came down from Camp II a couple of days ago and has already left for the lower altitude of Pheriche. At 17,500 feet, Base Camp is still at an altitude where the body is barely able to fight for its own survival, let alone battle any infection or virus. The Kiwi doc examines each of us in the medical tent, and as we settle into our tents, the initial diagnosis is pulmonary edema for Parry, pneumonia for Vern, and acute bronchitis for the rest of us. Jan immediately starts Parry on oxygen and says he needs to get to the medical facility in Pheriche as soon as possible. The oxygen level in his blood is less than half what it should be, but it's almost dark by the time she sees him, and it will be safer to have Parry remain here on oxygen overnight than for him to try to descend the uneven surface of the glacier by headlamp. His condition seems to stabilize with the oxygen, and Skip volunteers to watch over him throughout the night. They will leave, with Vern, early the next morning.

Vern and Parry are both coughing badly as Skip accompanies them on their way to Pheriche and the Himalayan Rescue Association (HRA) medical facility. Parry is on oxygen and moving slowly. Vern is clearly very ill despite his bravado. Skip is the only healthy one of the trio. Todd wants me to go with them, but I'm so exhausted I can't. "No way. I need to wait a day. I can't even deal with the thought of having to pack up again much less walk down there. I'll go down tomorrow.''

I feel stronger after just one night's rest at Base Camp, but I know it's an illusion created as much by the camaraderie as by any real healing. Mike, Hugh, Louis, and I spend the day resting, sorting gear, and coughing. If I'd been home, I would have been in the hospital, but here sickness is part of all our day-to-day lives, so I crawl out of my tent to take morning tea when it's offered and prepare my personal gear for the trip to Pheriche.

"Margo." Ong Chu, our Sherpa cook's lilting voice and broad smile attracts my attention as I finish my breakfast of granola and hot, lemon-flavored drink. "Would you like a bath to help your cough?"

This is an offer I can't refuse. "You bet!" I can't stop smiling. "I don't know if it will help my cough, but it sure will feel good." I haven't used anything stronger than baby wipes to keep clean for more than thirty days, and the image of a warm bath, especially right now, sounds like heaven.

"Where's the tub?" Half expecting Ong Chu to pull one out of the kitchen gear, I laugh at the image of bringing a tub into Base Camp on the back of a yak. My bright orange sleeping pad is all that separates me from the ice of the glacier as I take my "bath" in the cook tent surrounded by cases of canned goods and tanks of cooking fuel. I dip my washcloth repeatedly into the soup pot full of hot water resting precariously on the uneven surface of rock and ice and wash the dry, flaking skin off my arms and legs. I begin to relax for the first time in more than a week, soothed by the warmth of the water and this simple act of kindness on Ong Chu's part. They more than make up for the 50-degree air on my bare skin. But, even here Martha's voice begins to haunt me. "Yes, you made it to Camp II, and maybe you'll even get well, but you're too slow to make it to the top. You'll hold up the rest of the team, they'll be angry with you, and you'll be the cause of their failure, too."

I know I'm slow, maybe the slowest in the group, but when I begin to use my "Go Mode" and put one foot in front of the other, I've been able to complete each portion of the climb so far. Not bad for a woman who just six years before couldn't walk around the block without resting. I'm strong, and even more important, I believe I can make the summit. But no matter what my head or my heart tells me, my body says it needs to heal. Another painful coughing spell reminds me that I'm still in Base Camp on Mount Everest, and I'm not well, just clean. I need to get down to lower altitude to replenish my strength.

* * *

The trail from Base Camp to Pheriche leads across the Khumbu Glacier to Gorak Shep. Even with two relatively good nights' sleep, my body's weakness makes the normally easy early part of the walk feel extremely difficult. Mike and I leave together, but his pace is faster than mine and we soon separate. Reaching for my inner strength with every step, I repeat my mantra over and over again: "God's love, God's strength, God's will, I can." I've used this mantra on other mountains to keep me focused in long stretches of climbing. It's helped me reach most of my high summits. Today it's a lifeline I use to pull myself to medical help. Whatever is attacking my system is sapping my strength quickly. If it isn't stopped soon, I know my chance for this summit will be over.

From Gorak Shep, I follow the trail to Lobuche as it traverses through what a guidebook calls a "morass of morainal boulders." My fear is even more difficult to maneuver through. Gravity takes me down the steep, eroded slope of the Dugla hill to the floor of the valley carved by the Lobuche Khola. Coming around a bend in the trail, I see the village of Pheriche, which looks deceptively close. Every step I take is challenged by a strong headwind. I have to bend forward nearly double and once again repeat my mantra, digging deep inside to find the energy my legs need to take each step of the last mile to medical help.

To call Pheriche a town would be an overstatement. Five teahouses and assorted huts provide shelter from the wind, food, companionship, and a limited assortment of supplies. Its sparse vegetation and buildings made of stone or whatever wood could be carried from Namche Bazaar or Kathmandu, days even weeks away, offer a place to go for rest and recuperation from the altitude and work on Mount Everest. They also offer the simple luxuries of beer, soft drinks, and an odd assortment of international snacks left by expeditions returning from the mountains.

The Himalayan Rescue Association is situated just off the main path, in the midst of teahouses. It's a regular stop on the trek into Base Camp, and nearly everyone who comes through attends one of the daily lectures on high-altitude illness. After six hours of walking I drop my pack at a teahouse and head for the HRA, nearly collapsing with exhaustion and relief as I step into the small combination waiting/ treatment room.

Bill, the primary doctor, throws a greeting my way as he glances over his shoulder, "I know. You're sick, too." Turning back to his patient, he motions with his head toward a crate placed along one wall. "Sit down over there. We'll look at you in a minute."

Mike is being attended to by Melinda, a nurse from the States. She's taking his history while her husband Matt, a second doctor working at the HRA during the climbing season, listens to his lungs. I exchange smiles with Skip and count seven other people standing or sitting in the crowded room. There's barely space for the medical staff to turn around. Pulse rates and blood pressure readings are called out and noted in conditions that at best would be called primitive. Skip seems to be the only person besides the medical staff in the room who's not coughing.

"Take a deep breath. Now exhale." Matt reacts instinctively, lifting his stethoscope just before the deep, wet cough explodes into the room. "Now, another deep breath. And exhale." I automatically begin to take off some of the layers of pile and Goretex clothing I'm wearing and glance around the room, noticing the shadows cast on the stone walls and dirt floor. The acrid smoke from yak dung being burned for heat adds to an almost medieval atmosphere.

As my eyes adjust to the limited light coming from the open door and one small window, I'm startled by the sight of the large red sausagelike Gamow Bag stretched out along the floor. It's the life-saving device used to treat extreme cases of high-altitude pulmonary edema (HAPE) and high-altitude cerebral edema (HACE), a reminder that the body's inability to process the available oxygen effectively at altitudes above 10,000 feet creates an environment where disability and even death are sometimes only a breath away. I've heard them described before, but like hearing about a coffin in a mortuary, I never expected to see one up close. Now, here's one in front of me and people are looking through its clear top to check on someone inside. I glance up quickly and catch Vern's eye. He mouths the name, "Parry," and my heart skips a beat. For the first time since I stepped into the room, I notice the sound of air being forced into the artificial environment as Louis works the foot pump raising the pressure inside the bag, the equivalent for the patient inside of going lower in altitude.

For the moment it's determined that Parry has HAPE, Vern has double pneumonia, I have single pneumonia, and the others have varying degrees of bronchitis. Skip is the only one who has escaped whatever bug has attacked us and remains healthy. Experience, planning, and training can't prevent illness, and a successful climb always depends on the consent of unseen powers. Weather and accidents are always factors, but somehow, here in Pheriche, imagining that something like a simple virus could keep us from reaching our goal is demoralizing to me.

The weight of my exhaustion and the reality of my illness drain my energy and spirits. I'm about ready to give up. Everything looks hopeless as Parry, Vern, and I stay the night stretched out on the floor and wooden benches of the HRA. Although what could have been a life-and-death crisis has passed for Parry, the staff wants all three of us to remain for observation.

I drift off to sleep in the midst of coughing and wheezing. By morning, the important change in altitude between Base Camp and Pheriche is already beginning to have a positive effect on our bodies, and my spirits begin to rise. Parry, Vern, and I move to the teahouse. Our job now is to get healthy and go back to the mountain, to the challenges and fates Sagarmatha holds. Skip and the others stay for a couple of days and then head back up to Base Camp. For the three of us, Pheriche will be home for a while longer.

During the next week, Parry, Vern, and I form a close bond. We walk from the teahouse to the HRA for daily checkups, then drift to the "beach," a shelter built from discarded fiberglass sections that provides a warm place open to the sun and protected from the wind. The easy conversation, laughter, and back rubs the three of us share are as healing as the heavier air and the medications. Parry's youthfully freckled face breaks easily into a smile, which makes him look younger than his years and somehow belies his extreme fitness. At the same time he has a quiet maturity that communicates dependability and integrity. He is an easy man to trust. Vern plays his fiddle and harmonica with an enthusiasm that's contagious. Lean-bodied, with a full, dark beard and his head shaved bald, he reminds me of the Pied Piper when he starts his music. Children and adults are drawn out of their shelters and everyone joins in the singing. Vern expresses himself through his music while I use a portable computer to record my feelings. As I write, I realize how isolated I've felt from the others on the expedition and from my own inner sources of strength, too.

Every expedition requires an incredible amount of attention to detail and coordination, and mountaineering always demands a level of individual focus, determination, and self-confidence that lends itself to terms like "macho" and "loner." But nothing I've done before has prepared me for how separate I've felt here. Despite the bond with Parry and Vern, something is missing. Sometimes my inner mountains and crevasses seem more daunting, more of a challenge than even the highest peak on the planet.

When I hear on our radio link to Base Camp that Skip is taking Frank and John to Camp II and then up to Camp III, I have to get up and take a walk. I feel like a failure. Then one evening during dinner, Vern speaks up, "Seems like we're all still coughing more than we should. Maybe if we go down to Deboche, it'll speed up the healing. At least the change and exercise will do us good."

"Deboche?" My response is as instinctive as a mother's protection of her child, "That's going in the wrong direction. We're supposed to be going back up."

"Easy, Margo. Getting back on the mountain is what this is all about." Vern's gentle strength, experience, and logic are apparent as he and Parry discuss the pros and cons of going to an even lower altitude. Finally, I have to agree. It does seem to make sense. Besides, it will give me a chance to revisit the monastery at Thyangboche. The more we talk about it, the more I believe I have to go there as part of my healing. The sense of separation and the inner doubts I've experienced are certainly indications that something inside isn't quite right. I'm sure of one thing, I don't want to be alone in Pheriche with only Martha for company.

Deboche is one of many small villages trekkers visit in the Khumbu Region of Nepal: motley pearls along a string of well-worn trail that moves people and animals in their search for adventure at the top of the world. At 11,000 feet, it's low enough that trees, bushes, and giant rhododendron grow on the hillsides and between the buildings.

Vern was right. The excursion is just the change we need. I sleep twelve-hour nights and my spirit soars with the songbirds that gather in the trees. I feel stronger physically. I can see it in the way my body is holding itself upright and hear it in the spontaneity and fullness of my laughter and the absence of my cough.

For many of the people passing through Deboche we represent an unfathomable dream: climbers who have been on Mount Everest. Little do they know how much their interest and questions mean to the fragile grip I'm keeping on my quest for the summit.

"Yes," I say, "I've been on the mountain. Spent ten days living and working at 21,500 feet." I listen to my own description of having climbed on all seven continents and am still surprised at what I've accomplished. Me, Margo Chisholm, in Nepal and climbing Mount Everest. "Yes, it was cold and frightening. Yes, there have been accidents: At least one Sherpa and a member of the Spanish team were injured in the Icefall and were airlifted out of Base Camp." In response to their query about my being in Deboche, I listen to myself respond casually, "I'm down here recuperating from pneumonia and getting ready to go back to climb to the summit." Recovering from pneumonia? Returning to the summit? Do I really think I have a shot at that? *Yes, I do.* I smile as I hear myself answering with such resolve. I must be feeling better!

After a couple of days, we hike twenty minutes up the steep, muddy trail to the large Buddhist monastery at Thyangboche. Three years ago a fire destroyed many sacred and irreplaceable texts when it swept through the structure, just two days after electricity was installed in the facility. I visited the site during my first trek in the Himal, shortly after the fire. I wondered then if I'd ever be back, the thought of an expedition to climb Everest was too far beyond my reality then even to conceive it. Now I'm back, looking for something I've left behind.

The top floor of the Sherpa Cultural Museum serves as the main room for worship while the burned out monastery is being rebuilt. I enter the building and am drawn to the peaceful, quiet chanting of the monks and the ringing of their cymbals. I begin to feel a familiar, calm, almost physical presence. I'm comforted rather than afraid. It's my connection with the spirit of my friend, Jonathan Wright, the photographer and climber who first introduced me to the dream of being in the Himalayas nineteen years before. Killed in an avalanche in 1980, his spirit has been a significant presence on each of my climbs.

"Jonathan, where have you been?" I sense his response, as real as if he were sitting cross-legged beside me.

"I haven't gone anywhere, Margo. You've just been doing this one by yourself." It's true. I'd left Jonathan and God and my whole inner support team behind in this quest. I now know why getting up the mountain has seemed so hard, why I've felt so alone, and why Martha's voice has been so loud.

"Oh, Jonathan, I can't do it by myself anymore. I don't want to." My chest seems to expand with the warmth of his presence and God's energy. I feel more whole than I've felt on the entire trip, and as I sit, listening to the chanting, the tears that come are definitely of gratitude and joy.

Two days later, I lift my pack, swing it onto my back, and head up the trail toward Base Camp. I've rediscovered the source of my inner strength. That, along with my now healthy body and the camaraderie and closeness I have established with Vern and Parry, carries me through the three-day trek into Base Camp with a new resolve.

Back at the 17,500-foot altitude of Base Camp I feel some weakness physically, especially when I have to push uphill even the short distance to the toilet. During the expedition meetings and preparation and packing of the gear for our summit attempts, I begin to feel the hopelessness I experienced the evening before going to Deboche. My bronchial tubes feel tight when I breathe hard, and my chest hurts a little, but overall I feel strong enough to make it to Camp II and, I hope, beyond. The top is where I want to be, and I tell myself it's just a matter of putting one foot in front of the other.

When the climbing teams are announced, I'm assigned to the second group of climbers. Martha immediately speaks up. "See, I told you so. Todd's assigned you to the second team so you won't slow the first guys down."

I don't let her get to me. Sure, given my options I'd like to climb with Skip and Vern on the first team, but everyone on the second team has just as good a shot at the summit, including me.

While I select my gear for the final ascent, my excitement and fear build. I constantly feel Martha's desire to quit. She keeps up an almost nonstop chatter. "This is too hard. You can't do it. You need to find a way to justify not going. Don't you feel too sick to climb? Doesn't your body hurt too much?"

Her voice is loud and powerful, more so than usual, and I find it difficult to discover arguments with which to confront her. Why is it so hard? My mind races with the effort of fighting the fear and negativity. "Breathe, Margo." The familiar words move easily, gently through the chaos in my mind. They are Jonathan's words, words I have ignored since I left Thyangboche, trying instead to bull my way through life; trying to do it my way rather than listening to God's will for me. I don't know why this time I am finally able to listen. I am grateful that I can.

As the hours crawl by, the negative-self talk continues to soften, and I am able to stay focused on the summit. My renewed connection with Jonathan and God give me the extra boost I need. Together, we can make it to the top. Maintaining that connection is the only chance I have.

Friday, May 8, 1992, Base Camp
Oh, God, I want to get to the top of this
mountain! It's hard for me to want
something this badly, particularly now that the
odds against are even greater than they were
before. It's easier to not want it. But I do. That's
the truth. I want to summit. It almost makes
me cry to state it so clearly.

At 5:30 A.M., after a good night's sleep, I wake up to say, "Good luck" to our first team as they leave for Camp II. I long for Skip and Vern to summit, but I feel a huge loss as both of them walk out of camp. Skip has been such an inspiration to me on my path to Mount Everest and Vern's encouragement and openness with me while we recovered in Pheriche and Deboche are major parts of my being able to be back up here getting ready for my own summit ascent. When they leave, I feel as if they have taken some of my energy with them. My mentor walking off with my friend. Watching them climb through the Icefall, I feel excitement and sadness. I have to do this one without either of them. So I turn inside to find my strength.

Walking back to my tent, I pause and look around Base Camp. So many people's energy and activity have been focused on this single point in time, it's strange to think that in just a couple of weeks we'll break all of this down and leave for home. Our camp isn't the only one involved in preparations for the summit. Many groups of climbers have moved up onto the mountain today, hopes and dreams leading them through the Icefall, following the fixed rope past Camp I and into the Western Cwm. Prayer flags fly in the wind, carrying the wish for good fortune with them.

"What's going to happen on the mountain?" I ask myself, "Who's going to make it to the top? Will I be one of them? What's it going to feel like when I'm standing on top of the world?"

I spend the morning doing laundry, washing a month's worth of grime out of polypro and underwear in a blue plastic basin using powdered Nepalese laundry soap. Ong Chu, our kind and gracious cook, has once again provided me with hot water, and the rocks covering the glacier provide a natural washboard. The water in the basin quickly turns muddy, and I wonder if I am making my clothes cleaner or merely moving the dirt from one garment to another. At the very least, I end the process with the illusion that my clothes are clean. At least they don't smell as bad. After a leisurely lunch, I take my cup of coffee out into the sun, put Simon and Garfunkel on my Walkman, and spend the afternoon sharpening the points on my crampons and packing my gear in anticipation of climbing to Camp II in two days. In the evening I grow reflective and write in my journal, "How did I ever get here from being Miggie, that little girl in Greenwich, Connecticut? I'm forty-four years old. I sometimes think I should be over my past, and yet in so many ways I'm just going deeper and deeper into it. Climbing these mountains and finding myself—that's what my journey seems to be about today."

I cough. My whole body shakes as the memories from three weeks ago come flooding back. I stand up, frowning, feeling a twinge of fear as I walk back to my tent, and then smiling as a tingle in my spine indicates Jonathan's presence. Looking up at Mount Everest I talk to him, "How did this happen? Jonathan, how did I get here from that party in Aspen nineteen years ago when we first met?"

CHAPTER TWO

What's Wrong with Me?

Tuesday, August 14, 1973, Aspen, Colorado
I was moving to New York. Now I'm in Aspen
with an apartment, a gorgeous guy paying
half the rent, and a job to pay the bills. Things
sure have a way of changing fast.

"Jonathan. Jonathan Wright."

A lanky, twenty-something man turned toward us with a broad, welcoming grin. Even in that living room filled with healthy, tanned people who lived, worked, and played in the mountains of Colorado, he stood out. I was immediately intrigued, took in a deep breath and flashed what I hoped was at least a friendly smile in return as my hostess took my hand and led me across the room. Betsy dismissed the others standing around Jonathan with a polite but firm nod of her head. Putting her hand on my back to make sure I was facing him, she said, "Miggie Chisholm, Jonathan Wright." As we shook hands, I looked up at his face, towering a foot above my own, into eyes filled with a wisdom and ease that almost made me uncomfortable.

"Miggie is Barbara's sister. She's getting an apartment at Silver King." Turning to me, she continued, "Jonathan's looking for someone to share an apartment with. I think you two should talk. You just might be able to help each other out." Then she disappeared.

I took a sip from my drink, an excuse to break from the intensity of his gaze, hoping to find something else to talk about. I wasn't very enthusiastic about Betsy's proposition, everything was happening too fast, even for me.

"What I have," I said to Jonathan, "is a one-bedroom apartment. I hadn't really thought about sharing it. As a matter of fact, I've kind of been looking forward to living by myself. I've been in Denver for the past few years and was moving to New York when Barb suggested I come by for a visit. Now it looks like I'll be here a while." She had taken me under her wing when I arrived at her home less than a week ago. The past few years had been challenging but this move was going to be just the change I needed. I certainly wasn't looking for a relationship or a roommate. My nice one-bedroom would suit me just fine while I worked with Barb in her business and got my feet on the ground. "I really don't know about living with someone."

"I can understand that," Jonathan acknowledged, "but let me explain my situation."

While Jonathan talked, I tried to remember the last time I'd had roommates. Middlebury College. Was that just seven years ago? Seemed like seventy. There had been Middlebury, then The University of Denver, then the job in the tax department of a "Big Eight" accounting firm. Certainly didn't seem like that long. Filling the voids in time was the dark, empty feeling that came over me whenever I slowed down, whenever I was alone. I didn't know what it was, I knew only that I had to cover it up, stay one step ahead, or I would be lost. Lost, like during my depression at Middlebury. I tried to face it then and it was just too big. Too scary. Nobody knew what was going on inside of me. How could I tell anyone? I was too busy just trying to keep up appearances. I tried everything I knew to bring back the feeling I remembered from my last couple of years at Garrison Forest, the all-girl's boarding high school I'd attended. I wanted to be back there playing varsity field hockey, acting in school plays, writing letters to my boyfriend, being popular. But, the magic was lost. I had to find it again.

I let down my guard a little when I found out that alcohol and food took away some of my fear. In college, my drinking didn't seem like a problem—everyone around me was doing it. And my overeating was a joke, a part of my personality. I hid the hurt I felt when the fraternity guys called me FMFFQ, Fat Miggie the French Fry Queen. At 5 feet 2 inches and 125 pounds, I wasn't fat. Not even really overweight. So what if my clothes were getting a little tight? It was a coincidence that whenever one of the frat guys saw me in the snack bar in the Student

Union, I was eating French fries. After all, I was well liked—wasn't I? Besides, more food or a drink always helped take the sting from the emotional pain. Facing the world without some kind of buffer became harder and harder.

When I transferred to The University of Denver, skiing became part of my daily life. I skied whenever and wherever I could. The increased exercise and a temporary ability to control my eating kept my weight stable for a year or so, and I was still able to get A's by using other people's notes. I developed a wide network of friends who, like me, were ski bums by day and whatever we needed to be by night to let us have our time on the slopes. I never let my injuries interfere with my skiing, and I learned that a little marijuana worked just as well as booze. Better still, it didn't leave me with the same hangover I had when I drank. And the "munchies" made my indiscriminate eating acceptable, hiding the fact that it was out of control. I could not, however, hide the 20 pounds I soon gained.

Even after I graduated, no matter how much I smoked pot, drank, ate, worked, skied, no matter how much I did anything, I still had that emptiness inside. Two years later, when my job, my boyfriend, and everything else in my life no longer filled the void, I took what seemed to be the next logical step to change my downward emotional spiral. I decided to move. I'd go back to New York City. I could get a job there, and I'd be closer to my parents and old friends. Then Barb suggested I come to Aspen and check it out. "It'll do you good and I'd like you to meet my friends. The people in Aspen are great, you'll see. I think you ought to move here instead of New York. It's a much healthier place, and it would be easy for you to stay on a diet here. Everybody's fit and thin." My weight had risen to 160 and despite the shame I felt at my sister's words, they made sense.

Barb had always been the quiet one. Although attractive and athletic, she was painfully shy and had always seemed to get along with horses better than people. We dealt with life very differently: I compensated for my fear by being friendly and outgoing while she dealt with hers by withdrawing into her world of horses. Like many siblings we fought frequently for a number of years, but when Barb went to boarding school we grew closer. We had shared a house together with her three-year-old daughter Meg for a year in Denver before Barb had remarried. Meg was now six, and the idea of living in the same town with them again was appealing.

So, here I was, and someone was talking to me.

"Are you okay?" Jonathan had a quizzical look on his face.

"Sure." My own face flushed with embarrassment. "My mind kind of wandered there for a minute. I guess I've been more stressed than I thought. I'm really looking for some peace and quiet. That's why I was looking for my own apartment in the first place."

Jonathan's grin and eyes told me he understood, maybe more than I wanted him to, and he patiently began again. "So, like I was saying, I'm a photographer, and I travel most of the time. I need a place to live, but it doesn't make sense to get a place of my own when I'm only here three or four months a year. How about this for an idea? You get a two-bedroom at Silver King and I'll pay the difference and live in the second, smaller bedroom. I'll get a cheap, secure place to live and store my stuff and you'll get more living space for the same money."

This was beginning to sound interesting. A good-looking, fascinating man who traveled all over the world and seemed to do incredibly interesting things was asking to share my apartment with me. The possibilities were limitless! We talked for quite a while that night, and the more time I spent with Jonathan, the more something drew me to him. He was leaving for an assignment in Nepal in a couple of days and needed an answer quickly. Before the evening was over I heard myself saying, "Okay. Let's do it."

We were never to become romantically involved. Instead, Jonathan became my mentor of the spirit. He showed me a world I had never experienced through the way he lived his life. It was a place where people followed their heart's desires, where the heart was more important than the head, where gentleness and caring were the rule rather than the exception, and where death was a beginning and not an end. Jonathan didn't laugh at my ignorance or despair at my skepticism when we discussed spiritual matters. Shame and self-judgment did not exist in his world.

He shared his love of big mountains with me, especially the mountains of Nepal. I began to read about Nepal, the Himalaya, and Himalayan climbing. It was almost irresistibly enticing. Living in Aspen, I had mountains standing more than 14,000 feet all around me, and I could imagine the beauty, the wonder of being surrounded by peaks more than 20,000 feet high. But to see Mount Everest's 29,000 feet— there was no way in the world I could do that. And to think about climbing any of them was beyond even *my* active imagination.

That first year in Aspen my life seemed quite normal. I went to work, played with new friends, and reestablished my relationship with Barbara. I skied in the winter and did some hiking in the summer. Alcohol and pot were a regular part of my life without controlling it, and my weight was dropping seemingly without effort. I felt as though the black hole inside was gone. I had come to that safe place I needed to find. Jonathan was around just enough to be interesting, and while he was traveling, I didn't have to think about the things he stirred up inside my soul when he was at home.

My pragmatic, logical, left-brain side often rebelled against his spiritual, right-brain concepts. But Jonathan planted seeds of new ideas, then he left them to grow and mature in their own season.

Neither my lifestyle nor my job demanded much from me, and neither required much effort to maintain. Life was good and, for the moment, it was easy. I received a monthly income from a trust fund that had been established by my grandfather and laughingly called myself "dependently wealthy." With just enough money coming in to meet my basic living needs, a job was necessary if I was to live the way I wanted to. More important, I needed to have a title or business card to justify my existence. My identity was always wrapped up in what I was doing or said I was doing.

In addition to traveling all over the world to shoot photographs and climb big mountains, Jonathan loved to climb the rock faces around Aspen. My high school friend Leelee had come for a visit and stayed, living with us until she could find a place of her own, and we thought it'd be great fun if Jonathan would teach us to climb. So one warm, fall afternoon, we talked him into taking us to Turkey Rock.

The only thing I knew about rock climbing was what Jonathan told us as he fashioned "swami belt" harnesses for us and showed us how to attach them to the rope. He talked about climbing by feel. "You feel the rock to find holds, as well as look for them. You can't climb by sight alone. Use your touch. Make friends with the rock." And up he climbed.

Jonathan moved up the route easily, all the while describing what he was doing with his hands and feet. The grace with which he climbed and his comfort on the rock were mesmerizing. I was sure I would look like a total fool when it was my turn to attempt to haul myself up the face of the rock. I was also very afraid. I didn't especially like heights, there wasn't much to hold on to once you were on the rock, and I wasn't sure that Jonathan or the rope would hold me if I fell. When I fell is more like it.

"I don't know, Migger, this is really scary. Whose idea was this anyway?" Leelee asked as we waited below while Jonathan set up the belay.

"Ours." I hoped my voice wasn't shaking as much as my stomach. "It'll be neat. You'll see. Jonathan knows what he's doing." My mind screamed that I would surely die if I went through with this lunacy. I wished now I had remembered to bring a joint to smoke or something to drink to calm me down.

Only two things kept me there: my pride and my faith in Jonathan. I trusted him enough to believe that if he said I could do this, then I could do it. There was no going back now, my ego wouldn't let me, and I wanted to make Jonathan proud. I'd be damned if I was going to quit in front of two of my best friends.

Jonathan's big grin appeared over the top of the wall rising above us. "Okay. Which one of you is going first?"

Leelee and I looked at each other, our eyes reflecting each other's excitement and terror. "Go ahead, Migger. You're the one reading about mountains all the time."

"Me, I guess," I called up to Jonathan, hoping my voice sounded more excited than I felt.

"Okay. Tie the end of the rope into your harness like I showed you." He watched from the top as I fumbled with the rope and Leelee double-checked the knot. "Good. Now I'll take in the slack. Call out 'on belay' when you're set, and 'climbing' when you start so I'll be ready for you. I'll see you up here."

I moved to the base of the face, looking at where Jonathan had reached for his first handhold. It was six inches above where I could reach. I finally found something I could grab and shouted out, "On belay."

The rope tightened, gently pulling on my harness. I knew Jonathan was holding the other end. "Belay on." His voice was sure, confident. I was ready to climb.

"Climbing."

"Climb on."

And suddenly I was reaching for my second handhold. I'd left the safety of solid ground.

I had no clue about what Jonathan meant by making friends with the rock. Rock was rock. It was hard and rough and capable of tearing skin off my body. The idea of making friends with it was preposterous. As I struggled up that wall all I felt was a combination of excitement and pure terror. Only a 9mm climbing rope attached to some webbing around my waist was between me and severe pain, maybe instant death, if I fell.

I struggled up slowly, painfully looking for the bumps and weaknesses in the rock that would provide hand- and footholds. Halfway up the rock, at the crux move, I experienced the horror of knowing I was going to fall. My feet were slipping! I hollered up to Jonathan, "Oh, God, I'm going to fall. I can't hold myself!" I panicked.

Jonathan heard the fear in my voice and called to me, "It's okay, Miggie. I've got you. You won't get hurt if—"

My right foot came off the rock, and flailed in thin air. I let out a sound, more of a squeak than a scream, as my mind quickly assessed the situation and told me I was going to receive permanent injuries from this fall.

The rope, and Jonathan holding it on belay, caught me almost immediately. I wasn't dead. Not even hurt. I was very scared. As I rested with the rope bearing my weight, my heart pounded so hard it seemed to bruise my chest from the inside. I closed my eyes, leaned my forehead against the taut rope, and breathed deeply. My brain returned from hyperspace and began to appraise the situation. The system worked! I could trust Jonathan and the rope. It was possible to do this without dying, maybe even without being injured! I was a believer.

I glanced down at Leelee, 20 feet below me. She looked small but she was cheering for me. I looked up and saw Jonathan, once again peering over the ledge, grinning. It was the same smile I had first seen at the party when we met. Confidence and faith began to well up from deep inside as I looked up for the move I had been on when I fell. I reached out for the same stone pocket I'd had my fingers in and put my left foot back on the small outcropping from which it had slipped. Now I began to talk to the rock as I made my way up. "Okay, where do I put my fingers now? Help me out here. Okay, there's one."

By the time I reached the top of that short pitch I understood at least a little of what Jonathan meant by becoming friends with the rock. For the first time in my life I felt the immense satisfaction of reaching the top of a climb.

During my second year in Aspen I started a relationship with a new friend, one that would take me as far down as Jonathan's vision raised me up. It started out simply enough. I was at a party, we were introduced, and I fell in love. Early on, my new friend protected me from the frustrations of the world and gave me evenings of lighthearted fun and pleasure. All too soon the relationship took all my money, eroded my health, and filled my nights with unbearable loneliness, alienating me from the people who loved me.

Why would I stay in a relationship with a friend like that? Because the "friend" was cocaine, and the relationship was addiction. Cocaine made me feel as if I were on top of the world. Everyone was doing it and "knew" that it wasn't addicting. We solved all of the world's problems late at night under the influence of the drug.

While I continued quietly to find out more about the mountains and climbing, I also became increasingly dependent on food, alcohol, and drugs. It was more and more necessary to have something to eat or drink or smoke or swallow; some way to alter reality if only slightly; some way to try to fill the increasingly present black hole. I couldn't let people know of my strong interest in climbing because they might wonder why I never actively pursued it. So I didn't talk about it. I just read and dreamed a lot. The books I bought on the Himalaya, climbing, and Buddhism sat on the shelf along with my self-improvement books.

Whenever I felt so alone, so empty that even my addictions couldn't help, I would go to a granite rock I found standing in a meadow along the trail that followed Hunter Creek as it flowed out of the wilderness back country. I called it my God Rock, and it became a symbol for me of stability, a knowing beyond myself, a place of hope.

Something inside me continued to come alive whenever Jonathan was around. It was as if a fire inside me had been lit. Every time he came into town his spirit would feed the flame. Each time he left my life became a little darker than it had been. But as long as he was talking about his adventures or showing his slides, I was enthralled. I could almost see myself there with him in his world. However, when Jonathan actually invited me to join him on a month-long trek in Nepal, I was terrified.

"Oh, Jonathan, I'd love to go. But you know how picky I am about my food. I'd starve to death over there. I couldn't possibly survive on lentils and rice. Just make sure you bring back some great slides." My addictions had defined the limits of my comfort zone. I made light of it, but inside part of me was crying like a child who'd been told she couldn't go to the circus and didn't know why. I couldn't leave my cocaine and my alcohol and my food, even to fulfill my deepest desire. I buried a small part of my heart that day.

Things had not been good during my last couple of years in Aspen. My increasing cocaine use had resulted in a decreased appetite. At 105 pounds I was finally wearing a size 6, and had the body I'd always wanted. But I was as miserable as I'd ever been. So I took the "easy" way out and did more drugs. I ignored the fact that I had become too thin to be healthy and my hair was falling out. I couldn't see that I was spending more and more time at home by myself and that I'd been fired by my brother-in-law because of my drug use. Every time the bone-crushing, soul-destroying loneliness and depression hit, I swore I'd never do it again. My nightly resolution to stop or at least cut back on my drug use dissolved every morning.

Then one day in the winter of 1978 I stole some cocaine from my dealer. That I couldn't ignore. I had become a thief in order to support my habit. I was 30 years old, living in a resort town, going nowhere. It was time to get serious about life. My addicted mind told me the perfect solution, "Move to New York where your parents are close, can help you out, and you can get a real job again. Leave this atmosphere behind and you won't have a problem getting off the drugs." The problem, I persuaded myself, was Aspen. Just as it had been Denver, Middlebury, and Garrison Forest.

In the spring of 1978 I found a great job in New York City with a Fortune 500 company, moved into a small apartment I could afford, and began to make new friends. I loved New York. It was intense, full of life, and familiar. Greenwich, Connecticut, where my parents still lived, was only an hour's drive away. Close enough to run home when I wanted to; far enough away so neither they nor my old friends could interfere with my life in the city.

I desperately wanted to do well at this job. I even stayed off drugs— for a while. My life in the city was exhilarating, but soon the edge of this new adventure wore thin. Fear of failure began to take me by the hand every morning and sit next to me at my desk. I was terrified that someone in management would find out what I already knew: there was something inherently wrong with me, I wasn't as good as my coworkers, and my ability to do my job was all an act. I knew that when they found out, they'd fire me in a minute. I performed well but it took every ounce of energy I could generate. Soon the demands of living with this kind of fear began to overwhelm me. When the company brought forty account reps and technicians together at a large hotel for two weeks of high-pressure, competitive training simulations, I fell back on an old standby I'd learned as a child: I invented an illness.

We were divided into three-person teams, assigned different sales situations, and watched and critiqued on all phases of our performance. Every presentation, every project, became another opportunity for me to fail. The actual results and evaluations were irrelevant. My sense of impending doom became my reality. I wasn't good enough for anything. Finally, my old survival instincts emerged and I developed a serious "ear infection." I spent the final morning of the course in the emergency room of a nearby hospital while the other two members of my team made our big presentation without me. The shame and guilt

I felt from lying were easier for me to deal with than my fear of failing to measure up. Same as always.

By the time I was eight years old I'd found out a twisted knee or a sprained ankle got me attention and made me feel special in a way that my looks and achievements never could. But the attention always went away, and I was left feeling scared and alone until my next injury or illness. Faked injuries and invented illnesses were safe places to hide when I couldn't function in the world and couldn't let anyone know how scared I really was. I got sympathy that I interpreted as love. I got something that felt like respect. "See what a good job Margo is doing even though she doesn't feel well. See how well she copes with her problems." Each time I lied, I proved to myself that I wasn't worthy of people liking me unless I did something special to get their attention. In place of self-esteem, I built up a reservoir of guilt and shame. A reservoir carefully tended by Martha.

I didn't fail the training simulations. They didn't fire me. In fact, I received recognition for my accomplishment in overcoming such "obvious" physical pain. I got what I thought I wanted, but my shame, guilt, and self-doubts grew ever deeper. I had to work harder and harder to maintain my facade.

After six months on the job, I discovered that the husband of one of my coworkers had access to drugs in general and cocaine in particular. My body tingled with excitement at the anticipation of relief from my struggle. I knew this was what I needed: just enough so I could focus on my work. I knew I could handle cocaine this time. I could be around people who were high on coke; I could control how much I used. Plus, it was the easiest way I knew to diet.

I had put on about 20 pounds since arriving in New York. My eating grew more and more uncontrollable, particularly at parties, where I started smoking pot again, and at night when my loneliness was unbearable. Cocaine had always eliminated my desire, and need, to eat. I'd just do a couple of lines every now and then to keep from eating and to keep my energy up.

My control lasted about sixty seconds. Within a month or so I was requiring lines of cocaine and an unending supply of food to make it through the day at the office. The drugs didn't keep me from eating anymore. Soon I was doing lines in the workrooms where anyone could have walked in and found me. I was up, enthusiastic, and productive when I had a supply of coke. When I ran out, my desk drawers were armed with Twinkies and Snickers and potato chips. The supply was replenished every morning and gone by the end of the day. I was tired, negative, and full of excuses for the work that didn't get done.

Then I'd buy more coke and the cycle would begin all over again. During the next year and a half I developed a $1,000 a week cocaine habit and gained an additional 60 pounds.

In the spring of 1980, Jonathan called to tell me his wife had just given birth to a daughter. He was proud, filled with joy, and wanted to share his good fortune with me. We had maintained our friendship over the years even as the differences between our lifestyles had deepened. Somehow, simply knowing he was continuing to live his life with the principles I saw while we were in Aspen gave me faith that someday, somehow I'd be able to live that way, too. Jonathan's life seemed to be my last hope.

Six months later he was dead, killed by an avalanche while climbing in China. I was at my parents' house when Leelee called with the news. When I hung up the phone my body rocked of its own accord: rocked to protect me from the wave of grief and devastation that threatened to squeeze the air from my lungs; rocked to contain the keening moan that threatened to escape from my throat; rocked to keep from dissolving into nothingness. I had made Jonathan into a lifeline—my only connection with the possibility that I could ever live from a place of integrity again. When he died I felt as if that lifeline had been severed.

Now I had only my addictions to rely on. My behavior at the office became more and more unprofessional: I "worked at home" more frequently, accomplishing nothing; I ate continuously when I was at the office; I snorted cocaine in unlocked workrooms. Believing my dismissal was imminent, I had the presence of mind to leave the company before I was fired. I ran through my savings and created special needs to try to get more money from my parents. Survival now meant scheming about how I was going to continue my supply of staples: cocaine, pot, junk food, and booze.

For some people cocaine is a very social drug. For me it had lost most of its social aspects. I would arm myself with an eighth of an ounce of coke, a bottle of Grand Marnier, and a lid of pot, and hole up in my apartment with jigsaw puzzles, crossword puzzles, and Atari games. I pulled the blinds and didn't answer the phone. The eight-ball of coke was good for eight to twelve hours of escape. As soon as the coke ran out, I started eating. It was the only way I could survive until the next drug buy. Each time I said never again. Each time I repeated the process: It was still working for me.

There was nothing like the incredible feeling of the first line of the day. I craved it. Nothing will ever completely erase the memory of the euphoria that came with that first line. The rest of the day, and often the night, would be spent trying to duplicate that magical feeling.

It made me feel thin for a little while. It made me feel smart. It made me feel okay. It was an escape from the Margo I couldn't stand: a talented, bright, educated woman who was unable to hold down a job, weighed 180 pounds, and locked herself in her apartment several nights a week. I lied to almost everyone almost all the time because I could not stand the thought of having anyone find out the truth about me. I was behaving in ways that disappointed me and others more and more frequently. I hated myself and I hated what I was doing. I was caught in the middle and I couldn't stop. I was desperate.

Thursday, August 20, 1981, New York City
I finally did it. I've never felt better. I found out
how to handle my eating, and I've stopped
smoking, too.

"Are you eating again?" My mother's disapproval was evident in her voice as I stood peering into the open refrigerator. "Aren't those pants tighter than when you were here last? What are we going to do with you?"

I felt her judgment settle over my heart like a cloak. It mirrored my own shame. Despite the heavy cocaine use, my body had ballooned since I'd left Aspen. My eating was uncontrollable, and I heard in my mother's voice my own belief that there was something inherently deficient in me.

"I don't know," I mumbled, my words blurred by my efforts to keep from crying. The ensuing silence was heavy with unspoken judgments.

"Miggie. Have you ever thought about going to a 'fat farm'?"

I burst into tears. "Of course I have! Nothing else has worked. I'd go tomorrow, but I can't afford it. I know I need help, Mum, but I don't have a clue how I can get it or where to go."

"Miggie, if you find someplace that will help you lose weight, I'll pay for it."

My addict's mind believed that if I could just lose weight, I'd control my cocaine use, and my life would be great. Armed with the courage of Mum's promise of financial help, I'd find the place with the answer to all of my problems or I'd die trying.

I chose a program in Vermont that seemed to have the ideal balance between program and price. I would be there four weeks and could start within days. I was terribly excited when Mum okayed it. I knew this would be my answer: information, balanced meals, and psychological support in a structured environment. For the first time I heard the concept of eating in moderation. It seemed such a simple thing to do: just eat moderate amounts of food. I didn't have to feel deprived. I could eat the foods I loved and still lose weight. One of my roommates taught me about using laxatives. When I took a couple of them to clean out my system, I felt thinner. More important, I looked thinner and the scale registered less weight. As I packed to leave after an extended stay of eight weeks, I had lost 25 pounds and knew I'd received everything I had come for: information about the long-term solution and a quick fix for the short term. Things would be different now.

That night I partied with new friends in Vermont with a bottle of vodka and a couple of grams of coke. When I returned home I ate moderately for a while, but in a blissful state of denial, I juggled my excesses. As soon as I stopped one, I picked up another. I believed that in beating the odds I was winning at life. Drug use always increased my cigarette intake.

"If you continue to smoke cigarettes, the odds of your not getting lung cancer are zero." I was sitting across the polished desk of a naturopathic physician. I had been smoking cigarettes for twenty-three years, but he scared me so badly I knew I had to quit. So I gave up everything. Just like that. I went through a Smoke Enders program to let go of the cigarettes and went off coke and grass cold turkey on my own. I stayed off cigarettes and rarely used cocaine or pot, but my drinking and use of laxatives increased as my eating bounced in and out of control and my weight yo-yoed up and down. I hadn't found any real solutions. During the summer of 1983, New York lost its glitter, and I moved to a townhouse my parents helped me purchase in Greenwich. I barely maintained the financial and data processing consulting business I had set up three years earlier in the city where I shared an office with my father.

One day, as I talked about losing weight yet again, my father said, "Why don't you just eat less?"

I wanted to throw something at him. "God, don't you think I would if I could? Do you think I want to look like this? Do you think I'm eating this way because I want to?" I had a monthly commuter pass for the train and membership in the club with the best tennis program. My clients looked to me for advice. I had a nice car, stylish clothes, and appropriate friends. Outside, I looked the part of a successful, independent suburban businesswoman. Inside, the carefully glued-together pieces were rapidly coming apart. I skipped meals, ate huge salads, binged, then skipped some more meals. I continued to use laxatives. They did what I wanted them to: They made me look thinner.

For the next two years my food intake continued to be erratic and I increased my intake of Correctol to try to purge the extra calories or at least prevent the extra food I was eating from showing up on my body. Laxatives didn't make me thinner, they only made me look thinner, and they did it by leaching all the water out of my body. Over those twenty-four months I was completely obsessed with eating and not eating and how much I weighed and how I was going to lose weight. My white-knuckled control grew weaker. I slowly gained weight, once again approaching 160 pounds, despite increasing laxative abuse and attempts to diet. My ability to function in the world decreased rapidly.

I used sixty to ninety laxatives a day, five days a week. Correctol had become my drug of choice. I played a never-ending game of musical pharmacies to escape the raised eyebrows and unwanted questions that invariably accompanied purchases that were too large or too frequent to be considered normal.

I drank more and more. But I never looked or acted the way I thought an alcoholic would look or act. To me, I was happy, funny, and entertaining when I had a drink or two. I sometimes got a little bit loud after three or four or five drinks, but there was always someone else around who was a little louder. Certainly I was more at ease with people and in social situations after a couple of drinks. I began to spend more and more time with the people at Morgan, a local pub where my Happy Hour drink often lasted until closing. The ability to drive home with one eye closed while following the yellow line became a fine art, one we laughed about as we shared drinks the next evening. I didn't drink at home very often. There, I abused food.

I was a grazer: I ate from the time I woke up in the morning until the time I went to bed at night and sometimes after. It was not uncommon for me to wake up at four in the morning to devour raw hot dogs before I was fully awake. It was soothing, calming, not only the food itself, but the process of the eating as well. It was calming in the same way smoking had been before I quit. But after a while even the food and alcohol weren't enough to dull my sense of self-hatred. So I started taking Sinutabs and Nyquil as downers. They worked very well, and they were medicine, not drugs.

Before long, I was spending between two and five days a week unable to leave my house. I woke up hating myself, terrified of the world, knowing I was not able to make it to work. So I would pick up the phone, contact the office, and tell them the lie of the day.

I had to lie. I couldn't work. I didn't even leave the townhouse for days at a time. I couldn't tell the truth to anyone, especially my dad. How could I tell them I wouldn't be in because I took too many laxatives and got drunk the night before and didn't get home until after two A.M.? Often, I did what every good addict who's in denial does to cover tracks: I lied. I lied most of the time to everybody about everything. I reverted to what I knew so well: I made up illnesses and injuries and purposefully hurt myself to have the evidence to validate them. I banged my head against the wall hard enough to raise a lump as evidence of a supposed concussion. Soap in my eye caused the puffy redness that supported a scratched cornea. Breathing in a brand of perfume I was strongly allergic to created the congestion that confirmed a sinus infection. Never mind the real damage done by the self-inflicted injuries. The important thing was that no one discovered my lies.

My father, more often than not, would warmly sympathize and tell me to take care of myself. I'd hang up the phone with my guts torn apart. I'd just lied through my teeth to a man I loved dearly and from whom I received warm, caring sympathy in return. My mom had been ill much of her adult life: severe allergies, hypoglycemia, candida, migraines, fallen kidneys, a hyperactive thyroid, near blindness—the list was endless. So it was easy for my father to believe that I, too, was frequently ill or injured. But I couldn't live with the emotional pain that was growing inside me and the impending doom of the black hole that lurked just beyond the protective haze of the food and alcohol.

When I could, I would throw some clothes on, get in the car, go to the grocery store, the liquor store, the drugstore, and the video store. Then I would go back home with my bags of food, my stacks of videos, my bottle of Grand Marnier or vodka, my Nyquil, Sinutabs, and Correctol, and I would shut myself off from the world.

My days became a blur of food and drug-induced dozing, lying on a couch half-watching videos I could never remember because my mind was in such a fog. I would get up only to replenish the bowl of popcorn, make another sandwich, take another hit off the Nyquil bottle, pop another couple of Sinutabs, or sit on the john with my guts cramped up so badly I wanted to scream.

I had diarrhea continuously and was excreting clear liquid. It was humiliating but was the only time I felt anything but bloated to the point of bursting. The scale became an obsession. I weighed myself ten, twenty times a day. I was living in a state of extreme dehydration. I often had heart palpitations.

I got to the point where I couldn't stand how I was living and didn't seem to have any power to change it. I didn't see, couldn't face, the truth. I ate more, drank more, took more Nyquil or Sinutabs, and used more Correctol. My life was okay. It was my sister Barbara who had the real problem. She was the alcoholic who drank until she got stupid. She was the one who called everybody up at all hours of the night and fell over furniture. She was the one we all talked about, saying, "What are we going to do with her?" I didn't have a problem. I was just fat. In reality we were both dying—inside and out.

Thursday, January 2, 1986, Tucson, Arizona
It finally happened. Barbara went too far. Her
drinking behavior was just out of line. She
really needs help.

I struggled with my eating, drinking, and drugs; Barb concentrated on alcohol. By the time she came east for Christmas in 1985, her inappropriate behavior could no longer be ignored. The day before Christmas my mother gave her an ultimatum that resulted in her not drinking during the rest of her stay with the family. However, as soon as she returned to Tucson, where she was now living, she began again in earnest. On the night of January 18, 1986, the police gave her the choice of going into treatment or into the drunk tank. She opted for treatment and entered a facility close to her home.

"Margo?" It was one of Barb's counselors on the telephone. Since my sister had only been in treatment for a week or so, I wondered if there was something wrong. "No, nothing's wrong, we have what's called Family Week as part of the treatment plan here. We're inviting as many family members to come for that week as possible. You'll have a chance to meet the staff and experience some of the program, and it would really help Barbara to know that you support her. Family support is essential to your sister's recovery, and I know she'll appreciate it."

"I'll have to move my schedule around. But I'll be there if there's any way I can make it." It felt good to be needed and the counselor did say that it was important to Barb's recovery. "I'll do anything to help Barb with her problem." It was easy for me to be compassionate toward my beloved sister, her problem was so obvious, and it was embarrassing the family. In the middle of February, I flew out to Tucson, joining my father, Barb's husband, and her daughter Meg to spend five days helping Barb get better. My mother was too ill to travel.

During the first group session, twenty family members sat in a circle, scared, wondering what was going to happen. The counselor, Chris, told us that alcoholism was a family disease and that we, too, would need to heal. You could have heard a pin drop in the room. She said we were there to help ourselves, not, as she called them, our patients.

My mind began racing. This was not what I had planned. Give me information. Let me be compassionate. After all, I'm in a therapy group in New York. My shrink and I have been talking for years and I'm just fine. It's my sister who has the problem, not me. What about her? We're going to talk about her. Don't you know that . . . ? I suddenly felt sick to my stomach.

One look around the room confirmed that I wasn't the only one feeling uncomfortable. People were squirming in their chairs, two of my fellow group members got up to go to the bathroom. Chris calmly continued to talk.

"I'd like each of you to introduce yourself by mentioning a couple of things that you want to get out of Family Week." She emphasized that these were to be our needs, not those of our patient.

Always eager to please and get acknowledgment for how quickly I learned things, I put my hand up before anyone else had a chance to move and blurted out, "I want to get to know myself better and find out how to help my sister not drink." I was sure it was exactly what the counselor wanted to hear. Having the right answer always made me feel better. I even believed I was telling the truth.

But, as I listened to the others in the circle, I knew I had to speak again. I didn't know exactly what I was going to say. I only knew that somewhere deep inside me a truth was ready to escape. I looked around the circle. Some of the people were crying. Many had moved forward on their chairs, others were sitting with backs straight, arms folded in front of them. Somehow my hand raised itself and when Chris asked, "What is it, Margo?" I burst into tears.

"I need to tell you that I abuse laxatives and one of my goals for this week is not to do that." A dam inside broke. No one except my therapist had known about the laxatives; I was too embarrassed to tell anyone else and he hadn't seemed too concerned. Of course I'd never told him the truth about how many I was taking, but here, in this circle, I couldn't stay in denial any longer. I had to tell the truth. The secret was out, and I knew even then I'd never be able to close the door on it again. I didn't know then that I'd walked through that door to a whole new life.

It was not my conscious will that raised my hand that day and admitted my own unmentionable behavior. God was doing for me what I could not do for myself, allowing me to ask for help when I could not consciously admit I needed it. For the first time in my life I felt honored for speaking the truth, not the truth someone else wanted or expected to hear, but my truth. I felt the support of people who knew the pain I experienced as I faced my shame, my guilt, and my remorse.

At the end of Family Week, I stopped at Chris's office to say good-bye. We talked for what seemed like hours. I felt pain I didn't understand, and I couldn't stop my tears. I was terrified about going back to Greenwich, my town house, and my bar stool at Morgan, but I didn't know why. I felt truly defenseless and utterly vulnerable. What was I going to do? My life needed to be different but I didn't know how to change it.

Chris came around her desk, put her face 6 inches away from mine, and looked me directly in the eye. "You have an eating disorder. It is primary and progressive and it's going to kill you if you don't do something about it." She handed me the business card of a treatment facility that dealt with eating disorders and held me as I sobbed.

I called the Rader Institute's 800 number that night and arranged to enter treatment in ten days. Any doubts I had about the severity of my problem vanished as I returned to Greenwich and was still unable to stop my behaviors. Despite my resolve to quit, I put on 5 additional pounds that week. I watched my addictions rule my life and observed my destruction as though I were watching vultures on the carcass of a lion on some PBS special. I was hopeless and helpless.

Some days I didn't know whether I even wanted to stay alive long enough to get to treatment. Terrified, I couldn't imagine continuing to live the way I was eating, but neither could I imagine living without the food to protect me from my emotional pain and the laxatives I was convinced would offset the consequences of my eating. Surrounded by the fog of incomprehensible demoralization, I couldn't see how to survive without eating continuously.

I had little idea of what the treatment would involve. What I did know was that I was voluntarily going into a hospital for forty-two days without radio, TV, or recreational reading. I was going because if I didn't I was going to die. I didn't dare look behind me, the darkness was rapidly closing in.

TO THE SUMMIT

Wednesday, February 26, 1986, over Colorado
So, it begins. Am en route to San Diego. Less
than an hour to go. Took an Atavan in
Denver. Looked at the Rockies as we crossed and
felt that's where I should be going. I'm
scared.

The plane ride was a blur of vodka, Atavan stolen from my mother, and cashews eaten nonstop. Over and over again as I read the airline magazine and watched the movie I thought, "Nothing else has worked. Why will this be different?"

When I checked into the hospital at about 9:30 that evening, I immediately shut down emotionally. Cool, calm, and efficient, I completed the required paperwork and was fine until the admitting nurse leaned across the desk and said, "Hold out your right hand, Margo, so I can put this ID bracelet on your wrist."

I knew then I didn't have anywhere else to go. This wasn't a hotel or the health spa in Vermont. Weighing 160 pounds, taking ninety laxatives a day, unable to stop eating or drinking, I was an addict voluntarily admitting herself to a hospital for treatment of an eating disorder. I choked back my tears, sure that the staff member who took me to my room wouldn't know how scared I felt. I went to bed immediately and awoke the next morning with the primal terror of having no idea where I was. Then I remembered, and the fear was no longer nameless. I was terrified that the program might not work and even more terrified that it might. I didn't know which scared me more. That day I was introduced to the schedule, staff, and other patients. I spent time completing more administrative forms and medical questionnaires, giving blood for lab tests and being examined by a physician. I tried desperately to get a sense of this place and program. My fear was so strong that I looked for any way to be able to hide the turmoil going on inside, to look good. I answered their questions with enough truth to let them know I had some problems, but without revealing how desperately empty I really felt. If they found that out they'd tell me I was hopeless and ask me to leave. I didn't have any other place to go. I'd die if I went back to my old ways. I was up against a hard wall without enough energy to keep up the fight. Then I realized there was something very different here. The staff wasn't just caring, they told me stories about their experiences with food that sounded like mine.

One of the first things I heard was that my eating disorder was a disease. They told me I wasn't alone, and that it wasn't my fault. I didn't know whether or not I really believed them, but I felt as though someone had lifted a 500-pound weight from my shoulders. I still believed I was somehow morally defective, but here were people telling me it wasn't my fault. I had a disease and it was treatable. Not curable, but definitely treatable. Their stories were about people who felt the feelings I felt. Even those feelings I had had from the time I was eight and before. I began to experience an enormous sense of relief and hope, real hope for the first time. Within a couple of days, I had a roommate and was beginning to attend regular group and individual therapy sessions.

Sitting with a dozen other patients and staff in a circle of orange plastic chairs, I was told that the only way I could begin to win over my disease was to surrender to my powerlessness. The warmth that came from the caring staff in the otherwise cold, institutional room began to thaw through my protective exterior. But it wasn't until I was challenged by another patient during group that my hard shield was cracked. Sitting across from me there in that circle, she leaned forward, resting her elbows on her knees and looked directly at me. "Margo, I've watched you and heard your answers to the questions you're asked, but I don't know anything about you. You haven't told us anything about what's really going on inside. Who are you?"

I broke down. I cried for nearly twenty-four hours. I cried in group, in the hallway, in my room, during meals, on my bed before I went to sleep and when I woke up. Everywhere I went there was a puddle.

Through my tears I heard others say, "It's safe to let go, you don't have to hold it all together here. Trust the process, you will get better. Trust your tears. Trust God, Margo." Trust. I didn't trust anything except my addictions. They'd always done what I asked them to: take away the pain of the secret I carried around inside me. The secret that I was not enough, that I was not good enough, not smart enough, to deserve to be alive. "Trust your Higher Power," they said. I couldn't figure out what they meant. Religion had never worked for me, but I was desperate. I talked with one of the counselors, and she said this wasn't about religion; it was about faith that a power greater than me could and would help me in my powerlessness over food, laxatives, drugs, and alcohol.

Vulnerable and confused, I finally collapsed into a steaming hot bathtub. I turned off the lights and as the water soothed my body, I closed my eyes and began to talk to something or someone, I didn't know who or what. I just began to talk saying, "I don't know where to turn, I don't know who to turn to but God; if you're there I need your help. Jonathan, if you're around, I need your help. Whoever's there, help me." I soaked in the water and pleaded with the universe for some tangible sign, some image to use, something to trust. Jonathan's face filled my mind's eye. Jonathan, God, something or someone took me into its arms and held me, comforted, and soothed me. I couldn't believe it. Incredible. For the first time I felt a deep sense of hope. I knew I could heal and that there was a power greater than me I could trust.

That experience in the bathtub was the turning point for me. Trust. I remembered how it felt to climb up the rock toward Jonathan. Tentatively, slowly, I began to open up to the group. Little by little I let them in on my secrets. I found out I wasn't the only one who felt alone in a roomful of people. I wasn't the only one who was killing herself trying desperately not to let anyone know what was going on inside. Now I had others I could talk, laugh, and cry with about my pain and my powerlessness over my disease. Here were people who had been abstinent, the eating disorder version of staying sober, longer than I could imagine: some for thirty days, a few for a whole year. People who gave me hope that I could do it too. People who loved me, the me inside. People who told me they would love me until I could love myself. I believed them. I felt their love and I believed them when they told me I had just begun finding out who Margo is. That if I were willing, I would experience greater joy than I could ever imagine and the incredible freedom that knowing my truth would bring.

During the forty-two days I spent at Rader, I learned how serious this disease really was. In a meeting with the unit physician to go over my test results, he had not pulled any punches.

"Do you know what electrolytes are, Margo?" he asked.

"Pretty much. Potassium and sodium are the main ones. I know they're affected by how much fluid is in the body and that it's kind of hard on the system if they're out of balance." I had learned a lot of medical jargon to support my imagined illnesses over the years.

"That's right. And yours were way out of balance. Do you remember saying that your heart had been beating irregularly for a while?" My arhythmia had come out during my intake interview.

"Uh-huh. At least it used to. It used to go really fast and then kind of stop. I remember lying in bed one time with my heart thumping so hard and fast in my chest I thought it might explode. Then it just stopped. I don't know for how long; probably not very. I remember wondering what would happen if it didn't start again." I laughed nervously, remembering my fear and wonder when that had happened. I hadn't told him that story before. I was afraid he would think I was too sick to stay in treatment.

The doctor wasn't smiling. "Margo. You probably came closer to dying that night than you had any idea. The heart needs electrolytes to beat properly, and yours were way off when you arrived here. Given your history of arhythmia and the quantity of laxatives you were taking, you would have had a major heart failure before very long."

I wasn't sure I understood him. "You mean I would have died?"

"That's exactly what I mean," he answered gravely. "I don't think you would have lived another four months. You need to understand that you will die if you go back to that old pattern."

That conversation terrified me. I had to change my relationship to food, alcohol, and drugs if I wanted to stay alive. Otherwise, the intricate web of dependencies created in the familiar surroundings of Greenwich and New York City would kill me, or at least kill the newfound hope that was growing roots ever so slowly in my heart. I began to examine all of my attitudes and behaviors from my old life, even the people I hung out with and places I went. But if I couldn't go back, what else was there?

Creating my new life would be a lot like knitting a sweater using a variety of yarns. I could salvage a few strands that were still useful from old emotional blankets I used to hide behind. Some would come from beautiful garments perfect for a child, but unsuited to an adult. Some strands would be brand-new, spun from the self-knowledge I was gaining. But there was no pattern for me to follow, so during one of our weekly meetings I asked my counselor for help.

"Trust the process," she suggested. "The design will be revealed as you need it."

I talked with my sponsor in Overeaters Anonymous, too. "You'll start out, and if it doesn't fit, just start over and do it again," she told me. "Just don't eat compulsively, drink, or use drugs no matter what."

This was recovery: an uncertain process of sorting, discovering, and choosing without relying on substances or old behaviors to soften life's realities. I'd been warned it would be painful sometimes. Through tears and the seemingly constant raw vulnerability, I asked how long the process would take, and my trusted friends answered, "Your whole life." Then they added, if I did my part on a daily basis, I would experience things I'd never even dared imagine before. I had only to do this "footwork" one day at a time. I could do that.

Saturday, June 28, 1986, San Diego
I need to learn to trust myself. Becky says I'm
right where I need to be. I am growing more
capable and more responsible with each day.
Thank you, God, for the willingness to just be.

I remained in San Diego to stay close to the people who saved my life and the support structure that gave me so much hope. Being abstinent, clean, and sober with new friends was exciting. It had been so long since I'd felt anything but hatred and condemnation toward myself, my self-esteem and sense of worth grew almost daily. I realized that my old beliefs about myself and the world around me nearly always resulted in fear, resentments, and self-pity. Observing how I made simple decisions—even when to get up in the morning or go to bed at night—gave me insights about the values I really lived by and what I did when I was uncomfortable. The voices of my addictions whispered that I could eat or drink the uncomfortable feelings away. They told me that a binge or a drink or a drug, any drug, would take the edge off the feelings that came up when I faced my old attitudes; they'd always worked in the past. But my conviction that I could not do it that way anymore grew stronger. Every minute seemed to carry another opportunity for growth.

In the climate of Southern California I healed physically, too. I participated in sports again and felt the pleasure in exercise and competition I'd had when I was young. Volleyball games and even jogging became part of my regular routine. My stamina increased and I surrounded myself with friends who were also committed to a healthy lifestyle. By not eating between moderate-size meals, I reached a weight that was healthy and average. The exact number on the scale didn't matter, and for the first time in my life, I used it as a source of information about my health rather than as an instrument of punishment. I knew that as long as I abstained and ate in a moderate, healthy way, my body would be the size it was meant to be.

Professionally, I sorted through my options and interests. I knew I didn't want to go back into finance or computers. I really wanted to help others who felt as hopeless as me to find sobriety and abstinence, too. I set a personal goal of becoming a licensed counselor and defined a plan to follow. As I took preliminary entrance exams for graduate studies with people half my age I had to cope with back-to-school fears. Would my brain still function in classes? Each step in the application process became a challenge to overcome and a confirmation once it had been accomplished. After what seemed like months of inquiries, tests, and interviews, I was accepted into the masters program in Counseling Education at San Diego State University. I'd never studied without drugs and alcohol. How could I write papers and take tests without those props and junk food? What would I do if I failed, or even received a grade less than an A? The old voices said, "There's no point doing it at all if you're not going to get all As." It was doubtful that would happen, and the next thought was "So then why try at all?" Would I slip into a depression like I'd experienced at Middlebury when my ability to make easy grades abandoned me? I knew I'd need all the help I could get from God and my support group as I made my way through this new adventure. I began to explore other dreams, too. Where did I want to live? What about relationships? What about things I wanted to do, places I wanted to go that had always been "impossible"?

I decided to follow through on plans I'd made a few months before going into treatment to go on a safari. I'd talked about it for years but in a rare moment of clarity I'd finally realized that if I kept waiting for the perfect time to go and the love of my life to go with, it would never happen. On an alcohol-enhanced whim, I had asked a man who'd been my surrogate brother and good friend for many years if he wanted to go to Kenya with me, Impulsively, he'd said yes.

"I don't know if I can pull this one off, Becky. Do you think I'm ready?" I felt like the little girl sitting in front of the bookcase with the large glass doors at my paternal grandfather's house, looking at his collection of carved elephants. I'd dreamed then of going on a safari to East Africa but couldn't imagine ever really seeing those gentle giants in person. Now, I was leaving for my dream trip and was still unsure, "What will I do when I'm stuck out in Africa somewhere all by myself?" Becky had become one of my closest friends and was a mentor for me in recovery. I called her often to talk about my fears.

"Margo, you won't be by yourself," she said, reminding me once again of simple principles I used in my life every day. "Your job is to not drink or use drugs or eat compulsively. You're always in God's hands."

"I know, Beck, but . . ." It seemed like there were always so many "but's" in my thinking. My whole world had changed since I'd made the plans to go to Africa, and now I questioned whether I was ready to take the trip. I would have to face at least two potentially dangerous temptations: my friend enjoyed drinking and the food would be terrific and plentiful. Talking about my dilemma with Becky helped. My mind quieted. The fear that seemed so big disappeared like an early-morning shadow. I knew I was ready. I was in God's hands.

Every detail of the trip went perfectly, from the brilliant sunrise waking us in our tent on Lake Baringo to the sunset at Cotter's Camp in the Maasai Mara that turned the sky and clouds into a reproduction of the overleaf in an old family Bible. Flowers in full bloom stood out among lush green trees and golden brown grasses. We drifted above giant herds of wildebeest in a hot air balloon. And we rode for miles in the ever-present Land Cruiser, looking, I imagined, like some kind of mechanized turtle, our shoulders, arms, heads, and cameras stuck out of the viewing roof.

Hundreds of assorted animals filled our viewfinders and were recorded on dozens of rolls of film. Everyone we met—guides, expatriate farmers, and wildlife management experts, as well as fellow travelers and the indigenous Kikuyu and Maasai—were gracious and welcomed us into their homes and camps as friends they hadn't seen in a long time. I experienced the warmth of Jonathan's nurturing, peaceful spirit and the protection of God's loving strength in many ways throughout the trip. Each of them helped me to be strong against my addictions when the food and alcohol were so very tempting. Becky had been right. My job was simply to be there and take care of my recovery. The rest was up to God.

One afternoon I looked out through the trees, past elephants leisurely grazing in front of us, and saw Mount Kenya rising majestically in the background. Rugged, reaching above the plains and lesser hills, it called to me. I felt a strong desire to climb to its heights. I didn't know why. I couldn't ever remember wanting to climb a mountain before. My attachment to Jonathan's Himalayas was about their spiritual legacy, not about climbing. Now, here was this mountain, drawing me, calling to me deep inside, the way the miniature elephants had called to me when I was a young girl.

More than thirty years had passed before I answered that call. I wasn't going to let this one go without responding. If climbing a 17,058-foot mountain was supposed to happen, it would become a part of the new life design I was weaving. I felt as if I was being pulled by a force much greater than me. It was incredible to entertain a dream this big and to imagine how it would feel to accomplish it when at the moment I had no idea how. The questions of why and whether or not I could ever be in good enough physical shape to make it to the top of a mountain didn't even enter my mind until I got home.

After the trip, I lined the walls of my apartment in San Diego with photos from the safari. Every day the images of the animals, the people, and the flowers reminded me of the inner call to climb Mount Kenya. I didn't talk much about it because my attention was constantly drawn to the more pressing emotional issues I wrestled with and the practical career choices I was making. Still, it grew quietly, and when my self-doubt raised questions about my going, I learned to say, "Today I can take the next step toward this dream. If tomorrow I find out it's not the right thing for me to do, I can change my mind then."

Life in San Diego wasn't all sunshine and success, though.

My God now accompanied me into the depths of the dark, uncharted territory I was finding inside. Some days, just getting out of bed seemed like a major accomplishment. I learned to focus on the present, do the next indicated step no matter how I felt, and leave the results up to God. When I was at home alone, He filled the emptiness. He held my hand when it felt as if my very existence was threatened. When life was a struggle, He gave me hope along with my fears and the ability to go beyond the question, "Is this all there is?" I discovered a sense of belonging in the world. I could safely have dreams and believe they could come true. Slowly but surely the design for the fabric of my life was being revealed.

Recovery was no longer an intellectual exercise: Learn these principles and you'll have a balanced life. The emotional threads I pulled on every day were connected deeply to my past. Out of nowhere, a seemingly insignificant event or word, a level-two event on my emotional Richter Scale, would set off an emotional aftershock that would hit nine. I began to realize that most of my reactions to life were based on my history, not on the events of the present. I was surprised by memories and feelings I hadn't thought about for years, some I'd purposefully forgotten.

I talked with Becky about this phenomenon.

"Here's what's worked for me, Margo." One of the reasons I trusted her so much was that she rarely told me what to do; instead, she invariably shared with me what she'd done in a similar situation. "Each time a memory presents itself to me and triggers some strong feeling, I use it to begin to build an intimate relationship with myself at that age."

Soon I was learning about myself when I was four, eight, thirteen, nineteen, and thirty-five years old. I was concerned that maybe I had multiple personalities. Becky assured me that, in fact, what I was doing was finding all of the ways I'd left myself behind to get the acceptance and love I needed to survive. In the process I was healing, becoming whole. Another dream was being fulfilled.

I began dating and immediately found myself in the clutches of old beliefs about my sexuality and neediness. The voices inside said, "If you sleep with him, he won't go away." But they'd been proven wrong time and time again. My mind was still telling me I had to survive while my heart showed me I didn't have to give myself away, emotionally or physically, simply to avoid being alone. Free from that fear, I was able to see clearly for the first time how my expectations and actions with men corresponded directly to the nature of attention I received as a little girl, reinforced by each choice I made as an adolescent.

I experienced men, both friends and lovers, from a new perspective. In the middle of a first meeting I would check my emotions. Sometimes I felt as if I were thirteen with blood rushing to every part of my body, imagining the day or evening lasting forever. Other times, my nineteen-year-old would want to take a hostage, keeping him around as a distraction from having to feel the uncomfortable process of change. Frequently my four-year-old simply wanted to be held, the way she never was. Occasionally, even when I felt connected to myself and God, a fear would return that told me if I truly learned to hold myself and no longer needed to be held, then I would never be held again. Slowly but surely I was building a new foundation of experience based on my new belief in myself as a woman who could have dreams and fears at the same time.

During a visit with Leelee and her family in Aspen in the fall of 1987, she and I reminisced about our early days in Aspen.

"We did some crazy things back then, Migger," Leelee said with a laugh.

"That we did," I responded. "Remember the climb up Turkey Rock with Jonathan? We were both so scared at the bottom and so proud at the top."

"I sure do. Which reminds me: Alex went to Africa and climbed Mount Kenya and Kilimanjaro. She loved it. I thought of you when she told me."

Alex was a close friend of Leelee's and a high-powered lawyer in Boston who loved her career. And she had climbed a mountain. And not just any mountain. She had climbed Mount Kenya, the mountain that had called to me so strongly in Africa and stayed with me since that time. If she had done it, why couldn't I? This was all too much of a coincidence to be ignored.

I called Alex in Boston to ask her about her trip. "Yes, Margo, it was wonderful. Hard work but well worth it." When I questioned my fitness level, she replied, "I was able to train enough even with the long hours I work. You'd do great." Could this be? I tried to focus on what she was saying, but the negative voice in my head nearly drowned out her voice. This was my inner critic, Martha, at her best. It couldn't possibly happen and I wasn't strong enough anyway and on and on and on.

From somewhere deep inside a voice stopped the litany. "No, Martha. That's not the truth. I deserve it and this may be the answer." Once again God was doing things for me that I still couldn't do for myself. Events had come together in a way I could not have imagined: the trip to Aspen, talking about Turkey Rock, my affinity with Mount Kenya, Alex's climb. As before, I showed up and participated in life as best I could, and the Universe was giving me the key to unlock my dream.

I turned forty in January of 1988. When I was still active in my addictions I had dreaded even the idea of turning forty. It somehow signified the end of my youth; the end of any chance I had at achieving any of my dreams or goals; the end of any hope I had of changing. Now I embraced forty, wanting to celebrate and honor my being alive to begin the fifth decade of my life. I gave a dinner dance in my honor in San Diego, and my friends and I laughed and danced the night away. My dad, my sister Barb, her daughter Meg, and Leelee all flew in for the party. I was touched by the effort they made and honored by the people who had come together to celebrate with me.

I also gave myself a week at a vacation/health resort called Canyon Ranch. Barb had told me about it several years before and, intrigued, I had filed the information away for the future. Now was the perfect time. And I had sent for all the information about a Mount Kenya/ Kilimanjaro climbing trip that was offered the following summer. The week at Canyon Ranch would not only be a vacation but a gauge by which I would judge whether I could be fit enough by June to make the climbs.

Canyon Ranch was all I imagined and more: healthy food, hikes in the desert, satisfyingly sore muscles, daily massages, long nights of sleep, interesting people—and confirmation that I was indeed fit enough to plan to go to Africa in June. I reserved a space on the trip the day I returned home.

"Breathe. Just remember to breathe. And don't drink, no matter what." Becky's voice on the phone was reassuring. She always had such simple, practical advice when I came to her in a state of emotional upheaval. Even after two-and-a-half years in recovery the most basic things still troubled me sometimes, and her counsel helped me stay in the present.

"Beck, what is this about? I'm going on the adventure of a lifetime and I feel like crying. I don't get it." I had run all the miles I could, strengthened my upper and lower body with weight training, and gathered the necessary equipment. I even had a supply of music tapes for the Walkman to use while hiking. I'd learned that trick while jogging and wanted the familiar tunes on this adventure, too. All that was left was some last-minute packing and the trip to the airport.

"Maybe what you're feeling is gratitude, Margo." That wasn't even close to the possibilities I'd come up with. "Sometimes it looks a lot like sadness. Check your insides." She reminded me that I was having success in healing early childhood wounds, that I was feeling a sense of power from telling the truth and believing in myself, and that today I was preparing to reach out for a dream by going to climb Mount Kenya and Mount Kilimanjaro. "You've never honored yourself like this before, Margo. Recovery from addictions doesn't promise us that any of this will be easy, only that we can do it. I'm really proud of you."

After I hung up the phone, I let myself sit down, feel the gratitude, and cry. Memories and emotions from the past forty years washed over me in waves. First came the sadness and self-judgment from every time I'd said I wanted to do something then hadn't because I was too sick or too weak or too busy: the week at an Outward Bound course I'd canceled because I sprained my ankle; the bike I'd bought to exercise on and never ridden; the gyms I'd joined and never attended. Close behind these, though, was gratitude for the courage it took for me to go to Rader, to take that first trip to Africa to honor my childhood dream to see elephants in the wild, and my willingness to follow my heart's desire to climb Mount Kenya. There was so much to be grateful for today, I was getting all A's in my graduate program and was excited about becoming a counselor. So many parts of my inner emotional family were now my friends; they no longer had to run and hide for fear of how I'd abuse them or their feelings. I not only looked like a whole person most of the time, I really felt that way, too. The self-judgment still was the first emotion to show up, but maybe that would change someday, too.

CHAPTER THREE
Welcome to Africa

Tuesday, June 7, 1988, Nairobi
Sunrise over Africa. At least over a cloud bank
over Africa. Blue sky above, walkable, fluffy
white clouds below. Welcome back to Africa,
Margo.

"That's incredible! I can't imagine what it must have felt like to have been the oldest finisher of the Ironman. What a sense of accomplishment." My seatmate was also going to be one of my climbing partners on Mount Kenya and Mount Kilimanjaro. A retired corporate executive who was in his late sixties, Norton had phoned me before we left the States and arranged for us to meet in London. I was glad we had. His positive attitude and perspective were infectious, and I was fascinated by how actively he was living his life.

"Oh, what I've done really isn't much. All it takes is endurance and the willingness to go through physical pain. Anyone dumb enough and with a body that doesn't fail them can do it." Norton adjusted his tall frame in the cramped airline seat. We'd been flying for hours since leaving Heathrow and still had a feature-length movie between us and Nairobi. His voice had the polish of corporate protocol, understating his accomplishments. He paused and turned sideways in his seat toward me, "You know, what you've done, what you're doing on a daily basis, now that takes real courage. I've never had to face the issues you talk about. I don't know whether I could. You're the real hero."

I was speechless. What did he see that I didn't? How could I respond to a comment like that? I felt a tightness in my throat, the precursor to tears of gratitude. "Thanks." It sounded feeble, but it was from my heart, maybe deeper. I turned to look out the window. If I'd had a drink I'd have taken a sip.

My mind kept wanting to project me into the future—to the mountains; the other people who would be there; the guide, weather, food; and whether or not I had enough clothes—anything but sitting still, here. I somehow knew this trip would be more concerned with mental and spiritual strength than with mere physical endurance. Nevertheless, I wondered how I was going to handle sleeping bags, tents, and hiking long hours. I whispered a prayer of thanks for Norton's willingness to reflect back to me what he saw. It gave me a good alternative to Martha's critical vision.

The movie started, but Norton's acknowledgment had shifted something. It was as though my insides were a spinning top that he'd touched with his finger, and I wanted to see where it took me. So, even though I felt tired from my hours of flying and changes in time zones, I pulled out my journal and began to write about the past few weeks, especially the time I'd spent with Mum and Pop in Greenwich.

New awareness and insights continued to come to me on a daily basis. But each victory seemed to be built on a foundation of pain: the pain of change, of doing things in a new and sometimes awkward way. Some days the emotional work of reconstructing nearly forty years of faulty programming seemed overwhelming, like climbing inner mountains rising higher and more unattainable than Mount Kenya. I constantly reminded myself to take life one hour at a time.

Each experience helped me discover more and more about my new foundation. The anger, fear, and sadness, reflex reactions to the past, were sometimes so strong I knew they were markers, emotional signs that said, "Don't go this way: Danger." It seemed as if I didn't have a choice; I had to explore all of my inner territory to find out what was really true and what was not.

Anger, above all, seemed to be a key emotion for me. It frequently came out as judgment, sometimes as rage. With professional help I had walked backward through my life's disappointments, through the childhood that was not perfect but was certainly not bad. Back to an event that caused me to double over with emotional pain when I recalled it. As I faced its truth, I understood that I had minimized it to the point of nonexistence because I couldn't bear it any other way. There was no option for me now but to reexperience the sense of violation and betrayal of being fondled by my maternal grandfather when I was only six years old.

I had to acknowledge my anger at my parents for not protecting me if I was to be allowed to feel sadness for the part of myself I had set aside in order to perform as though nothing had happened, to maintain the approval of others, to survive. I knew I wasn't alone. Many children are molested every year, many much worse than me, but for the first time in my life I was able to hold the little girl I had been, to love her and tell her it wasn't her fault. Uncovering this truth was powerful, but I knew I had more work to do to completely open the door for healing.

On my way to London, I had stopped in Greenwich, resolved to talk with my parents about the new-found truth about my molestation. One day, then another, went by as I waited for the perfect time to tell Mother about my memories. Talking with her would be doubly difficult because it was her father who had touched me. Finally, after a number of false starts, I walked into her kitchen and knew this was the time. We were in her sanctuary, a place set aside, almost holy, where she was safe from the outside world. Her severe illnesses limited her freedom of movement, and extreme allergies took away all but the most carefully orchestrated contact with others, but here in her kitchen she had a sense of control over her world.

"Mum. There's something I need to tell you." My voice came out more high-pitched than normal—tentative, like a little girl's. Now I couldn't take the words back, I'd already said too much.

"Oh, Lord." Mum's words escaped, almost silently, propelled by fear and an involuntary preparation for pain. Then, instantly, she caught herself, her voice now smooth, controlled. "Of course, Miggie." She moved from the sink, drying her hands automatically on the towel she'd picked up somewhere along the way, and sat in her chair at the kitchen table. It had always been her chair, the one sitting sideways, the one that didn't commit either to the beauty outside or to the inner reality of her world, but kept her in the middle.

I took a deep breath. I knew my words would cut deeply and cause her to feel the pain she instinctively anticipated. I sat close to her in my seat, the one looking at the beautiful world outside, slowly drew in another deep breath, and told her about the molestation. About how I had tried so hard for so long to pretend it wasn't a big deal. About how much the little six-year-old inside me had blamed herself for it happening, that as that little girl, I needed to know I wasn't bad and that my mommy still loved me. I told her that I couldn't keep it a secret anymore, I couldn't pretend that it didn't matter. I had to let it out to break the powerful spell it had held over me for thirty-four years.

"Oh, God." Mum's body slumped forward. Her hands tried to cover the tears that streamed down her face. Then we talked. She told me about how hard it was hearing that her father, who had been so gentle and loved, whom she had held in such esteem, had done such a thing. And she said a great-granddaughter, also six years old, had said Poppy touched her "down there," too. The little girl had been told she must be mistaken and to forget about it.

Mum professed that she loved me and was glad I had told her, but there was something missing in her words. Her own need to survive got in the way of her heart. The loyalty to her father, the need to protect her image of him, and the pain she felt when she began to let it go were too much. My mother and I held each other and cried for a long time: our pain so real yet so separate. I wept for all the little girls who had been told their truth was a lie. She, for the truth she knew she couldn't allow to be.

Rather than the cleansing I had hoped to experience, I felt resignation. I reminded myself that talking with Mum had not been about receiving what I wanted from her. It was for me, for my little girl whom I'd abandoned so early. I looked at the new understanding I had of the intricate and overlapping threads of survival instincts woven between my mother and me and was able to begin to accept her in the whole truth of the woman she was—her courage and her weakness. The veil of resignation lifted. Now I could live my life more freely. I could love my mother without having to try to be like her or trying to receive something from her she couldn't give. That new life I'd been promised was emerging from the threads of my old one.

I closed my journal just as the captain was announcing our descent into Nairobi. It felt strange being in my skin, as if I were watching the person I'd always wanted to be. Sometimes, as at that moment, all I could do was shake my head in disbelief and thank God for the opportunity to live my life. I was returning to Africa, this time to climb mountains—incredible.

The plane touched down in Nairobi, and my fatigue disappeared as I smiled, anticipating the adventure to come. In the recesses of my mind, Martha's judgmental commentary ran nonstop: I would get lost in the airport, there wouldn't be anyone there to meet me, and besides, who did I think I was climbing Mount Kenya anyway? I fell into line behind Norton as we emerged into the tropical heat, walking past the intimidating gaze of guards holding machine guns.

As we completed the bureaucratic maze of customs, we were met by a ruggedly handsome, full-bearded man with a welcoming smile who introduced himself as Skip Horner, our guide for the climbs. I liked him right away, but I only half-listened as he laid out what we'd be doing between now and when we reached the base of Mount Kenya. Our first task was to kill time while we waited for the other members of our group. My focus shifted to asking questions about his life as a guide. I wanted to know about the stuff that excited my passions: the beautiful, exotic images of faraway places and marvelous adventures he described.

When I told him that the only climbing I had ever done was on Turkey Rock in Aspen, he surprised me by saying that he'd lived there, too. As we played "Who do you know?" and swapped small-town stories, it became apparent we had lived there at the same time and perhaps even gone to some of the same parties.

I shook my head and laughed. "I'm constantly amazed at how small the world is." That was an understatement! Here I was in Africa talking to an adventure travel guide about common experiences from fifteen years ago. "Did you, by any chance, know a guy named Jonathan Wright while you were in Aspen?"

"Yes, I knew him well." Skip's voice tapered off and got lost in a memory. "We were climbing together up on Independence Pass the day before he left on his last trip, the one to China." His answer took my breath away. I couldn't speak, but Skip did, "What? Is that a coincidence, too?"

"I can't tell you what a gift it is for me that you knew Jonathan. He's the one who took me to Turkey Rock. It's because of his life and his love for mountains that I'm here." I didn't believe in coincidences. What seemed like coincidences were simply miracles where God wanted to remain anonymous. I felt warm from the inside out, so filled with memories of Jonathan it was as if he were physically present. Skip smiled, and in his eyes I saw the same eagerness for the adventure of life that had been in Jonathan's.

The other members of the trip arrived, and we were finally complete. Six of us, including Skip, loaded our duffel bags and packs into the vans that took us to our hotel. Norton, Skip, and I rode in one, and the other three in the second. Mark, an early-thirties neurosurgeon who didn't look old enough to have an undergraduate degree much less be doing surgery on peoples' brains, and Janice, bright, witty, outgoing, and looking as much like a teenager as Mark, were a young Canadian couple planning to marry within the year. Laura, my roommate in Nairobi and tentmate-to-be on the mountain was a pleasant, attractive American woman with a marvelous sense of humor.

Laura and I spent the evening repacking our bags, sorting out what we thought we'd need while on the climbs. Skip had told us we could expect it to be hot and humid at the start, rainy and cool in the middle, and cold and snowy at the top, and he reminded us that if we didn't have something we needed with us, we wouldn't be able to go to a store to buy it. Our room was in total disarray, reflecting the chaotic sorting and resorting of clothes and other gear. Neither of us really knew what to expect on the mountain.

A knock at the door was followed by Skip's voice. "Laura. Margo. How's the packing coming?" We opened the door. He laughed as he entered, carefully picking his way among the piles. "This is what's known as 'root-n-rummage.' "

"Root-n-rummage." At least what we were doing had a name. I checked what I'd chosen one more time, especially sensitive to Skip's comments about the probability of rain and absolute assurance of cold temperatures. As I pushed my final T-shirt selection into the duffel bag, then cleared space off the bed so I could crawl in for some sleep, I was thankful we would have porters to carry our gear.

My body reacted to the time changes and excitement by waking me at 3:00 A.M. as though it were time to start the day. I managed to get back to sleep until 6:30, then I finally surrendered and swung my feet out of bed to get dressed. After breakfast we climbed into a Land-Rover for the drive to the bandas, the cabins that would be our starting place for the climb up Mount Kenya.

The four-hour trip took us from the urban paved roads of Nairobi to rough dirt roads approaching Mount Kenya. I saw grasslands greener than I thought possible, and small farms with patches of corn, tea, and coffee. At 17,058 feet, Mount Kenya's highest peak rises nearly 4,000 feet above the tallest point of the Aberdare Mountains, the massive north-south moorland range that's a major center for big-game viewing. Their rugged, volcanic origins had also made them an ideal haven for the Mau Mau rebels who fought against the British and colonists for Kenya's independence in the early 1950s.

Although the equator traverses its northern flanks, Mount Kenya wears eleven glaciers: permanent snow and ice fields, some of which can be seen on the ridges rising out of her rich, green, rolling hills like chipped teeth, discolored with age. Reports by European missionaries during the mid-1800s of ice on these mountains were discounted and disbelieved by the stately members of the Royal Geographical Society, safe and warm in their wood-paneled lounges in London. Nearly forty years would pass before these reports would be confirmed by "acceptable" sources.

The first serious attempt to climb Mount Kenya was in 1893. It wasn't climbed again until 1930, when a young British expatriate, Eric

Shipton, established new routes. Shipton went on to become a legend in climbing circles, some say the greatest mountain explorer of all time. The last unclimbed route on Mount Kenya was conquered in 1980.

As we drove through the grasslands and rain forest with its moss-laden trees, vines, and tangled growth, I began to feel a real sense of being an explorer and watched in awe as the mountain's peaks filled the windshield of our vehicle. I wasn't here simply to look, though, I was going to climb it. At 10,000 feet, we reached the bandas at the edge of what is known as the moorland zone. We had a night there to acclimate before starting our climb. At forty years old, I was here to climb my first mountain, my first two mountains.

The next morning I felt decadent as the twenty-three men who would be our porters and cooks for the next few days poured out of the odd assortment of vehicles that brought them to the bandas. They wore such an assortment of sweaters, jackets, hats, coveralls, and boots they looked like a walking thrift store. But, unlike the five of us, who were here for the first time and had varying amounts of apprehension about what lay ahead, they were seasoned professionals. They knew exactly what they were doing and where they were going as they arranged the various boxes, bags, and duffels that carried our clothes, tents, and food.

Before we had time to think about it, we were all following a trail through a magic kingdom of vegetation that grew larger than any I'd ever seen. Heather stood shoulder high and in abundance. Giant plants, called groundsels, had beautiful large star bursts of green and white leaves at the tips of their arms and reminded me of giant saguaro cactus of the Arizona desert. Grass grew in knee-high tufts.

The long pants and pile jackets of early morning were shed well before noon as the warmth of the African sun favored shorts, T-shirts, and even bare backs for some of the men. By early afternoon we had gained nearly 2,000 vertical feet in altitude, and clouds had closed in, bringing with them a significant drop in temperature and a fine mist. The mist turned into rain and we stopped to change back into long pants, sweatshirts, and rain gear.

My boots became waterlogged and my socks were soggy. Hiking through the tussock grass and over the irregular volcanic debris in our path was an ever-increasing challenge, and my attitude deteriorated with the weather. I wanted to find someone or something to blame for my discomfort, but instead, the tools I'd practiced in my recovery helped me adjust my outlook. I could hear Becky talking with me about staying in the present, doing the footwork, and leaving the results to God. I didn't have to ruin this trip of a lifetime simply because my feet were cold and wet. Proudly, I realized I was able to distinguish between physical discomfort and a real crisis. Not too long before I hadn't known there was a difference.

We made camp at Lake Ellis, surrounded by jagged ridges and higher summits. Sometime during the middle of the night, I crawled out of my warm sleeping bag and went outside to pee. Most of the clouds had been blown away, and zillions of stars filled a very black sky, making it seem even colder than it was. I stared out into the depths of space and said "thank you" to the Universe for allowing me to be here.

The second day of hiking took us up over a ridge and down the other side past Lake Michaelson and a small stream where we renewed our water supply, then up another, then down and up again. We scrambled along cliffs looking down more than a thousand feet into valleys carved by glaciers and erosion. We were following what's known as the Chogoria route to Point Lenana. At 16,355 feet it's the trekking summit of Mount Kenya, the highest point on the mountain that can be reached without technical climbing skills and equipment.

Sometime during the day I developed a severe headache and worried that it might be a symptom of high-altitude sickness, a dangerous threat to anyone climbing above 10,000 feet. Skip had told us that the best way to take care of ourselves would be to not push ourselves too hard and to drink plenty of fluids. At home the fluids I drank were cans of diet soda, and here I found it difficult to drink enough water to stay hydrated and knew the altitude was having an effect on me in other ways, too. One minute my face would fill with a smile so big I thought it wouldn't hold it, the next I'd be close to tears. My mood rose as high and dropped as low as the ridges we traversed, alternating between feeling great and strong to wanting to give up because my legs hurt so bad. A number of times I sensed Jonathan's presence, encouraging, prompting me to look up to see an incredible view as we gained enough altitude to see over another ridge.

We camped that night at 14,000 feet next to a frail-looking tin shelter called Minto's Hut. By the time we reached our destination, it was snowing quite hard. After dinner, I began to feel really lousy. My headache worsened and my stomach churned. I went to bed but couldn't sleep. Time seemed to stand still, and the night went on forever. I had to do something to get some rest as we were scheduled to get up at 4:15 A.M. to leave for the summit. I finally went outside, stuck my finger down my throat to get some relief, and fell into a fitful sleep soon after crawling back into my sleeping bag.

I awakened to the early call for breakfast with little appetite and what seemed like even less strength. As I walked around the outside of the hut, I watched my companions and the porters and willed myself to remember Becky's reminder from times I'd called her when I wasn't feeling well. She'd always said, "This, too, shall pass. You can do anything, one hour at a time, even this." I wasn't sure, but I knew I wasn't willing to miss out on any of the gifts waiting for me on this trip, and the summit was still up ahead.

We left camp in the dark at 5:00 A.M. to allow us to reach Point Lenana and still descend to our next camp in daylight. The circles of our headlamps stood out on the new snow and the rocks along our route as we spread out, everyone following his or her own pace. Skip and Mark led and soon were quite far ahead. Laura, Janice, and I held a place in the middle. Norton, in the rear, was slow but steady, greatly affected by the altitude, especially as we climbed above 15,000 feet.

The trail steepened considerably. I kept my head down, forcing myself to make the effort each step required, but glanced up just as the sun rose above the clouds that were now filling the valleys below. The sun surrounded us with its warmth and showed us where we had to go to meet our objective.

Picking our way through the snow, ice, and rocks, we scrambled across scree—rock debris sometimes as small as pebbles, sometimes as large as a man's fist—making our advance difficult. I argued with myself at one point, countering the voice that was saying, "You'll never make it" with my belief that together God and I could. I knew I could go as slowly as I needed to and began to use a rest step much of the time: lock the bottom knee, letting the forward leg rest momentarily, then breathe one full breath. Step, breathe. Step, breathe.

I reached the summit of Point Lenana in full sunshine, my face covered with tears, the wind and cold reminding me that I was standing more than three miles high on my first mountain peak. There were no words to describe the joy, gratitude, and satisfaction I felt. I could have a dream and realize it. I could accomplish hard physical work and overcome the negative voices that came from inside to attain a goal I wanted.

We stood taking in the 360-degree view, including the higher twin summits of Nelion and Batian standing out like fingers less than a mile across the Lewis and Gregory glaciers that filled the valley more than 2,000 feet below. The volcanic rock stood out, black against the brilliant white snow, while clouds hid most of the moorlands, forest, and plains. We took pictures of ourselves beside the tall metal cross that marked this summit like the hilt of some Arthurian sword waiting for the perfect knight to come along and claim his right to rule the land. I felt so strong, I imagined I could pull it out without a second thought.

We descended west, following the Nara Meru route down. The snow on this side was much deeper; in some places Skip had to cut steps with his ice axe. A misstep would have resulted in a slide with no chance of stopping until I reached the rocks at the bottom several hundred feet below. The challenge and adventure were exhilarating and pricked only slightly by an occasional needle of fear. We stopped at the base of the first ridge for a snack and looked back, still able to see our footsteps as they led off the summit, down to our current location.

The route was poorly marked as we continued down a very steep portion of loose rock and dirt, across a stream to our camp. The sight of the tents already set up, the activity around the cook tent, and the porters busy with their own preparations for the afternoon were as welcome as a lighted window at home. I slept solidly all night, collapsing from the combined effects of exhaustion and excitement.

The next day we continued our descent through the fantasy world of a vertical bog. The natural laws of gravity were suspended here in these moorland heights. Not only were we surrounded once again by plants that were larger than life, but everywhere we stepped the ground was soft and soggy. We were soon covered with mud, from trying to jump from one island of knee-high grass to another. Small streams ran clear and fast through deep-cut banks and randomly cut across our path, as we followed the erratic line of red-and-white striped posts that led us to the road head and the transportation waiting to take us to Amboseli for several days of rest and game viewing.

In the days after the climb, I floated between extremes: the ecstasy and sense of satisfaction of accomplishing this dream and a deep sadness that haunted me. I didn't want to drink or eat compulsively, yet Martha was telling me that because I didn't, I wasn't really a part of the group. When the others partied, I felt different from them and not safe talking about or showing what I was feeling. I found myself wanting to cry, but there was no place to be alone, so I took my emotions to my journal and wrote about them.

I wrote about my joy and sadness and felt the frustration and pain of the years I'd spent trying so hard to hold my life together, setting my feelings aside because they were "inappropriate," "wrong," or "bad." Alcohol and food used to take away the discomfort of having these feelings. Now I had other options. In my journal, all of my emotions could exist at the same time and not compete with each other. I didn't have to do anything with them or fix them. I could simply acknowledge them and their power and their place in my life, and then I could go to sleep anticipating tomorrow.

Tuesday, June 14, 1988, Amboseli Game Park
We finally got a view of Kili this morning. It
was cloudy when we got up but the clouds
rose as we were driving, and then there it was.
That famous snowcap with elephants walking
on the plain underneath.

Two more days of viewing big game in a variety of locations warmed my animal lover's heart and gave my body time to recuperate from the climb up Mount Kenya. As we approached the Kenya-Tanzania border, Mount Kilimanjaro dominated the horizon. I'd never experienced anything so overwhelming in scale. We traveled for hours and it didn't seem to get any closer. It was as if it were traveling south, too, staying just ahead of us.

Mount Kilimanjaro covers an area of more than 1,250 square miles, sprawling 50 miles long by 25 miles wide at its base. It has three peaks, Shira, Kibo, and Mawenzi. Kibo is the highest, at 19,340 feet, and was our objective. Our climb would take six days up and down, and at the summit, we would be 3,000 feet higher than we had been on Mount Kenya. Traveling through the lush countryside and small villages, I found it was easy to feel the awe in which this mountain was held by the trading caravans and lines of slaves as they moved from the heart of the continent toward the coastal center of Mombasa many years ago. It was more difficult to realize that, like Mount Kenya, Mount Kilimanjaro had first been seen by Europeans only a little more than a hundred years ago.

At the Kibo Hotel in Marangu, Laura and I unpacked all of our gear and spread it out across the red linoleum bedroom floor with its centrally placed flowered square. Separating the gear we would take with us the next day, we repacked. This "root-n-rummage" took me less time than the one in Nairobi, and I experienced the additional bonus of a sense of satisfaction knowing what had worked and what hadn't on my previous climb.

We left the next morning at 8:30 A.M., retracing some of our travel from the day before. In the small village of Moshi, we stocked up on vegetables, and the porters purchased their food for the trip. I felt as if I were on display as the children and adults in the village surrounded us, pointing and talking among themselves.

Our next stop was in Machame to visit the local butcher. While we watched, John, our Tanzanian guide and cook, selected a variety of cuts of beef for our meals from a carcass hanging in the open air. As we left the shop, he proudly held up his prize, a cow's snout. To our slightly warped amusement, it became what we fondly dubbed "cow lip soup" that night.

Soon after leaving Machame, what was loosely referred to as a road from the village to the beginning of the trail deteriorated rapidly. The ruts deepened, and the forest seemed to close in around us. Our driver, who was just learning to drive, wrestled our ancient Land Cruiser around every turn.

Recent rains had turned the dirt into mud. Twice we got stuck, even with four-wheel drive engaged all the time. One minute we'd be riding the high spots on the track, the next we were in the ruts and going sideways until we couldn't go any more. Fortunately, the road served as a riverbed, too, so it ran 3 to 4 feet lower than the ferns and trees surrounding us. At least we weren't riding on the side of the mountain. Each time we got stuck, we'd all pile out, grab branches and any loose leaves we could find, line the roadway with them, and stuff some under the tires. Then, we'd all climb on the bumpers, fenders, and side steps to add our weight for traction, hoping that we wouldn't fall or be thrown off as the driver rocked the vehicle back and forth until it gained enough traction to move forward again. By the time we reached the park ranger's hut and the beginning of the trail, we all wondered if it wouldn't have been easier to walk.

The trail we followed up the mountain, the Machame Route, was one of the least traveled. As soon as the porters arrived and loaded the gear, we started out for our first objective: the Machame camp. Our hike through the rain forest was filled with the wonder of bright red mushrooms, huge ferns, and mosses hanging from the trees, but the trail was a constant uphill push, and the wet, muddy ground made the going difficult. I was struggling with my eating, too.

At home I was committed to eating three meals a day and not having snacks in between. On Mount Kenya and now here, we were sometimes having four meals during the day, and Skip was telling me that I'd have to eat snacks like granola bars if I wanted to maintain my energy for the climb. I still found it hard to drink enough water to stay hydrated at these altitudes. Now I was questioning whether or not I would have to break my commitment to abstinence in order to finish the climb. Was my food program flexible enough to adapt to the requirements of climbing? I worried that I would use Skip's comments as an excuse to eat when I really didn't need to.

My food addiction was different from my alcoholism. I knew I couldn't drink alcohol, and besides, there was always something non-alcoholic available to drink. But, I *had* to eat. And here I had to eat at different times and in different quantities than I was used to at home just to have the stamina to make the climb. I really wished I had someone to talk to. It would have been so great to pick up a phone and call Becky for support. I felt more and more separate from the other climbers as my mind worked to "understand" and find a solution.

By the time we reached camp, my back and ankles hurt and my energy level was very low. The two Uniport domes there were intended to provide shelter for climbers, but it was cleaner, quieter, and warmer to stay in our tents. I was glad to have one to myself that night. As I lay on my sleeping bag I thanked God for my recovery and was astounded at how I was able to just put one foot in front of the other during the day. Right behind the gratitude was my fear of how to handle the issue of eating while climbing. I wasn't willing to give up the new life I'd created over the past two years, even for the summit of Mount Kilimanjaro.

That night, I found the place of balance and serenity in my journal. I wasn't eating more to stuff my feelings or to help me feel that I belonged. I was eating more because my body needed it as fuel if I was going to climb this mountain. It was essential for me to change my behavior here. That's what true recovery was all about: taking care of myself with discernment. I internalized the feelings of being separate and alone and found that God was waiting there for me. I was different from the others on the trip, I couldn't drink alcohol or eat everything I wanted anytime I wanted to, and it didn't mean I was any less than they were or that I didn't belong.

It began to rain about 2:30 A.M. and was still raining, although it was fairly warm, when we started hiking at 8:00 A.M. Walking in the lead with Skip, following cairns—trailmarkers made by stacking rocks—to find our way, I really enjoyed talking about the old days in Aspen and the changes that had happened in our lives since then. I soon took my parka off. The purple overshirt, shorts, and rain pants were all I needed to be comfortable. I liked watching and following Skip as he climbed, seemingly effortlessly over the uneven surface of this dormant volcano. I played with sexual fantasies but knew somehow that the role of this man in my life would not be a romantic one. Not only was Skip already with a woman he obviously loved very much, but my connection with him, as with Jonathan, had to do with mountains and my soul.

As we climbed higher, the temperature dropped and the rain continued. Combined with the increasingly steep terrain, they began to take their toll on me physically and mentally. By noon, when we reached our destination on the Shira Plateau, I was freezing and walking in small lakes, my boots squishing with each step. We waited inside the single Uniport hut there until the porters carrying the tents arrived, then I helped set them up. My hands were so cold they were nearly useless, even in polypro gloves. But the activity distracted my mind from dwelling on how uncomfortable I felt. Even though it was early in the afternoon, I was soon tucked away in my own tent, warming myself in my sleeping bag. I listened to music on my Walkman, took a nap, and read a book. But none of them took away the fear that lurked inside.

I was afraid of the cold, concerned that I couldn't handle four more days of discomfort like today's, especially as we climbed higher and higher on the mountain. And I was scared of not being able to talk with anyone about my fears. Wisely, I gave up trying to ignore the fear, prayed, and wrote in my journal. Except for one short, cold and wet trip outside to pee, I stayed warm and dry and grew more grateful by the hour for my ability to change my attitude. At last I was able to turn everything, including the weather, over to God.

By the time dinner was ready I was rested and free from most of my fear. We gathered around the cook fire, spreading our mittens, socks, and boots over rocks, sticks, and ice axes, anywhere they'd fit and catch some of the heat to dry. It was still raining some, although it looked as if the clouds were breaking up. The conversation that evening turned to poetry. Skip talked about some of Robert Frost's poems and how they moved him to tears. Such sensitivity contrasted with my image of Skip as the capable, friendly, yet restrained globe-trotting leader of adventure expeditions. I went to sleep trying to create an image of what it would be like to experience a trip like this with an emotionally vulnerable yet strong man—it might only happen in a dream.

When the first call came at 6:30 A.M., I was already awake in my sleeping bag, using my feet as natural heaters in an attempt to dry out my socks. They were still damp from yesterday, but I wore them anyway. The ground was soaked although the rain had stopped. The lingering clouds were still threatening, hiding Kibo and its summit still more than 8,000 feet above us. As we left camp, a rainbow arched over us and the sun broke through, giving us hope of good weather for this day's climb. Soon, however, clouds rose from the forest and moorlands below to envelop us in a fog that created an eerie, science fiction–like atmosphere. The trail was marked with cairns spaced just far enough apart for one to disappear in the mist before the next emerged. We followed one another, blindly trusting our leader, gaining another hundred feet in altitude, then another thousand as the terrain became increasingly barren.

We climbed over ridge after ridge formed by ancient streams of lava. The debris left from their freezing and refreezing made our cross-country hiking a real challenge. I listened to the music tapes I'd made at home and sang along with John Denver, the Eagles, Dan Fogelberg, and Neil Diamond as I scrambled up and down what could have been the ribs of a giant. Occasionally I would see Skip and his ever-present white cap or Laura's purple fleece off in the distance and was able to judge just how big the mountain really was and how far we still had to go.

I couldn't help but break out in a grin as gratitude bubbled up from deep inside. Here I was, Margo Chisholm, a forty-year-old woman who should have been dead from my addictions, but instead I was living in a tent, wearing wet socks and boots, and climbing over barren rocks on my way to the highest point on the African continent. One step at a time was how I learned to make it through a day in treatment. The same simple principles worked as well on this mountain as on the ones I was climbing inside. Show up, put one foot in front of the other, and extraordinary things can happen.

Our destination, the Barranco Hut, looked like a corn storage shed out of Iowa. Set among the boulders and scree in a deep valley, two-and-one-half miles high in the African sky, it seemed out of place and woefully barren compared with the majesty of nature all around us. Once again we hung our socks, boots, and outer clothes around our fire. This night the conversation turned to relationships, compatibility, and the meaning of life. "What would you do if you found out you only had one year to live?" someone asked the group.

I heard myself saying, "I'd keep doing this as long as I could." The intensity of my conviction surprised me. Seemingly simple and unrelated threads were coming together to form a common theme: Jonathan's influence in Aspen, the safari two years ago when I saw Mount Kenya and first felt the call to climb it, and now being here, in Africa again having met my goal on one peak, poised to complete the second. I knew that something important was going on inside, I just didn't know what it meant for the future. I had schooling to complete, a career track to follow, I didn't have time to climb mountains. Besides, I hated the cold! I was glad the conversation was only talk and not reality.

The clouds cleared to reveal a perfect new moon set in the deep black of the equatorial sky. Billions of stars winked back at me as I ate an orange in the doorway of my small tent and acknowledged that God and Jonathan's spirit were both with me. I scrunched down in the warmth of my sleeping bag and fell into a sound sleep.

It was freezing cold when I awakened, but the sky was still clear and for the first time in three days my socks were dry when I put them on. Once the sun finally rose over the ridgeline the air became quite warm. Oh, how grateful I was becoming for the little things in life: dry socks, sunshine, and the ability to change my own attitude.

We were directly below a tremendous rock face called the Breach Wall, which stands more than 4,500 feet high along the southwest side of Kilimanjaro. Our route took us around it to the east, up and out of the barranco, or valley, we were in, and across another valley to the ridge beyond with wonderful views of Mawenzi, Kibo's sister peak, and the Heim and Kersten glaciers. Below us, the tops of the clouds looked like whipped cream.

I was excited and nervous as I crawled into my tent at the Barafu Hut that night and I couldn't get to sleep. It was daunting to know that at over 15,000 feet we were higher than Mount Whitney, the tallest point in the continental United States, and that tomorrow I would be on Kili's summit. Martha's voice was active, too, judging my eating behavior, assessing whether or not I'd gained weight on the trip, and whether I was eating more or less than the other women. I was finally able to let it all go, get in touch with God, and even enjoy the beauty of the moon and the night sky when I went outside to pee.

I was just falling asleep as Skip rustled the side of the tent, "Time to get up, Margo. Kibo's waiting for us." Our summit attempt was about to begin. It was midnight, and I could feel the cold of the night, even inside my sleeping bag. We were leaving in the middle of the night so the snowfields would still be frozen and therefore more stable to climb on. I pulled out my polypro long johns, pink sweat pants, wind pants, gaiters, polypro socks, wool socks, hiking boots, two T-shirts, polypro top, pile jacket, down jacket, polypro gloves, and heavy wool mittens, adding layer upon layer, hoping I could still climb once I got dressed.

A quick cup of coffee and some granola, and we were off. The moon had just set and the circles of light from our headlamps seemed to be absorbed by the rock before they could provide light for our path. The wind had picked up during the night, and I was chilled by it despite the many layers of clothes I wore. The climbing was more difficult than I expected, and we still had 4,000 vertical feet to gain. We scrambled up loose scree and across slabs of rock that sloped downward. Patches of old snow intersected the route periodically, some quite wide with slippery, uneven surfaces. Fear began to make each step feel unsure, setting my emotions on edge. Jemss, one of our porters, didn't have a headlamp of his own and followed so closely he kept stepping on my heels. I walked a fine line between irritation and gratitude for being able to give him some light to see by. Janice slipped and was helped back up. Laura got terrible stomach cramps and nausea an hour and a half out of camp. Skip stayed with her the rest of the way. Moving from rock to scree to snow and back again, we entered that period just before dawn when the night is deepest. The temperature continued to drop.

I plugged away, putting one foot in front of the other. I never had a doubt about making it to the top. I felt God's and Jonathan's presence helping me with almost every step. When my toes or fingers or neck got too cold, my experience told me that they wouldn't stay that way. I knew I didn't have to be miserable just because parts of me were uncomfortable.

After more than six hours of hard work in the cold and wind, following the precarious route, we reached Gilman's Point on the rim of Kibo's crater in time to watch the sun rise over the opposite ridge, a mile and a half away. The welcome light began to fill the depths of the crater nearly 300 feet below. We were at 19,000 feet, but we still weren't at the summit. Our final objective was Uhuru Peak, still an hour's climb away. Its name means "Freedom" in Swahili, changed from Kaiser Wilhelm Spitze when Tanzania received its independence from colonial rule. As I trudged along the rim, my breath came in short, shallow bursts. A dry, hacking cough was triggered each time I took more than half a breath.

I watched Marc as he stood briefly on the summit, then went back, past me, to help Janice. I continued, the first woman in our group to reach the makeshift flagpole and metal box holding the summit log, and watched the downward slope of the massive snow fields disappear into the clouds that covered the plains of Kenya and Tanzania. I experienced a sense of humility and gratitude as the realities of what I'd accomplished over the past two weeks and where I was standing, at that moment, began to sink in. I felt very proud for being at the top of that mountain. Then, as my teammates arrived, other feelings emerged.

Skip came up holding Laura's hand. Marc returned with Janice. Jemss and Robert, another porter, arrived right behind them. All I could see were people in pairs, couples arriving on the summit. An intense sadness began to push my gratitude and perspective aside. My tears of joy were tainted with feelings of abandonment, being left alone when I was strong. The strong ones help the less strong. Who is there for the strong ones? I wasn't quite sure whether I was more grateful that I had made it to the summit, or sad that I had done it alone.

Almost immediately I felt a presence with me, and thought I heard a voice say, "I'm with you." It wasn't present like a warm body, but somehow I knew it was giving me something even more real and lasting, a sense of peace, joy, and inner healing I'd never known before. God's, Jonathan's and my own spirits were somehow joining together to let me know that, in truth, I wasn't alone.

And there was something else, too. Quietly yet powerfully from way down inside my heart, a lid was being blown off a box of incredible dreams that had been sealed tightly for years. I had a sense of truly unlimited possibilities. Something had changed. I knew I'd never be the same again.

"Okay, guys, group photo time." Skip's enthusiasm and supportive leadership were still present. "Come over here before we all freeze or get blown off this peak."

As we were assembling ourselves and our cameras, someone asked, "Where's Norton?" I felt stricken—I was so absorbed in my own emotions, I hadn't even noticed that he wasn't there.

"I haven't seen him in several hours, but John was with him." Skip's casual confidence set us at ease. "They were going real slow earlier this morning. I'll wait at Gilman's and if they don't show up in an hour or so I'll figure Norton couldn't make it and they turned around." John, one of our Tanzanian guides, knew the mountain well. "We'll all meet at the Horumbo Hut later. If they don't make it here, they'll meet us there."

We climbed back down to Gilman's Point and stopped for a break: trail mix and water. Even though we carried them in our packs, the water bottles contained a layer of ice, another confirmation for me of how extreme this adventure really was. Skip prepared to stay at Gilman's for a while in case Norton and John still made it there, while the rest of us followed the rim to Johannes Notch and the nearly 3,000 vertical feet of pebblelike ash cinders leading down to the Kibo Hut, the highest shelter on the Marangu Route. I followed Marc, catapulted down the steep slope by exhilaration. Neil Diamond sang "Soolaimon" on my headphones as I ran down the soft scree, arms extended like a bird's wings, banking through serpentine curves in the cinderlike soil with long sliding steps, laughter bubbling up and out. My incredible joy and energy felt better than any drug high I ever had.

After standing at 19,340 feet on the summit, the air at the 15,400-foot altitude of Kibo Hut felt almost like sea level. This hut was like Grand Central Station, filled with porters and climbers of all shapes and sizes. We had a lunch of peanut butter and jelly sandwiches and took a nap under the ever-watchful eyes of Jemss and Robert. Although I was still coughing and my sinuses were very dry, I felt stronger after the brief rest.

We still had a long way to go to reach the Horumbo Hut where we would spend the night. Located at 12,000 feet, Horumbo is actually a small village of sleeping huts surrounding a central dining facility. Expanded over the years to meet the demands of the large number of climbers approaching Kili's summit via the Marangu Route, it can house more than two hundred people. A long, well-worn trail took us down the mountain to the wide, barren, and relatively flat saddle that separates Kibo from its sister, Mawenzi, a rugged rock tower standing in stark contrast to the smooth slope of Kibo's crater. Continuing our descent, we were surprised to catch up with Norton and John and walked into Horumbo together.

Norton told us he had made his decision to turn around after only a couple of hours of climbing. He knew he was going so slowly he wouldn't have time to reach the summit and get to shelter, so he turned around, went back to camp, and after some sleep, he and John traversed around to meet us. I was inspired by his willingness to know and trust his limits, and his determination to find alternative ways to meet his objective.

As I sat with Norton, talking about his intention to make another attempt on the summit, a deep wave of emotions swept over me. I wanted to cry, wanted someone to hold me. I wondered why I felt so needy, so out of sorts after having such a powerful and fulfilling day. Martha said there really was something wrong with me, that I would never be able to really, deeply feel the joy and satisfaction of living a dream and be able to hold on to it.

I remembered a principle I'd learned at home: Keep it simple. I stopped trying to find some deep reason for my emotions. It really was simple. I was forty years old, had been awake more than thirty hours, and had spent more than half that time climbing to the summit of the highest mountain in Africa. Two years before I was dying and couldn't even walk up a flight of stairs without stopping. I joined the others for dinner and went to bed.

Exhaustion, excitement, and the altitude combined with my aches and pains from the climb and cramps from the first day of my period to make for a restless night. They also made me vulnerable to old behaviors. The next morning, when I joined everyone else at breakfast, I caught myself wanting to be recognized for doing a good job of showing up, and tried to get sympathy by lying about pains I didn't have. I knew now, though, that I could change how I felt on the inside by changing how I behaved. So, on the long trail down through the moorlands and into the forest, when Marc and Skip picked up their pace, I began to jog with them. The running lifted my spirits, and my mind began to look into the box of dreams opened on the summit.

What would I do if I really believed I could? There were other mountains to climb: McKinley in the United States, Elbrus in Europe, maybe an expedition in Jonathan's Himalayas to see how high I could go. There were river adventures, too: the Colorado through the Grand Canyon, the Bio Bio in Chile, and the Çoruh in Turkey. As I thought about them, it was easy to believe that time and money were the biggest hurdles I'd face, but I knew that wasn't true. My own inner doubts and fears were the real obstacles I'd have to surmount to reach these dreams.

When our group gathered at the hotel on our last night together, everyone was sentimental about the trip coming to an end. We had worked well together as a team and supported each other in making it to the summit. At the end of the evening, I followed Skip out of the dining room where we had our farewell party. I wanted to have a few words with him alone. "Skip," my voice was quiet, my emotions close to the surface. He stopped and turned. "Thanks for the incredible gift you've helped me receive over the past two-and-a-half weeks. Your encouragement and guidance were a really important part of my success on both mountains. I'm very grateful."

He beamed at me, his incredible smile framed in his full beard. "Margo, you're a good woman with a great attitude. I'd love to have you with me on other trips, too." I felt his affirmation all the way down to my toes as he reached out and hugged me.

"Right now, that's a dream of mine, too," I said, tentatively. Stepping back, holding both of his hands, I looked at him and smiled. Tears of gratitude rolled down my cheeks. "It's no accident that you were such a good friend of Jonathan's and that you were the one to take me to my first summit. I hope there will be more. Jonathan always wanted me to get to Nepal and the Himalaya. We'll see. I'm beginning to believe those kinds of dreams can really happen. They're happening in my life already."

The next day I shared flights with Laura to Addis Ababa, Rome, and London. Laura was going home to New York. I was on my way to Aspen for a few days before going to San Diego.

Thursday, June 23, 1988, In flight:
London to New York
Only time will tell what kind of long-term effect
this trip will have for me. I do know that
now I can do the kinds of things I've talked
about for so many years. I believe in myself
more than I did before. Recovery continues to
allow me more freedom, more options than
I ever dreamed possible. And more serenity. Who
would have believed it!

"Leelee, it was magic. Better than magic." We were jogging around the golf course off Cemetery Lane, the first chance we'd had to talk together since I arrived in Aspen the day before. "I was blown away when he said he was a friend of Jonathan's. It was just so perfect. The whole trip was perfect." I was riding a high and wouldn't remember the rain and cold and loneliness until I looked at the slides. I laughed out loud. "There is no way I could have imagined my life looking like this."

"It is incredible. I used to be so scared for you." Leelee's words came out between breaths. "Sometimes I called just to make sure you weren't dead. But I always knew you'd come out of it somehow. And you sure have! What a change!"

I took Leelee and her two boys, Michael and Matt, to visit my God Rock alongside Hunter Creek. I wanted to be able to share that special place with them and thank God for helping me find the willingness to continue to grow. He had helped me deal with the physical and emotional challenges on the mountain, adjust my eating in a way that worked for me while climbing, and had helped me open my box filled with new dreams.

I began reading a book called *Seven Summits*, about two successful businessmen, Dick Bass and Frank Wells, who had attempted to climb the highest mountain on each of the seven continents. Dick Bass had succeeded, and Frank Wells had come very close, missing only Everest. It wasn't the first book I'd read about climbing, but for the first time I thought, "If they could do it, maybe I can, too." A fleeting thought certainly, but one I didn't reject immediately.

Norton called from his home in California to tell me that on his second attempt he had reached the summit of Kili. I was so pleased for him and touched by his willingness to push himself to his limits. He was an important model. He invited me to attend a snow- and ice-climbing course with him sometime that summer on Mount Rainier. I knew I wanted to go, but I wasn't quite ready to commit.

Making my flight connections back to San Diego, I had mixed feelings about going home. I began to wonder how I would adjust to my ordinary life. Making my bed, keeping the house clean, and fixing healthy meals seemed like major challenges. Somehow life almost seemed easier on Mount Kilimanjaro. I knew I'd have to rely more and more on God to help me find the energy to do everything I'd need to do if I really wanted to live my dreams, not simply long for them.

CHAPTER FOUR

This Is What I Want to Do

Tuesday, July 26, 1988, Mount Rainier
Reality struck the dream: The bloom is off the
rose. This is the reality of what I want to
do. Pain and fatigue. Cold feet. No solitude. And
the sense of accomplishment at the end of a
day. And the beauty. Even sad and hurting, I
still feel drawn to it.

I arrived in Seattle on Sunday afternoon with ample time to drive my rental car to the Paradise Inn at the foot of Mount Rainier. The flight from San Diego had given me a great view of this 14,400-foot cone of volcanic stone and cinders. Rising majestically 45 miles east of Puget Sound, Mt. Rainier's perennially snow-covered summit is visible for more than 100 miles in every direction. Capt. George Vancouver had identified and named it during his explorations of the coastline in 1792, but the first recorded ascent of its summit didn't occur until 1870. In 1899, the government designated it a national park and it has held a unique place in American mountaineering ever since.

Mount Rainier supports the largest single-peak glacier system in the lower forty-eight states. Its easy accessibility and year-round snowcap make it ideal for learning snow- and ice-climbing techniques. Many American expeditions planning major ascents on mountains around the world, including Mount Everest, use Rainier's slopes for training prior to their climbs. That's why I was here, too.

I was approaching my new dream to climb like my annual Christmas wish list. I poured over adventure travel catalogues and folded back the pages of every climbing trip that interested me, then went through them again to narrow my choices. Fortunately for me, a trip to Cerro Aconcagua, the highest mountain in South America, was scheduled during my school's winter break. We would be establishing several camps on the mountain and carrying gear from one camp to the next on this expedition-type climb. Some days it was hard for me to believe I was even considering these trips, let alone planning for them.

I checked in with the Rainier Mountaineering Institute for an ice and snow course that would give me the additional experience and training I needed for South America. I rented crampons, an ice axe, and a pair of plastic climbing boots, and settled into my room. Afterward I walked around the grounds. The summit that was my objective stood starkly beautiful in the bright moonlight, an incredible mass of rock and snow rising 9,000 feet above me. Viewed from the safety of the trappings of civilization, its slopes seemed passive, belying the hard realities that lay between me and the summit. Norton had suggested this trip after we returned from Kili, then decided at the last minute not to come. He encouraged me to do it anyway, saying, "Margo, I know you're going to be doing a lot more climbing; this course will be really good for you." His positive vision and supportive attitude had been essential to my following through to be there.

Before I left San Diego, I'd attended one of my regular meetings of people in recovery and talked about my fears for this trip. I heard myself tell the others in the room that I felt as if I were at a watershed. With Rainier, I was consciously saying I wanted to climb big mountains, to set goals I might not achieve.

My old fears of not being good enough and not deserving to have what I really wanted were fodder for my inner critic Martha to tell me why I shouldn't be here and that I'd just make a fool out of myself during the next five days.

It took all of the courage and trust I could muster to stay at the base of the mountain through the night. Fortunately, my only tasks were to eat dinner and crawl into bed. Before I went to sleep my mind drifted back to a conversation I'd had a couple of months ago.

"Damn it, Becky, I'm forty years old. Why can't I do this without falling apart?" One more time I was on the phone, melting in a puddle of tears in my room, questioning my sanity.

"Margo, you're doing great." She rarely told me what I wanted to hear but she always told me the truth. "You're just exactly where you're supposed to be. You and God make a great team."

That's not the way it felt to me. "Yeah, right! If these are the results of recovery, tell God I quit!" I was lonely. My latest relationship had just dissolved. I felt fat and out of shape. I'd fed myself some junk food, felt like purging, and didn't want to get out of bed that morning. It bore little resemblance to my old behavior—I had had a moderate amount of popcorn and ice cream for dinner the night before, whereas three years before it would have been two bowls of popcorn, a quart of ice cream, a box of cookies, and a bag of potato chips—but I felt the same. The road was becoming narrower. Behavior that used to feel acceptable no longer did. "I don't want to go on the training hike I've planned for today. Not even a little bit. It won't make or break my experience on Mount Rainier, Beck, but why did I feel so good just a couple of weeks ago and today I feel like shit?"

"Feelings are real, Margo, but they're not reality." The simplicity of Becky's wisdom came through again. "You're doing such good work. Creating a new way of living isn't as easy as it sounds. Sometimes we feel the worst when we're having the most growth. Making a gratitude list really helps me when everything looks bleak. Maybe it'd work for you." That seemed reasonable. "I'm grateful that you're in my life and I love you very much. Why don't we check in with each other tonight?"

As always, I hung up feeling better. I knew that whenever I felt out of control and called Becky or one of my other friends in recovery, I had a different perspective when I finished. And when I felt overwhelmed, as though I couldn't ever reach the new dreams I had for my life, I would look at how far I'd come in just a couple of years. I would remember everything I was grateful for and I'd have hope again. So, on the eve of my adventure on Mount Rainier, I wrapped gratitude around me like a down comforter.

As I drifted off to sleep, pictures ran through my head of the countless days I spent lying on the couch in the den of my Greenwich town house, semiconscious from a half bottle of Nyquil and several ounces of vodka, watching videos I didn't remember, eating food I didn't taste. Countless nights in Aspen and New York, loaded on coke and marijuana, then no more coke but still too wired to sleep, no dope left to numb my feelings, swallowing Sinutabs to take the edge off. Anything not to feel the pain and self-hatred, the incomprehensible demoralization that filled my heart. Each time I did it, I hated myself more, and I had been totally powerless to stop doing it. A vicious, hopeless, self-destructive circle. How was it possible to get here from there? I didn't have an answer to that question. I only knew that I was blessed, and I slept like a baby.

Monday morning I was up early to meet my five companions and our guides, Paul, Dave, and Curtis, outside the Paradise Inn. The three guides were young, eager, and fit, and Paul had a strong physical resemblance to Jonathan that immediately made me feel comfortable. Except for the packs, food, and group gear we were loading into the vans, we might have been mistaken for just another group of picnickers as we stood in the bright sun wearing shorts and T-shirts. I glanced around the group: The other five clients, three men and two woman, were all in their late thirties or early forties. The men had extensive hiking experience but had never climbed on snow before. One of the women had done a fair amount of climbing and was using this course as a review before she went to South America to climb; the other had never been on a mountain. Assessing their physical conditioning, I noticed that I looked about as fit as they did. I might not make a fool of myself after all.

The clear blue sky and warm sun were nearly obscured by the dense foliage as we hiked through stands of Douglas fir. We crossed alpine meadows, full of bright white, yellow, and blue wildflowers sparkling with dew. The people in front of me looked like 45-pound packs with legs as they moved up the trail toting cooking pots, sleeping pads, and climbing helmets that hung like ornaments next to ice axes and snow shovels.

We stopped for lunch after we emerged from the last group of trees, having crossed the distinct boundary called the timberline. Cold air, chilled by the glaciers, greeted us, and we pulled long pants and jackets out of our packs to dress more warmly before the afternoon's hiking. The trip was beginning to really feel like work. We weren't even halfway through the first of five days, and already a hot, shooting pain, maybe a pinched nerve, had started in my left hip and radiated up my lower back. I was using every ounce of energy I had to continue moving my feet to keep up with the others. The plastic boots I'd rented felt awkward and clumsy on the trail and didn't seem to fit right. I hoped they'd feel more comfortable on the snow and ice. Despite the hours of weight training, Stairmaster, and jogging I'd completed between Kili and here, I still felt out of shape. Would I ever be able to make it as a climber?

I bit into the sandwich Paul had brought to me. "I'm thinking about trying to climb Aconcagua in Argentina in January," I told him between chews. "I heard this course will give me the skills I'll need to be able to make it. What do you think?"

"I think with what you'll be learning over the next couple of days you'll do just fine. I've never been there myself, but I know plenty of guides and clients who have." Paul's lanky body, easy mannerisms, and quiet voice reminded me a lot of Jonathan. The similarity comforted the uneasiness I felt. "The biggest thing will be your conditioning. You'll need to be really fit and able to carry at least forty pounds comfortably at sea level to make it. Aconcagua's a lot longer and harder than Rainier."

That afternoon we climbed through rocks, snow, and ice as we approached the Cowlite and Ingraham glaciers. The five other novices and I had our first instruction in self-arrest, a safety technique used by climbers to stop a fall on a snow-covered slope. Paul explained that whether we were climbing roped or unroped, this skill could save our lives or the life of a fellow climber someday. He showed us how to grab the shaft and head of the medieval-looking ice axe, while Dave and Curtis demonstrated on the slope in front of us. When my turn came to slide purposely down the slope on my back, adrenaline rushed through my system.

At first, the terror of sliding out of control blocked the techniques I'd just seen and heard. Then, I felt excitement as my axe dug into the glacier. Loose snow and ice chips sprayed around my head. I stopped sliding. Looking back up the slope, I saw the gouge left in the ice by my successful self-arrest.

I scrambled to my feet, waved my arms, and yelled, "Yahoo!" at the top of my lungs as though I'd just won an Olympic event. It didn't matter that I was twice the age of the guides and among the oldest of the clients. I could do this! As I watched Paul and Dave demonstrate other techniques and volunteered again and again to try them myself, the pains in my back and feet faded into the background. I felt proud and confident until the pain returned later, and close behind it, Martha's judgments and questions about whether this climbing thing was really something I wanted to do.

Later that afternoon we set up camp on a large snowfield, attaching the lines from our four-season tent to ice screws and anchors rather than stakes. I worried that the snow would melt underneath the tent and the water would leak in and soak the sleeping bags. The guides seemed to anticipate my unspoken questions and with each step explained what they were doing and why they were doing it. Waterproof tarps and the floor of the tent took care of the water problem, and the tent actually kept the snow from melting by protecting it from the sun. I was learning more than I'd ever imagined about the reality of climbing. This was different from rock climbing, different from hiking, even different from the camaraderie and pace of climbing in Africa. Some of what I learned nourished my dream, some made me question whether the hard work and physical discomfort were worth the fleeting moments of wonder and personal satisfaction.

We set up camp and ate, then sat on our Therm-a-Rests practicing tying knots and telling stories about climbing experiences. Sarah, Chris, and I, the three women on the trip, shared a two-person tent, a cramped but welcome buffer against the cold.

Throughout the next day, short waves of burning pain persisted in my back as we climbed 2,500 vertical feet on snow and ice toward Camp Shurman, a climbing shelter tucked in at the base of Steamboat Prow. The pain was so bad at times it took my breath away, yet I watched myself exaggerate it. The line between the real physical pain and my old ploy of using a physical ailment to cover my inner fear, self-judgment, and unhappiness blurred. I was pushing myself harder, doing more than I'd ever done before without any idea of what was normal or usual, and I didn't have an instruction manual.

At one point I stopped and was leaning into the slope, supporting my body on the head of the ice axe, when Curtis called out. "Margo. Everything all right?"

I had a hard time responding as I fought back tears. "Yeah, I'm okay, it's just my damn back. Hurts like hell. Sometimes I just have to stop and rest it a bit."

"The pain's not that bad." Martha sniped before Curtis could respond. "You're just tired and looking for an excuse to stop."

"Shut up!" I answered her silently. "Yes, I'm tired and, yes, my back hurts like hell. This is not the same as spending weeks on crutches with an invented injury. It isn't the same. I'm not the same!" I spoke with conviction.

Fortunately, Curtis wasn't able to hear the conversation I was having in my head as he moved across the slope to where I was standing. "You're a gutsy lady, Margo. I know a lot of guys who'd have stopped before now if they were you." Martha didn't have a rebuttal.

I had to smile. I believed him. I didn't know if I was gutsy, or stupid. I did know that if I didn't go on I'd never find out. "Thanks. You've made me a very happy woman." With his encouragement I was able to make it to camp to enjoy the sweeping panorama that spread out from the mountain.

The mountaineering hut that marks Camp Shurman was built in the early 1960s to house climbers, emergency food, and a radio. Constructed from metal highway culverts covered with stone, the structure stands like a ship's masthead splitting the Emmons and Winthrop glaciers as they flow past the rocky spine of Steamboat Prow. Exposed to the fierce wind and weather that rushes unobstructed across the Pacific Ocean to this ridge, even the outhouse is strapped down with strong cables securely bolted into solid rock. I doubted whether our frail-looking tents would still be standing in the morning. As the sun set, the sky turned a fiery red that reflected off Puget Sound. The lights of Seattle, over 75 miles away, sparkled in the twilight.

Still 5,000 vertical feet from the summit, we took a day off to acclimatize to the altitude and learn more about climbing techniques. The wind howled across the Emmons Glacier all morning, giving us an excuse to rest in our tents. Later, we gathered together behind the hut, protected from the wind, for more stories and "teaching" about mountains and climbing by the guides. I began to feel as though I were really taking part in an expedition. We were becoming comrades with a common goal. We practiced tying the bowline and other basic climbing knots and soaked up the warmth of the sun. By early afternoon the wind had blown itself out and we were able to move onto the glacier to practice crevasse rescue techniques.

More than 4 miles long and as much as 1½ miles wide, the Emmons Glacier extends from the crater rim to below the timberline in the White River Valley. When I was lowered into one of its crevasses, I could sense the power of this living, breathing force of nature. The whites and blues of the snow and ice were different down there from any I'd ever seen before. Glancing up at the deep blue sky through the mouthlike opening in the ice, I wondered what I'd do if I ever faced a truly life-threatening situation on a mountain. Deep down inside my soul I heard a distant, yet strong answer: I'd do whatever was necessary. I suspected that if I continued to climb, I would someday have that tested.

For hours I watched, then imitated the moves of the guides. I was reminded of climbing Turkey Rock with Jonathan and Leelee as I double-checked the bowline knot that tied my safety harness to the rope and called out "on belay" to let my partner know I was beginning to climb. Then I jammed the sharp toe points of the crampons strapped to my plastic boots into the ice and walked up the wall in front of me. Tired and fulfilled by a day of adventure and new perspectives I went to sleep anticipating the middle of the night wake-up call to leave for the summit.

It came at 1:15 A.M. so we could climb to the summit and back down before the sun made the snow and ice too unstable. At an altitude of 10,000 feet, everything is more intense, even the darkness. I'd awakened early for summits twice before, but on Mount Rainier, the black sky seemed to absorb everything: Our voices didn't carry very far and even the light from the stars didn't quite reach us. We roped together in threes for safety. Curtis, Von, and I leaned into the wind and fought to keep our balance as we skirted crevasses and scrambled across varying difficulties of snow and ice following the beams of our headlamps. By 5:00 A.M. we had climbed only half of the distance we had to cover, and the cold was setting in through my parka. Looking up, we could see the cloud cap, a self-perpetuating phenomenon that frequently swirls around the summit of Mount Rainier, blown by the winds aloft.

We kept going and at last stood on the crater rim looking down on the Cascades. The climb hadn't been technically difficult, only long. I had approached it with a somewhat cocky attitude because Rainier was 5,000 feet lower than Kilimanjaro, not appreciating the effort required to climb on snow and ice with heavy boots and crampons. That mistake left me unprepared for the difficulty of reaching the summit, and I was so drained I could hardly appreciate the accomplishment. Almost immediately we began our descent. We wanted to go all the way back to Paradise by nightfall.

The descent was hell. There was no question about it anymore—my rented boots did not fit properly. Blisters formed on my heels, and my toenails jammed against the unforgiving plastic with each step. Curtis kept up a brisk pace, and I didn't feel I could ask him to slow down. Martha kept telling me I should have known better than to come at all, that fitting my boots properly was my responsibility, and that now I'd just have to suffer through it. As we crossed the timberline and began the last leg toward camp, Curtis took my pack. Having someone help me because of a physical problem triggered deep, emotionally painful memories. The shame I'd touched when my back hurt two days earlier returned in full fury. I reexperienced the guilt that had always followed the initial attention I received when I made up an illness or an injury. "This isn't the same," I shouted to the voices inside. The shame lessened but it did not leave: An old movie, an image from my past, began to play across my mind's screen.

"Dad?" I'd said when he answered the phone in the office. I was supposed to be there by now but when my alarm had gone off, I'd known, once again, there was no way I was going to be able to leave the house much less get to the office. The effects of too much food, too much alcohol, and too many laxatives overwhelmed me with physical discomfort and emotional humiliation. Even as I bent over the toilet to vomit, I reached for the bottle of Nyquil to dull the shame. I'd rehearsed the phone call to my father for an hour. Which ailment would I use this time? The pattern had repeated itself so often I'd run out of ideas. A scratched cornea? I hadn't used that one in a year or so, it would work. The Nyquil had kicked in by then, and I was removed enough from myself to lie blatantly yet again to the man I loved more than anyone else in the world. I couldn't possibly have told him the truth or he would have hated me as much as I'd hated myself.

I tried to set the memories aside. "This is not then. That isn't who I am anymore." But they all but obliterated any sense of pride I had in what I was accomplishing on Rainier.

We reached the Paradise Inn, and I checked in my rental gear, too filled with shame to complain about the ill-fitting boots. Instead, I threw my duffel bag into the car, drove to a hotel in Seattle in physical pain with toes that were badly inflamed, feeling confused and off-balance. All night long I tossed and turned. My toes throbbed. The alcohol in the well-stocked minibar called to me like the Sirens, promising it would take away the pain, soothe me, and help me sleep. I put the pillow over my head and waited for sunrise. By the time I got on the plane for home I couldn't even wear my tennis shoes.

Arriving in San Diego, I could hardly walk and went directly to an emergency medical center. While I waited for treatment, I reflected on the past thirty-six hours: I had been awakened from sleep on a glacier on the side of one of the tallest mountains in the Western United States, climbed up more than 5,000 vertical feet, and down more than 9,000, all the while carrying a heavy pack and wearing ill-fitting boots. Then I spent a sleepless night in Seattle and caught a plane back to San Diego, and I still wasn't home. Despite all that, despite the exhaustion, the intense pain of my feet and the resulting blood poisoning, I knew I wanted more than almost anything to continue climbing. On Mount Rainier, I had experienced the limits of my experience, conditioning, and equipment, but I was willing to work on all three and improve. I felt pride in what I'd done, even if it hadn't been perfect. I still wanted to go to Aconcagua and climb other big mountains.

Saturday, October 3, 1988, San Diego
Despite all the food stuff, I am operating at a
level that does astound me. All I have to do
is stay out of my own way, off my own back,
and put one foot in front of the other.
Remember Rainier. Life is just the same. Rest
step. Slow and steady.

Each step I took toward my dream seemed to be matched by a shadow force that threatened to destroy the recovery program I'd fought so hard to maintain for my eating disorder. The shadow beckoned me to eat larger portions than I needed. I'd too often go to a movie and eat popcorn and candy and call that a meal. I self-prescribed laxatives because I felt bloated. And I wasn't calling my sponsor or friends regularly. Hiding out, keeping secrets, self-medicating: The next step would be to go on a binge and have to start all over again. Something inside me was fighting my recovery. I needed to find out what it was. If I didn't, everything I'd gained would be lost.

I confirmed my arrangements for climbing Cerro Aconcagua in January. I had to borrow money and struggled to write a letter to my father asking for a loan to pay for my climbing even though it was something that neither of my parents approved of, something they'd prefer I didn't do. Following my heart's desire was separating me further and further from them, yet I needed to take this next step toward my independence. I needed outside help to make my dream a reality, so I asked for it in business terms that met Dad's needs and mine.

To prepare myself physically, I ran five days a week, worked out with weights and a personal trainer, and spent hours on the Stairmaster carrying a 40-pound pack on my back. I took advantage of an outing to Yosemite National Park to test myself on hikes to the top of Yosemite Falls and Half Dome. My training was paying off and my confidence increased and, most of the time, I was able to resist the almost daily attacks of self-judgment that I wasn't doing enough and wasn't doing it perfectly.

Meanwhile, my graduate school program was progressing well. I earned almost all A's in my courses, learned to live with the B's, and advanced to practice counseling with student volunteers in individual and group sessions. As an assignment, I had to develop a personal counseling theory as a guide for the techniques I was using. I'd thought I'd be further along in my own process of understanding myself before I'd have to do those things. Now I was faced with the reality of helping others while I moved more deeply into my own issues. Once again, life wasn't presenting me with what I expected. I could fight it or surrender, trusting that God really knew better than I about how to proceed.

To work it out I went to my journal, which, from the beginning of my recovery, had been my primary tool for self-discovery. In its pages I not only recorded the activities and feelings that came with each day, I also used a variety of tools to integrate each new piece I picked up about myself along the way. One of my techniques was a written dialogue, whether with critical Martha or my four-year-old or the adolescent in me. Only half in jest, I again asked Becky whether I was developing multiple personalities. She assured me that my running conversations with these parts of myself were helping me in my recovery. As the conflict with my eating behavior became increasingly acute, I had one particularly revealing exchange with the part of me that said I had to be perfect, the part of me I called the "Ghost in White."

In my journal, I invited this perfectionist to have a conversation with me. I began the dialogue by writing a question as if I were talking with a tangible presence in the room. The exchange went something like this.

I wrote, *What is it you want from me?*

The Ghost in White responded, *I want you to behave like an adult.*

I continued the dialogue. *What does that mean?*

It means showing up all the time and never eating unhealthily and never missing a day of exercise and never fucking up and never fucking off and always doing it just right and . . .

My anger flashed and I wrote, *Now wait a fucking minute. Just shut up. I can't do that, and it doesn't mean that I'm not responsible or deserving of respect or good or lovable or any of that. It doesn't mean that I'm bad. It just means I'm human. And you're fucking not. No one can live the way you want me to. NO one! Not and be sane, too.* I was shaking from the intensity of this exchange, but my pen continued to write.

Our father can and does. What about him? Why can't you be like him? I didn't have a clue where this was coming from, but I needed to follow it.

I wrote the next thing that came out of my pen. *'Cuz I'm not him.* Then, from an even more revealing, more intuitive place, *Why can't you give me permission to not be like him? As long as you keep telling me I have to be like him or I'm not good enough, I'm going to have to look for a back door 'cuz I can't do that. I'm not him. I don't want to be him. That's not what I want from my life. And yes, I'd like to be able to be more like him. And I'm not. Somehow we've got to make peace with that, you and I. How can we go about doing that? I buy into your stuff and start believing that I'm not good enough unless I do it all like Dad. My heart doesn't believe that that's true. Yes, I'd like it to be true but it's not. Yes, I'd like to have my folks always like and approve of what I do and don't do. But it's never going to be that way. Let's sit down and talk about this. What are your feelings?* What are your feelings? I was writing in my journal, I was the only person present, sitting on my bed looking out on the lights of San Diego from my hillside home. I was asking this inner part of me to describe its feelings. And I trusted this process so much I didn't even pause as I looked back down at the page and watched the response.

We've got to be perfect. The words appeared on the page as clearly as though they'd been spoken.

I continued to write. *Why?*

Because . . . Because otherwise it's not good enough.

Now my handwriting bordered on scribbling. I could hardly keep up with the pace. *Good enough for who?*

For them.

Who's them?

Our parents.

Is it good enough for you?

I don't know. That doesn't matter.

Yes, it does. It's all that matters. The only thing that means anything is what matters to us and to God. I could hardly believe the strength and clarity of my convictions. I liked what was happening on the page. It continued.

The Ghost in White wasn't an ally yet, but it wasn't as defensive either. *What if they don't like what we do? What if they don't? Will that change that they love us?*

No.

Will it change that they'll always support our choices?

No.

I was amazed as the questions and responses continued. *Do you like and approve of everything Becky or Leelee does?*

No.

Do you love them?

Yes.

Well? Isn't the same true for Mum and Dad? Isn't it unreasonable for anyone to expect anyone to love and respect everything they do? I truly didn't know where that logic came from. I was impressed.

Yes, I guess it is.

Then my pen asked a really pointed question: *Can you give up needing to do it all perfect? Are you willing to start accepting that Dad is not going to like and respect everything we do?*

To start, I guess.

Suddenly, I was asking myself for a commitment. *Repeat after me: It only matters what God and I think. It doesn't matter what anyone else thinks.*

Magically, the pen responded. *It only matters what God and I think. It doesn't matter what anyone else thinks.*

It felt as if the dialogue was coming to a resolution but the pen continued to move. *Does God love us?*

Yes.

Well, what more do we need? I could hardly wait to read the response. *Nothing, I guess.*

I was grinning from ear to ear, but there was more. *Right on. That's a beginning. Now, given that we don't have to be perfect, what's this huge need for a back door? Why do we need to keep playing around with defining moderate amounts and appropriate foods and weights?*

Suddenly the energy in my body shifted, a new voice, that of my adolescent was now flowing out of the pen. *'Cuz I don't want to have to be adult.*

The dialogue shifted to this new focus. It had happened before, this one was simply going on longer than I was used to and was uncovering some really interesting perspectives. I didn't want to stop it, so I let the pen write, *You don't have to be.*

My adolescent was really defiant. *I don't want to have to do what they say I have to.*

I was confused. *Who's "they"?*

The Ghost in White and everyone else.

I reminded the adolescent of what had written itself a page or so before. *And she just said she was willing to make a start at letting that go, right? Can you do the same?*

The pen hesitated for an instant, but her reply was honest. *I don't know.*

Now I was really curious. *What's in the way?*

As her words formed on the page I knew they were the truth. *I want to eat what I want when I want it.*

I looked at what I'd just written and thought to myself, "That's my disease talking. I didn't invite you here. None of us want to do that. That's just disease." I was defensive and afraid. I wasn't going to listen to this voice. I wrote out another question to my adolescent. *Is that really what you want?*

No, I just want to feel good. A deep sigh escaped, I'd been holding my breath.

I continued. *Will eating make you feel good?*

I used to think so.

Is it making you feel good today?

No.

Remember that tomorrow. Eating is not making us feel good today. Not eating is making us feel good today. I knew that while I was writing in my journal to my adolescent I was really writing to myself. I continued. *I ate three moderate, average meals today. I didn't feel stuffed after any of them. And I feel good. No regrets. No 'I wish I's.' I feel better. I feel good. I don't want to walk out the back door tonight. Are you willing to padlock the door?*

What does that mean? Obviously she hadn't been listening during my talks with my sponsor and Becky.

My pen began to answer. *It means giving up the large amounts of ice cream. It doesn't mean giving up ice cream. It means giving up large amounts. It doesn't mean giving up food. It means not having our stomach feel too full. It doesn't mean feeling deprived. It means asking God to help us know what average is. It doesn't mean not enjoying food. It means feeling good after a meal. It doesn't mean having to do it perfectly. It means making the same kind of commitment to eating average portions of average foods at average times as I have to being abstinent. It doesn't mean that I'm hopeless if I slip. It means living by the principle that I eat average no matter what. Average looks like moderate with high moderate every now and then.*

What's every now and then? The adolescent wanted to find a loophole.

The pen's wisdom continued to surprise me. As the words tumbled onto the page, resolution and clarity came with them. *I'll know in my gut when I cross the line. Setting a number is about control, not about surrender. This has to come from surrender. It has to come from my not wanting to live this way anymore. It can't come from my doing it. I have to let God do it. I have to be willing to eat average no matter what. Am I? God, I'm scared to say yes. What am I scared of? What feels so scary? Having to show up. Having to do it "grown-up." But we don't have to do anything except eat average. And we'll probably want to. And that's wonderful. We don't have any expectation to live up to. Just God's will for me. What is that? Let's remember: To be clean, sober, abstinent; To not smoke, to live in recovery, and to be the best me I can be. I do those things on a daily basis. There's nothing in there about being perfect. Nothing about having to do anything. God loves me and that gives me everything I need. I don't need a back door to run out anymore. I don't need a reason not to succeed. I can take the risk and trust the results to God and know that whatever the results are, they are exactly the best thing for me, even when they don't look that way.* What I'd just written felt good to me, I wanted to find out how she was doing. *How do you feel?*

Again, the response was immediate and honest. *Vulnerable, shy, afraid, quiet, not stubborn. Surrendered.*

I continued, *I feel less scared, too.* Then my pen began writing again, this time apparently directed to the Ghost in White. *I really need your strength, you know. You're a part of this team, too. And I need you not to say "fuck it" when it feels hard. And not to say "fuck it" when the food is calling. It's hard for me not to listen when you say "fuck it." And I'm going to ask God to help me with that. 'Cuz I know you're not perfect any more than I am.*

The response came out freely onto the page. *You're right. I'm not. That's why I'm so loud. If I sound right enough you won't notice that I'm not perfect.*

Just when I thought the dialogue was finished, it started up again. *But I do notice.*

The pen seemed almost surprised. *Oh.*

I continued. *And you don't have to be. I love you just the way you are.*

I was set back by the next words the pen wrote. *Will you help me?*

My response was immediate. *Yes, I will.*

The Ghost in White continued. *What I need is the chance to say "fuck it" out loud or in a pillow or something. I have to let it out or I'll lay it on you. You gotta let me have my feelings without making them wrong. What is it my therapist says . . . go with the resistance. Well, I will resist. I can't give it up overnight. Are you willing to give me a chance to yell and kick when I need to?*

Yes, I am. Amazing, the power in these words. God was truly doing for me what I could not do for myself.

She continued, *I'll let you scream, and I won't make you wrong for your feelings. I apologize for that. I am wrong to make you feel wrong for having your feelings. It's just what they did to me.*

I could feel the remorse and sadness as the adolescent spoke again. *I know. I hate it. I don't blame you. If I give you a chance to have your feelings and support them, will you help me not to act on them, to know that we can find ways for you to express them without having to eat?*

The Ghost in White gave her support. *Yes, I'll do that.*

Then, I watched myself write, *OK, I will call my sponsor daily. I will eat average portions no matter what. I will pray before every meal. I will talk about the process of eating "average" on an individual level. I will allow my feelings to be there no matter what they are and not condemn them or the me who is having them. I am OK whatever I feel. I am allowed to have any feeling at all. No feeling is wrong or bad. Do you hear that, all of you? There isn't a feeling that any of you can have that is bad or wrong.*

The adolescent still had some questions, she spoke for all of the kids inside. *What if we want a hot fudge sundae?*

The pen wrote out my reply. *It's OK to want it. It's just that we don't have to have it. You can want it all you want. Do you get it?*

The following words formed on the page. *We understand. Hooray.*

I finished the writing with a note to God—a prayer, really. *I know You've been listening to all of this. We can't do it without You. Will You help? I know You will. I know that I haven't come this far just to have you drop me. I'm willing to work. To do what it takes. To make eating average portions my number-one priority no matter what. I can do that with Your help. OK, this feels*

like an adventure now, not a punishment. Let's keep it that way. We started an
adventure today that will save our lives. I want to continue it.

As the end of 1988 approached, the threads I was weaving into my
new life were beginning to make a distinct pattern. I had a tangible
sense of the healing results of my inner work. As a forty-year-old
woman, I was beginning to have a more realistic, balanced sense of
my value in the world and the power I had over my own life.

Anticipating Aconcagua, I purchased crampons, an ice axe, a pair of
plastic climbing boots that fit, and an expedition pack. I had flashes
of fear that I was pushing myself farther than I was ready to go. Then
I'd talk with someone who'd remind me that everyone on the trip
would want me to make it to the summit. I'd remember my successes
in Africa and on Rainier, and the fear would disappear. Showing up,
putting one foot in front of the other: These would be my only respon-
sibilities. The rest would be up to God.

I was packing to go to Greenwich for Christmas, and from there to
Aconcagua, when I felt a pull in my life's fabric. A key course I needed
to complete my master's degree was suddenly canceled from the
schedule. It would mean nearly a full year's delay in completing my
program. I was devastated. I didn't understand why this had to happen.

Then, an idea came to me. Why not use that time to do all of the
climbing I'd imagined? I'd get it out of my system and be ready to
focus on my profession without any distractions. Perhaps what had at
first appeared to be a major setback was a gift after all.

Still thinking that over, I came down with bronchitis just before
Christmas, another pull in the fabric. I was in and out of bed for nearly
two weeks. Each day I'd pump myself up in the morning, take medication, and try to believe that I could still make the trip to Aconcagua.
Every evening I'd feel worse and pray that some miracle would happen
during the night, that I'd wake up healed. When it became clear I
couldn't go and I finally called to cancel the trip, I slid into a depression.

Martha was saying, "See, I knew it. You can't complete any goals
that require long-term, consistent effort." Shame sliced like scissors
through the fabric I'd worked so hard to weave. Yet it held. Watching
competitions of amateur ice skaters on TV, I identified with their
emotions of having a goal, working for it, then achieving it; then I
wondered how it would feel to complete the goals I was setting for
myself. When I saw "Winds of Everest," a documentary about Phil
Ershler's successful ascent of Mount Everest, I cried, doubting
whether I could ever sustain the dedication it would take even to
begin to climb a "real" mountain like that. There was only one way
to find out. Was I willing to do the training I'd scheduled for today?

By the time the spring semester started, I had made up my mind to take the year to travel. Details fell into place. There was a bonus, too. Skip was leading a trip to Aconcagua a year from now and Norton was planning to go. I created an itinerary that included climbing in Mexico, Peru and Bolivia, Pakistan, Tibet and Nepal, time in Thailand and Australia, and then back to South America to join Skip's expedition. I'd be finished in time for the spring semester next year.

Monday, March 27, 1989, Mexico
I feel so good! I am filled with a deep joy at
being who I am. At being alive. I am not
beautiful and I am not thin, and I am an
incredible woman. And all it takes is showing
up. Just being there to participate. And I'm
doing it.

The trip to Mexico to climb didn't start well at all. My original flight had been canceled for days, but no one let me know until after I arrived at the airport. Shuttled between airlines, I was eventually on a plane, the wheels were up, and we were at cruising altitude. All the way from San Diego to Mexico City, Martha kept up her usual critical monologue: I weighed too much, hadn't trained enough, all the other climbers would have more experience than me. She harped on my equipment: my boots were wrong, my new crampons were the wrong kind, and I didn't have enough clothing or specialized climbing gear. Her voice increased my already heightened fears.

My disease told me a glass of wine would quiet Martha's voice and help me deal with any new problems that might come up during the trip. My older survival self said I should simply act as though I were sick and get on the next plane back home to avoid embarrassing myself. Instead, I prayed the simple prayer I'd learned in my groups: "God, grant me the serenity to accept the things I cannot change, the courage to change the things I can, and the wisdom to know the difference." Immediately I felt the self-judgment and fear drift into the background and my excitement and anticipation grow.

At the airport in Mexico City, I was uneasy with the cacophony of unfamiliar language and threatened by the presence of uniformed and armed troops. I made it to the baggage claim all right, but while other passengers selected their luggage and left, an ominous sense of foreboding crept over me. I had only one piece of luggage, my duffel bag, which contained my backpack and all my climbing gear—and it couldn't be found. I repeated the prayer for serenity, a mantra to give me courage, while I filed a claim for my luggage, changed some American dollars into pesos, and took a taxi to the hotel.

There I met my five climbing companions. Megan and Charlie were married, both geologists in their late twenties. They were joined by Megan's father John, a retired physician in his sixties. The other two members of the group were forty-something corporate attorneys, Dan, from Michigan, and Bob, from Orange County, California. Everyone had done some hiking or trekking; my experience put me about in the middle of the group.

That night we gathered to meet with Sergio, the scheduled trip leader, but instead of giving us confidence, he dropped a bomb. He announced that because he had just received an invitation to join an expedition to climb Mount Everest, he was leaving the trip and placing his assistant, Girardo, in charge. What he didn't tell us was that Girardo had never led a trip before. Since the trip was run by a reputable company, I trusted the change. My guides in Africa and on Rainier had proven themselves not only to be capable and worthy of trust as professionals but attentive to and aware of the needs of their clients as well. I reasoned that this trip was not likely to be any different. Still I couldn't shake a wary feeling in my gut. So many things had gone wrong already.

My duffel turned up at the airport the next day. Bob and Dan helped me retrieve it, and we did some sightseeing along the way. Our group had another day of acclimatizing to the 7,340-foot altitude of Mexico City, and although I enjoyed the camaraderie and the vacationlike atmosphere, I felt antsy. When we finally boarded the VW bus that would take us to the first trailhead, I was ready.

To reach 17,887-foot Popocatépetl located in the central highlands south of Mexico City, we drove past the airport and through cultivated but dry countryside. At Amecameca, with its large central plaza and prominent sixteenth-century church, we took a steep, winding road into evergreen forests to the Paso de Cortés. This 12,000-foot-high pass between the twin volcanoes, Iztaccíhuatl and Popocatépetl, was where Hernán Cortés and his troops first saw the Aztec capital of Tenochtitlán in 1519. Popo was first climbed during this expedition by Cortés' soldiers, who mined sulfur from the crater to make gunpowder used in conquering the Aztecs. Turning our backs on Izta, we drove the last few kilometers to the base of Popo and the Vincent Guerro Lodge at Tlamacas, situated at 12,950 feet.

I expected to find a tin, silolike shed like the ones on Mount Kilimanjaro, so the modern architecture of the Vincent Guerro Lodge, with its sweeping red tile roof, dark wood beams, and intricate stonework, was a surprise. We slept on built-in bunk beds, ate in a small restaurant with a good menu, and had conversations and read in a large central area with a circular fireplace where climbers from many countries were gathered. Through the picture windows were dramatic views of Popo's classic volcanic cone, its summit, Pico Mayor, and El Ventorillo, a major rock outcropping that marked the route we'd be taking on our climb.

We were met at the lodge by Guillermo, the assistant Girardo had hired. Guillermo did not speak much English, but it was not a problem during a short hike before dinner. The next morning, with lunches packed, we set out to climb to the crosses for which the Las Cruces route is named. It is one of two routes to the summit and although we planned to ascend Popo by way of the Ventorillo route, we would return on Las Cruces.

Popo's base is made up of scree the consistency of sand, so the first part of our hike was tedious and prolonged. At 13,000 feet, each step was an effort. I had a headache and some nausea, yet I felt my training kick in and appeared actually to be one of the stronger climbers in the group. John and Dan moved very slowly. I was concerned about how they would do on the sustained climb the next day.

On our second night at the lodge, we prepared ourselves logistically and mentally for the next day's summit attempt by sorting gear, filling our packs, and talking about what we'd read and learned from others about the climb we were about to make. The climb to the summit and back would take only one full day, but I knew it would not be easy. Girardo was not nearly as knowledgeable or helpful as Skip had been in Africa, and Guillermo's poor command of English forced him into the background, separated from the rest of us.

Martha complained that they must not know what they're doing and that we'd better not go tomorrow. If anything happened, it would be my fault, I should have taken the chance to hijack the van as we passed the airport on our way out of the city. I smiled at how loud the voice of my fear could be when I was unsure of myself and repeated the prayer which had been so effective when I first arrived in the country. "God grant me the serenity . . . ."

I answered the 3:00 A.M. wake-up call, still feeling slightly nauseated, and thought to myself, *It's going to be a long day.* I forced a little breakfast into my stomach and found myself in the front of the line of climbers as we headed back up the Las Cruces trail at 4:15 A.M. Soon, we branched off to our right, following the northeast ridge toward El Ventorillo. In the light of a full moon we scrambled up a long incline of small pebbles and arrived, at 14,652 feet, at the Quere-tano Hut, a metal and stone bivouac shelter just as the sun rose on a beautiful, clear day.

We put one foot in front of the other, sometimes walking on soft, slidy scree, other times climbing steep, difficult terrain. Hours after leaving the lodge, we reached the 17,377-foot level and the Teopix-calco Hut, where we stopped for food and water. At that point it was clear that John and Dan would not be able to make it all the way to the summit. Guillermo was directed by Girardo to lead them up El Ventorillo, a short scramble from the hut, then take them back down to the lodge. They would be waiting there long before we returned.

With Girardo in the lead, the five remaining climbers headed for the snowfield that would take us to the summit. First, we traversed a treacherous section of scree and loose rocks, setting off small slides even as we cautiously tested each step for safe footing. Crossing a saddle, we reached the snowfield. We put on our crampons, pulled out our ice axes, and clipped into a rope barely sufficient for four climbers, let alone five, then followed Girardo's footsteps onto the irregular sur-face that stretched ahead.

The area to our left was laced with crevasses, to our right there were steep drops. In between, along our route, were narrow gullies and knee-high ridges. Girardo called them sun cups. I called them every nasty name I could think of. If we stepped on top of the ridges, they collapsed under our weight. If we stepped between them, our feet got wedged in the bottoms of the troughs. It made walking precar-ious, and after I twisted my knee, I became even more afraid of falling and injuring myself badly. It slowed our progress to a crawl. We had climbed for more than ten hours by the time we reached the upper edge of the snowfield and walked 15 yards across rock and dirt to the summit. All of us were exhausted.

Instead of the exhilaration of Kili or my depression on Rainier, I felt a deep and quiet satisfaction knowing I had pushed myself through self-imposed limits to reach the summit of another mountain. I was comfortable inside as I shared water and food with my companions and looked across to Izta and into the haze toward Mexico City.

Climbing down past the crosses to the lodge took us only three hours. A sense of excitement about having made the summit grew as my strength returned in the lower altitude. I joined Megan, Charlie, and Bob in the dining room, and we began to relive parts of the climb.

In the middle of a sentence, Megan saw Guillermo in the doorway and looked relieved. "Where's my dad?" she asked him. We had been surprised when they hadn't met us upon our return and were even more surprised, now, to see Guillermo by himself. Without answering Megan's question, he turned around and headed for the room he shared with Girardo. We glanced at each other and shrugged. John was probably changing his clothes or going to the bathroom and would appear any minute. Five minutes later, Girardo and Guillermo reentered the dining room. Guillermo looked chagrined and Girardo was talking loudly in Spanish, obviously very angry.

"What's going on?" Megan asked, concern putting an edge on her voice. "Where's my father?"

Girardo scowled at Guillermo, then haltingly answered Megan's question. "He's still on the mountain."

"What?" Megan's concern became anger and her voice rose in pitch and volume. "What the hell are you talking about? He came down with Dan and Guillermo."

"No. Guillermo came down by himself."

I couldn't believe what I was hearing and jumped into the exchange. "By himself?" By now other climbers in the dining room sensed that something was amiss and were beginning to pay attention. "Where are the other two?" I demanded.

"They're still on the mountain," Girardo said.

The four of us began talking and asking questions at once. Finally, in his most restrained, lawyerly voice Bob said, "Girardo. What in the hell has happened?"

"John's still at the high hut. He insisted on spending the night there so he could go for the summit in the morning."

"By himself?" Megan shrieked. Charlie had his arm around her, as much for restraint as support.

"How could you leave him up there?" I fired the question at Guillermo who stood to one side. It was a straight, clean shot aimed at his heart. He remained detached from and seemingly unmoved by the ever-loudening conversation.

Girardo answered for him, "He wouldn't come down."

"Why didn't Guillermo make him come down?" Bob was cross-examining the star witness for the defense.

"He wouldn't come down," Girardo said again, as though repeating his answer would make us understand.

Megan was in tears. "We've got to go get him. He's sixty-two years old! You can't leave him up there. He'll freeze to death."

"No, he won't." Girardo was giving his best shot at impersonating a professional guide. "It's not that cold. He's inside the hut and he has a space blanket and a sleeping bag liner with him. Anyway, we're going to eat something and then go back up and get him." He wasn't convincing at all.

"But that will take hours." Megan's voice was tightly controlled.

"It's the best solution, Megan," Charlie said. "Right now it's the only one. Your dad will be okay." I could tell he really wanted to believe what he was saying.

Girardo and Guillermo turned to leave. I heard voices murmuring in the background, shock waves of questions and comments spreading among the other climbing parties in the room, out from the epicenter where a major explosion had just occurred.

Suddenly I realized Dan was still unaccounted for. "Wait a minute, where's Dan?" Girardo and Guillermo had almost made their escape. They glanced at each other. "He's down, right?" It wasn't really a question—there was only one acceptable, one believable response.

Girardo scowled at Guillermo again. "No, he's still up there, too. We don't know where."

That wasn't the answer I was expecting. I yelled, "What!!" Questions tumbled out of my mouth. "What do you mean you don't know? How could you not know? What the hell is going on?" Other voices joined mine in angry query.

"Okay, hold on a minute." As quiet as Bob's voice was, its authority carried over the noisy chaos, and the group quieted down. "Girardo. Tell us what happened."

He told us as much as he knew. He was caught in the middle between Guillermo and the truth and was obviously uncomfortable trying to explain someone else's actions—especially when they were as blatantly irresponsible as Guillermo's. "They got to the top of Ventorillo Peak okay and stopped at the high hut for some food and water on the way down. John refused to leave. It sounds like he wasn't thinking very well. He insisted that he would spend the night there, summit by himself in the morning, and meet us here at the lodge tomorrow. Guillermo couldn't do anything." Guillermo stood back, seemingly untouched by the crisis swirling around him, a classic "What did I do wrong" little-boy look on his face.

"That's crazy." Megan's voice was shaking with emotion. "Of course, he could have done something. You don't leave someone alone on a mountain overnight. Even I know that." She glared over Girardo's shoulder at Guillermo. "What were you thinking? You're twice his size. You could have carried him down!"

"Easy, Megan." Once again, Bob restored a semblance of calm. "Girardo. What about Dan?"

It was clear that Girardo was furious, but he tried hard to keep his anger buried. He said that while Guillermo was trying to deal with John, he told Dan to start down, that he would meet him at the Queretano Hut. Based on my experience with Guillermo's poor English, I could only imagine what Dan, tired from the climb, might have thought he'd said. Leaving John behind, Guillermo had descended to the Queretano Hut, only to find it empty. He waited for an hour, then returned to the lodge alone.

John would, at least, be safe in the hut. Dan was another story. He was an inexperienced climber, we knew he'd been exhausted, possibly disoriented, and now he was probably lost and in very real danger.

None of us had enough experience to initiate a search, especially not at night on an unfamiliar mountain in a foreign country. Bob, Charlie, I, and finally Megan agreed to Girardo's recommendation: the two guides would reascend to the hut and bring John down. As for Dan, he could be anywhere. Our only hopes were that he had returned to one of the huts and they would find him, or that he'd make it down to the lodge on his own.

All of us had been exhausted before we'd heard this news. Then adrenaline had pumped us up. As it wore off, we were more tired than ever. None of us were hungry but we had to eat. Long after Girardo and Guillermo started back up the mountain, we remained in the dining room talking among ourselves and with other climbers about what an absurd situation this was. The decision of our court was clear: The actions of Guillermo were unprofessional and downright stupid, and the lack of insight and experience shown by Girardo in his choice of assistants was no less appalling. Girardo's general mountaineering skills appeared adequate but his judgment and leadership were sorely defective. Two climbers from our group were now in unnecessary danger because of the inexperience and incompetence of these guides.

Finally we went to bed, but sleep did not come easily. Hours of frustration, anger, and fear passed slowly until John's noisy arrival at 5:30 A.M. stirred us out of our sleeping bags. Girardo and Guillermo had brought him down, complete with more misadventure, and we discovered at the same time that Dan had found his own way back earlier and was sleeping in his bunk. The crisis had passed. With everyone safe we settled in for a couple of hours of good sleep.

After breakfast Girardo held a group meeting. We thought we would hear a further explanation of what had happened, maybe even an apology. Instead, he criticized us for talking about the event with other climbers. Apparently Girardo had heard somewhere that a good offense was the best defense. He continued with his misguided attack, firing Guillermo in front of all of us, chastising John and informing him that because of his actions he would not be allowed to climb the second peak. I was openmouthed and uncharacteristically speechless. As far as I knew, public shaming went out with putting people in stocks. Moreover, both guides had made errors, while we, the clients, were reprimanded like school children. Girardo's believability as a guide dropped to below zero. Yet we needed him for Pico de Orizaba, at 18,851 feet, the highest mountain in Mexico and the third highest peak on the North American continent.

The next day we packed up and drove east toward Orizaba. It had an ominous cloud hanging over it before we ever saw its massive form. Girardo had withdrawn and hardly spoke to us at all, or we to him. We spent the night in the regional capital, Puebla, where I talked with Bob about how the atmosphere of the trip had changed. The enthusiasm of the group had drained away, our spirits depressed by the events on Popo. Not even the sensory feast of an Easter weekend fiesta and the press of pilgrims could revive our emotional energy.

The next morning, I began my day with some inspirational readings I'd brought with me and was reminded that my serenity would be in direct proportion to my acceptance. Acceptance, that was still the key.

As we drove to the trailhead, each of us was in a different state of mind. Dan said he would never climb again. John was not allowed to climb. Bob decided his trust issues with Girardo were simply too big to go back on a mountain with him, and Megan and Charlie were very ill with fever and intestinal problems. Girardo seemed to have given up caring about the trip at all, and part of me was looking for something to go wrong so I wouldn't have to decide whether or not to climb. Martha's voice was loud and clear. "Okay, Margo, nobody else wants to be doing this. Girardo doesn't know what he's doing and neither do you. Everybody else wants to go home. It's cloudy and snowing. You could die up there. What do you think you're doing anyway? Who cares if you climb this silly mountain?"

"I care." The voice came from my heart, a voice I was learning to trust more and more. "This is a big deal for me, and I'm proud as hell that I'm trying. I care a lot. I wish I weren't the only one. I wish Skip were leading this trip. But he's not. I can still put one foot in front of the other and turn the results over to God."

My resolve gave me a passion and clarity I was able to gain access to during the night in the ancient wood and metal structure that served as a hut at the base of Pico de Orizaba. It gave me strength when my doubts and fears talked to me ever louder. I had made my decision.

It was 3:30 A.M. and the moon was nearly full when Girardo and I began the climb. The night was still except for the sound of our climbing. Such power. One foot in front of the other. Over and over. At my own pace. In my own world with God and Jonathan adding their strength to my own. Scree, glacier, crampons, ice axe. Incredible sky, full of stars that faded into the background as the sun brought its warmth to us. The magic of the mountains, the magic of climbing. I had a sense of my own power, an indescribable feeling of deep, quiet joy. This was why I wanted to climb. It wasn't about getting to the top. It was about this part of the journey!

On the glacier, the weather deteriorated and clouds closed in on all sides. It was eerie, having the mountain slopes we'd already climbed disappearing below us, nothing but the ice, literally, in my face. Girardo commented nervously on the weather but kept moving toward the summit. He said we were forty-five minutes from the lower rim of the crater, another fifteen minutes beyond that to the summit. An hour later, he said the same thing. He worried out loud about the weather, and I worried silently about his ability to lead us down if a storm hit. I didn't think I had the experience to get myself out of trouble, and I didn't trust Girardo to be able to either. Up or down? I knew I was strong enough to reach the summit but not strong enough to hurry. I wanted the summit, yet I was concerned about the danger of descending in a storm with a guide whose abilities I did not trust. Girardo seemed unable to decide what to do. My head said up; my gut said down. I followed my instincts and said, "Okay, I'm done. We're out of here."

As we descended, the weather improved, and the storm we feared never arrived. I felt disappointment, and at the same time my heart was filled with pride at what I'd accomplished. I didn't know I could have such disparate feelings simultaneously. I was used to having one emotion at a time, always bigger than life, big enough to plug the gaping hole inside of me. Now the hole was shrinking. I had climbed well and learned I could trust my intuition when I didn't feel safe. The mountain had taught me something more about the truth of who I was.

Four days of rest and relaxation including a stay at an old sugar mill and plantation converted into a resort made a good transition from the mountains to home for the group. By the time we returned to Mexico City, we'd regained our sense of camaraderie to the point of having a comical awards ceremony after our last dinner together. The importance of companionship, survival through adversity, and the power to choose what was right for me all went home with me from the mountains of Mexico.

CHAPTER FIVE

Doing Ninth-Grade Work with a Third-Grade Education

Sunday, June 4, 1989, Cordillera Real, Bolivia
I'm scared of having the whole nine months go
up in flame if I don't get to the summit
tomorrow. That's not true. If I don't get to the
summit, it means I don't get to the summit—
period. The worst thing that could happen would
be not to try.

It snowed the night before I left the ancient city of La Paz for my ten-day trek into the Cordillera Real de los Angeles—the Royal Range of the Angels. It was not a particularly good omen, as omens go, but it added an incredibly beautiful mantle to the raw-edged mountains that reach more than 21,000 feet into the deep blue sky. Illimani, the giant towering over the city, was the ultimate prize we sought, but first we would explore Illusion, Condoriri, Huayna Potosi and other lesser known peaks along the spine of the Andes extending north of the canyon that is home to more than a million Bolivians.

Snow. No one in our group of nine climbers and two guides wanted to be cold and wet, yet we all came willingly into this environment to take whatever it presented. If any of us had wanted life to be predictable and easy, we'd have stayed in our homes in the United States. We had congregated in Lima, but stayed only long enough to catch a plane to the 10,900-foot altitude of Cuzco. There we spent five days acclimatizing as we explored the ruins at Macchu Picchu and the valleys surrounding that former capital of the Inca empire. My legs trembled after a day of hiking up and down the nearly vertical Mayan steps on Huayna Picchu. I'd entered a whole new level of climbing by joining this group; most of the others had more technical climbing experience than I did. But as we talked among ourselves I was glad to find out I wasn't the only climber with concerns about how my ability would fare when tested in the mountains.

It pleased Martha no end when I caught a cold after flying from Cuzco to La Paz, being bused into the mountains, and hiking for two days to 15,300 feet. Breathing through my balaclava lessened my coughing, but my nose was running and my lungs hurt. Menstrual cramps and emotions aggravated by hormones kept me on the verge of tears. Martha wanted me to use my cold as an excuse to cancel the rest of my trip and go home.

Besides, what was I doing taking all this time off just to climb— everyone knew there was no future in climbing: I should be focusing on my career or at least on finding a job. I knew that my dad, always the pragmatist, was silently waiting for me, at forty-one, to be productive and responsible, and that my mother, limited to the life of a near recluse by health problems, was openly fearful for my safety. Neither could understand my apparent disregard for my financial security.

I called on simple techniques I'd learned during the past three years to keep me focused on my dreams: Affirmations, a mental gratitude list, and remembering that if I'd kept on living the way I had been in my town house in Greenwich surrounded by laxatives, liquor, and lies, I'd be dead rather than climbing in the Andes. As I sat under the wind-swept sky, the Southern Cross floated among the brilliant stars at the highest camp I'd ever stayed in. I called on God, the spirit of my friend Jonathan, and all of my inner family to be with me.

The expedition would take us above 17,000 feet, where the breathable oxygen is approximately half that at sea level. The time it took for us to get to the base of the mountains allowed our bodies to adjust to the higher altitude, and we were able to do some training as well. Once at camp we practiced climbing techniques on glaciers and laughed while learning about running belays, shouting "wait" and "climbing" as we made our way through a system of ropes that looked like a spider web when we were done with it. The diversions kept me from dwelling on how bad I felt.

Martha's voice asserted that if I didn't do things perfectly, I had no right to be here. I countered that I'd proven myself with my climbing in Africa, on Mount Rainier, and in Mexico. God hadn't allowed me to come this far to drop me in a pool of self-pity. I would know whether or not to climb—just as I had in Mexico.

"Okay, everybody, this is how it is." I spoke slowly, lovingly, to myself, to all of the fears inside. "If we don't get to the summit, it only means we didn't get to that summit. There will be plenty of others, and we'll use what we learn on this one later. We'll take the mountains one step at a time, and that's how we'll take the rest of the trip, too. We'll do our best and leave the results up to God." Jonathan's presence became very real, and I told him I'd sure appreciate feeling him with me tomorrow.

The next day, after breaking trail through snow that sometimes reached above my knees, everyone in our group made it to the top of an unnamed peak and stood on its 17,600-foot summit. On the way down, each of us slipped at least once. When the lead climber on my three-person rope fell waist-deep into a hidden crevasse, I was too preoccupied with not falling or getting twisted up in the rope myself to notice. The first indication of a problem was his quiet, very polite voice saying, "Do you think maybe you could go into self-arrest? I'm in a crevasse." Fortunately, we were moving very slowly, the slope was gentle, and no one was injured. A potentially dangerous situation became a cause for much laughter during dinner that night as we recounted stories from our day. Exhausted, yet full of gratitude for succeeding on my first Bolivian summit, I went to sleep with a deeper sense of the trust I could have in myself and the others on the mountain.

The following day we moved our camp to prepare for our next climb. Others were ill with colds, too. Their debate over whether to continue with the trip or return to La Paz, combined with my own physical discomfort and the cold temperatures, sent my emotions on a roller-coaster ride. Questions flooded my mind: Why was I still so weak? Should I skip the next climb and rest? Did I want to climb if it would be cold and windy? Did I want to climb anymore at all? My emotions jerked my mind between past and future as I tried to figure out what to do. One minute I was a little girl who was far away from home and wanted someone to hold me, the next I was a sober woman choosing to face her emotional fears and physical limitations and climb to the summit of a remote mountain.

I sat on a rock overlooking one of the nameless lakes in the region, held myself, and talked with my inner family, Jonathan, and God. For as long as I could remember I had been afraid of putting any dreams of my own out into the world. Someone was sure to be unhappy. What if I changed my mind? Would I be considered a fool? Food, drugs, and alcohol comforted me in a world where I was sure I didn't belong. Without them, I'd learned that my life was about making choices, not necessarily being right or acceptable. I was still learning to trust my intuition, my inner truth, and God, but I felt an assurance rising up from deep inside. Whether or not I ever climbed another mountain, I, Margo, was okay. I heard myself say, "I'm not Superwoman. I'm not a mountain climber. I am Margo who occasionally climbs a mountain. I am Margo who catches a cold. I am who I am, not what I do." The next day I had an opportunity to test my new-found clarity.

Debilitated from my cold, I stayed behind while others made an attempt on Pequeño Alpamayo. As they followed their route, I hiked about an hour and a half above camp and watched as the two ropes of climbers inched across the glacier. The people moved like ants in slow motion along tracks left by other climbers on the long, flowing river of ice, and then became black spots on the white snow that surrounded them.

The sun warmed the air and highlighted the grandeur of the Andes, filling me with their wonder. I turned around. Wild, snow-covered peaks fell precipitously away from their summits down sharp-edged ridges into valleys, some cut into bowls by glaciers, some slashed by rivers. My eyes swept across barren rock to the sparkling surface of Lago Condoriri, up the other side of the valley to the cathedral-like spire of Condoriri peak. In the distance stood the rock face of the Black Needle, snow-covered Huayna Potosi, and dozens of unnamed peaks, solid and stark against the royal blue sky.

My body moved to the music of Paul Simon singing on my Walkman, as my soul danced to the rhythm of the mountains. Outrageous! I nearly shouted a prayer out loud, "Thank you, God, for this gift that has come out of so much fear and indecision."

During the next few days, our group practiced crevasse rescue. Once I had faced my own fears of getting hurt or making a mistake that would put one of my companions at risk, I really enjoyed the drills. I felt weak in the morning but strong in the afternoon, though never strong enough to feel confident about climbing anything. My internal landscape was as varied as the one surrounding me.

Again because of my cold, I missed the climb of Illusion. Carol and John Grunsfeld, a couple on the trip with whom I'd become friends and who were also ill, stayed behind, too. Instead of giving in to the disappointment and self-doubts we each harbored, we chose to make the most of the day and have a good time. We collected all of the little toy mascots we'd brought with us and took Pokey, Gumby, Dr. Pepper, Peffalump, and Orang with us to climb one of the lower peaks that surrounded our camp. Calling ourselves the "hospital rope," it took us two hours to climb to the foot of the glacier that formed part of the main route. At one point I was exhausted and told them to go ahead, but John encouraged me to keep going and promised to slow the pace to accommodate me. With their help I was able to climb through the emotional and physical barrier I faced and make it all the way to the rocky summit.

On that climb I came to the conclusion that I was a mellow, middle-age mountaineer. I liked the idea and the execution of mountaineering, but basically I enjoyed climbing easy mountains at an easy pace with people I liked.

While the others prepared to climb Huayna Potosi, Carol, John, and I returned to La Paz with Sarah, the wife of one of the guides. I was pretty sure I still wanted to climb Illimani, but knew I needed some antibiotics to help me heal first. Four days at the hotel Libertador gave my body the rest it needed. I also had more unexpected insights into mountaineering.

As Sarah and I walked between airline offices, money exchanges, and pharmacies, taking care of life and administrative details in this foreign city, we talked about mountains, climbing, and guides. Not only was she married to a guide, she led treks of her own. I was glad to get a woman's perspective on the world of adventure travel. Earlier I had told her about how wonderful the African climbs had been, and now I compared the current trip to those.

"As much as I love being in the mountains and climbing them and learning about climbing," I said, "this trip has been really hard, so different from my experience in Africa. This felt like an intense, get-to-the-summit-at-all-costs group. I hope it doesn't offend you—I know Geof's your husband—but he and John Culberson didn't seem to make any effort to connect with the rest of us. They kept to themselves at night and pushed us hard when we climbed. I don't have anything against being challenged. It's a lot of why I'm here. But I thrive on positive encouragement, not silent disapproval."

Sarah smiled and nodded in understanding. "Geof and John work very differently from the way I do. Every climber needs different things to get to the summit. Some work in isolation, some thrive on group effort. I encourage and teach from a place of support. They command and direct from a place of expectation. I believe that my way works for more people than theirs, but they'll no doubt continue to do what they know. They're more summit-oriented than people-oriented—and they're both very good guides."

"How much of this is related to gender?"

"There's probably some of that involved." Her eyebrows arched as her mind worked on my question. "But you said Skip was really supportive, too. I suspect it has more to do with what kind of people we are and what we've had to do to get to our own summits."

I realized I had just been given a big piece in the puzzle. On a climb, I had needs that were unique to me, that arose perhaps because I was a woman but more likely because I was Margo. My emotions gave me strength—I didn't have to leave them behind. I could choose guides who would support that. My job was to identify my needs and ask for what would meet them. With that attitude I could go as far as I wanted.

Standing outside the main cathedral in La Paz, looking up at Illimani rising far above the skyscrapers nestled in the protected valley, I knew I wanted to climb that mountain next.

Monday, June 19, 1989, La Paz, Bolivia
It's like trying to do ninth-grade work with a
third-grade education. You can't do it unless
you're superhuman, and I'm not. My head wants
to say failure and that's not what it's about.

Deborah, Steve, and I set off to climb Illimani under the guidance of Geof's assistant, John. The others in the group had left or were waiting in La Paz for our return. The road to the trailhead was carved out of the incredible mountains above La Paz, a route better suited to llamas than the Ford Suburban we were riding in. Perilous drop-offs distracted my attention from the intricately carved rock formations revealed around every corner. From time to time we caught glimpses of the glaciers, icefalls, and fluted snow ridges leading to the summit. Small villages, one of them home to Francisco, the head of our Bolivian camp crew, held tenaciously to the slopes, perched on terraces that also supported meager crops. The adobe brick homes were surrounded by rock walls, and everything blended into the mottled brown hillsides: houses, the people's clothes, even the llamas and sheep that watched us.

We hiked two-and-a-half hours to our first camp, an area nestled in warm sun near a pool that reflected the waterfall that fed it. Our beige dome tents were dwarfed by the sculptured ice of gigantic glaciers, and beyond them, the summit of Illimani looming far above. A nearly full moon rose above the ridge bathing everything with gentle white light. Despite this raw beauty, I sank into an emotional black hole until I got some food and cocoa into me and was once again able to appreciate where I was. I reminded myself that to keep up my strength at these altitudes I needed to eat small amounts of food throughout the day and drink a large volume of fluids.

The next day the four of us climbed for more than five hours up a steep scree ridge onto a glacier, then to Nido de Condores, the Condor's Nest. At 18,374 feet this was the camp we would use for our summit attempt. Deborah and I both had been very slow during our ascent, troubled by the altitude and unstable footing. John and Steve left us behind as they climbed rapidly, eventually moving out of sight. Unsure of the route, Deborah and I felt abandoned and afraid in this wild, untamed environment. We were angry and resolved to tell John what that experience had been like for us when we finally reached camp.

Our first order of business was to make lunch, but between bites of salami and cheese, Deborah and I had glanced at each other, lightning bolts meeting in our eyes. I spoke first and intentionally hedged my words. "John, I gotta tell you that getting far enough ahead of us to be out of sight for a couple of hours on the way up here was not the most helpful thing you could have done today."

John stopped chewing for a moment and shrugged his shoulders. "I figured you guys would push harder if I went on ahead as an example."

Deborah's anger showed itself. "That sure isn't what happened," she said. "I couldn't have pushed any harder. I was having a really off day and doing the very best I could. Your disappearing felt like a childish slap in the face and could have put us at risk on an unfamiliar mountain."

My courage grew with Deborah's directness. "That was my experience, too." I remembered the conversation Sarah and I had in La Paz. "I know that all guides work differently. You seem to think that the way to get people to do their best is to push them hard, but I do much better with encouragement than I do being pushed." I had to pause to breathe. At an elevation of 18,000-plus feet, my lungs were straining for air. "I'm pretty new at this climbing thing, John, and there's a lot I don't know and haven't experienced. A 'Hang in there, Margo' or 'You're doing great' motivates me much better than taking off and disappearing, assuming that my slowness is simply a matter of sucking it up and pushing harder." I couldn't tell if John was listening or not, but I needed to hear what I was saying so I continued. "I don't just cut off my emotions, put my head down, and go. It's important to hear I'm doing okay once in a while. I would have expected you to stay with us or at least wait every so often. What if we'd had an emergency? What works for you doesn't work for me."

Deborah nodded her agreement. "I was pretty scared when we didn't see you for such a long time. I got to thinking we were lost, and I almost turned around. It would have been really helpful if you'd been there."

"Yeah," said John. "I've heard this before." He was a quiet, closed man, and his candor surprised me. "I've been told it's different for men and women, too. Pushing myself is how I stay alive in the mountains, and I don't leave room for emotions. The wilderness is unforgiving."

"I absolutely understand that." My voice was becoming firm, more confident, less angry. "I know how easy it is to die on mountains. It's just that I have a different way of getting to my strength than you do, and I would hope that, as a guide, you could support my way as well as yours. I'm not exactly sure what it is I need to help me push myself past what I think are my limits, but being left behind like we were today sure doesn't do it."

He nodded and said, "I hear you guys, and I'll keep what you're saying in mind." He paused, taking time to clean a crack in the rock we were sitting on. Then he looked directly at me, and in a calm, firm voice, said, "But part of my job as a guide is to make sure people don't get themselves into situations where they endanger themselves and the people they're climbing with. Margo, based on what I've seen from you during the past month, I don't think you're fast enough to get to the summit tomorrow in a reasonable amount of time. I can't risk letting what I judge to be your limitations keep everyone else from being successful. I can't let that happen."

We'd been talking about encouragement. How did we get from that to "You can't go tomorrow?" I lowered my gaze. My fingers found their own crack to work on—something to keep my hands busy while I breathed into the shock of what I had just heard. Not go? Not try? What do you mean, I'm not fast enough? What do you mean I can't do it? I had a mental image of myself with my hands on my hips in stubborn, defiant anger.

I looked at John and saw regret in his eyes. "I'm sorry, Margo. I know how hard you've worked to get here, but I can't jeopardize Steve's and Deborah's chances for the summit."

I wasn't prepared for this. I could only nod to acknowledge that I'd heard his words. I didn't even want to make eye contact with Deborah. I sensed that John was right; I'd thought about not going myself. But this felt like having a lover break off a relationship before I could walk out on him. It took a little while for me to accept his affirmation of how hard I'd worked. More quickly than I could have imagined, however, my anger became relief and my body visibly relaxed as my bruised ego accepted his decision. I didn't have anything to prove in making the summit. I had reached high camp and now could enjoy my time here and be ready to pack up and climb down when they returned. Nevertheless, I didn't sleep very well that night and was awake at 4:00 A.M. when the others got up, dressed, and left for their ascent.

Deborah was back within an hour. Her cold had consumed her determination and she knew shortly after she started that she wouldn't be able to make it. By 9:30 A.M. the guys had returned, too. Steve hit a wall of physical exhaustion at about 20,000 feet and he and John decided to turn around rather than continue to push for the top. Quietly, as we packed up camp, each of us focused on our own feelings about not reaching the summit of Illimani. We descended the steep, unstable talus that formed the lower part of the mountain, and I began to sense I was in real trouble. I'd carried heavy packs before, and I'd descended steep boulder fields, but I'd never attempted to do them at the same time. Scrambling over the first ridge of loose scree, I constantly fought to catch my balance with ski poles. My fear of falling onto the jagged rocks below, combined with the heavy weight of my pack, sapped the strength from my legs. My quads were shaking after only half an hour, and I had to stop frequently to catch my breath and rest. The others, even Deborah who was ill, moved ever farther ahead. I was scared and felt totally out of my element. Martha was screaming, "You can't do this, you're going to fall and die. Your legs are giving out. What's wrong? You'll never get to Base Camp." Tears ran down my cheeks. Sobs threatened to explode out of my chest. The darkness of failure pulled me into its depths.

Our Bolivian guide Francisco finally reascended and took my pack to carry it down the worst of the scree. I was embarrassed and grateful, too. I don't know how I would have made it to camp otherwise. I took the pack back for the last hour, crossing streams and walking narrow trails. I kept moving in spite of my fear. Francisco, relieved of his double load, moved quickly toward camp. Although I was aware of John's silent disapproval of my slowness, he stayed with me and his presence was reassuring.

My terror on the precarious slopes and absolute inability to summon any inner strength left me limp and shaking by the time I reached our Base Camp. I felt beaten: by Illimani, by my own physical weakness, and above all by Martha. I had no strength left to fight her negative, critical judgments. Maybe, I thought, it was time to admit defeat and go home. On the drive back to La Paz, I chose not to make any decision for a few days to give myself time to regain some perspective.

Three days later I was walking up a hill overlooking the small, beautiful town of Copacabana, situated on the shoreline of Lake Titicaca. Both my body and soul needed a rest after the exhausting, frustrating efforts of the last month. At the top of the hill I watched local shamans dispense healing to those who could pay, then I walked over to a solitary rock outcropping to receive some healing from God and my inner family.

Martha's voice started before I could even sit down. She pointed out that I hadn't been able to complete anything I'd started for the past two-and-a-half weeks. I didn't want to believe her, but my heart and emotions followed her into the darkness. I couldn't find the strength in myself to counter her relentless pounding. Coming down off Illimani was the hardest physical thing I'd ever done. It was clear, very clear, that I was in over my head. At one point I'd even told myself, "I'm done. I don't want to do the amount of work necessary to be able to carry a 50-pound pack down steep scree without being paralyzed with fear or to exist at 20,000 feet on a mountain. I can't do the climbing, it's just too hard. I don't want to beat my head against the wall anymore."

Looking out over the town and Lake Titicaca, watching clouds building in the distance, I heard a quiet, calm voice come from inside my soul. It was Jonathan: "Margo. Breathe. And, listen to me. You haven't failed. It hasn't looked like you thought it would, but that isn't failure. It's just different. You've climbed to the summit of two mountains, functioned in difficult conditions when you felt lousy, tried things you've never done before, and shown up for life when it felt like that was too hard to do. You're exhausted. Give yourself permission to rest. I honor the courage with which you've walked through the last few weeks. I honor your willingness to feel afraid and show up anyway. I honor your ability to make difficult choices. I honor you."

Martha tried to argue. I told her I wouldn't listen. I felt Jonathan's spirit warm the chill that surrounded my heart. I could feel the beginnings of gratitude finding their way past my negativity. The truth was I wouldn't change where I was for anything. No, I didn't know how to do a lot of things, but yes, I was still stronger than I ever imagined

I could be. Both things were true and neither of them was the whole of my reality. I was left with a sense of the perfection of the Universe. It was, indeed, exactly the way it was meant to be. I could accept and even embrace the defeats as well as the blessings.

I spent some time sightseeing with Yolanda and Louis, Americans living in Ecuador whom I had met on the bus from La Paz to Copacabana. They encouraged me to ramble on about my dreams of climbing, the adventure of the past three weeks, and the failures I'd experienced, and they told me about their life as expatriates living in Ecuador. Louis's fluent Spanish gave me access to the lives and hearts of the children and adults we met. When they invited me to go skiing with them at Mount Chacaltaya, home of Club Andino Boliviano, the world's highest ski area, I said yes.

What a thrill! Nearly 18,000 feet in the Andes, I strapped on old skis that looked as if they'd never been tuned. Louis convinced the operator to start up the ancient truck whose drive train was used to power the "ski lift." It rattled to life, and we provided great amusement for some Bolivian Army troops standing nearby as we tried to master the intricacies of engaging the improvised hooks on the cable and landed in an inauspicious pile instead. Once on our way, though, the exhilaration of being on skis in the Andes kicked in, and the views of La Paz, Illimani, Huayna Potosi, and thousands of other peaks in every direction almost distracted me from the unloading point at the top of the cable. The slope was ungroomed and short, with patches of ice and exposed rocks. But the run was fun. Most important, I could now say that I had skied at the highest ski area in the world.

I returned to La Paz refreshed and ready for another adventure, a spontaneous three days in central Bolivia visiting the towns of Sucre and Tarabuco. This experiment in traveling alone and without an itinerary gave me a chance to face new fears. One step at a time I negotiated plane flights, hotels, and a short "train" trip on an old red-and-white school bus converted to run on rails. The same lessons I'd learned on the mountains helped me deal with getting out of my hotel room and mixing with people. Even when I was unsure of myself and uncomfortable, I knew I could make the choices required to take care of my needs. I wasn't trapped by my emotional ups and downs. Best of all, I hadn't wanted to drink, use drugs, or overeat through any of this. Amazing!

My plans seemed to be in constant flux. One day I was ready to pack everything up and head for home, the next I'd extended my stay for another ten days to finish my time in Bolivia traversing the Andes on some of the highest passes in the world. I talked on the phone with Becky and found out that international politics and low registrations had caused the trips I'd planned in Tibet and Pakistan to be canceled. Based on my experience on Illimani, I now knew they would have been far beyond my climbing capabilities. Once again, God was doing for me what I could not do for myself. When I talked with Sarah about these changes in my plans, she suggested a trek she used to lead from Kashmir to Ladakh in India as an alternative. I checked on its availability and they had an opening, so I signed on. I would have time in India I hadn't expected.

I spent a total of three more weeks trekking in the Andes. It was a time of healing, physically and emotionally. First, I joined a group led by Geof through the eerie desert landscapes of the Valley of the Moon and Palca Canyon. Some of us climbed a prominent rock outcropping called Muela del Diablo or Devil's Molar. We hiked from the remote village of Taquesi across a pass in the Cordillera Real, walking part of the way on paving stones laid down more than five hundred years ago as part of the major system of roads the Incas developed to connect their empire, which extended from present-day Ecuador to southern Chile through some of the most inhospitable terrain in the world. We experienced snow, rain, and almost tropical heat as we moved from one climate zone to another. In some places the trail was so narrow and steep the pack animals carrying our equipment had difficulty. One horse slipped off the path and tumbled more than a hundred yards before coming to a stop, miraculously uninjured.

On the last night of this trek, we shared camp with a group of climbers who were beginning the same trip I'd completed a month before. They invited me to join them for another chance to claim the summits I'd missed. I declined. Martha sneered that by not going I'd proved I was a wimp. "Just go home," she said, "and sit on the beach. It's all you're capable of." But it wasn't.

Then I joined Sarah and a group she was leading. We trekked for eight days, over nine passes at elevations above 15,000 feet. I felt strong, in body and spirit. I reveled in my strength, in the magnificence of the mountains I was traveling through and in the knowledge that I was exactly where I was supposed to be. We hiked through exquisite valleys, past tier after tier of towering mountains, and into herds of llamas. My serenity grew with each step as I let myself enjoy the present in this incredible country, experiencing intimately every change in the weather and terrain. As we moved from one valley to the next, sometimes we went from snow into bright sunshine, from barren scree to dense vegetation. My back ached on and off. Occasionally I wondered what my time in Asia would hold for me. As I ended my seven weeks in Peru and Bolivia, I knew I was a changed person and was ready for the next stop on my journey.

Friday, September 1, 1989, Over India
Looking out the window, watching the sky lighten,
I realize I am flying over India! The Himal!
My God, I am really here. Oh, Jonathan. I know
that you're here, too. I finally made it.

Sitting on the afterdeck of a houseboat on Nagin Lake in Kashmir, I took time to reflect on something that John, one of the guides in Bolivia, used to repeat, "I always feel better after I get out of bed." Since I'd arrived in New Delhi, my nose, ears, and lungs had been congested. When I awoke in the morning, I didn't want to get up. Martha had been pointing out to me that I was already sick and hadn't even started my trek yet and had almost convinced me that I should admit defeat. But I remembered John's words and found them to be true for me as well.

I watched brightly colored *shikaras* skim across the water, some filled with fruits, some with flowers, some with passengers. I listened to the sounds of birds singing, water lapping, and Muslims chanting their prayers. I began to feel grateful again, able to appreciate being on the edge of Jonathan's Himal, tucked up against Pakistan in northern India, ready to trek with fifteen others from Australia, the United States, and Canada. We ranged in age from eighteen to seventy-something, and everyone was ready for the adventure to begin. Having settled into the unfamiliar surroundings and made friends among the other trekkers, I could feel God's presence.

Our first day, we hiked over Margan Pass, nearly 12,000 feet high. The fertile countryside grew lush crops of corn, millet and wheat. Kashmiri children called out "Salaam, Salaam" as we passed, and our porters and camp crew sang folk songs. I was awestruck to be in the depths of a very foreign country halfway around the world from home, pushing my body to its limits, and choosing to walk into my fears. Yes, my sinuses were not right, I had a cough that hurt inside my chest, and now my right knee felt as though I'd strained or torn a ligament. Still, I was able to show up, participate, and feel the deep gratitude that emerged from my soul. I was living a life I couldn't have imagined three years earlier. I could so easily have been dead now rather than walking into the throat of the highest mountains on earth.

A light breeze played with the straps on my day pack as we started up toward Humpet Ridge. We walked through a beautiful grove of white-barked trees unlike any I'd ever seen. Their shade was a welcome relief from the already rising temperature of the day. During the next few days, as we hiked closer to the Himal, the land became more barren. The lush fields disappeared, replaced by rocky cliffs, and there were fewer villages. Temperatures swung through extremes, sweltering heat during the day, frost at night, and the trail became rougher. When Martha brought up the pain in my knee, I told her the worst that could happen was that I'd go home, cancel Nepal, and take all of my memories with me. The amazing part was I really believed it!

Coming around a gentle bend in the trail I heard the herdsmen's whistles and whoops signaling an approaching Bakarwal caravan with its enchanting harmony of bleating goats and pony bells. Since this was an ancient trade route, used as a major thoroughfare by these nomads for centuries, we'd been swallowed up and spit out by many of these already. I smiled in anticipation of seeing the stiff gait and curlicue horns of hundreds of goats, dust kicked up by their hooves swirling around them and the ponies carrying children, sick goats, and possessions. The herdsmen always had unkempt beards, dusty turbans, and dark clothing. Some sat straight in their saddles, horses at a walk, with young children riding on their shoulders. Others rode at a trot in their characteristic style, leaning far back with legs and arms extended in front, swinging ropes and whooping and whistling at the unruly animals.

As I rounded the corner, the caravan appeared, backed by snow-capped peaks. I was deeply touched—I was in the Himal, Jonathan's Himal. His spirit filled my heart as I stopped and breathed in the reality of where I was and how far I'd come to be here. It all seemed impossible, and I heard Jonathan's voice saying, "Welcome. Welcome to my world and the realization of your dream. Welcome."

My dream? My dream was to climb, but my knee grew more painful with each step. I had concerns about being able to get over the next pass, let alone to the mountains in Nepal. What did he know about my dreams? Through that day and into the next, mixed feelings pushed and pulled at my heart.

On the trail and in camp I wanted to talk to someone about the debate going on inside. With doubts, questions, and fears bottled up, I felt like a pressure cooker. Sometimes tears would run down my cheeks while I walked. At one camp I found a rock down by the river where I was able to cry, and as my feelings released I could feel the fear behind them. It seemed that some part of me was creating a problem so I could perform in spite of it, and by performing well enough, be okay, even if I wasn't able to climb. My old ideas were still alive and well.

We crossed fast-moving rivers, holding on to each other's wrists with all our might as the biting cold water tried to drag us downstream. One woman slipped, her legs swept out from under her. But we never lost our grip and pulled her across safely. We walked on the Bhot Kol glacier as we crossed from Kashmir into Ladakh from Muslim into Tibetan Buddhist territory. The trail took us through the town of Pannikar and across the pass known as Lago La. The twin peaks of Nun and Kun, both over 23,000 feet high, watched us move toward the valley beyond.

I did a lot of thinking about Jonathan's affirmation of my dream becoming reality. One night I sat in a grove of trees. I could hear the Nepali crew singing in the cook tent. The light of a full moon reflected off a small waterfall and stream in front of me. I visualized taking my nineteen-year-old self into my arms to give her the unconditional love she had never received. She was the part of me who had always been aware of the judgment of others. She was the part of me who always felt like a failure. She was the part of me who wanted a problem as an excuse, something to overcome and to blame for not being "strong enough."

I closed my eyes and whispered my love for her, stroked her hair, and told her that we could choose our own path. We could climb or not climb, we were terrific no matter what happened, and we didn't need anyone else to tell us that. I told her we didn't need to have a problem to overcome and that we'd walk more slowly and take more time to look at the scenery so our knee could heal. She still wasn't sure she trusted what I was saying, but she was willing to try.

I noticed that when the trek entered the sphere of Buddhist influence, a soft serenity pervaded the people and the countryside. The Rangdum Monastery was important to the region, and I looked forward to seeing it but wasn't prepared for the way it dominated the wide valley it occupied, sitting on top of the only raised portion of an otherwise flat expanse. Around it grew tundralike tufts of grass fed by a small stream coming from some distant glacier. Mountains cradled the valley, their fluted ridges carved out by eons of wind and rain emphasizing the quiet serenity of this place and the people who inhabited it.

As the sun set, I watched the shadow of the mountains creep up the natural pedestal on which the monastery sat, then climb the face of the massive structure itself. I was filled with the presence of Jonathan's spirit. The monastery was a symbol of the expansion of my life view that Jonathan had started in Aspen. Our discussions of Buddhist philosophy and teachings had broadened the narrow perspective of the world I'd been raised with and allowed me to begin questioning the traditional life views I'd been taught. Change had been too threatening back then. Just the idea of it plunged me deeper into my addictions. Too fearful to consider that what I thought I believed was actually someone else's truth, not mine. Jonathan's words and ideas, his mirrors of my soul, had been filed away. Not thrown away, but carefully stored in a safe place far enough from my conscious mind that I wasn't distressed by the questions they raised.

Now, as I sat in front of my tent watching the monastery in the fading light, the importance of the time with Jonathan emerged like the stars beginning to shine overhead. I felt his essence embrace me. He'd planted seeds that were now bearing sweet fruit in my recovery. They had been in suspension all those years while I ran from life, from myself, from my fears, with drugs and alcohol and food. Like his spirit, the seeds were hearty and survived.

The next morning some members of the group walked half an hour across the valley to the monastery. I was filled with an almost overwhelming excitement, about to be in a place I'd been drawn to for fifteen years. A dream coming true. I entered the dark main room where the 108 books of Sanskrit Buddhist scriptures lined one wall. I saw statues of a variety of gods, offerings of yak butter carvings and seeds and nuts in front of them. A photo of the Dalai Lama hung on the wall. Surprisingly, the space felt oddly familiar and comforting, as though I'd been here before. Something inside breathed out the word, "Yes."

I sat cross-legged on one of the prayer rugs, taking in the sense of the space as my companions looked around for an hour or so and then left. Eyes closed, I focused on the sounds of drumming and chanting coming from other rooms. The thick intervening walls dulled the sounds, but they still touched my soul with a tangible energy. The last time I had heard these rhythms and atonal chants was at Jonathan's memorial service in Aspen in 1980. Tears trickled down my cheeks as I gave in to the sadness I'd carried with me since he'd died. Soon I felt a shift, sensed his presence beside me, and the grief became comfort. For an instant, I believed that if I opened my eyes, I'd see him sitting in a lotus position, looking at me with the serene smile that so often adorned his face.

I didn't hear any words, only saw his smile and the love it projected directly into my heart. My tears came faster, but now they were tears of joy and gratitude that I was finally here, at Rangdum. With the realization of the dream came the knowing, at a new level, that I could not go back to my old ways: the ways of avoidance and pain and incomprehensible demoralization. The path of my life led forward into sunlight, into the truth of myself rather than away from it. I was discovering the strength, love, and wholeness Jonathan had seen in me when I couldn't see anything but a black hole that terrified me. I sat and meditated and felt the mix of joy at my life's journey and grief for the parts of me I was leaving behind. My tapestry was becoming as rich as the finest fabric in Rangdum.

My hours in the monastery were a kind of spatial warp. I knew I'd experienced something important and yet wasn't sure exactly what it meant. At the moment, there were more immediate issues to deal with. We still had a major pass, the Kanji La, to cross, and days of hiking ahead before we'd reach the town of Leh, the end of the trek. Being in the present was still the key.

A four-hour hike the next day took us to 13,800 feet. We set up camp on rock platforms laboriously dug into the face of a cliff overlooking the river we'd traversed a number of times to get here. The immediate challenge was finding enough places for tents, people, and horses alongside the gorge. We slept three people to a tent to fit everyone in.

At 17,300 feet, Kanji La was the highest pass we crossed. Clouds obscured many of the peaks within the Karakoram Range that extends into Pakistan, but the views as we hiked down the deep gorge on the other side of the pass were breathtaking. Thousand-foot-high walls of reddish brown rock and sparkling quartz towered above the trail. We followed the stream, which led us, over the next two days, to the road and Jeeps that transported us to Leh, warm showers, and clean sheets. As I completed my stay in India, the gratitude and sense of connection I experienced at the Rangdum Monastery deepened, and I left for Nepal eager to find out how my dream was going to manifest itself.

Saturday, October 7, 1989, Kathmandu
Thank God this room has a tub. The flight was
cloudy so I couldn't see the mountains but
what clouds! I really am in Kathmandu!

After months of anticipation, my introduction to Nepal was inauspicious and frustrating. I felt none of the powerful connection with the mountains I experienced flying into Cuzco or La Paz, and my first impression of Kathmandu suffered greatly from my having to move from one hotel to another, then finally to a third trying to meet up with Bill, the guide for the trek, and Eric and Art, the other two climbers on this trip.

I took time to soak in the bathtub in my hotel room, letting water wash away the errors and fears and frustrations of my first few hours in the city. As my body relaxed, I closed my eyes and climbed into the rocking chair on the porch of God's cabin next to Hunter Creek. I could feel myself being held in God's loving embrace. I was safe and cared for and loved. Gratitude and wonder replaced the fear and frustration. When I opened my eyes and looked around the room, I told myself, "I'm in Nepal. Tomorrow I'm leaving on a trek into the Annapurnas that will last twenty-nine days! How's this even possible?"

Martha jumped into my head and said, "Big deal. You could have been here in 1975 with Jonathan, now he's gone and you're here all alone."

I stepped out of the tub and grabbed a towel. "I'm not alone. God's here. And Jonathan. And the energy from everybody back home." Deep down inside, though, Martha's words hurt. I really would have liked to be sharing the experience with someone I loved. Something else to add to my list of dreams. I continued talking with Martha as I got ready for bed. "Today I'm able to live this dream, in the city Jonathan told me so much about, the one I saw in his photographs and experienced through his heart. I'll take his memory and his spirit with me to experience the wonder and the power of the mountains he loved so much."

As I turned out the light to go to sleep I said, "Thank you, Jonathan, for opening my heart to life's possibilities. I didn't understand then, when you first told me. I was too afraid. But your words got through and have lived inside me all this time. Thank you."

"You're welcome." I heard his response clearly in my heart, and the words filled my soul with the warmth and love and kindness of his spirit.

I met Bill, Eric, and Art for breakfast at 6:15. Bill and Eric looked like climbers, compact, fit, big smiles. Their shorts and T-shirts revealed bodies hardened with a lot of exercise. Art looked more like Ichabod Crane, tall and thin, bespectacled, and dressed to hike in a white shirt and gray slacks. I wondered who had packed his bags for him. But all three had much more climbing experience than me. At least I held the record in the group for trekking.

The guys were nearly beside themselves and made cracks about the luxury of this trip as seven Sherpas and twenty porters loaded up our gear in Dumre. "Hell, all we have to do is get ourselves to the mountain. This'll be a piece of cake." We headed up the well-traveled trail through rice paddies and manicured fields. Soon we were soaked with sweat from the heat and high humidity. Overhead, billowing monsoon clouds parted every once in a while to reveal snow-covered peaks in the distance. Most of the peaks surrounding us, including the Annapurnas, soared higher than 20,000 feet. Many were over 25,000 feet. One of them, Manaslu, at 26,658 feet was the world's eighth highest. We scrambled across precarious suspension bridges and past children playing on hand-powered ferris wheels as we made our way out of the bamboo and banyan trees of the southern slope of the Annapurna Himal and climbed steadily toward our goal.

At 21,060 feet, what is generally regarded as Chulu West is actually one of a cluster of peaks that are part of the Chulu massif, immediately northeast of Annapurna and just off the trail to Thorong La, the highest pass on the Annapurna circuit. Chulu is one of eighteen peaks in Nepal that can be climbed with a trekking permit. For a climber like me, they offered a chance to test my mountaineering skills without requiring the massive support and cost required for bigger mountains.

My knee was holding up pretty well, but painful blisters were forming on my toes as we moved into the more irregular terrain of the true mountain valleys. Still, I was grateful and proud of my body's ability to keep up with Bill's pace, and I found that changing the type of socks I wore helped my toes. My heart soared as we moved from the Hindu villages of the lowlands up to the Buddhist shrines known as *chortens*, prayer flags, and "Namaste" greetings at higher altitudes. Martha was wonderfully silent. All three men were openly supportive, and yet I felt separate from them. I was a climber whose focus was as much on the process of trekking and climbing as on reaching the summit. The guys simply didn't understand, if the summit wasn't the goal, why come?

Still, I was amazed at how I was able to allow myself to be a beginner with them. It was as though their support and acceptance of me honored my growing base of climbing experience, and I felt free to ask questions and listen to the answers. One afternoon, Bill spent more than an hour going over the map with me when I got turned around.

In Manang, at 11,600 feet, my body rebelled. I had constant foot pain and also menstrual cramps. Bill was supportive, even allowing that we might be able to take a rest day when we reached Base Camp, but his closing comment was "You may just have to bear the pain." Art said that making the choice not to climb would be more painful for him than any physical problem. Eric kept his thoughts to himself. My experience cautioned me to take each day one step at a time and not to project how I might feel at one moment into the future. We moved up to Base Camp for Chulu, 16,400 feet.

As I'd hoped, we rested there one day. I put fresh moleskin on my feet to try to ease their discomfort. A Nepalese crow, known as a gorak, cawed as its shadow passed overhead. I looked up to find it, saw the mountains surrounding me, and was almost knocked over by the physical sensation of joy and gratitude at being in Nepal. Long ago I had sat cross-legged on the floor in Aspen, hunched forward in excitement, looking at slides Jonathan had brought back from his first trip here, listening to the love of this place in his voice as he told me what I was seeing. He had left on the trip only days after we'd taken the apartment together, so I hadn't known him very well, but the beauty of his images and the emotion in his voice as he showed the place and the people he loved so well spoke volumes about the kind of man he was.

The very first slide had been an image that touched my heart deeply. In the foreground was a tree in silhouette against a great peak of rock and snow with a double summit that looked like a fish tail. "Wow! That one takes my breath away. What mountain is it?"

"Macchupucchare," Jonathan said. "It's a part of the Annapurnas."

"God, I'd love to see it in person someday." I wasn't aware of the irony in my comment as I sat there with a cigarette in one hand, a bag of marijuana at my feet, and a vodka and orange juice on the table beside me. But I felt an immediate fascination with this place, its people, and these incredible mountains that was to stay with me. And I felt a longing: the empty longing that comes with wanting something we believe in our hearts we cannot have, wanting something we know is beyond our ability to have or do. Even then, my addictions had smothered any belief I ever had that my dreams could come true. It had been exciting to think about someday going to the Himal, while underneath the excitement was the knowledge that I would never be willing to travel that far away from the drugs and the alcohol and the food.

My mind came back to the present. "I'm really here," I breathed softly. "That's the victory. The climbing is a bonus." I worried what the climb to Camp I tomorrow would bring: biting cold and a heavy pack, steep scree, and mixed climbing in the couloir—the slash in the face of the mountain that was our access to the summit. Yet I was greatly relieved by the memory of where I'd come from. I'd already won at the game of life simply by being here. It didn't matter how well I performed tomorrow as long as I showed up and put one foot in front of the other the best I could. I could do that. That was how I lived my life these days—it would work on a mountain as well.

Straight out of camp the next morning, we headed up steep, unstable gravel. My pack weighed about 35 pounds, and as the slope steepened I found the going tough. Each time I put weight on my foot, the gravel moved, threatening to carry me sliding all the way back to camp, and my whole body tensed, remembering Bolivia. "Breathe, Margo," I told myself. "This isn't Illimani, you don't have to panic. You're doing great." I focused on staying in the present, planting each foot as carefully as I could, and relaxing when it slid before finding a solid purchase on the rock under the gravel. The more I relaxed, the easier the climbing got. "Yeah," I said under my breath as I began to feel a rhythm in the climbing. "Yeah," as I was able to take in the wonder of being here, climbing in the Himalaya. "Thank You," I said to God, the words a part of the rhythmical breathing that kept me moving.

At the base of the couloir we rested, drank some water, and looked up at what was to come. The climbing was mixed, rock in some places, snow in others, and steeper than anything I'd been on up to this point. It wasn't technically difficult, but standing at the foot of it, I had no idea how I would get to the top. "How ya' doin', Margo?" Bill asked.

"Good." I tried to allay my own apprehension as well as answer his question.

"Okay, let's go." Our *sirdar* or head Sherpa, Ang Puri, started up.

"Leave enough space between you and the guy in front so you don't get hit by any rocks they kick off," Bill said. "Some of this stuff is pretty loose."

Art followed Ang Puri, moving quickly and confidently, with Eric following him more slowly, seeming very unsure of himself. Bill called out directions from below, dodging rocks loosened by Eric's attempts to gain solid footholds. "Easy, Eric. The footholds are there, you don't need to make them." He gave me a nod. "Okay, Margo. Go for it!"

I started up, remembering to use my ice axe in my uphill hand for balance rather than to lean on, bending my ankles so as many of the points of my crampons were in the snow as possible. I planted the metal points carefully on the hard surface of exposed rock, breathing hard but rhythmically: one foot above the other, keep breathing, concentrate on foot placement. I edged carefully past Eric who had stopped, panting, to rest and get his bearings. "Way to go, Margo," he said. "You're a strong lady."

I smiled a "Thanks" and reveled in the sense of pride his words stirred in me.

An hour later we were all at the top of the couloir and moving slowly along the long, low angle slog to Camp I through the deep new snow. The last hour to camp was the hardest work of the day. "God, it's just like life," I thought, as I picked up my right foot and raised it high to clear the foot and a half of snow that encased it. "It isn't the crises that are the hard part. It's showing up on a daily basis, one day after another, one task after another. It's the slogging that's so hard."

That day was an enormous confidence builder for me. I felt strong, competent, and proud, especially given the hard work of the last hour. My technique had been good in the difficult places, my determination strong when it all came down to slogging. Bill had said I did great and, most important, I thought I did great! My soul sang as I ducked through the tent door out into the cold to pee. The wind shifted and blew snow all over my exposed butt, and I laughed out loud. I felt alive and proud and free—free of the addictions that had ruled my life for so long, free of the fears and disappointment of Bolivia, free for the moment of the doubts and negative voices that had been such constant companions during my life.

I returned to the tent I was sharing with Bill, and as I snuggled into the warmth of my bag, I heard Bill snoring softly. I wondered if he ever had the same kinds of feelings as I did, the mood swings, the doubts, the fears. Did other climbers not have them or did they just not express them?

At seven the next morning, we set off for the summit. The snow was deep and we would have to slog through it, but our packs were light. After climbing for three-and-a-half hours, I didn't know how I could keep going. I leaned over my ice axe, resting as best I could, and focused on my breathing, searching inside for the strength I needed to continue putting one foot in front of the other.

Tears came to my eyes. I asked God to help me. Ahead, I could see the summit.

"Okay, God, let's go." I took a deep breath, picked up my left foot, and extended it toward the boot print the men had made before me. Once again I sunk in past my knee. I choked back a sob. "Oh, God, stay with me. I don't think I can do this. Jonathan, are you here?"

"I'm here, Margo. You're doing great. Just breathe and step, breathe and step." Jonathan's spirit filled me with warmth, as it always did, and I began to believe, again, that I could keep going.

In only a few minutes, though, my fatigue overwhelmed me. I felt unsteady on my feet and called for a rest stop. The fear drained me even more. I could only climb for fifteen minutes before calling for another rest stop. When we stopped, I kept my knees locked because that was the only way they would hold me up. I leaned over my ice axe for balance.

"I've told you all along you couldn't do this." Martha's voice sounded strident and righteous in my head. "You might as well quit now and go home." The quiet pride of yesterday swirled into the black hole that waited like a predator to swallow up and destroy the light of my heart. "You're so lazy," Martha chastised me. "You'd be okay if you had only trained harder or had more determination or had hydrated better or . . ."

"Shut up, Martha. None of that stuff is true." I spoke aloud, and Ali, the Sherpa who was climbing with us, looked at me questioningly. I shrugged.

She did shut up and left me alone to agonize. "It isn't going to happen," I admitted to myself softly. What was wrong? I had felt fine this morning. Why had I run out of energy? I had no answer, but after several minutes, I knew I couldn't continue. My legs had no strength left, and my balance was deteriorating.

"Bill," I shouted. No response. "Bill." Louder that time, but still he didn't hear me. I gave it all I had. "BILL!" He turned, and I motioned him over.

"I'm done. I haven't got another step in me." I couldn't look him in the eye, and stared down instead at my green plastic boots surrounded by bright white snow.

"What's wrong?" he asked.

"Nothing's wrong. I'm just done. I've run out of energy." I fought back the tears. "I can wait here for you guys to summit and come back down. It's warm enough." There, I'd said it. The decision was made.

"Are you sure?" he asked.

"Yeah."

Bill told the others, made sure I had enough clothes to stay warm for several hours, then led the team, minus me, toward the summit, an hour and a half away. Mesmerized, I watched the line of men grow smaller as they slowly walked away, moving ever closer to the summit I would not reach.

I knew I'd made the right decision, yet the disappointment and frustration were acute. I'd given this mountain everything I had. I didn't cop out or fake an injury because it was hard. I just ran out of gas. No excuses. No inventions. I simply couldn't do any more.

I turned around to find a place to settle into, and was struck motionless by the magnificence of the scene laid out before me. I was standing eye to eye with the snow-covered peaks of the Annapurna Himal. They rose in wave after wave moving to the horizon and beyond, range upon range of powerful monuments to creative forces. I was filled with a sense of wonder. This grandeur and my connection with God, the mountains, and the possibilities of life were the reasons I was here. The summit had been the dream, but being in this place at this moment was the true victory.

The sun was bright in the clear blue sky. The thin air at 20,000 feet gave everything a richness and clarity, even my heart. Bravo, Margo. The "failure" of not reaching the summit became a gateway to a new level of acceptance of myself and the perfection of the Universe.

Two days later, as we approached Thorong La, I was increasingly sure I did not want to attempt the next day's climb of Thorong Peak. I had another cold and cough, and had asked myself some difficult questions: "Do I have to be sick to give myself permission not to climb? Am I afraid of not getting to the summit or of looking like a wimp? Or do I just not want to work that hard? Does it even matter that I'm sick?" I had an answer that I didn't have before: "The only question that has any meaning is 'Do I want to?' not, 'Can I?' or, 'What will they think?' or 'What does it mean if I don't climb?' Simply, 'Do I want to?' "

When we arrived at Base Camp for Thorong, I was still wrestling with that question. Bill made the decision for me. "Margo, it really doesn't matter what you want to do," he said. "You're not well enough to climb, and you're going down first thing in the morning."

I was at ease with his decision, but of course Martha chided me for letting someone else make the choice. She said I'd never be able to take care of myself. I preferred to believe that if I were ever faced with a similar choice, I'd be the one to decide next time. Meanwhile, I took advantage of the extra time to rest, read, and relax and when the guys returned from the summit, I was ready to complete the trek. We still had a week of rigorous hiking ahead of us, passes to cross, and Macchupucchare was waiting for us before we'd arrive in Pokhara, our final destination.

With four days to go, I ran out of reserve energy. In the town of Tatopani, named after the hot springs it contained, I lay in my tent, in tears. Not even soaking in the naturally warmed water sounded good. We had walked more than eight hours that day, and I had to fight back tears the last couple of them. At one point I was walking so slowly and gingerly that Bill asked me if I was okay.

"I'm just real tired and my feet hurt like hell."

"What makes you think you'll ever be able to climb if you wimp out on a day of walking?" he threw out as he left me in his dust.

"See!" Martha immediately latched on to Bill's words.

"Asshole," I thought, not sure if I meant Bill or Martha. Maybe both.

He called at my tent that night. "I need to talk to you about something," he said. "May I unzip your tent door?"

"Can't it wait until tomorrow?" I felt wiped out and certainly didn't want to take any more shaming from him.

"No. It needs to be now." Bill unzipped the tent without waiting for my okay. "It has to do with why you're so tired." He hunkered down in the doorway. "I've been watching you for almost a month now, and you're just not eating enough. That's why you ran out of gas on Chulu, that's why you've been fighting that cough, and that's why you're so tired now. Do you realize you're not as strong now as you were when we started?"

"I know." I felt as though I had done something terribly wrong.

"You're eating up your own muscles because your body's not getting enough food. Look at you, your pants hardly stay up anymore." I'd noticed I was thin, but had enjoyed the feeling of my clothes being too big. "You'll never make it as a climber if you can't keep your body nourished."

His last line drove deeply into my shame, but I was able to laugh at the irony of the situation. Here I was recovering from being a compulsive overeater, and I was having difficulty finding ways to eat enough! Who made this one up?

I increased my calories during our walk out as we ascended and descended a seemingly endless series of ridges, each one with stairs carved into the trail. I felt stronger and more balanced emotionally, and was grateful once again for the recovery that allowed me to be open to change, to listen to others and their experience, and to live my life so fully. Now I saw humor in my fears about how I was going to handle my food issues when I went to Africa. In my mind, I made a mental note to take nuts and peanut butter with me to the Khumbu region to supplement my meals. It would be a good trial to see if it would be possible for me to eat enough to keep my body strong.

As we climbed the steps leading to the village of Chandrakot, my excitement grew. At last I would be able to see Macchupucchare. It had captured me in its spell when I first saw the pictures Jonathan brought home to Aspen. I felt his presence very strongly and noticed that my pace had quickened. Ang Puri signaled me from the porch of a teahouse by the side of the trail, inviting me to join him for a rest stop. I stepped onto the wooden porch, dropped my pack, and picked up the bottle of Fanta he had waiting for me. Thirsty, I guzzled half the bottle before something caught my attention from the periphery of my vision. I turned my head, and there, rising up through rose-colored clouds into a baby blue sky, was Macchupucchare. Jonathan's mountain. I left the porch and walked around behind the teahouse to be with the mountain by myself. It was real. I cried with loud sobs of joy and gratitude and awe: It was real. This was not a photograph.

I felt Jonathan's arms around me, holding me, surrounding me with faith in myself and trust in my dreams. "I knew you'd get here, I just didn't know when. Welcome. Embrace this mountain and what it stands for. Embrace your dreams and what is to come into your life." He knew what I couldn't know, and didn't dare to believe, about the dreams that had already become reality and those I had not yet even imagined. "It's okay to have longings and dreams, Margo. It's okay to believe in yourself. You've earned the right. Honor your heart. I'm right here with you." The beauty of the mountain and the newfound feeling of wholeness inside filled me with a sense of peace I had never before experienced. Anything was possible.

Saturday, November 18, 1989, Namche Bazaar
Walked up to the top of the Kala Patar Guest
House for tea. Our tents went up in their
backyard. Couple of guys playing cards with a
Sherpa turned out to be from San Diego.

A full week between treks gave me a chance to fulfill another lifelong desire. A highlight of my trips to Africa had been watching the elephants from my grandfather's collection come alive in their natural habitat. One of my favorite photographs was the one I took of them grazing among trees with Mount Kilimanjaro in the background. Now I had a chance to stay in Royal Chitwan National Park and not only see more elephants up close, but ride them as well. Seated on the very boney back of the gentle gray giant, its ears sweeping at my legs, I marveled at being able to fulfill this desire, too, on this trip where many dreams were coming true.

Afterward I returned to Kathmandu and met a new set of companions for a twenty-one-day trek into the Khumbu region of Nepal, famous as home to the highest mountain on earth, Mount Everest. Bill was still going to be our guide, but this time I was going to have another woman on the trip, Marguerite, along with her husband David and a young man named Greg.

Our immediate challenge was getting to Lukla, the tiny airstrip carved into a hillside that was the main access point for most people going into the Khumbu region. Weather made the Royal Nepal Airlines schedule anything but dependable. It took three days of trying and a number of hurried, futile trips to Tribhuvan International Airport with all our gear before we were finally able to depart.

Jonathan's love for the Khumbu, its Sherpa people and their mountains, had been transferred so completely to me that the first sight of Namche Bazaar, its main village, almost took my breath away. It was bigger than I'd imagined, and much bigger than when Jonathan had seen it in the seventies. The ever-growing number of Western trekkers had spurred its growth. There were many Sherpa-owned teahouses. Some three stories high and whitewashed, making them stand out against the barren hillside. Each one had numerous windows trimmed in green or blue or red. They were laid out in rows around a U-shaped, walled nook that formed the site of the village and provided sleeping, eating, and tent space for trekkers and climbers alike. Shops selling everything from Tibetan artifacts to ice screws to cinnamon rolls lined the narrow streets, which echoed with a cacophony of different languages. I was entranced.

Like most trekkers and climbers, we would spend two nights in Namche, using the rest day to acclimatize before going higher into the valley. Our Sherpa crew was already pitching our tents in the courtyard of the Kala Patar Guest House. Greg went inside to the dining room for a cup of tea while I rummaged in my pack for an additional layer of clothing.

"They're from San Diego?" I looked over at the two men playing cards with a couple of Sherpas on the other side of the room.

"That's what they said," Greg replied. One of them looked up and smiled. I introduced myself and sat at their table to chat. Bart and Glenn had met on the plane from Los Angeles to Bangkok and decided to travel together. They seemed well suited to each other, and I felt a warm and welcome ease and companionship I hadn't experienced since I left the States for Peru and Bolivia.

Their card game forgotten, we talked animatedly, overlappingly about all kinds of things, jumping from subject to subject like popcorn in a frying pan, discovering that we shared many philosophical and metaphysical beliefs. Balboa Park in San Diego and which beach had the best sunset blended into discussions of reincarnation, movies, and homeopathy.

"Okay, enough talking." Bart unfolded his tall, lean frame from the chair in which he had been sitting. "Let's take Margo out on the town." I waved good-bye to Bill and Greg.

As Bart, Glenn, and I walked around Namche, poking our heads into shops, bargaining for jewelry, chatting with Sherpas and Westerners alike, I felt a gratifying connection. I'd been living my dream of climbing and trekking around the world, but so much of my time had been spent around climbers and trekkers who gave so little expression to their feelings that I was soul hungry. Now, in Namche Bazaar, a place Jonathan had talked about with such affection, I'd met two men with whom I could speak from my heart about my feelings, my physical dreams and soul needs were being fulfilled together.

After dinner, Glenn and I walked together up the hill behind the teahouse and found a spot to sit where we could look out over Namche, watching the lights in the windows and tents extinguish, one by one, as tired trekkers went to sleep. I remembered a time in 1975, in my bedroom at the Silver King Apartments in Aspen, after I'd told Jonathan that I wouldn't be able to go with him to Nepal. As I lay on my back in the dark room, wide awake from the cocaine I'd snorted earlier, fuzzy-brained from the marijuana I'd smoked to mellow out the hyperactivity of the coke, tears spilled silently from the corners of my eyes, falling to the pillow, creating growing circles of wetness. I felt empty inside. And hopeless. I had said "no" to the thing I wanted most in the world. "I can't go. It would be impossible for me. I'd starve to death. I can't eat lentils. I'd get sick. I'll go with you next year." I reached for the marijuana pipe on the bedside table. Just another couple of tokes. That would make me feel better.

"Margo. Yo, Margo." Glenn's voice lit up the darkness into which my mind had traveled. I looked at him and smiled.

"Where'd you go?" he asked softly, looking straight into my heart. "It felt like a long way away."

"It was," I answered. "A very long way. A place I never need to go again." Smiling, I took his hand, answering the invitation in his eyes.

He said, "How about that back rub I promised you?" I'd spoken earlier about being skin hungry, missing hugs and back rubs, and Glenn had offered one.

"Perfect," I replied, and we walked back down to the teahouse.

Glenn and I had a wonderful, gentle love affair over the next few days. We spent hours talking, touching, and nurturing each other, and when it was time for our group to move up the valley to the Thyangboche Monastery, Glenn and Bart went along. Gorgeous pine forests and groves of rhododendron trees in bloom added their rich magic to our rocky path. Although I felt a little strange about doing it, I left Glenn behind and kept up with Bill and Greg as they scrambled across a hillside to pass a Yak herd heading up the trail. Clouds engulfed us like fog at the Monastery. It was eerie and mysterious to hear yak bells ringing, then watch the huge animals emerge from the mist right in front of us.

The clouds lifted to reveal the classic view of Nuptse, Everest, Lhotse, and Ama Dablam as well as the hundreds of other peaks that surrounded us. As if on cue, the sound of ceremonial horns and bells drifted up to us as though they knew the celebration that was going on in my heart. I had wondered if I would ever be able to experience pushing myself physically and being supported emotionally at the same time. I had wondered if it could ever happen. It did that day, and that night, too, as Glenn shared my single tent with me, holding me, making love.

The Thyangboche Monastery had been a beautiful spiritual center in the Khumbu for centuries, but just a few months before we arrived it had been destroyed. A fire caused by faulty electrical wiring had left it a charred relic. Jonathan used to speak with reverence about this monastery, and I'd expected to feel a strong sense of his presence there but didn't. I couldn't connect the burned-out ruins with the beautiful photographs he'd shown me and the stories he'd told. I felt sadness and a deep sense of the loss: for the Sherpas who'd lost so many spiritually significant artifacts, for me in losing this part of Jonathan's world.

Greg wasn't feeling well the next morning, but we headed for Dingboche anyway. By the time we stopped for lunch, he was very ill and we took the afternoon to rest. Glenn and Bart continued on to Dingboche and with luck I'd meet them again in Kathmandu. As a precaution, we'd exchanged phone numbers for home. My time with Glenn had been perfect, physical and emotional nurturing freely expressed and received. Although I felt a twinge of loss as I watched them heading up the trail, my focus was now on Island Peak and making it to my first summit of a Himalayan mountain.

A pattern of sunny mornings, cloudy afternoons, and overnight snow or frost had now established itself. The higher we climbed, the colder it got. I was following Bill's suggestion to eat and drink more, and had a positive attitude that I didn't know whether to attribute to my time with Glenn or my new eating habits. Whichever it was, I was grateful.

The next morning, Greg was strong enough to hike to Dingboche. I stopped by a chorten on a hill overlooking the town, and Jonathan's presence wrapped its warmth around me. Standing by this small Buddhist shrine, I felt a healing. The self-inflicted wound of turning down the invitation to come here in 1975, the shame I carried about old behaviors, the self-hatred that still dug at me were healed in the presence of God and Jonathan and myself.

That afternoon I walked over the ridge to Pheriche and back. I stopped again by the chorten and listened to John Denver singing on my Walkman. Turning in a circle I could see ten major peaks including Island Peak or Imja Tse where I hoped to be standing in two days. I could see part of the route we'd take, and when I got back to camp I talked with Ang Phurba about the mountain. He said it looked as if the weather would hold for us and the climb would be easy.

"Easy for you, not for me," I said with a laugh.

"For you, too." He smiled and I almost believed him.

Greg and I were standing together in front of our tent at the Base Camp for Island Peak, staring at the clouds as they sailed across the sky. The weather had been so bad all day we hadn't been able to see the tops of any of the mountains around us. Bill and Marguerite both were sick, and David had gone back to Dingboche with them. Convinced of Ang Phurba's skill and guiding ability, Bill descended with the couple, leaving Greg, Ang Phurba, Ang Pasang, and me to climb tomorrow. It had to be tomorrow or not at all. Greg and I continued to stare at the sky, quietly dealing with our individual doubts and insecurities.

Greg, although young, had been very supportive and able to share some of his own questions and negative voices with me. Bill had been distant and had had a hard edge to him since we'd left Kathmandu, and Marguerite and David had kept very much to themselves, so I welcomed Greg's openness. He made it safe for me to be vulnerable, and when I gave voice to Martha's nagging negative garbage, her energy dissipated. Greg told a bad joke and we laughed, harder and longer than the joke warranted, a response to our tension and nervousness. The gods must have liked it, because the clouds parted almost instantly, revealing an astoundingly dark, royal blue sky and the massive, glacier-covered mountains in front of us.

"Damn," Greg exclaimed, "we're really going." It was hard to tell if he was angry or excited.

We rose at 2:30 A.M. and were moving by 4:00 to be able to make our round-trip to the summit and back before dark. I was still plagued by a cough. Deep breathing triggered it, so coughing spasms stopped me in my tracks every few minutes. Under the pale, cold light of a new moon we followed a well-trodden trail. My pack felt very heavy. Twice, Ang Phurba offered to take it, and both times I shook my head. My pride was winning the battle with my good sense. He said nothing but continued to stay right behind me until, while I was hacking yet again he finally walked around in front, unbuckled the waist belt of my pack and removed it from my shoulders. Not saying a word, he clipped my pack to his and continued up the trail. I didn't argue, and felt a huge improvement in both my strength and the coughing.

We made a quick stop for water at High Camp. When I stood up, I felt a familiar, flowing warmth between my legs. "Oh, God, not now," I thought. My period had caught me completely off guard. I had no Tampax, no pad, nothing with me to catch the flow of menstruation. I mentally rifled through my pack: food, water, camera, an extra layer of pile clothing for the descent, nothing. There was nothing I could use. I could turn around and give up the chance to stand on my first Himalayan summit, or I could get messy.

Martha, speaking my mother's words, was adamant. "You have to go back. You can't bleed all over yourself like this. It's too embarrassing. And it's dirty. Tell them your lungs hurt and you have to turn around. Tell them anything. Just go back to camp before they find out." The thoughts brought back feelings of shame about having a period.

"Mummy. Mummy. I'm bleeding. Help!" Tears of terror and confusion had coursed down my eleven-year-old cheeks as I knocked loudly on my parents' bedroom door early one fall morning.

"What is it, Miggie?" My mother opened the door and stood, tall and elegant in her dressing gown, looking down at me with concern.

"Where are you bleeding this time?" she asked, leading me into her bathroom.

I wrinkled my nose. "Down there," I said, using the euphemism I'd been taught practically from birth. "Down there" was a place not to be discussed unless absolutely necessary. Everything "down there" and anything that happened "down there" was unclean and impolite.

"Let me see," Mum said. She raised the hem of my nightie. When she saw the blood on my inner thighs, her mouth pursed in disapproval. "Oh, is that all? It's just the curse." She walked over to the bathroom cabinet and left me with my horrified thoughts. Curse! What curse? Why was I cursed?

"What curse?" I finally asked, my voice shaking. She matter-of-factly explained the workings of a woman's body, the tone of her voice conveying clearly her own shame around the whole subject. I learned a little bit about monthly cycles and having babies and a great deal about how messy and inconvenient and unclean the whole thing was—and especially how important it was not to talk about it with anybody.

I'd worked hard since I started my recovery to unlearn that lesson of shame, and although its voice was still loud, I had no intention of allowing it to keep me from climbing this mountain. "No more, Mum. I'm a woman—a strong woman—and I'm proud of it, proud of all that goes along with it." Perhaps not entirely true yet, the words affirmed what I wanted to believe as I made my way up Island Peak, aware of the continuous flow of blood out of my body and choosing not to let it get in the way of my dream of standing on the summit.

We scrambled up a steep couloir above High Camp, then jigged right to follow the route up a steeper, more exposed section. The climbing was not technical but any misstep would have led to serious injury. The final half pitch leading to the foot of the glacier was narrow and even more exposed, requiring full concentration. The sun shone on us, giving energy and warmth to our cold, tired bodies as we put on our crampons and stepped onto the glacier.

I felt strong and capable and offered to take my pack from Ang Phurba. He just shook his head and pointed the way up the glacier. Its surface was firm and provided us with an easy forty-five-minute walk across a couple of snow bridges to the foot of a steep section that led to 300 vertical feet of very steep climbing. The slope appeared nearly vertical, the snow in the couloir was quite soft, and climbers preceding us had left big buckets—solid, stable footholds—for us to use as we clipped into the fixed line and slowly climbed toward the summit ridge. I'd been concerned about how I would do on this kind of steepness at close to 20,000 feet and was proud and grateful for the relative ease with which I climbed. We stopped for food and water at the top of the pitch and my eyes were drawn to the narrow summit ridge, which undulated the length of a football field to the summit.

Moving again, I looked down, past the crampons that kept me on this three-foot-wide ridge. The mountain fell away 60 degrees on my right side, 80 degrees on the left. The grade to the summit was not steep, but a missed step or a crampon caught on Goretex could mean a very long slide and almost certain death. I'd never experienced this kind of exposure before, and my heart rate, already rapid from the effort of climbing at 20,000 feet, increased even more. Carefully I put one foot in front of the other. I wondered if I was leaving a trail of blood in the snow, but I was too scared to look back.

The slope steepened. Then, suddenly, it leveled off. I looked ahead and saw Ang Phurba waving from 10 yards away. My first Himalayan summit. I did it!

I covered those last 10 yards and hugged Ang Phurba. Soon Greg and Ang Pasang joined us. The four of us hugged. We beamed with joy and pride. I moved away from the others to thank God privately for all that He'd given me during the past three-and-a-half years while taking in the panorama of higher peaks surrounding us. "Oh, Jonathan, thank you for all you have given me in life and in death."

The descent was surprisingly easy, marred only by my growing awareness of the quantities of blood flowing down my legs. What was I going to do when we got to camp? The old shame began to rise. "I'll deal with it then." I answered my own question from a new belief in the strength of who I was: a worthy, capable woman in the world.

Despite the fatigue of twelve hours of climbing, Greg waited patiently outside our tent while I made a somewhat futile attempt to clean myself up. My polypro long underwear was stiff and sticky with blood from crotch to ankle, and all the Baby Wipes I had brought with me made only a slight impact on the dried blood on my legs. Finally even Greg's patience wouldn't last much longer. "Margo, what are you doing?"

"Just a sec." I couldn't quite bring myself to tell him what was going on, but neither was I consumed by my mother's shame. Martha was still speaking her old disapproval, but the words didn't have the impact they used to. I pulled on my spare pair of long underwear and a clean pair of socks. I put the stained clothes in a plastic garbage bag, put it in the bottom of my pack, and crawled out of the tent.

"It's all yours," I said to Greg. I walked away from the tent and felt as though I'd left a piece of my own emotional garbage behind forever.

Our group walked up the valley to the village of Lobuche and from there made the day trip to the top of 18,192-foot Kala Patar from which much of Mount Everest is visible. We were blessed with a clear though windy day, and as I stood looking in reverence at the black rock pyramid, I thought what a miraculous thing it was for me to be so near to Sagarmatha, Mother Goddess of the Universe. This Sherpa name for Everest described her grandeur perfectly. I remembered Jonathan's attempt on the mountain in 1976 and all the stories he had told me about it. I could see the bottom of the Khumbu Icefall with its jumble of giant blocks of ice and huge crevasses. I created in my mind an image of the Western Cwm, the huge, high, glacial valley at the top of the Icefall, which led to the foot of the Lhotse face. Jonathan's photographs of the Cwm had held a special attraction for me. I'd hoped to be able to see it from Kala Patar, but Jonathan's images would have to suffice.

The walk back to Namche Bazaar and the flight from Lukla went smoothly. Soaring mountain peaks, Dal sheep, and good weather combined to give me the perfect end to a successful trip. I'd walked through another layer of fear and shame and come out the other side more whole. Knowing I'd been on a Himalayan summit made me sure I would be able to make it to the summit of Aconcagua.

CHAPTER SIX

A Miraculous Forty-Second Birthday

Friday, January 5, 1990, Las Penitentes, Argentina
I have so much concern, read fear, about carrying
weight for so long. We'll see what happens, I
know I was okay on Chulu. I am so afraid I don't
have the endurance to pull this off.

The guidebook described climbing Cerro Aconcagua as "a strenuous, high-altitude ascent for experienced mountaineers only." The mountain was known for its fickle weather and strong winds, which I feared more than anything else about the climb. When I first saw its powerful profile reaching nearly 3 miles into the sky above our bus and realized we would hike for three days before even reaching Base Camp, all I could do was shake my head in amazement. Here I was, a middle-age American woman who only two years before hadn't climbed anything more strenuous than a flight of stairs, and I was going to climb that mountain. I actually believed I could get to the summit. I wasn't so sure about being able to carry the heavy pack I had with me. Each member of our expedition would be required to make multiple trips with equipment and supplies to establish the support camps we'd need to reach our goal.

Glenn and I had reconnected in Kathmandu, then went together to Thailand where we spent an incredible week together playing and making love. We left Bangkok, each honoring the journey our dreams were leading us toward—Glenn to Bali, me to Argentina—not knowing if or when we'd ever see each other again. Our love affair was over for now. Before returning to San Diego, I carried my memory of the time we'd spent together with me as I celebrated Christmas at a resort in Australia, returning home for five days over New Year's.

As one calendar year passed into the next, I restocked my supply of hugs, 12-Step recovery meetings, and telephone calls. I also washed the clothes I'd need for Aconcagua, repacked my duffel bags, and put new batteries in my Walkman. Then to the airport again: This time my destination was Mendoza, Argentina, where I met the rest of the expedition.

I felt almost at ease and something of a veteran. I already knew four of the nine other people on this trip. Skip, the trip's organizer and guide, and Norton had been with me on Mount Kenya and Kilimanjaro. At seventy-one, Norton had become one of my heroes, pushing himself to the limit running triathlons and climbing big mountains. Bob had been on the ill-fated trip in Mexico to climb Popo and Orizaba, and he had since become my personal attorney. Because of my traveling during the past six months I hadn't known he was coming on this trip. His quiet nature and wry humor was a pleasant and welcome surprise. Scott was an exuberant friend from San Diego whose recovery experience would provide the two of us with the chance to have our own "meetings" while on the mountain. Two of the other climbers were women. I still hadn't experienced a deep level of emotional safety while climbing—maybe I would with them. The other members of the group were friendly and supportive, and we all seemed to be rapidly building the level of bonding necessary for us to complete this climb successfully.

In Mendoza, Skip called a meeting to propose that we change our route to the summit. The Vacas approach would have far fewer people on it and would provide more challenging climbing than the established Ruta Normal. This group reacted differently to a suggested change from the climbers in Bolivia. The latter had been quiet, intense, and driven. Their summit orientation and individualism had brought a focused rationality to discussions about changes in timing and routes. The Aconcagua group, in contrast, was outspoken, emotional, and humorous. They wanted to get to the summit, yet were much more willing to consider every aspect from the point of view of what would give us the most complete experience.

Although I believed that each climber created his or her own experience on a mountain, I'd noticed that the attitude of the guide affected my ability to get the most out of a trip. Skip's supportive and encouraging leadership style seemed to attract people who wanted to get to the summit but enjoy the process of climbing as well. Skip understood that the mountains each of us climbed inside were sometimes more challenging than the ones rising above us. Now I was grateful for the bronchitis that a year ago had kept me from attempting Aconcagua with an unknown guide. The universe, once again, had placed me in Skip's hands.

The desolation of the mountains and valleys surrounding Aconcagua emphasized its remoteness. From Mendoza, we drove to Las Penitentes, a ski resort closed for the Argentinean summer but open to climbers who acclimatized at its 9,000-foot altitude before leaving for the base of the mountain, 4,000 feet higher and an arduous 30-mile hike away. We took advantage of our time at Penitentes to explore a valley and climb a ridge to get another look at our objective. The area was a landscape devoid of life, yet it had a beauty all its own. Crisscrossed paths left by explorers, adventurers, and others traversing the continent gave a sense of its history. Daniel, Skip's Argentinean assistant guide, told us that only about 30 percent of the 2,000 or so climbers who attempt Aconcagua each year make it to the summit. Women comprise roughly 10 percent, and their success rate was far lower: only about ten out of two hundred.

I was determined to beat the odds. Physically, I was in the best shape ever, but my apprehension about carrying a pack weighing 30 or 40 pounds on sustained climbs at the altitudes we'd reach gave Martha plenty of data with which to question my ability and conditioning. I told her what I knew to be true: Only time would tell how I'd do, and the rewards would be worth whatever discomfort I'd have. I couldn't imagine anything that would keep me from the summit of this mountain, not the cold, not painful feet and shoulders, not even wet clothes and boots. Nothing could keep me from my dream as long as I had the support of God, my inner family, and the encouragement of a supportive guide.

The night before we left Las Penitentes, we all crowded into Skip's room for "root 'n rummage." Crates of fresh fruits and vegetables, canned goods, and odds and ends lined the walls needing to be sorted and repacked for mules to haul to our Base Camp. On this expedition-type climb, we didn't have any Sherpa or porters. From Base Camp, we would carry all the equipment and supplies on our backs to camps higher on the mountain. The lighthearted kidding among us didn't quite hide what each of us was thinking: "Will I be able to handle my part of the load? Will I be the one to let the group down?"

Over the next three days, we hiked over barren ridges and up valleys filled with glacial debris, making our way toward Base Camp at 14,000 feet. The stark beauty of this part of the Andes came from its harsh simplicity. Dust, rocks, and the occasional scrub bush holding tenaciously to life formed a uniformly brownish gray landscape, broken every now and then by a swift river of dirty glacial water. Some of those we crossed on foot. Others would have swept us away if the arryaros, or muleteers, hadn't seated us on the backs of their animals. Because our gear was carried by the mules on the walk to Base Camp, we had only water, cameras, and rain gear in our light packs. The second morning, as we prepared to leave camp, Skip suggested that we prepare ourselves for the physical and mental toughness of the climb ahead by adding some extra gear to our packs to get used to their weight during the next couple of days. It was as though he had read our minds and knew our fears. Before I went to bed, I watched shadows from the arryaros' fire dance on a rock wall and felt Jonathan's presence with me. With that as a secret weapon, I knew I would make it.

Our small sleeping tents with their bright blue rain covers surrounded the larger yellow kitchen tent at Base Camp, giving a sense of order and comfort to this temporary staging area. As the arryaros left, leading their mules back down the way we'd come, I felt a gaping void, an almost tangible sense that now it was just the mountain and us. Mountaineering expeditions are sometimes compared to military campaigns where the mountain is the enemy to be conquered. I had a sense that this expedition was more like a mystic traveling into the wilderness in anticipation of a revelation. I began to let myself be drawn into the mystery called Cerro Aconcagua.

Our first day at Base Camp was a rest day, time to settle in, let our bodies adjust to the higher altitude, and sort everything that needed to be carried to Camp I into manageable loads. We would start with fairly light packs, 25 pounds or so, and increase the weight with each trip to allow us to build up our strength. By the time we moved everything up the mountain, we ought to be ready to take the next step higher to Camp II. As I walked among the stacks of supplies, the sleeping tents and the cooking tent, it occurred to me that the base of this mountain was roughly the same altitude as the summit of Mount Whitney, the highest point in the contiguous United States. I watched the light of the sun move across the barren landscape, the browns and grays of the volcanic residue enhanced by subtle lavenders and reds as Aconcagua revealed its beauty. That night the moon was nearly full.

The second night at Base Camp, my tentmate Linda and I sat inside our "home," ready to crawl into our sleeping bags, waiting for the moon to rise. A progression of hues shone through the clouds, changing them from orange to pale peach. Linda was easygoing and well-educated and had already demonstrated her superior strength on the walk in. We had talked quite a bit during the long days on our way to Base Camp and I liked her spirit and determination.

I replayed the day in my mind: We had made our first carry to Camp I, and I had climbed well. Slowly, smoothly, I'd placed one foot in front of the other, carrying my share of the equipment, cooking gear, and food with an energy that felt as if someone had tripled the amount of adrenaline in my body. At 16,800 feet into the Andean sky, I'd been filled with the sense that there was nowhere else on earth I would rather be, nothing else I would rather be doing. Now, in my tent, back at 14,000 feet, I closed my eyes, breathed in the spiritual presence of Jonathan and Glenn and felt again that sense of fullness. When I opened them, the moon filled the sky in front of me: a magnificent, enormous yellow ball.

"Linda, look." I moved aside so she could see.

She looked up from the book she was reading. "Oh!" Her voice was reverent. Then, as she let out her breath, "Wow."

The next day the wind blew hard, much harder than it had blown before. Wind was one of the things I feared most about climbing, more even than being cold. And Aconcagua had a reputation for its wind. Climbers told horrendous stories of what it could do to people and equipment, how it turned a moderate climb into an epic descent, a relatively comfortable day of climbing into an agonizing effort to stay alive. Throughout the day I shadowboxed with it and struggled to stay upright under nearly 40 pounds of gear. The last steep, unstable pitch leading to Camp I was especially dicey. A gust hit me in midstride. "Damn," I said, fighting to retain my balance. I swore again, angry at the wind and frightened by its seeming desire to blow me off my feet. My inner voice spoke calmly in my head. "Breathe, Margo. Breathe and put one foot in front of the other. Just take a step. One step." I could do that, wind or no wind.

When I reached the area where we'd set up Camp I yesterday, Skip was right behind me. I hadn't noticed him as I climbed, too absorbed in the hard work of getting there. The relentless wind had nearly blown down the Junebug tent we'd erected to protect the gear we'd so carefully carried up there. It took an hour at this altitude for all of us to build a wall of rocks and reanchor it. As I was taking a rest, Skip, too, stopped for a moment.

"Don't much like the wind, do you?" he asked.

"Not even a little. It makes everything so much harder. I just got madder and madder today."

"I used to hate it, too." The hood of his parka flapped erratically as though the wind were using it for emphasis. "It made climbing cold and uncomfortable. But resisting it took so much energy I figured I could either waste my energy hating it or get into the heightened excitement and sense of adventure it brought and draw energy from that. Now, I've come to almost like it." He turned away to add another rock to the wall.

I watched him move slowly, saw his body respond when my unseen nemesis pummeled him. Could it be as simple as he said? Through my thick wool hat, the wind sounded like cars passing on a freeway. I had no power to change it, that was for certain. My friend Kelly often told me, "You can't change the way life happens, but you can change your attitude." This was exactly the same thing. The proverbial light bulb went on in my brain. I didn't have to fight the wind, I could accept it. What a concept! So very unlike the way it used to be when I believed I couldn't change myself so I withdrew from the world and hid. The truth was, the wind was blowing. I didn't have to like it but neither did I have to be miserable about it. If I embraced the wind, I could draw energy from it rather than using my energy to rail against it. Was it my imagination, or did the wind back off as we hiked down to Base Camp?

On the third day, we were to complete our move to Camp I. That morning I awakened in a primordial emotional ooze: exhaustion, ela-tion, and fear swirled around me. I was in tears before I was even out of my sleeping bag. There was no reason for the intensity of the emotions, nothing I knew to do to address them, so I did what I had been taught: show up and do the best I knew how. I got dressed and walked into the kitchen tent to get some coffee. Skip was working with one of the stoves. He looked up, smiled, and said something cheerful.

I practically burst into tears. Fighting hard to hold my rampant emo-tions in check and losing the battle, I said, "It's one of those days, Skip. I am emotionally off the wall for no reason. I guess I'm just giving you a warning. Approach with caution." I managed a rueful smile.

He stood, put his arm around my shoulders, and said, "Too bad it's a tough day for you. I trust your attitude, Margo. You'll do okay."

I loved it! I was able to be out of sorts emotionally, grumpy and on edge, and talk about it rather than fight it alone. The attitude of the climbers in Bolivia and Nepal hadn't given me room to be vulnerable. That had taught me important lessons about trusting God and myself, but here, I welcomed being able to acknowledge what was going on. Being able to express my emotions felt more whole and more honest. In spite of the emotional burden that had been added to my 40-pound pack, I did just fine on the final carry to Camp I. There I helped set up the tents and haul rocks for more walls to windproof them.

That evening after dinner it snowed, but not enough to prevent us from making our first carry up to Camp II the next morning. "Ninety-eight, ninety-nine, one hundred. Phew." I stopped, the weight of my body and pack resting on my straightened right leg and the ski poles I used for stability on the slope. As I let my bones absorb the weight to give my muscles a rest, I concentrated on my breathing. In through my nose, deeply into my diaphragm and chest, then out through my mouth with force, as if I were blowing up a balloon. This was pressure breathing, a technique that allowed my lungs to absorb as much of what little oxygen there was in this rarefied air. Twenty breaths, then another hundred steps. I was more than four hours into this carry and that was the pace that worked best for me.

The raw simplicity of the mountain invited each of us to make our individual, inward journey. The route was not difficult but required hours of toil on the gray-brown rock. The steepness of the slope never let up, varying from 30 to 35 degrees. Pebbled scree created uncertain footing, especially with us carrying heavy packs and bracing ourselves against the wind. I would rather have been walking in crampons on a glacier, but that was not the nature of Aconcagua. It was a giant rock heap, desolate, barren, and windblown. I kept my head down and watched my footing, moving so slowly I was certain the others must be way ahead. I was concentrating so intently I nearly walked into Scott, who had stopped to take a rest with Jordan. Only sixty-seven steps into my count of one hundred, I kept going. A smile broke out on my face and I felt a rush of adrenaline: I had just passed two of the guys!

At Camp II, we stashed the food we'd carried, taking as little time as possible. The wind was blowing with even more force here at its 18,800-foot altitude, and although the cold was not unbearable, it was uncomfortable. We wanted to get back down to Camp I to rest from the exertions of the day. Upon our return, we learned that Norton and one of the women, Hope, were preparing to retreat to Base Camp. Norton said his spirit was absolutely willing, his body just wouldn't make it any higher. His level of acceptance and willingness to take care of himself continued to be an example for me. I cried as Skip gave him a hug just before they left.

After the effort of making the carry to Camp II, we rested for a day. We were all glad we weren't climbing. Skip even cooked us a breakfast of pancakes using the bottom of an overturned pot as a frying pan. We devoured his special, creative treat and spent much of the day in one tent or another playing cards and dice. As the day progressed, the wind picked up, making traveling even the short distance between tents an exercise in maintaining balance. Two climbers from another group returned from higher on the mountain and reported it was "god-awful." I felt strong, but not strong enough to fight a force this power-ful and unrelenting. I prayed for the wind to blow itself out; instead, it became worse.

In bed that night, I couldn't hear Linda talk, even though we'd moved our sleeping bags right next to each other. The wind shook the walls of the tent so violently the nylon fabric screamed in defiance. The pitch and volume rose each time a gust hit, drowning out our words completely. We kept our hands and heads pushed against the vibrating upwind wall, so it wouldn't collapse on us. At midnight, gusts were still roaring over the ridge 1,500 feet above, sounding like huge freight trains careening down the rock face and smashing through camp. I couldn't imagine trying to climb in wind like that. "It's not possible," I thought. "I can't do it. What if it doesn't stop? There's no adventure in this, it's just plain scary." Not even remembering Skip's words could quiet my mind. I must have slept, though, because I was awakened by a deafening silence. I looked at my watch; it was 2:00 A.M. I stuck my head out the door. The black sky was filled with stars and everything was in its place. I slid back down into my sleeping bag, turned over, and whispered, "Thank you, God."

Thursday, January 18, 1990, CAMP II, Aconcagua
What a miraculous way to spend my forty-second
birthday... Again, the most difficult thing I
have ever done... I went through every emotion
imaginable. And the determination never left.
Discouragement so strong sometimes. And always
the determination. As always, it came down
to me and God.

"Happy birthday to you. Happy birthday to you. Happy birthday, dear Margo. Happy birthday to you-o-o-o!" I was awakened by Skip and Wally greeting my forty-second birthday with a lovingly off-key rendition of the familiar song, accompanied by a cup of coffee and two Nestle's Crunch bars. An appropriate and greatly appreciated birthday treat in this barren place full of rocks and freeze-dried food. I snuggled further into my sleeping bag, giving the coffee a chance to wake me up and thought back to where I'd been on other birthdays. They had always been a time to celebrate. However, as I became older, the celebration was less about festivity and joy and more about drinking and doing drugs. The day I turned thirty-eight had been spent at home "celebrating" on the couch with a bottle of vodka, piles of junk food, and a stack of videos, afraid to leave my house. Now, only four years later, I was taking risks that were inconceivable to that woman lying on her couch, loaded with alcohol and food. I smiled as the pride of being sober flooded through me. Packing my personal gear and getting dressed, I thanked God for the depth and richness being added to the wonderful tapestry of my life.

We packed up camp in bright sunshine and headed to Camp II following the same route we'd taken two days before. With the set of cooking pots and two tea kettles strapped to my pack, I must have looked like a tinker carrying her wares. The humorous image lightened my 40-pound load a little, but not enough to counter the instability the heavy and awkward pack added to my slow ascent through the steep scree.

Skip smiled as he passed me easily about an hour into the day. "What a place to spend your forty-second birthday, although maybe not the nicest way."

I had to stop to catch my breath and called out after him. "Considering I couldn't walk up a flight of stairs without stopping when I was thirty-eight, it's an incredible miracle just to be able to attempt to do this."

"I love that attitude!" he said over his shoulder as he continued to climb.

Our encounter gave me new energy as I continued placing one foot carefully in front of the other. It was like walking on gravel over concrete, only the surface was sloped like a roof and we were now climbing above 18,000 feet. I called on the rhythm of the rest step, so familiar to me after using it on mountains on four continents. I even had my own name for it, "Go Mode." Lift the right foot, then put it down, test the scree, hoping it wouldn't slide. At the same time, plant the pole in the left hand for balance and keep the left knee locked to give those muscles a momentary rest. Next, transfer weight onto the right leg, knee bent to absorb the movement of the pebbles that always came, no matter how stable I thought it would be, sometimes sliding back half the distance I had stepped forward. Then, repeat the cycle with the other foot. Add deep, rhythmical breathing with each step, and the progress up the mountain became automatic, efficient, reassuring.

Bob and I climbed together most of the day, his presence a comfort. We climbed in sync, almost as if the mountain itself were keeping time. Once, Bob's foot slid back almost to where it had started, his back hunched under his heavy pack. "Damn," he said. He caught his breath and said, "Damn," again. He repeated the word a third time when he reset his foot and it slid again, halfway to its starting point. "Damn." Swearing was not a normal part of Bob's controlled demeanor.

Remembering the powerful effect of Skip's encouragement on me, I called out, "You're doing great, Bob." I didn't have the energy to look back, but the swearing stopped.

Continuing up the seemingly endless slope I heard my inner cheering section. Images of Jonathan and friends in San Diego appeared in my mind, encouraging, applauding, helping me through the three hours and forty-five minutes it took to get to the lunch spot and six and one-half hours in all to arrive at Camp II. Two days before, we'd made it in five. The difference was the extra weight. I marveled at how my soul found ways to keep me climbing.

When I finally sighted Camp II ahead, I saw that Skip, Daniel, and Wally were already there. They had their packs off and were going through gear and food, but they weren't unloading: they were adding what we'd left two days before to their already full loads.

As soon as I got within earshot I called out, "What's going on? What are you guys doing?"

Skip looked up. "Rather than spend the night here, I want to go directly to Camp III today. It's only a couple of hours of traverse, and it'll give us a rest day before the summit attempt. I think it'll increase everyone's chances to make the summit."

As tired as I was, it still made sense, and I trusted Skip. Since the beginning of the trip, he had consistently demonstrated an ability to see our capabilities in a way that we could not and to know what would support us in pushing through our limits. If Skip said going all the way to the next camp was the best thing to do and that I could do it, then I would certainly give it a go. Taking only the extra supplies we'd need for the next three days, we left the rest of the food cache for our descent.

The route to Camp III was mostly a low-angle traverse across a snowfield. Even with the greatly decreased steepness and the solid footing of crampons on good snow, I went through a constantly changing, flowing blend of fear, fatigue, and discouragement. But never once did my determination leave me. Skip carried a huge load, yet managed to disappear quickly ahead of the rest of us as we plodded on, exhausted, taking care not to catch sharp crampon points in the material of our full-legged Goretex pants.

After an hour or so he reappeared from the direction of Camp III and sang out, "Happy Birthday to you-o-o-o. Lest we forget!" as he passed by. It was so unexpected and felt so supportive that once again the physical effects of additional adrenaline rushed into my system. He walked back to the end of our straggling, spread-out line of climbers to take the pack from Bob, who was near exhaustion. Only Daniel and Wally were ahead of me as we moved slowly over the snowfield, but I was fast approaching my own limits.

I stopped to rest. My count had dropped to twenty steps and ten breaths. I leaned on my ice axe. Tears of fatigue fell on the inside of my goggles. "Shit. I don't know how I'm going to get there. What am I going to do? I can't do this." A sob escaped from my throat, and I turned inside to my greatest source of strength. "God, I need You here. I can't pull this one off on my own. Please, give me the strength to get to camp." I had no idea how far it was, but as I breathed deeply, I found the determination to continue.

Skip passed me, carrying Bob's pack and again sang part of the "Birthday Song," breathing energy into me with every note. When he returned a short time later, I was stopped for the third time, again in tears. As he passed me he said, "I know you're doing okay, and can make it. It's not far. I don't have to take your pack." He took Linda's instead.

"But wait," my insides cried. "I'm not doing okay. I can't make it. I need help. Take mine." My heart was wiser, though, and didn't give the words voice. I took a deep breath, repeated my prayer for God's help, inhaled strength from my own pride, and walked on. My "Go Mode" carried me to Camp III that day—nine hours total. Too exhausted to feel proud of the accomplishment, I dropped my pack and helped set up the tents. Then, even in my exhaustion, I looked around and knew why I was here. All of the hard work and discomfort were worth it. The magic of being able to live life at this intensity was unmistakable. As shadows cast by the setting sun played across our tents, Skip acknowledged the hard work of the day. He rewarded our willingness to push beyond our limits with hot water bottles for our sleeping bags, a very tangible luxury at 19,600 feet on a cold Andes night. This was, indeed, a miraculous way to spend my forty-second birthday.

The next morning I felt as if I had been run over by a truck. All of us stayed in our tents most of the day, out of the wind and biting cold. Camp III was nestled among sandstone ridges that had been carved by the wind into goblinesque shapes, then broken by the force of freezing and refreezing. Whenever I went outside to eat or pee, I watched fabulous clouds float over the peaks and valleys that ran to the horizon.

Not far from our tents was a cliff from which we could see both the high Berlin Camp and Base Camp of the Ruta Normal. The vast numbers of tents in each one made us grateful for Skip's route change. Earlier in the day he'd seen a line of thirty-five or forty climbers, all dressed in identical red parkas and blue wind pants, walking two feet apart at exactly the same pace, marching toward the summit. A true climbing machine. We'd met only a handful of other climbers on our route and were grateful for the sense of being almost alone on this great mountain.

As I prepared to go to bed that night, I watched what looked like a storm forming and thought that a weather day would suit me well, allowing me to recover even more from the hard work of getting this far. I knew it was my fear talking, Martha had been telling me all day about the cold and the wind and harping that I wasn't eating enough to have the energy I'd need to reach the summit. But my desire to stand on the top of this great mountain was strong, and I knew I could put up with whatever discomfort I would face tomorrow, especially with God's help. In my sleeping bag I whispered a prayer, "Hang with me, God. I can't do this on my own."

The next morning was clear and cold, but calm, the first day since we'd arrived at Base Camp that the wind wasn't blowing at all. We ate a quick breakfast, packed only emergency clothes and the water we'd need for our climb, and started creating a long series of switchbacks up a steep pitch of scree. We then joined the other route, merging with groups of climbers ahead and behind us, and made a long traverse across an increasingly steep slope leading to the Canaleta. Many climbers have described this as the most disheartening part of an already difficult ascent. It certainly was for me. Rock debris of various sizes made progress slow and unsteady. Already drained by the extraordinary effort required to move at all at 21,000 feet, I felt how easy it would be to make mistakes. The mental and physical effort were excruciating.

I leaned on my ice axe, precariously balanced against the steep slope, still only halfway up the Canaleta. My legs hurt and were shaking. My arms felt as if they were encased in lead, too heavy to lift. I could not imagine climbing for one more minute, let alone the hours needed to get to the summit. Then, like a wave rolling up on a beach, the deep, soul-level desire to get to the top swept back into my being. I ate some gorp, took a swallow of water, and let a full, deep breath fill my lungs. With a whispered, "Okay, God, let's go," I continued inching upward. Two steps, stop and breathe. Six steps, stop and breathe. Two more steps and stop to breathe. Seven hours after leaving Camp III, I stood on the summit of Cerro Aconcagua, 22,835 feet high, the top of South America.

We saw a cross on the summit that was layered with items left by legions of climbers before us. Were they gifts left by pilgrims in gratitude for successfully reaching the summit or amulets for protection during their descent? Our fatigue, the cold, and weather rapidly closing in on the mountain kept our time on the summit very short. Grouped around the cross tightly for warmth, we had our picture taken to commemorate our success. Yet I knew that we were only halfway through this climb. True success depended on returning home safely. During the descent, every step lower in altitude gave us more oxygen, and the Canaleta and slopes of scree weren't nearly as daunting. We moved quickly, taking less than half the time we'd spent getting to the top. A little over ten hours after leaving Camp III, we returned, jubilant and exhausted. I slept soundly, the sweet sleep of a successful summit.

The next day we rested, recovering physically and taking time to appreciate the beauty of our location on the mountain. We melted snow for drinking water and meals, played dice, and crowded into Skip's tent to tell stories. About 8:00 P.M. I walked around the sandstone walls rising above us and let the fullness of having spent my birthday here sink in. Argentina was on double daylight savings time— the clocks had been set two hours ahead—so the long shadows and soft glow of the setting sun washed everything in a magical light. I had realized a dream, a dream that four years before I didn't even know I had. One step at a time I'd get back to Base Camp, then to Mendoza, then on with the rest of my life. I couldn't imagine what I'd dream of next.

After another good night's sleep, we were ready to descend. The morning was bitterly cold and windy. Fingers exposed to the air without gloves became numb in minutes. Even with extra layers of socks and mittens, my fingers and toes ached with the cold. We decided to save time by skipping breakfast: hot chocolate would have to tide us over until we stopped for a break later. On the way down we needed to clean up the cache for Camp II and pick up our additional equipment still at Camp I. We felt confident that we could cover the more than 6,000 vertical feet in one day, but could we carry all that gear, adding it to our already heavy loads? The only way to find out was by doing the best we could. None of us wanted to have to climb back up the mountain the next day.

My body rebelled under the weight of my pack, and my pace on the long traverse down to Camp II was agonizingly slow. Skip stopped at one point, waiting for me, and asked, "Margo, are you okay?"

Even though every step was a major effort, I was feeling well and wanted my answer to sound reassuring. "Feels kind of like the air has glue in it." I smiled at the image as I added, "Otherwise I feel great. Just tired."

We divided up the remaining food cache at Camp II. I tore open a package of cookies and ate six of them in quick succession. I felt strength returning to my body almost immediately. My extreme fatigue had at least partially been a result of low blood sugar, probably from not having breakfast. For once, cookies may have saved my life—at least I like to think so.

With the site cleared, we proceeded down the mountain. I walked much of the way from Camp II to Camp I with Skip, and by the time we reached the final lengthy slope of soft scree, we were laughing and nearly jogging, intertwining our paths in figure eight's as though we were skiing. Our playfulness helped release some of the apprehension about the hard work still ahead.

At Camp I, we ate lunch and pitched in together to pack up the gear and food remaining. Each of us shouldered an oppressively heavy pack for the final trip to Base Camp. I guessed that mine weighed close to 60 pounds. I couldn't lift it to my back without assistance or stand up without help if I put it on while sitting down. None of us could have carried another ounce.

Struggling up a small rise, I grumbled to Scott, "This is supposed to be downhill!" Halfway between Camp I and Base Camp, we stopped for a break. Selecting boulders for seats, we rested without taking off our packs: it would have been too difficult to get them back on again. Although I'd descended this route twice after making carries up to Camp I, this day it seemed like a whole new trail, double the length I remembered.

"Okay, let's go!" Scott's voice was much more energetic than I felt as I fought to get to my feet. The two of us climbed slowly, haltingly, up another rise, each step a conscious effort. As we came over the crest we could see the tents of Base Camp. We were home!

A Miraculous Forty-Second Birthday

Monday, January 22, 1990, Base Camp, Aconcagua
Growth and accomplishment. Tail busting and huge
rewards. Tears and grins. Sobs and yells of joy.
And I'm glad it's behind me instead of ahead of
me. Good on you, Margo.

I had been holding in my tears since arriving in Base Camp. Physical and emotional exhaustion masked my feelings of pride, gratitude, and joy. Martha told me to make up something to avoid helping with the dishes. "It's harder for you than it is for them." I had hoped that Martha would die on the mountain. I would have been happy to leave her there, but here she was, as negative as ever.

I followed her advice and wasn't at all graceful when I told Skip I didn't have the energy to do the dishes. I had been selfish, insensitive to how hard he'd worked all day, not supportive as part of the group effort. Still, it was the best I could do that night. I would make amends in the morning.

A night's rest and the healing effect of the lower altitude gave me a better attitude. It was amazing how motivated we were to get to Mendoza where a real bed and a hot bath awaited us. We had every-thing packed before the arryaros arrived with their mules. With the mules carrying our gear, we were able to push hard over the rough terrain and multiple rivers we had to cross. We were only going to take one-and-a-half days to hike the distance that took us three to come in. Nine hours and 20 miles after leaving Base Camp we stopped for the night.

I was the last one into camp, and fatigue had turned me into a needy six-year-old. My feet and ankles were sore from the long day of hiking. Being a human mule had caused a pain in my hip that radiated all the way down my leg. I wanted to be held, to cry on someone's shoulder, but I knew we were all exhausted. Martha was relentless, though, and I was too tired to resist. She convinced my whole inner family that people would care more about me if I exagger-ated the injuries. Rather than asking for the support I wanted, I re-verted to my old behavior by moving more slowly than I needed to with a worse limp than the pain required. It worked. Skip let me cry in his arms and Linda stroked my head. Their attention and sympathy temporarily filled the hole inside and I felt better. We wolfed down hot food and collapsed into our sleeping bags under the stars, too exhausted to put up the tents.

Embarrassment at my charade didn't hit until the next morning, and

I wasn't able, then, to tell anyone. The truth was it got me what I wanted when I didn't know any other way to get it. I was learning how to live differently, but I wasn't perfect yet. I knew I needed to stay watchful for my old behaviors. They would separate me first from the truth of the woman I was becoming, then from God, and eventually from my abstinence and sobriety.

The next day we hiked nearly 10 more miles before finally reaching the buses waiting for us. They took us to the amenities of Mendoza. In a tub I washed away layers of dirt from my body. Clean, I rested my head on a soft pillow. The fullness of what I'd accomplished and the satisfaction and pride of having successfully climbed the highest mountain in South America began to emerge.

I had scheduled two trips following Aconcagua: rafting on the Rio Bio Bio, a major whitewater river in Chile that was soon to be blocked by a large hydroelectric project, and a trek led by Skip and his wife Elizabeth through Patagonia at the southernmost tip of the continent. These seemed like excellent ways for me to make the transition from the hard physical effort of the mountain to the everyday life waiting for me in San Diego.

In addition to the bath and bed in Mendoza, a few days' rest in Santiago added to my healing. By the time I climbed aboard the overnight train that took me from Santiago to Victoria, I felt emotionally balanced, physically healthy, and ready to be pampered by good service in beautiful surroundings. The river trip promised to be a wonderful combination of powerful and exciting rapids, good weather, and the company of other adventurers in an exotic setting.

I didn't expect to climb on the Bio Bio trip, so the only footwear I packed was my running shoes. In fact, my feet were like hamburger after Aconcagua, and I was looking forward to soaking them in water. So I was surprised when we spent 16 hours one day climbing to a 16,000-foot summit. Scrambling up the slopes of Callaqui, a massive cinder cone covered by snow at the top, I was pleased to find it challenging but not difficult. It was good for me to be able to watch others push themselves past their preconceived limits as they strived to reach the goal. The hardest part of the climb for me came when the river guides brought out a bottle of champagne on the summit to celebrate the accomplishment. I felt left out and diminished, even with my recent successes. I was grateful that those feelings passed quickly, and I could see the incident as a graphic reminder of how alcohol had been a part of my celebrations for years and how much the old ideas about how to be a part of everyone else's joy were linked to my doing whatever they were doing, too.

The whitewater was intense in spots, and the names given to the sets of rapids rarely revealed their characteristics. Lost Yak, Lava South, and One-Eyed Jack all proved challenging in the unusually high water caused by heavy rains. Boats hung up on rocks and flipped passengers out into the frigid, roiling water. All in all the trip more than lived up to the brochure copy for adventure travel. It was great fun, and the adrenaline-pumping action stirred up my fears and excitement of knowing that as a middle-age woman I was willing to try new and challenging adventures.

Serene, quiet times balanced the action. I slept to the gentle singing of the river as it flowed by, sunbathed leaning against the warm tube of a raft, and soaked in a natural hot spring within 3 feet of the ice-cold river. One night we returned to the pools after dark and as one of the boatmen rang his temple bells under the brilliant stars, my mind was filled with images of Jonathan, the monastery at Rangdum, and the summit of Island Peak. Memories about the last eight months swirled slowly and easily around me like the hot water. Wonder, gratitude, and peace flooded my being.

How different it was from the nights spent in hot tubs in Aspen in the seventies. Then, vodka, marijuana, and cocaine flooded my system, and I worked harder at not being present in my body and my life than I ever did at simply enjoying the warm, soothing waters. I remembered how my insides would vibrate, always wanting more. People around me would be laughing loudly, rock-and-roll always blaring from the stereo. We worked so hard to have a good time. It had been a ruse, a game, a fantasy—and it had almost killed me. On the Bio Bio, as we left the womb of hot water and quietly walked the half mile back to our tents, I gave thanks for the difference. I knew without a doubt that no matter what my dreams were to hold for me it would be possible to get there.

I returned to Santiago to meet Skip and Elizabeth and the others who would be on the trek in Patagonia. We flew to Punta Arenas on the southern tip of Chile. Looking across the Straits of Magellan, I could see Tierra del Fuego. I thought about the explorers who had taken their ships through that passage. I felt like an explorer myself, going to the literal ends of the earth and into the furthest reaches of my heart and mind to find, experience, and celebrate my truth.

Patagonia, known as a land of extremes, held a special fascination for me. On my trip its legendary weather, changeable and unusually fierce, was abnormally mild. Spectacular mountains, enormous glaciers, and lovely streams all helped to create a beauty that rivaled anyplace in the world. One evening we stood outside our tents watching the setting sun bathe the surrounding rock formations with a warm golden glow.

"Los Cuernos," Skip said quietly.

"What?" I asked, not sure what I had heard.

"Los Cuernos," he repeated. " 'The Horns.' The formation you're looking at is called The Horns of Paine."

"Got it," I said, then added mischievously, "So if those are the horns and they're called los cuernos, and your last name is Horner, then we could call you El Cuernador. Right?"

He laughed softly. "Yup, I guess so. And you could be Margita."

The names stuck, and we referred to each other by them for the duration of the trek.

The quality of the light and the colors and shapes of the clouds in Patagonia were unlike any I had ever seen before. I reveled in their magnificence. I watched guanaco, gray fox, and kestrels playing in their natural habitat and laughed at the antics of penguins in their rookery. I felt the force of the wind that whipped up 2½-foot waves on lakes with ice floes floating in them, and in an ice cave at the base of a giant glacier, I saw my hand, undistorted, through nearly a foot of blue ice. I crossed mountain passes carrying extra loads for those who were less strong and knew that my sore feet and stiff knees would get better.

Sitting in my tent in a light rain our last night out, I realized that in a couple of days I'd be celebrating my fourth anniversary in recovery. I recalled how scared and alone I had felt walking up to the admissions desk at the Rader Institute. I didn't have a clue then that four years later I'd have completed nine months of mountain climbing and adventure travel on four continents. I wouldn't have believed it if someone had predicted it. I spoke to Jonathan about the wonder of it all. "Think of everything I would have missed if I hadn't surrendered. How is it that by admitting my powerlessness over drugs, alcohol, and food, I'm able to live this life today?"

Two days later I was on the long journey from Santiago to San Diego, gazing out a plane window at the clouds that looked like giant cotton balls and fingering a miniature silver ice axe pinned to my jacket lapel. Skip and Elizabeth had given it to me the day before. He'd had some made in Kathmandu and was giving them to "special people." It was extraordinary to be considered a special person by someone for whom I had so much respect. Four years earlier the only people who acted as if I was anything special were the ones who wanted something from me. What a big part Skip, and Elizabeth as well, were playing in this ongoing, newly evolving dream of mine. Skip had invited me to join him climbing in Russia in June, and I had already begun rescheduling my life so I could. I wanted to take advantage of the supportive environment he created, which allowed me to climb and at the same time grow and get to know myself better. I was struck yet again by the perfection of my life. I continued to be given exactly what I needed in order to be the best Margo I could be.

Nearing home, however, Martha brought me kicking and screaming back into her reality. While I was reflecting on my trip and Skip's invitation to climb Mount Elbrus, Pik Lenin, and Pik Kommunizma with him, she reminded me about the decisions and details I would need to address in the weeks to come. Self-doubt and fear immediately began to erode my joy and gratitude. I was returning to the real-life challenge of pursuing my chosen career in counseling. This, like my climbing, was a dream that filled my heart, but like all dreams, it brought with it the fear of pushing myself in a way I had not done before. I battled the fear with an ever-deepening faith in myself and in my Higher Power. I had climbed the highest mountain in the Western Hemisphere. If I could do that, I could take the necessary steps to follow my career.

CHAPTER SEVEN

I'm Not the Same Person I Was This Morning

Wednesday, November 28, 1990, Miami
Hunkered on one of my duffels... I feel excited
and alive. I'm going to make an attempt at
something that only two other women have pulled
off. Incredible! Sometimes even I am amazed
at what I want to do!

En route to a snow- and ice-climbing course on Mount Baker in Oregon, I stopped to spend the night with Skip and Elizabeth. Before dinner, Skip walked me into the woods surrounding their place to pick wild blackberries for our dessert while Elizabeth set the table on the porch. Their home reflected their warm natures. Elizabeth's fabulous rugs, antiques, and Waterford crystal combined with artifacts collected by Skip during his travels around the world to create an eclectic environment that was both welcoming and elegant.

As the sun set and night settled in, we lingered at the table, laughing as we recalled memories from the rafting trip we'd shared on the Çoruh River in Turkey. The great whitewater and some of the villagers we'd met along the way were especially memorable: the old man who wouldn't stop asking us questions about ourselves and America, and the women, so quiet and demure when men were around, covering their faces and hands, yet so animated and warm when the women from our trip got a group of them alone. I had been disappointed when the climbing trip to the Soviet Union that Skip had planned fell through at the last minute. But the canceled climb had given me time to rent a car and drive by myself through some of the historic places in Turkey I wouldn't have seen otherwise. I enjoyed that time, and it had been a valuable experience for me to be on my own in a foreign country.

While Elizabeth prepared the blackberries, Skip and I cleared the table. I was moved by how full my life had been. "It's been an incredible year," I told Skip. "I thought I'd get the adventure-travel bug out of my system with the nine months I spent climbing and trekking and running rivers but all it's done is make me want to do more. There are so many places I want to go, things I want to do, mountains I want to climb. Makes it real hard to think about finishing school. A career would only get in the way." I laughed and shook my head at the irony. Fantasizing about the possibilities of traveling rather than working, I asked, "What trips do you have scheduled for next year?"

"I'm going to Vinson in early December. It's the highest peak in Antarctica." I admired the ease with which he talked about traveling to such remote places and climbing big mountains. He referred to Mount Vinson as casually as I might talk about the local market. "Why don't you come along?" he added.

In my belly, an entire colony of butterflies took flight. Immediately, intuitively, I wanted to go. Just as quickly, Martha's voice caught my desire in a net. "You can't do that." The force of her conviction and practicality instantly deflated my excitement. "You have to be responsible and finish school, get an internship and earn some money. You can't afford it. Vinson is so extreme you couldn't handle it. It's in Antarctica, for God's sake!"

Still, I couldn't say no outright. "I'll have to check out my school schedule," I hedged, straddling a bar stool to include Elizabeth in our conversation while she cleaned the berries we had picked earlier. "December is when I'm supposed to graduate. I don't know whether they'd let me leave before the end of the semester. It sure is intriguing, though." Martha groaned, frustrated at my lack of commitment to what I "should" do.

"Well, I'd love to have you." Skip handed me a bowl of berries. "You have enough experience, a great attitude, and you certainly proved yourself on Aconcagua. I think you'd really enjoy this trip."

He left the room, returned momentarily, and handed me a brochure describing the trip to Vinson. "Here, this'll tell you more about it."

Martha argued loudly while I devoured the itinerary. "What a trip!" My eyes lit up with excitement. "God, I would love this!" My voice tapered off, leaving the "but" unspoken.

"Yes, you would," Skip answered, his voice coaxing. "And what you really ought to do is come with me to Everest in 1992."

Had he really just said I should climb Mount Everest? "Yeah, right." I laughed so hard I lost my balance, tipping over the stool and landing on the floor, but still laughing. "Me on Everest! Skip, you've got to be crazy. I don't have that kind of experience."

"You could by then." Skip wasn't laughing. He sat down on the couch, casually stirring the bowl of fresh berries he was holding. "I've been invited to be a guide on a commercial trip to Mount Everest in 1992. I think you should come along. In fact, you should think about climbing the 'Seven Summits.' You could be the first woman to do it. I know you're capable of it. You've proven you have the physical ability. Having the inner dream will make it or break it." He spoke so quietly and deliberately, I knew he was serious. "If you climb Vinson this December, you could do McKinley with me in June of 1991, Elbrus that summer, and Kosciusko and Everest in the spring of 1992. I don't know of any other woman who's making the effort to string the seven together, certainly no American woman. You might as well be the first."

Late into the night I was still grilling him on details: logistics, costs, training. Martha raised every question she could think of to undermine his vision. The more Skip and I talked, the more excited I became. The next morning I left without making any commitments, although I knew in my heart that Everest and the Seven Summits were going to be my focus for the next two years. As I drove to Mount Baker, I thought and prayed about every issue that worried Martha or me, and talked to Becky by phone and wrote in my journal. Two days later, I called Skip from Bellingham, Washington, to tell him I wanted to go for it. I'd begin to work out my schedule for Mount Vinson as soon as I got back to San Diego.

Each new skill I learned at the course on Mount Baker affirmed the tiny flame of belief that I might, just possibly, be the first woman to climb the Seven Summits.

The four and a half months between Skip's suggestion and my sitting in the airport ready to head to Antarctica were filled with more questions than answers. Glenn had returned from his travels and we had reconnected, dating for several months, then going our separate ways again. How would I ever have a relationship if I was so focused on following my dream of climbing? What did I think I was doing even considering the idea? How would I support myself and pay for the trips? How could I have a successful career if I was off climbing mountains? Who would take care of my house while I was away?

But I only needed to take one step at a time, and I completed all of my graduation requirements early in order to go to Mount Vinson. If my final exams and projects were accepted, I'd have my master's degree as well as the third of the seven summits when I returned.

It didn't seem to matter that I'd only been climbing for two years and that I hadn't started until after my fortieth birthday. Skip had been persistent, and I trusted his judgment. I didn't know which scared me most: anticipating the climbs, believing that it just might be possible for me to be successful in completing all of them, or realizing that someone else believed in me so much he could see me on the summit of the world's highest mountain.

Monday, December 3, 1990, Flying to Patriot Hills
We just passed Adelaide Island, halfway down
the peninsula. Craggy small peaks of ice
rising right from the sea. Pack ice going on
forever. I am so grateful for the chance to
be here. Remember that when I'm cold.

As airplanes go, the DC-6 wasn't very pretty. Designed for long-distance utility, ours had the patina of a 9/16-inch open-end wrench buried in a mechanic's tool box. I half-expected Jimmy Stewart to be our pilot, wearing a World War II leather flying jacket and scarf. Instead, it was hard to distinguish the flight crew from the passengers. When our flight engineer wasn't winging her way to Antarctica, she rowed rafts carrying clients through big whitewater in the Grand Canyon. Those of us occupying the eighteen passenger seats in this four-engine transport were definitely part of the world of adventure travel: members of two expeditions heading to Mount Vinson and a couple from Germany on their way to the South Pole. Curiosity, the unknown, and a desire to participate rather than observe life bound all of us together.

At eighty-one, Klaus was almost twice the average age of everyone else on board. His wife Carla, seventy-five, was animated as she talked about other adventures they'd enjoyed together around the world. I was drawn to their openly affectionate manner. Broad smiles, casual touching, and whispered exchanges accompanied their conversations. My hope of someday being able to experience my dreams with a partner was given a new life and I noticed that this time Martha wasn't arguing.

The seven climbers on board were from New Zealand and the United States. Kiwis Rob Hall and Gary Ball were joined by an American, Gary Kopff. Our original team of three had been expanded to four by a last-minute addition in Punta Arenas. As I settled back into my seat watching the endless parade of whitecaps passing underneath us, my mind drifted back over the past few days. Skip had brought up the possibility of adding an additional member to our team while he, Steve, and I were completing our "root 'n rummage" in his room. Steve was a beguilingly intense partner in an international consulting firm with an elfishly dry humor and a big heart. During the brief time the three of us had spent together, we'd already formed a close bond. My first response was to protect that and reject adding a newcomer. Skip certainly didn't have to consult with us. He was the trip leader and we were his clients. Another client might mean the difference between his breaking even financially and being able to pay some bills at home. He never made us feel like paying guests; every step of the way we were colleagues. But we had to be able to trust each other. The Vinson Massif didn't give any room for errors in judgment. Skip was asking whether we were willing to trust Woody with our lives.

"I spent an hour or so with Woody this afternoon." Skip's voice was matter-of-fact. He might as well have been going over the checklist. "He's heading for the South Pole but would like a shot at Vinson and wants to climb with us. He's in good shape physically and his climbing experience seems to be okay, but this isn't my expedition, it's ours. How do you feel about having him join us?"

I'd had some conversations with Woody, a sixty-ish banker from the West Coast, but they'd centered around who we knew and what we'd done rather than who we were. "You'd be a better judge of his climbing ability than me, Skip. He does appear to be in great shape for his age, and he seems like an interesting guy." An interesting guy? I didn't have a clue what to look for. "Steve, what do you think?"

"I think it would work fine." He'd been listening to me, brow furrowed as he contemplated Skip's question. "I'm for it."

"Me, too."

"Then it's agreed." Skip stood up and turned toward the door. "I'll go give him the news."

I went back to work sorting the gear and food spread out around the floor, ignoring a nagging sense that there were questions I should have asked. I trusted Skip. He'd led me to three successful summits, and his easy, competent manner was reassuring. I hoped Woody wouldn't take away from the playfulness and sense of ease that Skip, Steve, and I had already developed.

A couple of days earlier, we'd been shopping for food in Santiago when Steve reached for a box of detergent. "Here, Margo, this is for you." He looked straight at me as he set it into the basket I was pushing. "You know of course that women climbers are supposed to do the laundry for the men."

Without missing a beat, I gave him my best, wide-eyed-innocent look. "Shall I get some fabric softener, too? I'd hate for your polypro not to be soft enough." He had laughed and put the detergent back on the shelf. The light teasing among the three of us tested our limits and boundaries. I'd slipped right into it, feeling an inner strength and security I hadn't noticed before. It even allowed me to initiate pranks like tweaking Skip's nose with the, "What's this spot on the front of your shirt?" trick I'd learned in the fourth grade. Skip and Bob had worked hard to catch each other with creative variations of this on Aconcagua. It was fun to continue the tradition.

Still pushing the cart, I glanced at Skip, then at the cookies lining the aisle. "Skip, are you going to share your cookies with us this trip?" On every expedition, he packed a tin of chocolate chip cookies that his daughter Sidney baked for him. He always saved one to eat on the summit in her honor.

"In your dreams, Margo." He was already moving to the next aisle. "If you want cookies, get your own." Then from around the end of the display, "You're not wearing my sunglasses, either." He meant the pair of star-shaped yellow plastic child's sunglasses he had bought to wear on the summit.

Skip's devotion to his family and ability to be playful increased my appreciation of him as a guide. He brought a lightheartedness to the physical risks and trying emotional work of an expedition. That and his caring support helped me access my own strengths in spite of the inner conflicts I still faced. If I were to make it up all Seven Summits, he would be an important part of my journey.

In Santiago and again in Punta Arenas I'd talked with Skip, Steve, and other climbers about enduring hardships in extreme and exotic environments and listened carefully as they told stories about climbing technically difficult peaks. Even though Skip and Steve teased me with comments about my size, strength, and emotional balance as a woman, I felt grounded, knowing my experience spoke for itself. Compared to the men around me, I was a rookie, but I was willing to honor that and myself by not trying to be like them. I could be me, Margo. That was enough.

The evening before we had left Punta Arenas, a group of the climbers had gone out for dinner. I sat next to Rob Hall. Before dinner was served, he passed out key chains carrying the name of a prominent New Zealand corporation.

"What's this about?" I asked.

"They're our sponsors." Rob's eyes were lively and his face was framed by a full, dark beard. He was very tall and very lean, with a gentle soulfulness I found appealing. His partner, sitting across from us, smiled. Gary was as extroverted as Rob was quiet. Blond, powerfully built, and handsome, Gary was the more outgoing, public half of their successful guide business.

"Sponsors for what?" I asked.

"Our attempt to do the Seven Summits in seven months."

"Seven months?" I asked incredulously. "Is that possible?"

"You bet. We summited Everest on May 10, then did Denali, Elbrus, Kilimanjaro, Kosciusko, and Aconcagua. We need to be on top of Vinson by December 10. Today's the 2nd, that gives us a week. We'll get it. It's been a pretty exciting seven months." He spoke about the details of this astounding achievement with a relaxed, understated confidence and lightness that I greatly enjoyed. It was clear that although the goal of completing the Seven Summits in seven months earned them their sponsorship, it was the whole experience that Rob was enjoying. "Climbing is so much more than just standing on a summit. If you don't enjoy the process, what's the point? I have a hard time with clients who are only summit driven. Gary and I provide the experience of climbing for our clients, not just getting to the summit."

This professional, world-class climber had just given voice to the words that lived in my heart. "That's it exactly. Climbing feeds my soul in a way that nothing else does."

"How did you come to be here?" Rob asked.

"There's a long story about how it all started but basically it feeds my insides. I really want to stand on top of Vinson, but just the idea of being on a mountain in the Antarctic with no one else around for hundreds of miles excites me." My words tumbled out, carried by the force of my passion. I caught myself, then smiled and added quietly, "It would also be very cool to be the oldest woman to have climbed Vinson."

Rob gave me another of his characteristic "You bet's" and grinned so widely his eyes all but disappeared. He understood. "Life's about being happy and fulfilled *now*, not ten years from now. There are no guarantees, so I'm going to live the best I can today. I don't want to wake up ten years down the road regretting the things I didn't do. And what I want to do is climb."

"Absolutely." My heart was full. Rob had confirmed the validity of following my fledgling dream of being the first woman to climb the Seven Summits and of experiencing the mountains in the way that I loved. I didn't have to do what my parents or society wanted me to. Life could be about my living my heart's desire, now, not later.

Gary Ball's voice rose above the sound of the engines as he pointed out features of Cape Horn, the Antarctic Peninsula and Adelaide Island, and the crazy-quilt pattern made by the pack ice we were now flying over. He told me that Aristotle had been one of the first to postulate a continent at the bottom of the world, and that its name derived from "anti-" or opposite-arctic after the constellation "Arctus," also known as "Ursa Major," which points the way to the North Star. Later, it was called "Terra Incognita" or "hidden land," because it defied identification for so long. Gary said its size is more than twice that of Australia, and that one glacier, the Byrd, is almost as wide as the English Channel. In one trench, the ice has been measured to a depth of 15,670 feet. Much of the continent's land mass actually lies below sea level, having been pushed down under the tremendous weight of the ice it carries.

He continued to tell us that Antarctica has some of the most inhospitable weather conditions in the world, creating an environment with the smallest number of species of flora and fauna found anywhere on Earth. Winds average 50 mph along the coast, and temperatures, which regularly run below 0 degrees Fahrenheit, have been recorded more than 20 degrees colder than anyplace else on the planet. Snowfall figures are unreliable because blizzards and foglike blowing snow constantly redistribute the ground snow. One valley in the interior is so desolate and dry that scientists have used it to test equipment to be sent via satellite to Mars.

Listening to Gary's descriptions, I really began to question why I was going to a place where I had to wear my down jacket just to stay warm in the plane taking me there. Already my hands and feet were cold. Martha complained, "You know it will be this way or worse for the next couple of weeks. What are you doing?" From the climbing I'd done, I knew I didn't do well in extreme cold and actually dreaded it. I looked around the cabin at everyone else bundled up and wondered if they shared my concerns. I hoped this trip would increase my tolerance for cold. I reminded Martha that cold was a fact but misery was optional. As we flew over the Ellsworth Range, I saw the Vinson Massif, its high point, extending more than 16,000 feet above sea level.

The awesome desolation and wind-swept ice broken by jagged mountains and lines of crevasses astonished and unnerved me.

We landed on the blue-ice runway of the staging base called Patriot Hills used by Adventure Network for people going to Vinson and the South Pole. A swarm of people surrounded the plane, unloading gear, refueling and reloading it with the gear from an expedition that had just returned from Vinson. Skip stopped to talk with a couple of the climbers who were leaving. As I walked toward the main building, he motioned me over.

"Margo, this is Todd Burleson." I smiled and offered my hand to Todd as Skip continued. "Todd's the leader for the expedition to Everest I'm guiding in 1992." I caught my breath. Skip said, "This is the woman I was telling you about, Todd. She'd be a great addition to the expedition. She should have six of the Seven Summits by then."

In the few minutes we had to talk, Todd said that Vinson, in addition to being a marvelous climb in its own right, was a great training ground for Everest. More important, he confirmed that with Skip's recommendation and my completing the schedule I'd set out, I'd be welcome to join his expedition to Everest. "It would be great to have the first woman to climb the Seven Summits reach her goal on one of my trips," he told me.

Me, Margo Chisholm, a member of an expedition to climb the highest mountain in the world. It was hard to believe. Yes, I had at least three major mountains to climb before I got there, a lot of training to do and even more money to raise, but the dream could be real—and it was mine.

By now six or seven of the departing climbers had gathered around. I questioned them about their experience: the weather, the route, did they make the summit?

"We made the summit, but the weather was pretty bad all the way," one volunteered. "I'm ready to get off the ice. This place is too cold for me," and he made his way to the waiting plane.

"Yeah, but the climb was still fabulous," said another. "It's an incredible place." The smile on this face, despite his fatigue, spoke volumes about his experience on the mountain. "You going to the Pole?" It was more of a statement than a question.

Only two women had climbed Vinson, but it annoyed me that he assumed I was there to go to the Pole rather than to climb. "Why would you think that?" I asked as neutrally as I could, glancing at Skip, yet my response obviously made the climber uncomfortable.

"Well, uh, I don't know," he said. "I guess because not many women have climbed down here. I didn't mean any offense."

I shrugged, "No offense taken. But two weeks from now I'll be the

*F*rom here: a lost soul in an oversized body, dreams seemingly lost forever. On the right is my niece Meg, 1981.

*T*o there: a strong soul in a strong body, dreams coming true in the Antarctic. Camp I, Mt. Vinson, 1990.

Toilet facilities never seen at any hotel. A two-holer over a crevasse at Camp I on Pik Lenin, 1991.

Complete exhaustion with another 500 feet yet to climb. The foot of Heartbreak Hill, Denali, 1991.

Natural refrigeration. The kitchen at Camp V, Denali, 1991.

Creating a home under extreme conditions. Putting up a tent in high winds. Camp I, Aconcagua, 1990.

Jonathan Wright's spirit was with me as I sat for hours in my first Buddhist monastery, living out my dreams. Rangdum Monastery, Ladakh, India, 1989.

My grandfather's elephants come alive as I ride one. Nepal, 1989.

Skip Horner and me at the 18,481-foot summit of the highest mountain in Europe, my fifth of the Seven Summits. Mt. Elbrus, 1991.

At 19,340 feet, pictured from the right: Laura, Mark, Janice, Skip and I stand on the roof of Africa. Mt. Kilimanjaro, 1988.

Antarctic Airways provided the transportation from Patriot Hills to Base Camp. Mt. Vinson, Antarctic, 1990.

Ice blocks create a wind break for the tents. Camp I, Mt. Vinson, 1990.

The watchful eyes and prayer flags of a Buddhist chorten quietly bless the village of Namche Bazaar. Khumbu Valley, Nepal, 1993.

A mani stone, carved as a memorial to climber and guide Gary Ball, who died on Dhauligiri in 1993, supports the photo of Tanner and Shea Daily. Foot of the Khumbu Glacier, 1995.

I climb one of the many ladders that facilitate the route through huge seracs and yawning crevasses in the ever-changing Khumbu Icefall. Mt. Everest, 1993.

Dehydrated and weak, in front only so I don't get left behind, I lead a line of team members through a whiteout toward Camp II. Western Cwm, Mt. Everest, 1993.

I establish a personal high altitude record at 23,500 feet between Camps
II and III, strongly aware of the difference between this "high" and those I
had searched out only seven years before. Lhotse Face, Mt. Everest, 1993.

Credit: Rob Hall

oldest woman to have summited Vinson." My voice was strong, tinged with pride.

"Good for you," a third climber said. "That's great." He nodded in affirmation, smiling his approval.

I smiled in return. God, I wanted that mountain!

It was warmer than I'd expected when we arrived, my cold-weather sleeping bag would be overkill in the 20-degree temperature. But from what Todd's group had said, I knew I'd be grateful for it once we began climbing. An even bigger surprise for me was the amount of daylight. We'd arrived at six o'clock in the evening and by nine it hadn't gotten any darker. Clocks lose their meaning in Antarctica. There are only two seasons: light and dark. At this time of year, the sun followed a low arc across the sky, never quite going below the horizon. There would be no darkness for another two months. It was midnight before I climbed into the tent I was sharing with Woody, and the sun's angle had hardly changed since our arrival. I had brought a sleep mask with me to trick my mind into thinking it was nighttime, but I didn't know whether it would really work.

I wasn't sure how much sleep I could get anyway since a cold was settling into my chest. First Bolivia, then India, now here. It seemed to happen too often to be a coincidence but I had no idea what the connection might be. Was it a natural response by my body to travel, the altitude, or being out in the cold? I could only shake my head in frustration and believe it would pass. It had on the other trips. I'd taken some medicine for the congestion, but Martha reminded me of every cold I'd ever had in the mountains. "I've come a long way, Martha. This doesn't have to be like Bolivia. You've been with me on Island Peak and Aconcagua, too, remember? Go do what you've got to do. I'm going to sleep." Then, as I felt myself beginning to drift off, I added, "God, she's in your hands. Good night."

"Margo. It's time to get going." Skip's voice pulled me out of a deep sleep.

"Okay, thanks. I'll be right there." I took off the sleeping mask. The sun seemed to be in the same place it had been the night before. My cold had worsened. Part of me hoped that bad weather would keep us from flying to Base Camp, but our duffel bags and boxes of food were loaded onto the Twin Otter, one of two planes used to ferry people to Vinson's Base Camp, and we were airborne by 11:00 A.M. During the flight our pilot, Warren, mentioned that they were looking at using another glacier as a site for Base Camp and a new approach to the summit. We were likely to be one of the last expeditions to use the current route.

Gazing out the window, I felt intensely drawn to the raw-edged beauty of Antarctica. Mountains rose up like the dorsal fins of some prehistoric monster. Shadows added mystery to the massive wind sculptures, crevasses, and other variations in the surface caused by the shifting ice. The underlying rock occasionally burst through, black as deep space against the white background. Sometimes the ice was draped with frozen sheets, glistening in the low angle of the sun. As we began our descent toward the Vinson Massif I delighted in the knowledge that I was not just a tourist, content to fly over the miles of ice and snow, having it be enough to say I'd seen it. I was a climber, preparing to walk into the middle of this wilderness. I was here to climb to the summit, not to look at it through the window. The deep growl of the props as the pilot throttled back for landing triggered a shot of adrenaline through my system, and my heart began beating faster.

We unloaded quickly. When the small plane departed from the makeshift runway, loose snow sloughed off the skis and was blown back in the wash from the propellers settling on us in tiny crystals sparkling in the sun. For a long time after it disappeared from view I could still hear the engines. Then an almost tangible silence absorbed the last of the sound. It felt as if our lifeline back to Patriot Hills had been severed. We would be here for two weeks with only a radio for contact with the outside world. For two brief periods every day—8:00 A.M. and 8:00 P.M.—Patriot Hills would be listening for any communication from us. I felt as desolate as we would have looked to someone flying overhead: red, blue, purple, and black specks against an endless background of white.

"Listen, Skip, it's early in the day and only a couple of hours' easy walk to Camp One." Steve's words broke through my momentary sense of total isolation. "Why don't we do a double carry and sleep there tonight?"

I responded instantly. "No. I don't feel well, and I don't want to do two carries." Still, I knew Steve's idea was a sensible one.

The Kiwis, Rob and Gary, declared their intention to go all the way to Camp II in one day. With only a week to meet their deadline and the weather always uncertain, they were taking advantage of the calm winds and virtually unlimited daylight to push hard. They moved out quickly carrying heavy packs and dragging even heavier sleds behind them. The third member of their team struggled to keep up.

Skip said, "Margo, I want you to carry light so you don't aggravate your cold." He knew I'd really need my strength as we got higher on the mountain. "Take only what you'd need if for some reason we can't complete two carries today. We'll get everything else on the second load."

Orange plastic sleds stored at Base Camp made it possible to haul more than double the weight we could carry on our backs. Getting used to the rhythm of the sleds' weight pulling back while we tugged them forward was awkward as we started out, but with each new step we became more accustomed to them and within two hours were at Camp I.

As we set up our tents, we could see Rob and the two Garys climbing up the fixed ropes toward Camp II. I was putting gear into a tent when Skip said, "Margo, there's not much left at Base Camp, and I want you to rest. Steve and Woody, you'll go back down and get the rest of the gear. Margo'll melt water for hot drinks and soup, and I'll go up and work on the fixed ropes in the couloir." Todd's team had mentioned wishing the fixed ropes extended lower in the couloir, and Skip had brought extra rope with us to complete that job.

I wanted to argue, tell him I could go back to Base with the guys and help haul gear, too, or go with him to help with the ropes, but my strength was ebbing fast and I knew it was my ego talking. My body knew that staying put was the right thing for me, and Skip had my best interest at heart.

Steve and Woody left camp with empty, drooping packs and sleds that slid around in front of them on the gentle downward slope. I heard Steve curse as he tried awkwardly to swing his sled behind him but succeeded only in overturning it. I smiled somewhat guiltily at his predicament. It appeared that as big a help as the sleds were on the way up, they were a pain in the ass on the way down. I wondered briefly why they didn't ride them down but surmised quickly the danger involved in an out-of-control sled ride down the ice far outweighed the advantages.

I set to my own chores. Unpacking the lightweight single-burner stove, its fuel bottles, and the pots used for melting snow and cooking, I swung out the stove's spiderlike legs, attached a fuel bottle, and pumped up the pressure. It took me several tries to prime the burner before the loud but comforting and familiar pffft-pffft-pffft sound of the flame announced that it was doing its job. A piece of cardboard provided a marginally stable surface on the ice, while a thin metal windscreen kept the flame focused on the pot. I sat bent-kneed on a second piece of cardboard, the stove between my feet, and added snow carefully to the small opening of the kettle. In spite of the cardboard base, the legs constantly needed readjusting as the reflected heat melted the ice around them.

Shadows from the ridge above shifted closer as the sun followed its arcing path near the horizon. Anticipating colder air, I pulled out Steve's down jacket—mine would arrive in the second load. On the walk to Camp I I'd experienced the vagaries of Antarctic temperatures. The air was probably no more than 10 degrees, but in the direct sun I had sweat running down my back. From time to time a light breeze had blown across the ice, though, instantly turning the sweat to frost and making me shiver in a windchill below zero. The climb was a continual rhythm of hat on/hat off, jacket on/jacket off. Now, as the shadows reached my cardboard seat, I stood up and put on Steve's jacket. It wouldn't be good to wait until I was too cold.

Skip was a 4-inch-high moving spot at the foot of the couloir. Watching him, I reveled in the experience of being alone in such peaceful, desolate beauty with only the low growl of the stove for company. I thought, "I'm in Antarctica!" and realized suddenly that now I had been on all seven continents.

I lifted the lid off the kettle and put another hunk of hard snow into the opening. It caught on one side and knocked the pot off the stove, spilling almost all the water. "Damn!" I couldn't believe it. More than an hour of melting gone to waste.

"You can't even melt water." Martha's words were scathing. "First you're not strong enough to do the same work as everyone else, and now you can't even heat water right. Some climber you are!" I felt shamed to my core. Maybe she was right. Maybe I really didn't belong here after all. Maybe I was really just a middle-age dreamer.

I began the process again, hoping there would be at least some hot water when the guys returned, but Skip appeared shortly. When I told him what had happened he said, "There could be a time when that water means the difference between life and death. We don't have enough fuel to waste any of it. You have to be more careful." His words, though not harsh, invoked the seriousness of my error.

I didn't answer. There was nothing for me to say. It took two more hours to heat enough water for dinner and hot drinks.

In my sleeping bag at 3:00 A.M., I was still talking to myself. "It was a mistake. Nothing more. This is not about who I am. It was a lesson, only a lesson, to be more careful." At last I slept peacefully, having let go of the shame.

When we woke up at 11:00 A.M. it was snowing, but not heavily enough to keep us from moving gear up to Camp II. Snowstorms are very rare in Antarctica, and this one reminded us that we were not in charge of the weather. My head was still stuffy and there was pressure in my ears, but both lessened as soon as I began moving around. A climbing schedule of sorts began to take form, with us leaving camp whenever we were ready, doing the day's climbing and chores, then sleeping until we got up. The never-ending light really made concepts of night and day irrelevant. We left about 4:00 P.M., walking for forty-five minutes up to the fixed ropes, then putting on crampons for the steep pitch up the couloir.

By the time I reached the bottom of the fixed rope, I had developed a cough that caused a tight, sharp pain in my chest. It felt as if my lungs might explode. I kept my breathing shallow to avoid triggering it as we started up the fixed line. I hadn't been on terrain this steep before, with or without a fixed line, and I felt awkward and bumbling, finding it very hard going. I tried walking duck footed, feet pointing out to the sides, then sideways, crossing my feet one over the other, all the while sliding the ascender up the rope with each step. This was the first time I'd used an ascender, a mechanical device that grips the ropes on a downward pull but slips freely upward providing protection against a fall. The tenuous attachment to the mountain gave me a great sense of security but I could not find a rhythm that eased the awkwardness and fatigue I felt as I inched my way breathlessly, trying not to cough, up the couloir.

Halfway up, my right foot burned as if cramping. It had happened some while I was running but never severely enough to do anything about. Now the burning sensation deep between my third and fourth toes became a sharp spasm that forced me to stop and take off my boot to massage the pain away.

I was furious. "First the cough and now this foot thing. I don't need this, God." The ascender that attached my harness to the fixed line helped me balance on my left foot, crampon points imbedded solidly in the hard snow. I wrestled the outer shell and liner off my right foot. "What if I drop it?" I fought the rising panic. "Breathe, Margo. You're not going to drop it. Just be careful." I ran a carabiner, an oval-shaped metal snap link, through the laces of the loose boot and attached it to my ascender, relaxing with the assurance that it would not fall. It took both hands manipulating my foot before the spasm released. I forced the boot back onto my foot. The effort triggered a second painful, though short-lived, spasm, and then a cough, an explosion of pain that brought tears to my eyes. "This is just ludicrous," I said angrily. "I'm in a 60-degree couloir on a mountain in the Antarctic. I have to take my whole boot off because my foot is cramping, and now my chest feels like it's going to explode. Who made this up?!"

Still muttering and swearing under my breath, I looked up at the distance to the top of the couloir. I had no idea how I was going to get up there and lowered my head in dejection. "I can't do this."

"Yes, you can." I was no longer surprised when God gave me a strength that seemed, only moments before, impossible. I trusted it, and began once again to take one small step at a time toward the top of the couloir. This time there was an amazing difference in the rhythm of my climbing. I couldn't take any credit for it. I hadn't consciously dug down and found added strength—it was just there.

At the top of the couloir I looked down to Camp I and beyond, seemingly to the edge of the ice itself. Then I climbed down a short, steep pitch and followed a traverse to Camp II. Rob and the two Garys were still there, forced by the weather to take a rest day. We unloaded our packs, ate a little, then headed back to Camp I to get some sleep. My cough had worsened on the traverse to II, and at times, the pain almost took my breath away. It eased on the descent, however, which I took as a positive sign.

The trip down the couloir was almost fun without the weight of the loaded pack, but by the time I reached camp and my tent I was ready to collapse from exhaustion. I crawled into my bag after 4:00 A.M.

By 4:30 P.M. we were trudging up toward the fixed ropes once again. Our packs were heavier than on the day before, but now we knew what to expect in the couloir, and I was more comfortable with the ascender. Moving slowly and purposefully, using the duck-walk movement, I climbed steadily up the fixed lines. Physically, I was more tired than I had been yesterday, but my inner family and Jonathan were cheering me on, an almost tangible help in lifting first one leg then the other.

I reached the top of the couloir an hour and a half faster than the day before, in spite of the heavier load. Four times I had to stop to rub a cramp out of my right foot, but my frustration was eased greatly by the view as I sat astride the narrow ridge at the top of the couloir and took a couple of photos. Bravo, Margo! my inner family cheered. Slowly and carefully I began the descent and traverse to Camp II. My legs felt like wet noodles, and I didn't want to make a stupid mistake. On the traverse, my chest was tight and my cough excruciating, but I felt much better overall and knew I was recovering from whatever bug had invaded my lungs.

After a little more than six hours of steady climbing, I arrived at Camp II. Skip and Steve had climbed strongly and fast, well ahead of Woody and me, and they had one tent set up and the stove burning by the time I came in. Woody had started the day climbing strongly but had slowed to a crawl, stopping frequently. He reached camp an hour and a half after me. On our first carry up the couloir, Skip had asked me to stay behind Woody while he and Steve went ahead, and even moving as slowly as I was I had been frustrated by his slow pace, aware that it would be difficult to stay warm moving that slowly when we were higher on the mountain. As I helped Steve set up the second tent, I wondered about Woody's ability to do the sustained climbing necessary to reach the summit and how his slow pace would affect the rest of us.

Woody and I rested the next day while Skip and Steve made a light carry to III, marking the route through the icefall just below it. Their round trip took just under three-and-a-half hours. Both felt strong and welcomed the exercise. Woody spent most of the day in his sleeping bag and behaved as if he wasn't quite all there, as though he had left part of his brain at the bottom of the couloir. He was an impressive man in many ways, but here on the mountain he seemed somehow over his head. I didn't know whether to attribute it to his not having climbed in a while or being unfit or afraid.

The next day, a 30-knot wind and blowing snow forced a rest day. It was a dozing, healing, daydreaming kind of day that provided needed rest for body and mind alike. We all had more energy the third day, even though we were in the shadow of an ice serac the size of a small building and the overcast skies and –12-degree temperature made the hour-long process of breaking down Camp II a stiff-fingered, cold-toed procedure. We stashed everything we could in our packs so we would only have to make one carry to Camp III rather than two and were glad that the sun broke through the clouds on the diagonal traverse above camp. My pack was heavy. The higher we climbed, the steeper the slope became. Mentally I reviewed self-arrest techniques as I followed Skip. He kicked steps into the ice, occasionally dislodging chunks that slid nearly 2,000 feet to the valley below.

My heart was pounding from effort and fear when Jonathan's presence came to me. "Breathe, Margo. Don't forget to breathe." I felt a confidence, ease, and sense of belonging I'd never experienced before. The process became fun, and I laughed out loud as I front-pointed up the last section, too steep to use any but the two points on the front of my crampons. The angle lessened, and we picked our way around and across crevasses and debris in the icefall leading to the shelf holding Camp III. When we arrived at camp, Skip, Steve, and Woody set up the tents, and I took on the job of cutting snow blocks to build walls to protect our tents from the wind.

The extreme cold and dryness of the climate created a layer of snow several feet deep that had the consistency of Styrofoam. It made an ideal surface for walking in crampons and the perfect material out of which to cut building blocks. I headed for an area, not far from our tents, which Gary and Rob had apparently used when they built their own walls the day before. A series of rough steps in the snow marked the quarry. Following the patterns already there, I used a snow saw to cut blocks that measured roughly 10 × 10 × 20 inches, piling them beside me. Skip and the others stacked them, forming walls around the tents. It was a new experience for me, and I enjoyed the physical activity as well as the addition of another skill to my climbing résumé.

Two-and-a-half hours after arriving in camp I took a break, holding a cup of hot chocolate, warming my hands and my insides. We'd pitched our tents within five feet of a large crevasse, with the Kiwis camped slightly above us. We expected their return from the summit anytime. Seven Summits in seven months—what an achievement! I thought about my own quest as I looked off into the valley now more than 2,500 feet below. From where I sat I could see the narrow saddle at the top of the couloir above Camp I, and Flamingo Peak, a perfect black-rock pyramid rising like an island just a mile from Base Camp. Beyond it there was only wind-sculptured ice.

This mountain was somehow a rite of passage for me. Even Martha recognized it. She had been strangely silent—no "If they only knew . . ." no "I'm not good enough . . ." when I'd arrived at Camp III, or "What if I can't . . ."—only the knowledge that I'd worked hard and performed well. I felt like a true mountaineer: I deserved to be there. I smiled as that truth filled my heart, and I breathed in deeply, taking in the stark beauty spread out around me.

The Kiwis' return from their summit success only added to my joy. They made their goal with no time to spare. During our rest day at Camp III, I helped them take down their tent as they prepared for their descent. A joking, friendly atmosphere prevailed, giving us great expectations for our own success. My only concern was the cold, which I knew I could handle with clothing and acceptance.

Monday, December 10, 1990, Camp III,
Mount Vinson, Antarctica
Morale is high among us all. The wind is pretty
much gone; the cloud above Shinn is dissipating;
the barometer is up; I'm coughing less; Skip has a
good feeling about the weather. It all bodes well.
I want this mountain, God. And I already feel
victorious. What a difference between Bolivia
and here. In only a year and a half.

On summit day we were up at 7:00 A.M., an early start in Antarctica. I hadn't slept well because of summit jitters, and my cold had kept me tossing and turning all night and aware of Woody rustling around, settling in, snoring. Thin clouds appeared ominous. We ate a quick breakfast, secured the camp for our return, roped up, and began climbing through another icefall. By the time we reached the top of it, we'd broken out of the clouds and were greeted by bright, warming sunshine and a view of the summit that made it seem tantalizingly close. We knew we still had hours to climb before we'd be there.

We climbed steadily, carving out switchbacks up the long face. The high altitude and freezing temperatures controlled each footfall; Woody struggled to keep up with the rest of us. If he couldn't make it, none of us would. Skip talked with him about how he was doing and even though he was having enormous difficulty, we all reached the top of that portion of the climb and dropped our packs. We still had a half-hour climb to the 10-foot, nearly vertical step that was the final obstacle between us and the summit, but I'd felt the strength of my whole inner family working hard and cheering with me with each step I took, and now, this close, I knew I'd make it.

Feeling the effects of the altitude and the exertion of the climb from Camp III, we picked our way slowly and steadily up the rock-strewn slope that led to the final short headwall. Skip stopped at its base. "Margo," he said, "I want you to be the first one up—to be alone up there." I looked at Steve who nodded his agreement.

The honoring and acceptance of these men touched me deeply, and I wept as I climbed onto the 16,864-foot summit. At –30 degrees, the tears immediately became drops of ice on my face and the backs of the outer mittens I used to try to wipe them away. Steve came up next, and he broke out in tears, too. His father, who'd died two years earlier, had been enamored of the Antarctic, and for Steve this was a triumph for his father's spirit as well as for himself. Skip joined us and broke out his cookies, then Woody arrived, slow and triumphant.

Joy and gratitude were reflected in our photos taken next to the stake with small flags on it and an upside down ski pole that together marked the actual summit. Skip wore his yellow star-shaped glasses and a cookie-filled smile, my face was hidden behind glacier glasses, Steve's was frozen in a balaclava, and Woody's grin told its own story. It had taken us just under eight hours of climbing to get here from Camp III. We expected our return to take about half that long. Thirty minutes after we arrived on the summit, we departed. We needed the exertion of climbing to keep our bodies warm in the extreme cold.

"Slow and careful, Woody, there's no rush." Skip had descended the steep 10-foot pitch from the summit, kicking steps for the rest of us as he went. Steve and I watched as Woody started down, placing his left foot in the highest step Skip had cut. Woody was obviously exhausted from his effort to reach the summit. As he crossed his right foot over his left, lowering it toward the next step, he realized this technique was not going to work. He paused, balanced precariously on the points of his left crampon, then brought his right foot back to its original position on the flat ice of the summit. He stabilized himself there for what seemed like a full minute, contemplating how to approach his descent.

"Try moving your right foot behind your left," Skip said. "It might feel more secure." His concern was evident in his voice. The majority of climbing accidents happen coming off a mountain. Too often climbers use all of their resources and reserves to reach the summit, not thinking about how they'll get down. The ice steps were large enough to be stable and safe, but to a mind dulled by fatigue, extreme cold, and limited oxygen, negotiating them was a daunting task.

Woody began again. He planted his left foot, then lowered his right behind it to the second step. Transferring his weight, he lowered his left foot another step. He was bringing his right foot behind the left when he slipped. He spun around and began to slide head first down the rock-strewn slope.

"Oh, my God," Steve spoke softly in a voice strangled by horror. I couldn't move. I felt my heart racing, my mind's eye slowing time, recording frame after frame as the catastrophe in progress revealed itself.

Sliding out of control, Woody's body picked up speed rapidly. Skip hurled himself at Woody in a heroic effort to slow down the slide. Instead, both bodies, one across the other, slid even faster. They careened like pinballs off rocks imbedded in the ice. Woody's head hit one with a sickening thud. As quickly as it started, it was over. Neither of the men was moving.

"We've got to get down there," Steve and I exclaimed, nearly in unison. Perhaps 100 yards below us lay two bodies, half our expedition, including our guide.

"Come on, Margo." Steve moved quickly toward the face we had to negotiate.

"Careful." The word on my mind escaped automatically as he front-pointed down the steps.

"You, too." Steve was looking down, focusing on his feet, and he didn't look up as I started down after him.

I safely reached the last step and turned to see Skip lift an arm, then his head, slowly forcing himself to sit up. Beside him, Woody's body was limp, a red stain spreading from his gray wool hat. "Oh, God," I thought running, "don't let Woody be dead."

Steve called out to Skip to stay down, but he struggled slowly to his feet. Standing, Skip's body wove back and forth. His royal blue Gore-Tex pants had a large tear on the left thigh with what appeared to be red long underwear bulging through the material. As I got closer, I saw that the "long underwear" was exposed muscle. A crampon point or ice axe had sliced an ugly gash, deep and long, into his leg.

"Skip . . ." Steve's concern and compassion were evident although his voice had the edge of authority an emergency situation brings out in some people.

"I'm fine." Skip began to examine the client he'd just ridden down the slope. "We've got to help Woody."

"You're not fine. Look at your leg." The wound was severe but wasn't bleeding, a positive result of the extreme temperature.

Skip glanced at his leg and repeated, "I'm fine." Then Woody's head moved slightly, and he let out a faint groan. We dropped our medical debate to give our full attention to Woody, and Skip brought the edges of his torn Capilene together to cover the gash in his leg.

Woody didn't appear to have any broken bones but as we questioned him he didn't know who we were, where we were, or what had happened. He obviously had a concussion.

"We're too exposed to the wind up here. We have to move down to the packs. We'll figure out what we're going to do there." Skip had no way of knowing how his injured leg would perform. "You guys help Woody. Let's get moving."

Woody was unable to stand up, and there wasn't anything available to create a litter: He would have to down-climb. His bleeding came from a fairly superficial scalp wound and had stopped on its own by the time he was sitting up. Two heavy wool caps had probably saved his life. Steve and I helped him crab along down the ice, sliding on his butt using his hands for stability and our ice axes as foot rests to prevent him from sliding out of control. Skip was using all of his strength to get himself down.

The reality of our situation prompted me to breathe out a prayer: "God, please don't let anything happen to Steve. And stay close. If Skip gets any worse we're in big trouble." I was strong, but not strong enough to move anyone down Vinson by myself.

"Move your foot to the axe, Woody. Now the other one." Steve was almost yelling. We had to get to lower altitude. At 16,000 feet we were working at an oxygen deficit and it was getting colder by the minute. As our adrenaline wore off, exhaustion set in. But Woody was in shock, his responses very slow, sometimes nonexistent. "Woody! Move your feet." Frequently we had to move his feet for him with our hands. We kept shouting at him, though. He needed to stay awake and moving if he was going to get down alive. "Hit the pole, Woody. I know you don't understand. It doesn't matter where you are. We'll tell you later. Just keep hitting the pole."

It took us more than two hours just to make our way to the packs. By the time we reached them the wind had picked up, the sun had moved, and we were shrouded in shadow. The temperature dipped, the windchill factor driving the cold even more deeply through the clothing we'd worn to the summit. Woody was shivering. As I moved his uncooperative legs one more time I thought, "Dear God, what are we going to do?"

We put on our heavy down-filled parkas. Skip checked Woody, then turned to Steve and me. "At this rate there's no way we'll get him down. I've got to get to Base. With luck, Hall and Ball may still be there. If not, I'll radio for help. The two of you, do what you can for Woody and take care of yourselves until I get back up here with the help we need." He paused, reflective, as if he were playing back what he'd just said. Then he asked, "Margo, what do you think?"

Everything in me resisted second-guessing Skip, so I chose my words carefully. "Do you really think that's the best way to go?" My gut told me that staying this high without the additional equipment at Camp III could only lead to disaster. "I think we can get Woody down the couloir, then, if we have to, haul him on a pack the rest of the way to Camp III. With you going down to Base, there's no way of knowing when help could reach us: eighteen hours, twenty-four hours? Probably more." I looked at Steve, wanting him to understand my point. "At least this way we'll be doing something. I'm absolutely willing to do everything we can to get Woody down, but I'm not willing to stay here and freeze to death just waiting."

Steve nodded. "I agree."

"Sounds like a good idea, Margo." Skip's voice was stronger.

Our immediate obstacle was the couloir: eleven pitches top to bottom, each requiring a belay. We lowered Woody to the end of the length of rope, then set up another belay and repeated the process. Skip belayed while Steve moved down the slope with Woody, cajoling, badgering, ordering, doing whatever was necessary to keep him moving. I kept the ropes untangled, then used my ascender to move down to Woody and Steve. Skip followed, down-climbing without protection. For the first five pitches there were rocks we could use as anchors, then there was only ice, and Skip had to set up a boot/axe belay for the remaining six.

When we reached the bottom of the couloir, Woody was stable enough to begin the long walk ahead of us. Wobbly and confused, with Steve by his side, he continued slowly hour after hour, reaching deep inside for the strength to make it on his own to camp. I stayed with Skip, who moved more slowly with every mile, yet continued without complaint. His ability to function as a capable and caring leader in the face of his own severe injury and life-threatening injury to a client deepened my already great respect for him.

Twenty hours after we had left Camp III, Skip and I returned, too tired even to eat. He immediately struggled into his tent without saying anything. Steve was already in his bag, and Woody, too. I was scared. I sat outside the door to the tent I shared with Woody, drinking the last of the water I'd carried to the summit, letting the emotions of the day wash over me. Woody was already asleep, snoring loudly. "God damn it! Why does he have to snore?" The fear eating away at my insides momentarily turned into irritation with Woody. I was afraid to go to sleep knowing that if Woody had a concussion, it was dangerous for him to be asleep too long. Also, I was really concerned about Skip. How would he get down to Base Camp tomorrow with that leg? We had only two narrow windows of time each day for radio calls. Every hour was important.

Woody had stopped snoring when I climbed into the tent. He woke reassuringly when I gently shook him, then fell right back into what seemed to be a restful sleep. My exhaustion was matched by my gratitude as I pulled my own sleeping bag around me and immediately went to sleep myself.

"Anybody awake?" Skip's voice passed easily through the walls of our tent, quietly demanding a response.

"Yup." Talking triggered a cough. My throat was scratchy. I rolled over and saw that Woody wasn't awake, but he was breathing. At least he was alive.

"Steve and I have a plan."

"So what is it?" I coughed again. I was exhausted, I ached all over, and my cold had settled back into my chest. I felt like shit and couldn't imagine doing anything but lying right where I was. How about a rest day as a plan? Even in my fatigue, I knew that wasn't possible. We had to get down to get medical help and it wasn't going to be easy.

"I'm going to take Woody all the way to Base Camp today. We both need to get down, and we need to get a plane here. You and Steve will do a double carry from Three to Two today, then continue down to One and Base with double loads tomorrow."

I answered, "Okay," turned back toward the wall of the tent, away from Woody and the world that needed me to be strong, and cried. I couldn't find anyplace in my body or my head or my heart that believed I could do what Skip was describing. I breathed deeply, feeling the exhaustion, each of the places that were sore, and the congestion in my chest. My breath seemed to go all the way to my soul, and it touched a strength that came alive. Okay, I thought, I'll do it. I don't know how, but I'll do it, and I began to get dressed.

Steve brought me a hot drink and checked on Woody. I said, "Steve, I don't have a clue about how I'm going to be able to pull this off today. But I'll do whatever is necessary so all of us get down."

He smiled and hugged me. "We can do it. We have to. Together we can do anything." I could sense his fatigue and was grateful for the strong bond that was forming between us.

After forcing down some hot chocolate and a granola bar, Skip and Woody headed toward Base Camp, carrying only what they needed, including their sleeping bags in a summit-size pack Skip always carried with him. Woody was close to being helpless: clumsier than ever and almost incapable of any coherent thought or organized action.

As they disappeared behind a serac, Steve and I began to pack up camp and sort the equipment for two carries. An hour later, we swung heavy packs across our shoulders and started down. I had been concerned about the steep section just above the icefall, but Skip had cut big steps for Woody, and I had no problems, even with the extra weight. The sun finally appeared from behind the rocks above, and its presence was warming despite the cold temperature. My confidence level was way up. I figured that Skip and Woody would almost be to Camp II by now. We all just might make it.

Exiting the icefall, I looked down the route all the way to Camp II. My confidence dropped into my crampons. Skip was almost to the camp but Woody was far behind him and had apparently become disoriented. He was walking in the wrong direction. "Woody," I yelled as loudly as I could. "Go right. Follow Skip." He didn't change his course.

"Woody! Turn around, go toward Skip." He heard me this time but instead of turning toward Camp II he haltingly began walking back up the hill.

Steve came out of the icefall. "They'll never make the radio call."

"I'm going to run down and catch Skip."

"With that load? What are you, nuts?"

"Skip needs to go down by himself and leave Woody with us. He's got to make that call to get medical help for his leg and for Woody, and Woody's way too screwed up to make any time. Look at him, he's walking back toward us. My pack isn't as heavy as yours, and it's all low angle from here."

"Well, okay. Be careful." His voice trailed behind me. I'd already started down as fast as I could.

"Skip," I hollered. "Wait up." A light breeze blew my words back into my face. Skip was moving surprisingly well, but his injured leg was stiff and slowed him down considerably. I passed Woody and told him to stop climbing and wait for Steve. He didn't give any indication he'd heard me as I continued down the slope as fast as I dared. I finally stopped to catch my breath and yelled as loudly as I could, "Skip, wait up." He heard me this time and turned around, watching me trying to run to where he'd stopped.

"What's Woody doing?" Skip had just spotted him slowly climbing back up the grade he was supposed to be descending. "Woody. Woody! Turn around. Woody!" Frustration put an edge on his voice. By this time I'd reached him. "Damn, what's going on?"

"He's really out of it, Skip, and even if he weren't he'd be too slow for you to make the scheduled call." I gasped out another suggestion. "Steve and I think you ought to leave him with us and head down yourself. We'll take care of him. You get a plane here. It's the only thing that makes any sense."

I could read the doubt on his face "We'll be fine," I argued. "Steve and I are both healthy and strong, and we'll keep an eye on Woody. There's nothing you can do for him that we can't. You need to get that plane here."

He thought some more, then nodded. "Okay. It's a good plan. You guys take care."

"We will. Don't worry. Just take care of yourself and get to that radio sched." I walked with him the short distance to Camp II, dropped my pack onto the ice, and sent him on with a hug.

Steve led Woody into camp and we fixed a place for him to sit while we unloaded our packs, set up a tent, and brewed some hot drinks. We helped Woody get into his sleeping bag with orders not to come out of it, then headed back up to Camp III to retrieve the rest of the gear. It was a beautiful afternoon, with the sun feeling almost warm. Our confidence and adrenaline levels were high. Partway up the traverse we stripped off our Capilene tops and laughingly took "sunbathing-in-the-Antarctic" photos. The trip up felt almost easy without packs, and we let ourselves laugh and joke and enjoy the beauty around us.

At Camp III we quickly packed the remaining gear, then sat for a few minutes on the spot where my tent had been, looking down for the last time on the magnificent view of Flamingo Peak and the ice beyond. I put my arm around Steve's shoulder and relaxed against him. "Pretty incredible, isn't it."

He put a hand on my knee. "It sure is." The bond that had formed between us on the summit had become even stronger with the life-threatening accident and hard work of the past two days. "I'm glad you're here to share it with."

"Me, too." Then the realization of what was still ahead of us hit me. "God, I hope Woody stayed in his sleeping bag. What if he had to pee and wandered off? I'd love to be able to sit a little longer, but we've still got a night and a long day ahead of us after we get this stuff back down to II."

Steve agreed that we needed to get moving, and we helped each other adjust the heavily loaded packs to our backs. "Hey Steve. Are you limping?" I was walking behind him on the descent and noticed him favoring his right side.

"Toe hurts like hell. But I'll be okay."

Great, I thought, what if Steve isn't able to make it down with his load? "I sure hope Skip makes it down for the radio call tonight. We need all the help we can get."

"You're right about that one." Steve was keeping up a steady pace, even with his obvious pain. "And I thought getting to the top would be the hard part!"

"Me too." It was so much like life. I always thought that once I arrived somewhere, life would be easy. What I'd found was that even in recovery, each step simply opened up new vistas, greater challenges, more choices. Vinson wasn't any different: stay in the present, take one step at a time, trust that there's a power greater than myself holding everything together. Life and mountains, there was magic in how they were fitting together for me.

At camp, Steve glanced over his shoulder. "You check on Woody. I'll get the stove going for dinner and hot drinks."

To my relief Woody was still in our tent, although disoriented. I worked with Steve to fix a soup and rice combination and dished it into the cup Woody was holding. After he'd eaten, Woody wanted to rinse his dishes.

"There won't be enough water for that, Woody," I said. "Just clean them out the best you can for now. We'll wash them at Base Camp." He wandered off to the tent, but returned, cups in hand, an hour and a half later when Steve and I were finishing filling the last water bottle. "Woody! We'll get them clean tomorrow." Exasperated, I said. "Steve, you've got to deal with him. I'm at the end of my rope."

I don't know what Steve said. I didn't really care. I just wanted to get into my sleeping bag, and when I did, I passed out. Earlier, Steve and I had decided that he and Woody would start down at 10:00 A.M. He'd help Woody down to the top of the couloir and the fixed rope and get him started down. He would carry Skip's heavily loaded expedition pack, leaving it clipped onto the fixed ropes, while I took down the tents and packed the rest of the equipment. He'd come back for a second carry, and together we'd get everything down to Camp I. From there we could use the sleds for the last haul all the way to Base.

The electronic whine of my alarm jarred me out of a deep sleep. I had set it for 8:00 A.M. to help get Steve and Woody off by 10. I wished I could have had another couple of hours' rest, but that was a luxury we couldn't afford until we were safely down. Just one more day, then all we'd have to do was wait for an airplane out of Base Camp, to Patriot Hills, then on to Punta Arenas, and for me to Greenwich for Christmas with the folks. First I had to get through today.

We packed Skip's large pack with as much loose gear as it would hold. Steve struggled to get his boot on. His toe, severely frostbitten, was ugly, swollen, and very painful.

I cringed just watching him force his foot into the plastic boot. "Are you going to be able to make it?"

"We're too close to stop now. I'll be fine." His stoic determination matched his physical strength.

"I'll be ready to go by the time you get back. Take it slow and easy. We should start looking for the plane. I'm sure Skip's gotten through by now."

"I sure hope you're right." He turned to Woody, who was standing still, not registering any emotion or awareness that anything was happening around him. "Come on, Woody, let's get you down the ropes. We can tow you from the bottom to Base Camp, if we have to."

I pulled down the tents, folded them, and stuffed them into their protective sacks. I had buried my emotions but I could feel them pushing toward the surface as I imagined what it would feel like to get to Base Camp, to be able to relax while someone else worried about cooking and packing and being responsible. My exhaustion and stress were getting to me, but I knew I couldn't indulge myself now.

Steve arrived just as I finished packing. "How's it going?" he said.

"Great. Everything here's ready to roll." I stood up, and Steve helped me to swing my pack onto my back. "How's the foot?" I was surprised he'd made it back so quickly.

"Okay as long as I don't think about it." He was obviously in great pain and pushing through it.

It seemed like forever just to make the traverse and climb up to the fixed ropes at the top of the couloir. Once we were there, we found Woody still waiting at the top. We had four packs now, and decided to leave the largest and heaviest attached to the fixed ropes to be collected later. It didn't have any essential gear and would be only one long day's climb from Base Camp.

"Come on, Woody, let's get going." Steve and Woody started down while I secured the extra pack, then followed. Slowly, painfully, we inched our way along the rope. The snow had deteriorated since we'd come up, having been melted and refrozen by the changing temperatures. It was slippery slush in some places, hard ice in others, making the descent tricky, even with the fixed line. I'd negotiated the slope below the couloir and was almost at Camp I when I heard the throb of an engine. I stopped walking to see if my ears were playing tricks on me.

"Steve. Woody." I yelled back to them. Steve was close enough to hear me. "Listen!" An orange-and-black Cessna came into view flying low along our route toward the couloir and Camp II. It appeared to be flying through a haze. I hadn't even noticed the ground fog we were moving into. Steve and I screamed and jumped up and down, but the plane droned on, then disappeared. We were sure that it would return. It didn't. "What do you think? Did they see us?"

"I don't know, Margo. It sure seems strange that they didn't circle or anything. Maybe they were radioing our position to someone they let off at Base Camp." I could tell he was trying to be hopeful. "I'll lay odds we'll meet someone climbing up to reach us as we head on down."

"Man, I hope so." We had reached Camp I and were watching the sky hopefully, willing the plane to reappear. It didn't. "I'll load up the sled with the extra gear and get started. Can you wait here for Woody to make sure he gets here? I'll send whoever I meet on up to help you out." My expectations were so high that tears began to run down my cheeks. Adrenaline pumped me into an almost frantic pace as I loaded the sled with more than 50 pounds of gear and lifted my own pack, nearly 40 pounds by itself, onto my back. I looked over my shoulder and saw Steve sitting, still searching the sky. Hope. It was as good a drug as any I'd ever taken.

Soon the fog closed in so completely, I couldn't see 5 feet in any direction. The temperature dropped drastically. I pushed on. After a while it seemed I should have reached Base Camp. Was I lost? What happened to the plane? What happened to the people it dropped off who should have been here to help us by now? And where was Steve? I came to a place where the trail turned 40 degrees to the left, abruptly, and there was a spot where a tent had obviously been set up and taken down.

"Oh my God, somebody took the Weather Haven." The Weather Haven was the large, community tent at Base Camp, and was the marker I had been looking for. Into the thick mist, I said, "Oh my God, I'm lost. I'm in the middle of the Antarctic—and I'm lost!" I couldn't see anything. No one knew where I was. I'd never felt so alone. Oh my God. Oh my God! Panic had my chest in a vise. I talked to myself out loud, countering the fear. "Easy, Margo. Don't lose it yet."

I continued walking for a few minutes more. I was going uphill, it didn't seem right. I didn't trust that this was the main trail that would lead to Base Camp. It seemed to be taking me too long, and in the wrong direction. What if I was heading into the middle of nowhere? I reversed course and rounded the bend in the trail, back the other way. But wait, I had come from there; it couldn't be this way. I turned again, and followed the trail up the gradual rise below the empty tent site but decided it wasn't right either and turned around another time, all the while dragging the sled behind me, making tracks in the snow.

Since leaving Camp I, I had moved through optimism to despair to tears to trudging; from God-supported strength to acceptance to anger to fear, and now I was close to panic. Reaching the abandoned tent site for the fourth time, I stopped. "Breathe, Margo. This isn't getting you anywhere. Just breathe for a minute and think." I had to reassure myself that I wasn't going to freeze to death; I had my down parka and pants. "Okay, death is not going to happen." I spoke my thoughts out loud as if the words would ground me somehow, bring me back into my power. "God, what is this about? I've worked my ass off, now I'm lost out here by myself. Where is the damn Weather Haven?" I screamed my exhaustion and frustration into the blanket of fog, tears staining the inside of my glacier glasses. "I don't want to be out here by myself."

I took several deep breaths, releasing the emotions with the words. "Okay, that's better. I know Steve and Woody are somewhere behind me. The worst that can happen if I continue back-tracking is I'll end up back at Camp I, get some sleep, and do this again when the visibility is better. The best that can happen is that I'll run into Steve and not be alone anymore." I decided to continue back up the trail I had come down. I'd been walking for more than four hours since leaving Camp I on a trip that should have taken less than three.

Within minutes the sun broke through, clearing the fog, and there was Steve towing his sled behind. "I've never been so glad to see a friendly face in all my life!" I was too exhausted to cry. Then I realized Steve was alone. "Where's Woody?"

"He's coming. The fog seemed to be clearing ahead of me and I've been following your tracks. He's following mine. With two sets of sled tracks he'll make it okay."

With the ground fog lifting, we could make out the established trail more clearly. Twenty minutes past where I'd turned around, there was the Weather Haven and Skip. The three of us hugged each other tightly. He was obviously as glad to see us as we were him.

"Where's Woody?" Skip's concern was evident as he looked over our shoulders.

"Not far behind us," Steve said. "He's doing okay, just moving slowly. Where's the plane?"

"It's weathered in, ten miles away on the Nimitz Glacier with Hall, Ball, the doctor at Patriot Hills, and Warren all jammed into a three-man tent in a blizzard." Skip told the story. "I missed the radio call last night but talked to Patriot Hills this morning, and they took off right away. They flew over Base Camp but couldn't land because of the ground fog, and chose to land in the next valley over to wait while our weather cleared. They figured it wouldn't take more than a couple of hours. Now they can't take off because of a storm there." I shook my head at the image of four large men scrunched into a three-man tent with the wind howling outside.

My heart sank as I realized that their desire to help us had put them there. Gary and Rob had only been in Patriot Hills a few hours when Skip's call for assistance came. Despite being tired from their own climb, and without taking time to celebrate their enormous feat, they immediately flew back to Base Camp to help us. Their generosity was impressive but didn't come as a surprise. It was their nature and the unspoken code of the mountains to help another climber who needs it. Now they were stuck.

We had another round of hugs when Woody arrived an hour and a half later. At last, we were all down off the mountain, safe and relatively sound.

Three days later I stood outside the Weather Haven, shielding my eyes from the glare, watching the Cessna on its final approach. The waiting had been uneventful but long: time filled with crossword puzzles, scheduled radio contacts, and inventing new meals with the same old food. Our hopes were raised each time voices broke through the static on the radio, then dashed as weather reports of ground fog here and blizzard conditions on the Nimitz continued. Laughter always emerged, though, at the outrageous, sometimes embarrassing, jokes told over the radio by Gary Ball.

"Gary, there's a woman listening," I reminded him after one particularly graphic sheep joke.

"I haven't forgotten, Maggot." His smile came through the radio loud and clear as he used the nickname he'd bestowed on me two days before. "Just thought you could use some proper Kiwi educating."

Two days earlier, I'd walked out to the blue barrel marking the end of the makeshift runway and wept in solitude. I'd reached the end of my rope and needed to find an extra length somewhere. All three men, although remarkably fine, were affected by their injuries. As the only uninjured one in the group, I took responsibility for doing everything I could so they could rest and heal. Yet I was severely exhausted and wanted just to fold up in someone's arms, to be comforted and taken care of.

At the end of the runway, I collapsed, one more time, into the place where God and Jonathan and my inner family gave me the strength to do what I thought was impossible. I breathed into their essence, into my Truth, and felt the calming energy that was always there for me. They comforted the little girl who only wanted to go home, to stop working so hard, to give up responsibility. I gazed out across the ice at the exquisite, desolate beauty of Antarctica. I felt strong and capable as a mountaineer. I'd done things on this mountain that would have been impossible for me a year ago. The same sources of strength that filled me now had allowed me to access an internal power—physical, mental, and emotional—that I'd never felt before. I turned and walked back to the Weather Haven, smiling, holding my head high, knowing I could do whatever was necessary to care for myself and support the guys until our plane arrived.

Now, two days later, here it was, touching down on the ice. Scott ushered Skip and Woody into the four-seater, and Warren took off for Patriot Hills as quickly as possible for the hour-long flight. They would finally have the medical attention they needed. Gary dashed up the couloir to "rescue" Skip's pack. He and Rob would ride the third shuttle back to Patriot Hills after he returned. When Warren and Scott came back for Steve and me my heart filled with relief and gratitude as we rose above the ice. Although I wouldn't be entirely at ease until Gary and Rob were also back at Patriot Hills, an enormous weight lifted from my soul. We'd done it. A successful summit, an accident that might have had tragic consequences, an epic descent. I knew I would never be the same and was open to whatever adventures were waiting for me as I made my way toward the rest of the Seven Summits.

CHAPTER EIGHT
A Perfect Day in Paradise

Monday, January 7, 1991, San Diego
My wonderful feeling is being eroded by the way
I'm eating. It's about comfort. A soothing to
the discomfort I'm feeling about putting myself
out there publicitywise. A soothing comfort
just to life itself. A soothing comfort. Period.

When I returned home from Vinson, I gave my life over to my quest for the Seven Summits and all it entailed. Daily revelations, reflections of the pattern now evolving as the fabric of my life, sent my emotions reeling. When it would have made sense for me to savor my personal triumphs, I instead struggled constantly with food. Even with five years of recovery from my eating disorder, I still, all too often, related to my disease in a way that kept it active in my mind rather than dormant. Questions about what I ate, how much I ate, and why I ate it became weapons I constantly used to beat myself up emotionally dragging myself down every time I felt I was making progress toward my dreams.

Popcorn and ice cream became elements in an elaborate, surreptitious scheme to comfort myself, like a little girl who pulls her old satin-lined "blankie" off the high shelf in the closet. These foods and other old behaviors seemed to ease the distress caused by the changes, challenges, and success I was experiencing, and I chose those behaviors all too often, despite knowing that the perceived relief was illusory and that I would pay a price in the long run.

Giving up alcohol and drugs was easy compared to recovering from my eating disorder. The people in my 12-Step recovery groups pointed out, "Margo, if you don't take the first drink, you won't get drunk." It had worked perfectly. I'd been able to learn a whole new way of living in the world. But I had to keep eating, and the limits were harder to maintain. I'd succeeded in learning to define what abstinence looked like for me and how I could still nourish my body. I'd learned how to eat in a way that gave me enough strength to reach the summits I was climbing and still remain abstinent. But now at home I found myself pushing all of the limits I'd set around foods and behaviors, even occasionally using laxatives. I remained abstinent, but according to its technical definition rather than in its spirit. My self-judgment became more destructive than my behavior.

Sometimes I prayed about letting go of my disease more completely, sometimes I wrote about it in my journal, and sometimes I talked about it with Becky and others whom I trusted.

"Damn it, Beck, why does it have to be so hard?" We were sitting on the beach "catching rays" in what had become part of our Sunday ritual.

"It doesn't."

At times, Becky's clarity and the simplicity of her answers really angered me. I took a deep breath. "Well, it feels hard. God, I hate struggling! I surrender and surrender and surrender, and I still go back to the old patterns. I go out for lunch to justify eating big portions. I bring home videos, have a bag of popcorn, and finish off a pint of ice cream. Not all the time, but often enough that it's showing in my sanity and in my body."

"As long as you entertain your disease, your eating will be a struggle, Margo. I wish I could tell you something different, but that's my experience. Don't cut your eating disorder any slack. Surrender. You can't ever win, it's bigger and much more powerful than you. It'll win every time until you're dead."

I knew she was telling me the truth. "It's so much easier on a mountain. Here my 'real life'—career, bills, talking to people about what I'm doing—feels like a distraction from the satisfaction I get when I'm climbing. I always believed that the closer I got to living my dream, the easier this stuff would become, but I think the road's getting narrower instead of wider."

I was experiencing myself very differently in the world since I'd committed to the Seven Summits. Newspapers and television stations interviewed me—even my hometown paper, *The Greenwich Times,* wanted to do a feature. I overcame my fears of what people would think of me, as well as my doubts that I deserved their interest. I discovered I enjoyed being interviewed, seeing articles in print, and acknowledging that I did have something to share. But there was always the nagging sense that somehow I wasn't doing enough, wasn't being enough. The cycle repeated itself time and again. I'd have some positive experience, then I'd judge it, question my value in the world, and finally find some old belief that could, if I let it, destroy the path I was on.

"I'd just like to feel peaceful," I told Becky, "and satisfied, really satisfied, with an interview or when someone says they admire what I'm doing. But my head keeps saying, 'If they only knew the truth about you . . .' "

"I understand." Becky was in the middle of sending her truth out into the world in ways that made my climbing mountains seem easy: writing a book about what she believed, founding a treatment program using her principles, and having others entrust their lives to her ideas. "Some days, I have to *act* like I trust God, because it doesn't feel like I do. Sooner or later my attitude changes, the feelings change, and life looks different. As long as I'm still alive I get to feel the good along with the hard stuff. You do, too—I've been with you while you've gone through it."

I was grateful for the history I had with Becky. She gave me perspective when mine got buried.

"You'll grow through this, too, Margo. You're doing incredible things, and your disease, that part of you that helped you survive for so long, is scared that it's losing you. It's fighting for its survival. Let it die. You don't need it anymore. Let the truth you're learning about yourself be your foundation rather than the lies you used to believe about yourself. They're comfortable because they're familiar. You simply used to give in to your disease, now you've learned to struggle with it. The next step will be letting it go. You'll see."

Wanting to be feminine and liking to work out hard, to put in the physical effort required to get me to the top of the highest summits in the world also seemed like a conflict. One day, as I completed the final lift of my third set of squats with 175 pounds, I grunted loudly and felt the strain in my legs and the sweat dripping off the end of my nose. Breathing hard, I replaced the bar on the rack and backed off, with an intense feeling of satisfaction.

"Good going, you little stud muffin." Don, my trainer, had dubbed me that several months ago as we worked on what he called my "superhuman" legs. I hadn't been comfortable with the label but knew he meant it as a compliment. "Great job! Now time for your run."

I headed out the door of the gym dressed in running tights and a T-shirt. I was aware of my sweat giving off the scent of healthy exercise. As I turned the corner toward my standard 5-mile loop alongside Mission Bay, my mind flashed an image of my mother. Her disapproval pressed more heavily on my heart than the weights I'd just been lifting.

Always neat and tidy, always socially appropriate, my mother was a lady in all aspects of her life. She couldn't understand how having fun was more important to me than staying clean. As a little girl, I'd run into the house on a Saturday afternoon, shirttails out, knees of my pants muddy, pigtails askew, sweat cutting paths in the grime on my face. Giggling and overflowing with tales of my day, I'd say, "Mum, guess what we did this afternoon!"

"Look at you. What a mess! What would people think? Take off those filthy clothes and take a bath. I don't understand how you can get that dirty. And why do you sweat so much? It's simply not ladylike." Although her words always splashed cold water on the fire of my enthusiasm, I'd usually try again.

"But Mum, we played kick the can, and I hid in a—"

"Go on. Upstairs with you. You can tell me about it when you're clean and dressed for dinner."

Dejected, not understanding what had just happened, I'd go upstairs and do as I was told. I knew she loved me, but her love couldn't overcome her aversion to dirt and sweat. I learned to believe there was something wrong with me because I ran and played and got sweaty and dirty. I was not a "lady."

I ran rhythmically on the path by the bay, thinking, "God, help me to let it go. I've bought into so much of what Mum said. I can be strong and still be okay as a woman. Help me to allow my softness and sensitivity to exist alongside my strength. I want to be comfortable being who I am. I want to like the woman I am, to accept without shame my body and my sweat and my sexuality. Being feminine isn't always dressing in frills or skirts. It doesn't have to be one or the other. There's nothing wrong with how I am as a woman."

I aimed other thoughts toward my mother, too. "Mum, I love you a lot and you give me so much, but I don't want to be the kind of woman you are. I don't want to be rigid and put off by my natural bodily functions and afraid of the truth of who I am. I celebrate the woman I am with my strong body and sensitive spirit: sometimes forceful, sometimes vulnerable, sometimes salty with sweat, and sometimes salty with tears. I'm not you, Mum, I'm Margo, and I celebrate me."

Despite my strong words, or maybe because of them, I was compelled to comfort myself with popcorn and ice cream for dinner that night. I'd made a lot of progress in the past five years toward becoming a woman I could respect, and I no longer ate from the time I woke up until the time I went to sleep. Yet, I still held on to the last bit of my disease.

I had a similar process of discovery in my career. I was supposed to be accumulating hours of supervised counseling for my Marriage, Family, Child Counselor License, but one large hospital couldn't take me. Neither could a second; a third replied with a rejection, too. What was this about? I had my M.S., but all the doors seemed to be closing. Had I made a mistake? Was this not really God's will for me? Was I not meant to be a counselor? Or was it simply that it wasn't going to look the way I thought it would? Certainly, that had been a constant theme in my recovery: I had to let go of my will and let my life take its natural course. Do the footwork, but then release control of the results and trust the process.

So, what was I going to do about my career? What was the lesson in the internships falling through? Was I meant to make Everest the focus for the next year, and put the career on hold? Was there something else I was supposed to be doing? I took the questions with me on my next run.

Running had become my meditation time. The rhythm of my breathing, the measured pace of each foot hitting the ground, and the mantra that had come into my head out of nowhere one day, "God's love, God's strength, God's will, I can," combined to create a quiet center from which answers to difficult questions often revealed themselves.

That day the images that appeared in response to my questions were not at all what I'd thought they'd be. I had expected visions of jobs at treatment centers or psychiatric hospitals or with private therapists. Instead, I invisioned adventure travel: mountains, the Pacific Crest Trail, the Grand Tetons, fifty-two peaks in Colorado over 14,000 feet high, the Zambezi River, giving a slide show in a school auditorium in Idaho. Could I make a living doing what I most loved to do? Could I climb and hike and travel and run rivers and make a living sharing those experiences with others in a way that touched them and motivated them to be the best that they could be?

It certainly seemed as if those doors were opening and others weren't. My running pace quickened unconsciously as the possibilities expanded and my excitement grew. Could this be my path? I would so love it! Could it be? I'd never know if I didn't try.

I decided then to do it. I would walk through the open doors, write letters, put myself out there, and schedule more workshops at Canyon Ranch. The hurricane that had howled inside my gut for the past two days blew itself out, and I felt calm. I had a direction now. I had no idea where it would lead, but I had a direction.

The very next day I received a call from the *San Diego Tribune* requesting an interview with me, and a local television talk show expressed interest in my being on their program. Another journey had begun. I had climbed three of the Seven Summits, Mount McKinley was next on my list. I'd let God handle my schedule, I had training to do.

Wednesday, June 5, 1991, Camp 1, Mount McKinley
Sitting on an Ensolite pad minding the stoves. A
perfect day in Paradise today. Almost too
perfect. Very hot at times.

"Yeee-hah!" It was three o'clock in the morning and someone in the Fantasy Ridge expedition's camp was yelling.

I had just fallen asleep after humping gear nearly 2,000 vertical feet, up the tediously long slog known as Ski Hill, to the 9,500-foot level of Camp II. "What the—" I was tired, more than tired, and my first reaction to being awakened was to be mad. Then I heard the roar. An avalanche—a big one, judging by the sound.

"Do you hear that?" Linda asked.

"I think it's close." Adrenaline couldn't motivate my tired body to get up and look. The opportunity passed quickly as the roar faded, and I was left with a racing heart.

Four nights had passed since I'd arrived on the first of two single-engine planes that brought the six of us to the 7,200-foot altitude of Base Camp. We'd flown from Talkeetna, the small Alaskan frontier town used as an operations base by the air taxis serving McKinley. Four of us, Bob, Jordan, Linda, and me, had climbed together on Aconcagua. The fifth member, Rex, had been on the trek in Patagonia and, of course, Skip was with us, so this trip was a reunion with friends. We'd faced other challenges and achieved mutual goals together, and we welcomed the opportunity to climb together again.

Bright, warm sunshine, clear, cold nights, and just a little light snow tossed in for good measure made for good conditions as we began to move our gear up the mountain in stages, just as on Aconcagua and Vinson. Here we could use sleds the full length of the Kahiltna Glacier: 11 miles of ever-increasing slope that would take us to Camp III at 11,000 feet.

On a clear day, Mount McKinley can be seen from both Fairbanks and Anchorage. At 20,320 feet it is the highest summit on the North American continent. It also happens to be the highest summit any-where above 50 degrees north latitude and has the greatest vertical rise of any other mountain on earth, 18,500 feet from tundra to summit. Denali, meaning "The Great One," was the name given to the twin peaks that top this mountain by the native people who hunted along its flanks. Denali is the name preferred within the climbing community and by the increasingly large number of tourists who visit the large national park surrounding it.

Dr. Frederick Cook took credit for having reached Denali's lower, north, summit in 1906. Members of his own party disputed the claim, however, and photographs allegedly proving his accomplishment were later proved to have been taken from a point much lower on the mountain. During a barroom debate on the matter in Fairbanks, four "sourdoughs," prospectors who'd come to Alaska for the gold, decided to try to climb Denali themselves. On April 3, 1910, they successfully reached the lower, north, summit while carrying a 14-foot-long spruce pole, which they planted close to the summit, complete with a large flag, hoping it could be seen from below as proof of their accomplish-ment. The slightly higher, south, summit was climbed three years later by a group led by the Episcopal Archdeacon of the Yukon, Dr. Hudson Stuck. The next expedition to Denali wouldn't come until the 1930s, when planes were first used to drop supplies. Today the West Buttress route following the Kahiltna Glacier on the south side of the mountain is the most heavily traveled. It was first explored in the 1950s, using ski-equipped planes to establish a base camp on the glacier.

During the first forty years of its climbing history, nearly 250 people succeeded in reaching Denali's summit. In its second forty years, the number grew to nearly 6,000. Still, only about half of those who get to the glacier ever make it to the actual summit. Climbers are drawn to Denali like moths to a flame, her relative accessibility and well-established routes offering a prize within the grasp of many mountain-eers. But the mountain can be deadly. Like every other major peak, she controls the destiny of everyone who steps foot on her. Treacher-ous winds and fierce storms are matched by extreme temperatures that fluctuate from +80 to –60 degrees. Long climbs on glaciers present the constant threat of hidden crevasses, and her snow-covered slopes are susceptible to avalanches. Added to these is the physical strain put on a human body venturing into the rarefied air of 20,000 feet. Dehydration, exhaustion, and high-altitude sicknesses can kill climbers as readily as falling off steep ridges or into giant, seemingly bottomless, crevasses.

A sense of easy companionship had pervaded Base Camp. A steady stream of climbers heading out of the landing site formed what looked like trails of worker ants, moving ponderously in line down to the main glacier. Each member of the team carried a large pack. Most trailed heavily loaded sleds behind. Those returning were exhausted from having spent two or three weeks in this harsh environment. Some skied down the glacier, most trudged wearily, but everyone reached the base of Heartbreak Hill, the aptly named 300-foot rise directly below the landing area.

We took two days to acclimate to the altitude, sort our gear, and practice some crevasse rescue techniques in the shadow of the incredibly rough, almost fearsome mountains rising around us. Denali dominates its closest neighbors, 17,400-foot Mount Foraker and 14,573-foot Mount Hunter and the thousands of other peaks within the Alaska Range. The scale of every ridge seemed more grand than anything I'd seen before. The combination of ice, snow, and exposed rocks against the blue sky provided a sense of magic and wonder that sometimes took my breath away. Standing at the shelf we'd carved out of the ice for our kitchen, we had a view that went on forever. Since climbing Vinson, I felt comfortable with the routine of camp and took an active part in setting up tents, sorting the wands we'd use to mark our route, and preparing meals. We experimented with some funky "snowshoes." It was rather like hooking oval-shaped upside down pie plates with straight sides to our boots, but they helped keep us from sinking into the snow on the glacier. Fear and self-judgment were never far away, but my confidence and the companionship of the group helped my attitude tremendously. Another distraction was Vern Tejas, the first man to complete a solo winter ascent of Denali, who was guiding a commercial group. Skip introduced me to him as Vern was playing the fiddle he always brought with him on a climb. The music was beautiful, the performer almost comical. His lean frame clad from the neck down in red polypro and bright blue running shorts, he stood in the snow, his shaved head and full, dark beard offset by an 8-inch tail of hair. I was in awe of this climbing legend, with his easy, playful style that set people at ease and welcomed them into his world.

On our third day we made our first carry of supplies to Camp I. It took us nearly four hours to cover the distance, gaining only about 400 feet in altitude but taking several miles to do it on the long, sloping ascent up the glacier. The greatest task of this day was keeping the rope connecting Skip, Bob, and me from sliding under the sled directly in front of me. The rope, a lifeline against possibly fatal falls into crevasses, was a new ingredient for me, and I struggled to maintain just the right amount of tension: too tight and Bob was dragged backward or I was pulled forward onto my face; too loose and the rope became caught under his sled. I was sore after the hard work of the first day's carry with a heavy load. I knew my jerky pace would smooth out as I got more practice pulling a sled and climbing while roped to others. If I experienced pain, I could get beyond it. And I knew that I could be uncomfortable with the cold and the wind we expected farther up and still function, still participate, still make the summit. I was exhilarated that we'd finally begun our climb, and I looked forward to the days ahead.

The next day, we moved the rest of our gear to Camp I, climbing through ground fog reminiscent of Vinson, then clouds and fairly heavy, wet snow. We feasted on a dinner of brown rice with cheese, onion, and sun-dried tomatoes, and after everyone had his or her fill, I sent Skip off to bed while I finished the dishes in the snow. Participation, anticipation, and gratitude filled my heart when I thought about our carry to Camp II tomorrow and saw the changing light on the mountains as the sun swung around its elliptical course. Here, too, at the opposite end of the earth from Mount Vinson, the sun touched the horizon but never quite set in its summertime dance of eternal light.

The intense sun during the day raised the temperature and softened the snow on the Kahiltna Glacier, making it more comfortable and safer to take advantage of the long hours of daylight and climb in the evening. We left about 5:00 P.M. for the carry to Camp II at 9,500 feet. Traveling in two ropes of three climbers each, our group inched its way for an hour up the glacier to the foot of Ski Hill, the steepest portion of the climb to Camp II. It felt like trudging through eternity, and at times my tears came without warning. I couldn't find any rhythm in my gait, I was angry at Skip for speeding up the pace, and Martha was angry at me for "being such a wimp." Neither Skip nor I deserved the anger, whether spoken or not. God got me to Camp II. The way I was feeling I couldn't have done it on my own.

As we moved back down the mountain, my right foot cramped, forcing me to stop, pull off my boot, and rub it out before I could continue. "Shoot," I muttered, "not again." It was just like on Vinson. Although cramping had not been a problem during my training at home, it clearly was a problem on a climb. I would have to address it before Everest. "Nothing I can do about it now," I said to myself, putting my boot back on. "Let's go, gang." My inner family infused me with energy and, warily, I continued to put one foot in front of the other.

On our fifth morning of the expedition, we all slept in and after a late breakfast spent the afternoon leisurely working on equipment and packing the sleds for our move up to Camp II that night. Our activity took place among the tents, within the perimeter of the ice-block walls we'd built for protection from McKinley's legendary winds. Some in the group had done laundry and spread their clothes out on the tents to dry. The sun was warm, and everyone was enjoying the lazy pace of the afternoon and the sight of ridge after ridge of black rock rising out of the pure white of the glacier and into the majestic peaks towering far above us.

Suddenly, the gunshot sound of an avalanche breaking loose ricocheted across the glacier. From the loudness and the growing roar, I knew that, like last night's, this one was big—and close. I looked up and saw the chute, directly behind camp, that had given way. A boiling white cloud filled the space where moments before there had been ice and rock. As the avalanche swept down and hit the surface of the glacier, it rebounded in a great storm of snow billowing from the surface of the ice, pushing a gale-force air blast before it. The mass of driven snow—spindrift—filled the air like spray blown off a wave in a hurricane. Our camp stood directly in its path. Linda and Bob grabbed some of the clothes spread around to dry, and everyone dove for cover. I closed the flap on our tent just as the wind blast and spindrift reached us. It felt as though a giant was blowing out the candles on his birthday cake, and the tent was one of the candles.

"Well, Margo, you said you wanted to see a big avalanche." Linda was smiling. I answered with a smile of my own and was very glad to have another woman on the climb.

"Wasn't it great?" As far as I was concerned, I'd already received more than I'd come for. My mood had shifted 180 degrees from the day before, when physical pain and emotional discomfort had nearly overwhelmed me. I could hardly wait for whatever else was in store as we made our way, one camp at a time, to the summit.

This night's climb to Camp II seemed far easier than that of the day before, even though both my sled and pack were heavier. It was my attitude and energy level that made the difference, and I was grateful for the improvement. We arrived at Camp II after midnight and went about our routine, now comfortably familiar. I smiled with contentment as Linda and I said our good-nights.

In the morning I didn't feel well. As we prepared to move out for Camp III, I told Skip, "I feel lousy and will need to go slow." Once again my monthly cycle seemed to be at cross purposes with what I needed to do on a mountain.

"Margo, it's not fair to slow everyone else down. Just lighten your sled so you can keep up." Skip's statement was very reasonable, but I was too proud to take much gear off the sled. Five steps out of camp, I knew the load was too heavy. But I kept quiet. It was a wonderful day, and I only felt miserable. For several hours, I was able to put one foot in front of the other almost automatically, but Martha harangued me. "You can't do this. You can't just tell them you're exhausted and have cramps. If you were sick they'd understand. Then it'd be okay not to be able to make it. If something was wrong, they'd feel sorry for you instead of being impatient at your slowness." The thoughts had been born many years before, but the fatigue and pain were real.

I called for a number of rest stops and imagined wrath and judgment from the others. I heard Skip's words in my head, "It's not fair to slow everyone down." Almost reflexively, I reverted to the familiar behavior of inventing physical ailments: I faked dry heaves and dizziness to justify my slow pace because I had lost faith that it was okay simply to be what I was—emotionally off and physically exhausted.

Finally, as the slope steepened, even Jonathan's spirit and God couldn't give me the strength to haul my sled one more step.

"I'm in pretty big trouble, Skip." It was the third time I'd called for a stop in 20 minutes. I just wanted to lie down.

I could hear Skip's impatience in his voice. "You'd better make up your mind if you're going to leave the sled behind. It's got your tent and the kitchen on it, so if it's not going to get there today, we need to put that stuff on another sled."

Defeated, I answered, "I can't get this sled up that hill."

Skip loaded the essentials from my sled onto his and anchored the abandoned sled with a picket to be retrieved later. His sled was now overloaded and top heavy. It overturned at the slightest excuse. Time after time, swearing out loud, Skip was jerked backward by the pull as the sled turned over. On a couple of sections of the route, he resorted to making two trips, one with his pack and one carrying the sled on his back. At one point he slammed his ski pole against the snow in frustration and kicked the sled, muttering under his breath. I felt responsible: I should have acknowledged that I needed to carry lighter. I had thought I could macho my way through it, and I couldn't.

When we finally arrived at Camp III, late in the evening, I collapsed onto my pack. I held my head in my hands. I was exhausted and ashamed. I couldn't stand up. I couldn't even get my water bottle out to drink. I talked to myself: "Just sit, Margo. Breathe." Skip stood silently 10 yards to my left, his body language communicating anger and frustration as he struggled to untie the knots on the ropes that held the makeshift load on his sled. The knots were frozen tight with snow, making them difficult to untie, and he had to remove his gloves to work the knots out and free the gear. As I watched him shake his bare hands and tuck them into his armpits to warm them, I reminded myself that making a mistake did not make me worthless. It didn't mean I didn't deserve to be here. It didn't mean I needed to go home. It didn't mean I was a failure. It didn't mean I couldn't get to the top of this mountain. I breathed in the truth of my thoughts. "Okay. I need to take care of myself." I reached for my water bottle and a Power Bar and refueled my body until I felt strong enough to help Linda set up our tent.

Skip, Rex, Linda, and Bob went down to bring up the rest of the gear while Jordan and I stayed at Camp III. He dug out a latrine, and I got the stove going to have hot water for the climbers when they returned. There would be no overturned teakettle on this night! The semilight of the night sky reminded me of the Antarctic. As my watch ticked past 10:00 PM., the rich peach color of alpenglow shone on camp and the surrounding peaks, backlighting the bright colors flying from the trail-marking wands of each expedition: ours were fluorescent pink; others were lime green and black, bright orange, and deep red.

I sat in the vestibule of Skip's tent, protected from the wind, yet basking in the glory of God and Mother Nature. I was proud to be able to deal with the stoves, proud to have recovered so quickly from the frustration of the climb up here, proud to be a mountaineer. My soul was filled to overflowing. If I hadn't been exhausted, I would have been making the second carry with the others and would have missed this quiet, spiritual time. It was a special night, and it was my bonus for being willing to continue to show up, regardless of what it looked like or how it felt. My trip to Camp III had certainly not been dignified or pretty, but I got here.

Skip returned, leading the others, with an enormous smile on his face. He, too, had been reveling in the beauty of the evening and shared with me how much he loved this: being on a mountain, carrying a reasonable load, on reasonable terrain, with enough wind to keep him cool, surrounded by the exquisite beauty of an Alaskan summer night. I apologized for the difficulty with the sled and said I would go down to get it in the morning. He put an arm around me. "I was mad at the sled, not at you. I'm glad you're here, and you're doing great." We looked out over the route he'd just climbed, enjoying both the company and the view.

"Hey, guys!" It was Chip, the leader of the Fantasy Ridge expedition, just rounding the corner into camp. "I found a wand of yours an hour or so down the trail. It was attached to a sled, and I thought you might need it so I brought them both up. Are you missing one?"

Once again the Universe had smiled broadly on me.

"Bless your heart!" I hugged him as I spoke. "You've got a backrub coming any time you want." It was the best reward I could think of offering.

For two days we were trapped in our tents while the weather did its thing. Weather. The dictionary has two definitions: the scientific one about the state of the atmosphere, including temperature, moisture, wind velocity, and barometric pressure, and a second: "bad, rough, or stormy." The second definition fit perfectly. Wind and snow made travel impossible; even going to the bathroom was dangerous. Walking on white snow, in white clouds, with wind driving white snow in our faces, we had no depth perception and footprints disappeared as soon as they were made. It would have been easy to lose our way and walk into a crevasse or slip off the edge of the mountain. We moved cautiously from tent to tent, and only when absolutely necessary for food or water. Linda and I passed the time talking, reading, and writing in our journals.

With too much time to think, I worried, evaluated, and projected the wind, freezing temperatures, and physical discomfort into a failed summit attempt. We were only about a third of the way up the mountain and Martha was already telling me I might not be able to make it the rest of the way. I stopped the cycle by reminding myself that I wasn't alone, that God, Jonathan, my inner family, and my five companions were here, too. Together we were strong enough to make it. I also took action. Snow had blown in under the sides of the tent's vestibule, burying our overboots and packs. I dug them out, delivered meals to other tents, and listened as guides visited Skip, bringing their stories from other mountains and other climbs on McKinley.

The combination of a break between storms and the necessity of getting higher on the mountain if we were going to have any shot at all at the summit pushed us to make a carry partway to Camp IV to create a cache we could pick up when we made the move. Finally, the next day the weather cleared enough, and several expeditions left at the same time for Camp IV, 3,000 feet higher on the mountain.

Seven ropes, each linking three or four climbers and their sleds, moved at a crawl, breaking trail in untracked snow up the steep slope of Motorcycle Hill. Each rope looked like a string of beads: climber, sled, climber, sled, threaded together by the safety of the rope. For our climb we used team pursuit tactics, the technique developed by cyclists on a track. When the leader of the first team in line tired from the immense effort of plunging through the knee-deep snow, his entire rope moved aside, allowing the second rope in line to assume the burden. The first then fell in at the end of the long column as it passed. Skip's strength, and that of one or two of the other leaders, was awe-inspiring. Even in midline, where the track became well established, I struggled with the weight of my pack and the tugging of the sled I was pulling. In the uneven footing of the new snow, it was almost impossible to maintain a steady pace that was neither so fast it created slack in the rope ahead nor so slow it created backward pull on the climbers in front of me. Even above Motorcycle Hill, and past the surprisingly calm edge of rock known as Windy Corner where the steepness of the route was greatly decreased, the going was difficult and slow. It took us more than eight hours to reach Camp IV.

The well-populated plateau at 14,000 feet had been christened Denali Village. Nearly fifty of the hundreds of climbers on the mountain were there, regrouping, resting, and waiting to move higher. The bright colors of the various tents were a welcoming sight as we covered the last hundred yards and claimed a couple of vacated snow platforms as our own. We untied from the ropes, dropped our packs, and unhitched our sleds. It had been a full day on anybody's time clock, but in this office in the skies of Alaska our work had only begun: tents had to be put up, gear unpacked, and stoves started for hot drinks and dinner.

Fifteen minutes into the chores the sun moved behind a ridge overlooking camp, and the temperature plummeted. By the time the tents were up and the stove was roaring, we were all chilled to the bone. I felt colder than I'd ever been on a mountain, even on Vinson. Linda, an exceptionally strong woman who had been carrying very heavy loads and seemed to be growing stronger as she moved higher on the mountain, became frighteningly hypothermic. She lay on the floor of the tent, shivering violently, unable to feel her toes. I unpacked her sleeping bag and Therm-A-Rest and helped her take off her outer layers of clothing so she could get warm inside her bag while Skip and Rex worked on dinner.

"Anything we can do to help?" Jordan called through the thin tent wall, carrying the concern of the others.

"No thanks, Jordan. We're fine. Go get warm yourself. I'll be out in a sec." I could hear his teeth chattering through the nylon that separated us.

"Margo, I'm scared. I've never been so cold. Don't leave me alone." Linda's voice was pleading from within the cocoon of her sleeping bag. "Don't go." Her shivering increased; her fear was palpable and disconcerting.

"I won't. I'm right here, Linda." I rubbed her body through the loft of the sleeping bag. She seemed soothed by the contact, and as her shivering lessened, I stopped the rubbing but left my hand resting on a shoulder. I felt her body relax and her breathing ease into the quiet rhythm of sleep. It was only then that I fully realized how cold I was and tended to my own care. Swathed in my down jacket, legs stuck in my sleeping bag, I watched Linda sleep and was struck by how truly hostile this environment was. We were here only by the grace of the mountain, and she could swipe us dead as easily as a horse swatting flies with its tail. Climbers do not conquer mountains; mountains allow us to walk on their crowns, to revel in their beauty. This was not a place to take anything for granted. My toes tingled as they returned to life. I pulled my wool hat down low over my ears and crawled out into the brittle night air. Laughter echoed from around this temporary village, constructed at the acquiescence of the great goddess Denali. "God, I love it here!" I spoke the words out loud from the fullness of my heart.

We all slept hard and well that night, and the next day descended to retrieve the cache we'd left two days earlier. Once in a while I'd let myself look at the grand scale of the mountains around me, rather than where I was going to put my boot for my next step. Peaks rose above us, with ridgelines leading toward the summit and trailing down to the tundra far below. Even in mid-June, snow covered much of the landscape, the mountains resembling peaks of frosting on a cake. When we returned to camp, I tended to details, resetting tent lines hurriedly tied the night before, melting snow for water, and organizing food. Taking care of these chores made me feel like more than just a client: I was a working, valuable member of an expedition team. At last I crawled into my tent and stretched out on my sleeping bag, tired from the climb to retrieve the cache and the work I'd done around camp but filled with a great sense of accomplishment and satisfaction.

An hour earlier Jordan had acknowledged the amount of work I was doing. "I gotta tell you, Margo, you're workin' harder around here than anyone except Skip."

"Thanks for that, Jordan." I appreciated the acknowledgment, although I was a little embarrassed. I wasn't doing it for recognition, but recognition felt good. "I like doing it, and it makes me feel useful." Skip seemed to be pushing me harder on this trip than on any before, and I was responding by expecting more from myself. I was grateful to him, though sometimes I hated it.

"Dinner!!" I roused myself at the sound of Rex's voice. Feeling stiff and tired tonight, I didn't relish the thought of carrying a load up the head wall in front of us. I felt as if I were seventy rather than forty-three as I struggled out of the tent, groaning as I stretched out my body.

Skip chuckled as he watched my awkwardness. "A little sore, Margo?"

"I think perhaps you're trying to kill me." My wince broadened into a smile.

"Nope, just trying to make you into what you want to be and what I know you can be."

I patted his arm in thanks and acknowledgment as I continued on to dinner. For the first time, I felt deep inside that I really might be able to climb Mount Everest.

Three nights later, Linda, Skip, and I were standing on a knoll above Camp V at 16,200 feet, awestruck by the glory spread out below us. Linda and I had our arms linked comfortably around Skip's waist, his on our shoulders. We were speechless, tanned faces content in the warm, golden light of the late evening sun. We drank in the beauty of this magical place. In one direction, clouds moved and changed above the Peters Glacier. In another, we looked down on Camp IV, perched on the edge of the cliff known as The Edge of the World. Mount Hunter appeared mystically through the clouds. There was almost too much beauty to take in all at once. When Skip and Linda said good-night, I stayed behind, soaking in the view, while scenes from the last four wonderful days ran through my mind. Hard work, good weather, and good energy had been mixed with liberal quantities of fun, out-loud laughing, and a wonderful sense of belonging with this group of friends on an expedition.

I embraced the strength I had experienced on the carry to Camp V two days before. I'd been unsure about going. Martha had seemed to want to keep me in camp with reminders of the excruciating foot cramps I'd experienced in the couloir on Vinson that was so much like the one in front of me that day. My fear of not being able to make it to the top with a load conspired with Martha's strong belief that I had no right to be there at all.

Vern Tejas's assistant, Dolly Lefever, encouraged me to make the carry and reminded me that I didn't have to do it perfectly. "So if you get tired, you can drop your load at fourteen-six or even fifteen thousand feet. It's not a big deal. Go for it, Margo. You'll regret it if you don't." I knew she was right. Her persuasiveness convinced me to show up and do the best I could. I thought again of how much climbing was like life. The two had become woven together—each one teaching me a lot about the other.

I made the carry and made it strongly. Clipped into the fixed line, I'd enjoyed the climb at my own pace, feeling the strength in my legs and my heart. I'd discovered pleasure in the hard work, four hours of tedious climbing, and still I hadn't been tired. Jordan was practically knocked off his feet by the majesty of the dramatic view that opened up around us as we stepped up on the ridge from the head wall. He was considered a financial wizard in the field of commercial real estate at home, and his career was the love of his life, leaving little room for relationships. He took one trip a year with Skip, allowing the mountains of the world to replace work for a few weeks. Jordan looked back at me and said, "This is the best thing I have ever done."

As my attention returned to the beauty of the magical night, now above Camp V, a shadow skated over my soul, and I saw in my mind's eye the Margo of five years before: lying on the couch, surrounded by food and drugs and laxatives. She was unable to walk out the door into the world, lonely, without any hope. I held her image close to my heart. "Thank you, God," I whispered, overwhelmed by how far I'd come. Without the willingness to stay alive through the pain and hopelessness, I would never have found my dream. The horror of my past brought an even greater sense of wonder and life to the beauty around me that night.

The next day, both the weather and my attitude changed. Four expeditions were at Camp V preparing to climb the 800 feet to Camp VI at 17,000 feet. Although the wind was blowing hard, all of the expeditions needed to stage some gear up to the higher level. Skip, Rex, and Linda opted to carry ours, while Bob, Jordan, and I stayed behind.

The three of us stayed inside all day, talking, reading, and playing cards as my intestines became more and more upset. I made a dozen or more cold and windy trips to the latrine, each one resulting in increased discomfort and a deepening lethargy. It was easy for me, in that condition, to put off the chores I knew we should be doing. Another expedition had displaced our kitchen. It needed to be set up again and snow melted so there would be hot drinks for the returning climbers, but I couldn't bring myself to do the work, and I didn't ask Bob and Jordan to do it. When our three companions returned and had to take care of it themselves, Skip's disappointment and irritation were evident in his silence. Linda told me that the climb had been very trying. They'd stopped short of Camp VI because of high winds and had to stash the loads they'd carried to be picked up later. My guilt and remorse ran deep.

I felt as I had when I was a little girl and had disappointed my mom and dad. Their silence frequently was far more eloquent than any words. I'd learned to anticipate guilt even when I hadn't done anything wrong, believing I'd never be perfect enough to please them. If they ever did suggest I'd fallen short of their expectations of me, it only reinforced what I already knew.

I had been working hard, feeling good about my participation and progress as a mountaineer. Now the old belief that I was a failure if I disappointed someone I cared about was ample fodder for Martha's harangues. She told me loudly that I was weak and selfish and lazy and that she had known all along I didn't belong here. The tears of an adult Margo came from a place deep inside where a little girl felt only sadness and shame.

After dinner I lay in my tent, wrapped in the warm down of my bag, and did my best to tune out Martha's judgment, to hear instead the comforting words from my inner family: "Margo, you don't have to be Superwoman. You aren't a guide. You're a strong woman who was tired and ill today. It's appropriate that you rested."

The next day I apologized to Skip.

He said, "It doesn't feel like an expedition when stuff like that happens, Margo. It feels like me doing all the work instead of us being a team. It won't work like that." His tone of voice reflected his displeasure.

"I'm sorry," I said quietly. The tasks on a mountain needed to get done, and if I was too ill to do them, I needed to ask someone else. To leave them undone was a serious, possibly life-threatening error. "It won't happen again, Skip."

"Good." He nodded, the anger gone from his voice. "I believe that."

We broke camp early the next morning. My fingers and toes went numb quickly as we took down the tents, fixed breakfast, and waited for the wind to die down up on the ridge leading to Camp VI. They warmed up rapidly, though, as we began moving. This was my idea of true climbing—steep, difficult, windy.

In some places the ridge was only a foot or so wide and the wind blew in gusts. I used my ice axe for stability and leaned into the wind, setting each crampon carefully. I moved strongly and well, continuing along the ridge until I stepped with confidence into Camp VI. It offered a view down onto the glacier that gave me a view of the route we'd followed in a broad sense rather than as daily pieces. I could look at my recovery in the same way. All the small events added up to the journey I'd taken to get to 17,000 feet on the fourth of the

Seven Summits. This was the nineteenth mountain I'd climbed in three years. Where was my larger quest taking me? What would I see when I looked back?

Skip walked toward me as I looked out over the peaks and clouds. "Margo, I just heard some news that'll be important to you."

"Yeah? What is it?"

"Junko Tabei walked up Kosciusko last month. She's the first woman to make the Seven Summits."

My heart dropped. My dream of being the first woman to climb the Seven Summits was over. But what did that really mean? Only that I wouldn't be the first woman. "Thanks for telling me, Skip. I'm glad she got them all." My dream to climb was still alive; the gifts I experienced in the process of following my dream were still there, and weren't they, after all, the real point? "You know, climbing the Seven Summits is a wonderful dream, but it's the joy of climbing, it's times like this, that fill my soul." Nothing had really changed.

Skip smiled. "Margo, you're great. Tomorrow's the Summer Solstice, how about we summit on the solstice?"

I smiled and nodded, "Let's do it."

On June 21, 1991, Mount McKinley gave us a gift. This mountain, infamous for its horrendous weather, not only offered its summit to us, it gave us clear skies, calm air, and warm temperatures—almost 20 degrees above zero. A perfect day in paradise.

Six-and-a-half hours of climbing took us first on a traverse across the Autobahn's slope to Denali Pass, a rise of about 1,000 vertical feet. Always dangerous, the Autobahn's name recalls the out-of-control speeds of the famous German highway, a prediction of what awaits any climber who slips on its surface. At Denali Pass, we were still 2 miles and 2,000 vertical feet from the summit. We climbed the West Buttress ridge past the Archdeacon's Tower and onto the Football Field, the aptly named, slightly bowl-shaped approach to the south summit. We hiked its length to the base of the final 800-foot wall leading to the narrow final ridge with its dangerous overhanging cornice of wind-swept snow, then to the last 10-foot rise to the small platform that is the highest point in North America.

Two other expeditions had summited ahead of us, and we waited a few yards below for them to vacate the small plateau. We wanted to be there with just the six of us to share the hugs and hollers of joy, to feel the gratitude, take in the grandeur, and let the tears flow. Once on the summit, we took a lot of photos. Each of us spent some time alone with Denali's energy, I was aware of the energy of the solstice as well. Reluctantly, we left the magic there and headed down the mountain. We were only halfway through our climb. We would sleep at Camp VI, then retrace our steps through each descending camp until we reached the airplanes that would take us to Talkeetna.

My experience on Vinson had persuaded me that what guides say is true: The most dangerous part of any climb is the descent. After spending weeks getting to a summit, the climber wants to get home. The temptation is to relax: Every cell in her body says, "I want to rest. I can't walk another step." But she must. Her climb isn't complete until she's home. The edge of awareness that's so much a part of an ascent may be dulled by inattention or fatigue, allowing basic, even simple, mistakes to happen. Climbers have even been known to forget to tie themselves into their rope and have fallen to their deaths.

Our careful descent to 17,200 was uneventful, although the wind picked up, dropping the temperature and reminding us of how extraordinary our summit experience had been. I focused my attention on not catching a crampon on my Gore-Tex pant legs. I'd always been strong climbing downhill, and I found it true on Denali as well. I was grateful that my knees were holding up.

It took a little over two-and-a-half hours, less than half the time we spent getting to the top. Soon after we arrived at Camp VI, tired but in high spirits, the stove was pffft-pffft-pffft-ing happily. Rex melted snow for hot drinks. I was grateful for his willingness to tend to that chore. It had been mine the night before: a cold job, in air chilled by the shadow of the ridge above. Fatigue spoiled our appetites, so dinner was a brief affair. Our celebration would come after we got off the mountain. My sleeping bag was warm and welcoming, taking me quickly into a deep, dreamless sleep.

"Margo, Linda, I have some hot drinks for you." Skip was generously providing morning room service. He wanted to get off the mountain in two days. Today would take us to Camp III at 11,000 feet. Tomorrow we'd have dinner in Talkeetna.

We had slept for nine hours and roused ourselves in the chill of a clear Alaskan morning to pack up. Though much of the food was gone, everything that came up the mountain in our multiple carries had to go down in one, making our packs extremely heavy. As we retraced our steps down the ridge toward 16,200 feet, Bob was moving especially slowly, asking for breaks the rest of us did not seem to need. Clearly he was feeling the effects of his enormous effort on summit day. My own fatigue was manifesting as irritation with Bob, which normally would not have happened.

When we reached Camp V, we stopped briefly for a drink of water and a last taste of the view from this magnificent aerie. Then it was on to the fixed ropes leading down the steep head wall to 14,000 feet and Camp IV. Unroped from each other, but clipped into the fixed rope on the face, we each began to descend at our own pace. Every step for Bob became a Herculean effort. He was unsteady on his feet, in spite of the security of the fixed line. Halfway down, he sat for a rest and didn't get up.

"What's the matter, Bob?" Skip hollered up from below.

I was only a few feet above Bob, my own descent halted by his lack of movement. But even from where I was standing, trying to hold my position on the steep slope, I couldn't understand his mumbled response.

Skip called, "What'd you say?"

More mumbling.

"Bob, I can't hear you. What is it?"

"I'm tired, goddammit!" Bob's voice was uncharacteristically hostile.

"We're all tired. Get up, Bob. We've got to keep going."

"I can't."

"Come on, Bob. Get up and get moving. You've got people stacked up on the rope behind you. Get up." Now Skip's voice carried an edge of irritation. The steepness of the slope made it difficult for those of us above Bob to pass him safely. His refusal to move affected a growing number of climbers.

"I can't, goddammit. My ankles won't hold me up."

I'd seen his ankles buckle a couple of times as he'd descended the first half of the ropes. "Bob," I said, "you don't have a choice." I spoke quietly, almost gently, hiding my own irritation. "You can't just stay there. You've got to go down. Come on, I'll help you get up." I knew what it was like to be tired, not to be able to take another step, to be embarrassed and not care. Bob was competent, strong, a survivor. And now he was more than tired. His exhaustion was visible as he sat, slumped over his knees, his pack still on his back.

"I can't," he said again.

I looked down at Skip and shrugged. I didn't know what else to do.

Skip shook his head. Sloughing off his pack, he banged it into the snow, then clipped it in to the fixed lines so it wouldn't slide to the foot of the head wall. Quickly he climbed up to where Bob was sitting, expressionless, a condemned man without hope.

"What the hell are you doing?" The only times I'd heard Skip yell like this were when Woody was so slow on summit day on Vinson, and when I couldn't pull my own sled load up to Camp III. He was angry, but mostly he had to get Bob moving. "You've got people waiting behind you and a team relying on you, and you're sitting here like a lump. Get your ass off the snow and walk down this mountain."

"Don't you get it?" Bob was still looking down. "I can't."

"You damn well can and you damn well will. Give me your pack. I'll get that to the bottom. You just get yourself down." He hitched Bob's pack to his back and almost ran down to where he'd left his. He jury-rigged them together and looked up the hill once again. Bob hadn't moved.

"Bob! Get up, now! There isn't any time for this wimpy bullshit." Skip was digging deep into his bag of tricks, hoping he knew Bob well enough to get him on his feet. As exhausted as he was, Bob was no wimp. Skip was praying he would fight.

Bob slowly got to his feet.

I followed closely behind him, watching as he descended slowly, painfully, ankles wobbling, to the bottom of the fixed lines. The line of climbers, now fifteen strong, that had built up behind him passed by without a word as he sat in the snow with his head in his hands. I stayed with him for a few minutes but my patience had been eaten away by my own fatigue, and I rose with a shake of my head. "Get it together, Bob," I mumbled as I started down the last half hour to Camp IV. We still had 3,000 vertical feet to go before stopping for the night.

Skip, Linda, and I sat on our packs at 14,000 feet and broke out the sausage, crackers, and cheese we'd left there with the gear we didn't need at the summit. We ate our fill, resting, waiting. Bob finally arrived half an hour later. We cajoled him into eating something while we packed up the remaining gear and placed it on the sleds we'd also stashed there. Bob's pack went on a sled as well. It was all he could do to carry himself. Rex had moved on ahead. He was going all the way to base in one day to make a connection to Anchorage, and Jordan had gone with him.

Tied into a single rope, the four of us continued down to Camp III on the mostly low-angle route. It was evening by now, and the heat of the day had sabotaged our stable footing by turning the snow to slush a foot deep in places. Boots slid on the surface and feet slid inside boots, causing blisters to form. The only words spoken were occasional obscenities as, time and again, one of us slipped and had to do a quick dance step to keep from falling.

At one point I raised my head and looked out on a sea of clouds with the sun just setting behind them. It was almost midnight, and it was only because our day had been so long that we were blessed with the vision of the miraculous colors of the sun floating, reflected in the ocean of clouds. I thanked God out loud, and the remaining couple of hours into camp were not quite as painful.

We didn't have the energy to brew hot drinks when we reached camp at 3:00 A.M. We fell into our sleeping bags, thrown unceremoniously into the tents we'd hurriedly erected, and slept until we woke up naturally. We took the time then to melt water to hydrate ourselves and eat a quick breakfast. We wanted to make Base Camp that evening so we could fly out, but we had to go 4,000 vertical feet and more than 8 miles to get there. The planes quit flying at 9:00 P.M. so there was no time to lose.

When I put on my boots that morning, I counted eleven blisters on my feet, two of them the size of silver dollars. Even with liberal applications of moleskin and Second Skin, it wouldn't be a comfortable day. I knew the exact step when the largest of them broke, triggering the sharp, raw pain that comes only from an open blister that is continuing to be rubbed. I had neither the time nor the energy to feel sorry for myself, as Skip kept up a pace that felt like a forced march.

"Skip! Slow down!" I was at the end of his rope—and mine. "I can't keep my balance going this fast!" Two hours into the descent from Camp III, the snow had once again deteriorated into deep slush. We were practically running down the mountain without crampons. My boots sank in, sometimes as deep as a foot, then slid precariously on ice. "I need to stop and put on snowshoes."

"We're not going to stop until we get to Two," Skip answered, bulling ahead. "We have to stop there anyway to load that gear, and I don't want to take the time to stop now to find the snowshoes. Come on, Margo, pick it up."

I swore under my breath.

"I agree," someone nearby said.

I was angry and tired and hot and my feet hurt. Why was it so damn important to get down in time to fly out tonight? What was wrong with one more night in a tent? Nothing, as far as I was concerned, but I wasn't at the head of the rope. It was the first time I'd been really angry with Skip, and I didn't understand his obsession with getting off the mountain. I kept on going, almost at a run, arms extended wide to keep my balance, sled tugging awkwardly at my waistband. My ego and my anger kept me going. I could keep up!

We pulled out the snowshoes when we reached Camp II, and they helped a great deal: I didn't sink in nearly as far in the deep slush. Several more of my blisters had broken. My feet felt raw, like some sick butcher's idea of hamburger meat. With 2,000 vertical feet left to descend, there were still a number of miles, too many miles, to go. And at the end of it all was Heartbreak Hill.

I lost track of the hours but it was about 8:00 P.M. when Skip radioed ahead asking for planes to meet us at Base Camp. It would be a bit past the deadline but we hoped they'd make an exception.

"Skip, your planes are on their way." The operations center had come through.

It was good news and bad news. The flight from Talkeetna was about a half hour and planes can't wait at Base Camp—they either sink into or freeze to the snow. That meant we had, at the outside, an hour to climb our last obstacle. Heartbreak Hill is infamous. Not overly steep or particularly long, it is the last stretch everyone travels into Base Camp after a 17-mile descent from the highest point in North America.

We stopped at the base of it, trying to force down some cheese, having no sense of how we were going to get to the top. Skip was carrying an enormous pack and hauling an even heavier sled. Linda, too, was doing heroic duty. Bob was speechless from exhaustion despite his light pack and lack of sled. And I was done in—physically, mentally, and emotionally. I looked up the hill and felt Jonathan's spirit but still knew I simply didn't have the strength to get both me and the sled to the planes. The shame of having left my sled on the way up to Camp III washed over me once again, and I felt like a failure.

The radio crackled again. "Plane's on the way. Better hurry up." Hurry up? Christ, I wasn't sure I could even get up that hill at all, much less hurry.

Skip stood up. "Okay, let's do it." His voice carried echoes of weariness.

I wiped tears from my cheeks, took a deep breath, stood up, and said to my team inside, "Listen up, everybody. Somehow we gotta get up this hill. I can't do it on my own. I need all of you to help."

I noticed two people walking down the hill from Base Camp as we were psyching ourselves up to climb the last 300 feet to the landing strip. They weren't roped and didn't have packs, which was very unusual. The fantasy that they were coming to help us entered my brain and left just as quickly. There was an unwritten law that everyone hauls his own loads up Heartbreak Hill: it's Denali's final challenge. Still, it was a nice fantasy.

They appeared to be heading for us when we started walking. I turned to Linda. "Do you think they're coming to help us?"

"No," she answered. "It wouldn't make sense."

"I know."

She was already moving, third in line on the rope that Skip led up the hill. Our group moved slowly but surely, one step at a time, breathing rhythmically. I was grateful for what felt like thick air at 7,000 feet. Still, I didn't have the energy to do anything but put my head down and plod.

"Hey, can we help?" I thought I must be hallucinating, but no, there were those two mysterious people we'd seen approaching earlier. "We heard you on the radio and figured we'd help you make your planes."

Skip's voice boomed with gratitude. "You guys are outrageous! Thank you!"

"Wow," said Linda, "this is great."

"Bless your hearts," I added. "You're life savers."

They each took a sled and a pack. Our pace improved dramatically, helped as much by the lift in spirits as by the decrease in weight. We heard the first plane approaching as we reached the lonely toilet situated about 50 yards below Base Camp, out in the open, right next to the runway. In perfect timing for us to walk up to it, the plane landed and turned around, ready for take-off again. We threw in half our gear, and Linda and I climbed in. Almost before we'd fastened our seat belts, we were gaining speed and lifting off the glacier. We watched the second plane land and knew that Bob and Skip would be close behind. The two of us laughed all the way to Talkeetna, our fatigue forgotten in the exhilaration of being on our way to a real meal and a soft bed.

CHAPTER NINE

I Have Five of the Seven Summits

Monday, July 22, 1991, Moscow
I keep waiting for the childlike excitement I used to
get when I first started traveling. It's not there.
I guess I've gotten sort of jaded. Yet my heart is
full. I don't want to let the Seven Summits
become a mission that gets in the way of where I
am. I'm here to experience the Soviet Union, not
just to climb. I don't want to be so narrow-visioned
that I miss it. Stay open, Margo. With your
eyes and your heart.

The most outstanding feature of the room in Moscow was the bathtub. European in depth and American in length, it immediately called out to me. Hot baths were one of the great pleasures of my life, but as rare as it was for me to pass up a good soak, I was just too tired. By the time I'd flown from New York to Moscow via Copenhagen and Stockholm, checked into the hotel, and met the other eight members of our group for dinner, all I wanted was to go to sleep. It was nearly midnight when I fell into my bed, but at 1:30 A.M. my mind was once again wide awake, leaving me staring at the ceiling as my roommate, Nola, slept soundly in her bed. At 4:00 A.M. I was sitting next to the window in the early morning light, writing in my journal.

Everything I knew about the Soviet Union I had learned in school and from television. I didn't know any Russians, and I'd been taught they were our enemies. Now I was in their country. My mind retained images of the Russian Bear and "duck-and-cover" nuclear attack drills, but, the Iron Curtain that had separated the Soviet Union and the United States for so long was coming down. Since the Berlin Wall had been dismantled, the news had carried messages of peace, political change, and even the beginnings of a capitalistic free market for individuals in this heartland of communist uniformity.

In some ways my path and theirs were similar: old beliefs that had controlled us were breaking down. Freedom was a new concept for them, and a new way of life for me—one that was allowing me to live from my heart and follow my dreams, a way of life that had taken me, incredibly, to the Soviet Union. I'd never imagined my dream would someday take me there, ready to climb the fifth of my Seven Summits. Martha wanted to focus on my equipment and preparations: Had I trained adequately, did I have the right clothes, would six months really be enough time to prepare myself for Everest after I returned home? With the success of McKinley, I had only three obstacles between me and the ultimate prize. Although Mount Elbrus was the highest mountain in Europe, it was not a technically difficult climb. I'd walked marathons on ice getting here, another long, slow ascent wouldn't stop me. The sixth summit would be Mount Kosciusko, a day hike on an improved path to the highest summit in Australia. The seventh, the toughest, the goddess of all mountains, would be Everest.

While I waited for Nola and the others to awaken, I flipped back through the pages of my journal. Following the weeks I'd spent on Denali, I'd taken a healing trip on the Tatshenshini River in Alaska before returning to San Diego. On the river, easy conversation over an early-morning cup of coffee blended with watching nature. A grizzly sow and her two cubs traversed a velvety green hill. Gray clouds straddled the snow-covered peaks that rose out of the moraine that cradled the flowing ribbon of water. All of it soothed my mind and spirit as well as my body. I listened to the tall tales of the boatmen over a campfire after dinner, heard the loud reports as house-size chunks of ice broke off the Nanutak Glacier, and spent quiet hours writing in my journal with nowhere to go and nothing else to do.

Early in my recovery I believed that by the time I had attained five years of sobriety and abstinence, my life would be perfect. I'd be doing everything I ever wanted, be in a loving relationship, and be filled with self-confidence all the time. I thought I'd be wise, witty, and never have to struggle. Recovery would eliminate all my character defects and make my life easy. In short I'd be "fixed." I'd held on to the fantasy for as long as I could. I'd since passed the five-year mark and my life truly was blessed, but it didn't look anything like what I'd imagined. The self-doubts still spoke loudly and some days were a definite emotional struggle. I was certainly not "fixed," and life was still life. Mountain climbing and adventure travel still often seemed simpler than dealing with day-to-day challenges.

When I returned to San Diego from Alaska, I had a difficult time motivating myself to maintain my physical conditioning for Elbrus and was obsessed with wondering whether I'd disappointed Skip with my performance on McKinley. Some of my inner family were grappling with the fear of not having done well enough and wanted to eat the feelings away; some trusted the process and gave me permission to feel whatever I needed, supporting me in staying abstinent. As my departure for the Soviet Union grew closer, I went home to Greenwich, hoping it would give me a boost before climbing my next summit.

Mum's kitchen, with its familiar table and the big sliding glass doors that kept the outside safely at bay, was still the place where I relaxed most easily into my little-girl fantasies of warmth and acceptance. I walked in, the first morning, looking for coffee. Mum was standing at the sink. I poured myself a cup and automatically slipped into my chair, prattling on for half an hour or so about San Diego, my roommate, the cat, and the weather, while she straightened up towels and wiped off the counter for the third time. As I began to tell her about the beauty of McKinley's knife-edged ridges and high-altitude views reaching out forever, and the exhilaration of standing on the summit, she sat down in her chair. She listened quietly, her hands absentmindedly exploring the surface of the table as I reviewed my itinerary in the Soviet Union for the next five weeks and shared what I knew about Mount Elbrus and Pik Lenin.

I noticed that she hadn't said anything for a while and assumed it was because I was dominating the conversation. "Whew! I don't know whether it's the coffee or my excitement about the trip, but something's sure got me wound up this morning," I said. She was usually quiet when I talked about my climbing, but today she seemed distant. "Are you okay, Mum? Are you feeling all right?"

"I'm just fine, Margo." She was staring blankly out the window. Her voice was soft and controlled, foretelling the seriousness of what she was about to say. All of my kids inside sat up straight, scared, waiting for whatever was coming. "But I don't think you have any idea how I worry about you and your climbing. I just don't understand why you do it." Her head turned from the window toward me, but her nearly blind eyes lowered as if to watch her fingers trace circles on the table in front of her. "My heart would break if something happened to you out there in those places you go to. I try not to think about it or say anything, because I know you're going to do it anyway." She paused, her resignation and fear engulfing me like some primordial flow. Then, exhaling deeply, she continued. "You've already broken my heart twice doing what you said you needed to do, so why should this be any different? I'll just have to deal with whatever happens when it comes."

"What?" I was in total shock. Broken her heart? What'd she mean, broken her heart? And, twice? "What are you talking about?"

"You told me my own father had molested you. Then you told your father that he should send me away to a nursing home so he could be rid of me. If those didn't break my heart, I don't know what would."

"Mum, I've never said anything like that to Pop."

"It was in the letter you sent him for his birthday." Mum was fighting back tears. "He started to read it to me, even though he wasn't supposed to." She hesitated, then continued, still looking down at the table. "He thought it was to both of us, so he read a few words out loud. Then he said, 'Oh, shit,' and threw it on the floor. It was about how hard his life was because of me, and how you could make it better by sending me away. You were planning how to get rid of me so your father could . . ." Tears were flowing down her cheeks.

"Mother! Stop! Stop!" I couldn't believe what I was hearing. "That's not what the letter said. It wasn't anything like that." I could feel how deeply her fears had twisted my words. "I wrote the letter to Pop for his birthday to tell him how much I respect him and how much he's given me during my life. It wasn't about you. You and he heard stuff that wasn't there." I wept now, too. Mum's fear had taken my honesty and the truth by which I was living my life and distorted them until they broke her heart.

She said, "I know I'm a burden to your father. I know he'd be happier if I went to a home. I know."

"Mum, stop. Pop loves you. He'd be miserable if you weren't here. You're the love of his life. Maybe your life hasn't looked the way you guys wanted it to. That doesn't change the way he loves you, Mum. You've gotten it all twisted around." I was crying, filled with my own hurt as well as my mother's pain. "What you said is simply not true." I pushed my chair back, stood up, and walked around the table to her. She sobbed as I put my arms around her.

We cried together for several minutes. Then she patted my arm and straightened up in her chair, leaning away from me. "I'm okay. Now

I understand. I realize I misinterpreted what I heard. I'm sorry I upset you." Clearly, she wanted the conversation to be over.

I was still shaking from the depth of emotions that had been touched. "I love you very much, Mum. It has never been my intention to hurt you."

"I know that," she replied quietly. I didn't believe her. As I left the kitchen to find a safe place to be with my own emotions, Mum was staring out the window again.

Later that night, I lay, wide awake, in the bed in the guest room of my parents' house. All afternoon I'd mentally reviewed the letter from which she'd drawn her conclusion. It had been a deeply personal one I'd written Pop for his birthday last spring in lieu of buying one more present for a man who already had everything. In it I honored him for being the kind of man he was, for the loyalty he brought to a marriage which had been so affected by Mother's ongoing, debilitating illnesses. It seemed that despite my good intentions, my words had been misinterpreted and caused pain I had never intended.

In that letter, I also acknowledged the importance of the role Pop had played in my life. I'd written the things I'd tried to tell him in person over the years that he'd always made light of. His modesty and integrity had been important models for me. In my experience of the world, his kind of loyalty, acceptance, and strong sense of ethics was highly unusual. I thought that if I wrote my words, he'd be able to hear the truth of them in a way he couldn't when I spoke them. I'd been mistaken.

He called me after he received my gift. He spoke a polite, "Thank you for the nice letter," but added, "You're wrong about me being exceptional. I'm just like everyone else I know. All my friends behave the same way I do, and I'm just sorry that you don't have that kind of people in your life. Maybe you should find some different friends." Then, in a tone that was stern and sharp, "And don't ever send a letter like that to the house again. I started to read it aloud to your mother until I realized it would have been devastating for her to hear what you said. Don't ever do anything like that again." I'd hung up the phone with tears in my eyes and an emptiness inside.

I realized I'd asked both Mum and Pop to exceed their emotional capacity. While I'd spent the last five years uncovering my heart's truth, they'd spent their entire lives behaving and responding to life the way they thought they were "supposed to" rather than following what their hearts might really want. I knew I had to accept them as they were rather than try to make them the way I wanted them to be. Another old belief had to die. Another little-girl fantasy of mine had to be set aside. A wave of sadness washed over me, then a peaceful warmth settled in: If I stopped trying to change them, I could love them even more. I wasn't willing to change my path to make their lives easier, but neither would I ask them to be different for me. A couple of worn strands were pulled out of my tapestry and its strength held.

I had left for Elbrus knowing I was creating an enormous new freedom for myself. Once again, facing difficult pieces of my life brought me unexpected gifts. I was in the Soviet Union, and my roommate and Moscow were beginning to stir. It was time to put my journal away, take my shower, and join the group downstairs for the trip back to the airport.

Fewer than twelve hours after arriving in Moscow, we were on a two-hour flight to Mineral'nyje Vody, a busy city in the central Caucasus named for the healing mineral waters found in the surrounding area and used as a holiday center by vacationing Russians. The bus trip from the airport in Mineral'nyje Vody to the Baksan Valley at the foot of Mount Elbrus showed me that even though the Soviet Union was a superpower, a lot of the country remained very much Third World.

We drove for hours through beautiful countryside interrupted by small, subsistence villages filled with friendly but tired-looking people. The women wore faded, shapeless dresses, their hair hidden under the ever-present babushkas knotted under their chins. They seemed bent over by the weight of their lives as they sat on stools in front of small, weather-worn wood or mud-brick houses. The men stood in groups, smoking cigarettes, clothed in patched wool jackets and pants of indeterminate color. With dulled eyes, they watched our bus drive by.

All along our way, rural poverty was evident. Buildings in great disrepair or abandoned in midconstruction formed small complexes surrounded by wood and stone fencing. Goats and dogs and chickens inhabited dung-covered, grassless ground. Yet, when we stopped at a small village bazaar, the indomitable nature of the human spirit shone through the smiles of these people. I could have been in Bolivia, India, or Nepal: the details and clothing were different, but the essence was the same.

As we approached the base of Mount Elbrus through the Baksan Valley, the countryside came alive with lush green fields and brightly colored wildflowers. The formidable Caucasus Mountains, their rugged, high passes capped with snow and blanketed with glaciers, flanked the valley, forming a natural wall extending nearly 600 miles from the Black Sea to the Caspian Sea. The range protected the regions to the north from exploration and foreign domination for centuries and became home to fiercely independent and somewhat isolated peoples who could tolerate its harsh terrain and tempestuous weather. Even today, tourist access is limited to a few major areas. The Baksan Valley is one of these and besides being a vacation resort, Soviet style, it is the most popular approach to Mount Elbrus.

Soaring thousands of feet higher than the alpine peaks surrounding it, Mt. Elbrus is an extinct, double-coned volcano located only 60 miles from the subtropical climate of the Black Sea. The name, Elbrus, is derived from an ancient Persian word meaning "snowy mountain." Its twin peaks reach altitudes over 18,000 feet and take the brunt of the notoriously changeable weather and violent storms moving from south to north, keeping most climbers from its summit. The first record of a summit success was in 1829, when a Kabardin guide and a company of Russian soldiers approached its summits from the north where the Malka River and "Narzan" mineral water flow.

Since the 1930s, Prielbrusye, as the area around Elbrus is known, has served as a popular destination for Soviet citizens. They come in organized groups sponsored by labor unions or sports clubs, some for the opportunity to climb, some to ski, and some simply to enjoy the change from factories and cities. The valley has a series of camps and "hotels" developed to support tourists and Soviet vacationers alike.

The small hotel we would use as our Base Camp for Elbrus was surprisingly comfortable, a three-story building with only six "rooms," each one really a suite with a large living room, fair-size bedroom, and large bathroom. The bottom level also contained a large dining room and a common room with TV and pool table. The hotel was surrounded by a forest of evergreen trees, and after Nola and I dropped our duffel bags on the floor of our suite, she opened the large French windows.

The happy babbling of a stream immediately filled the room. Nola said, "Nice," and leaned out the window to get a wider view. Nola was the only other woman on the trip and would be my roommate for the duration. As always, the presence of another woman on a climb—especially one my own age—was most welcome, and we had talked extensively during this day of travel. She worked in the administration of a school system in New York State and was an avid and skilled rock climber and mountaineer. My first impression was one of determination and strength.

After spending hours traveling through nondescript airports and the poverty of the countryside, I was delighted. "Nola, look at this tub!" I shouted from the bathroom. "Will this ever feel good when we get back from the mountain!" The first hot shower or bath after a multiday trip was a frequent fantasy of mine during the climbs themselves. Here we were blessed with both: a shower to clean off the dirt and a huge, deep tub to soak away the fatigue.

On Elbrus, climbers are assisted in their approach to the summits by a series of chairlifts extending almost all the way to a large hotel/hut nearly 14,000 feet high on the mountain. Our group took an acclimatization hike the first day, riding the chairlift from the base to 9,000 feet, then hiking up to 11,200 feet. It was rainy and cold when we reached the top of the chairlift, and I was struck by the difference between our high-tech, multicolored Capilene and Gore-Tex clothes and the lightweight, olive green and brown cotton clothing and marginal rain gear of the Soviets. It was another spotlight on the reality of life for the majority of people in this superpower country.

By the time we reached our destination, the sun had appeared from behind the clouds and we picnicked in comfort on a blanket of wildflowers. Bread, sausage, and cheese were augmented by the unexpected luxury of a can of paté Nola had carried up secretly as a surprise for the rest of us.

She'd pulled it out of her pack with a flourish, saying, "Look what I've got!" and I laughed at her childlike pride. I liked her more every day. She had a bright mind, entertaining humor, and caring heart. As I savored a piece of bread slathered with paté, I let my body relax into the meadow. All around us, the raw-edged Caucasuses slashed across the sky, their harsh beauty somehow both tempered and emphasized by the soft, bright meadow of grasses and flowers.

There was an easy camaraderie within our group. Ed, though self-admittedly uptight, had a marvelous humor about him. He was seated a few yards to my right, involved in an intense conversation with Lyn, whose strong religious beliefs were a primary focus of his life. Larry, Michael, and Skip sat together slightly above us, Skip talking animatedly, gesturing with his hands, while Michael grinned broadly and Larry laughed out loud in response. Michael was a softspoken, gentle-hearted, Southern-accented mountain guide and mental health worker with enormous physical strength. Larry was a teacher and had gone to grade school with Skip. He'd come to climb this, his first mountain, to be with his long-time friend rather than because of a love for climbing, and his bright humor was enormously engaging. Tod sprawled amidst the flowers, chewing on a daisy stem. He was battling cancer and demonstrated a deep strength of character by choosing to dive into life rather than retreat from it. The ninth member of the group, Guy, also sat off by himself, appearing lost in thought. He was a Vietnam vet who had remained in Asia following the war. Although he was now married and had a daughter he adored, Guy had an air of mystery about him that invited my invention of exotic stories about the years he spent in Bangkok. He was the only one of this group who would continue on to Pik Lenin with Skip and me.

Our second morning, we rode the cable car up to Priut Mir. At 11,800 feet, it was a large, crude building containing a number of dormitory rooms, with various numbers of bunk beds, and a big community dining area. It provided an opportunity to acclimatize before moving up to Priut Odinnadtsati, "Refuge of Eleven," or Priut Hut. At 13,780 feet, Priut Hut would be the jumping off point for the summit.

We dumped our gear and hiked to the higher hut, the exercise helping our adjustment to the altitude. We hiked in pairs or groups of three, talking, getting to know one another better, and simply enjoying the day. Compared to my other trips, it was a rare pleasure to be in the mountains on snow without a heavy pack and without being concerned about time or a destination. Scattered clouds moved in and out keeping the temperature comfortable as the route rose alongside the still-active ski trails higher on the mountain. I was filled with joy watching birds flying overhead and skiers making their turns, laughing and falling their way down the slopes. The white of the snow contrasted with the black rock and our bright Gore-Tex clothes, their colors heightened by the low-angle afternoon sun.

At the top of our climb, Priut Hut looked like a large Airstream trailer: a multistory, sausage-shaped, aluminum-covered refuge. We mixed with the Soviet and other occupants there as we had lunch, the cacophony of languages sounding like laughter to my untrained ears. On our descent, we skated and glissaded much of the way down, sliding, with arms extended like surfers' to help our balance, chortling with sheer pleasure. As we arrived back at Priut Mir, my soul sang a song of thanks, and I had a smile in my heart that matched the one on my face.

After a dinner spiced with good conversation and belly laughs, I stood outside looking at the skyline of the Caucasuses silhouetted against a sky dominated by the rising full moon. I sensed someone behind me and turned to see Skip approaching. He put an arm across my shoulders, and I slid mine around his waist, the two of us joined in silent appreciation of the magnificence surrounding us.

"Here we are again," I said quietly, giving a slight squeeze to this man, the guide who had become my mentor and friend.

"Yup," was all he said as he squeezed my shoulder lightly.

I appreciated the simplicity of his response, and I found myself anticipating the journey ahead. Skip was guiding me into physical places where Jonathan's spirit was present and my soul could run free. I silently thanked God for all of the miracles in my life.

The next morning, we moved our gear up to Priut Hut. Riding the chairlift as far as it went, we balanced our heavy packs awkwardly in our laps, then climbed the final thousand feet. Many Russians walked around on the snow in the warm sunshine wearing bathing suits or shorts with no shirts, reminding us that this was a vacation resort. Nola and I giggled at the irony of us in our climbing gear and them in their bikinis. I was glad to be moving higher on the mountain and felt strong, humming along with John Denver as his heartfelt songs came through my headphones. I put one foot in front of the other on a beautiful mountain surrounded by vacationers and other climbers who shared my appreciation of where we were and relished the simple sense of enjoyment that was becoming the theme of this trip.

There were four American men sitting in the sun outside the hut when we arrived. They'd summited the day before and planned to descend a bit later. One of them introduced himself as Glenn Porzak, president of the American Alpine Club. I'd heard that he was making a bid for the Seven Summits and that he'd been up Everest, so I asked him where he was in the process.

"This is number six," he said. "I've only got Kosciusko to go."

"That makes it pretty much a done deal," I responded. "Congratulations."

"Thanks. I'm pleased about it." Glenn's response was low-key but his satisfaction glowed brightly behind his modesty, and we continued to talk about his climbs. He'd been climbing for a long time and had earned his six summits over a number of years.

"I'm hoping Elbrus will be number five for me," I said. My climbing history was very different from Glenn's, but I was proud to be able to say I'd climbed four and pleased to feel a true part of the mountaineering community.

Glenn asked for details. I told him that Kili had been my first mountain in 1988, and his surprise was evident. "You've only been climbing for three years and you've already got four of the seven? That's pretty amazing. What started you climbing at your age? It's pretty unusual."

"It's a long story," I said with a smile.

"I'm not in any hurry. I'd like to hear it." His genuine interest encouraged me, so I told my story as briefly as I could while we sat in the sun at 14,000 feet on Mount Elbrus in the Soviet Union. His three companions listened as well.

"Wow," one said when I finished.

"That's astounding."

"Bravo, Margo."

The positive reaction and support of these men who had such strong climbing backgrounds filled me with pride. We spent another half hour swapping stories of other mountains. When we parted, I wished them well. Glenn gave me a hug. "You've done an amazing thing. I wish you the best of luck on Everest." He lifted his pack to his back, and the four of them headed down the mountain.

After they left, our team reassembled to picnic in the sun before climbing up to the Rocks of Pastukhov, a landmark at 15,748 feet. We carried very light day packs, and I moved well, legs strong, my breathing rhythmical as John Denver once again sang in my ears. That afternoon I chose to climb by myself, with only my inner family and spirit guides for company. The physical effort and quiet reflection were satisfying. It was a joy to walk unroped, totally at my own pace, and let myself savor the soul-filling essence of this sport for which I had such a deep passion.

It took us only two hours to reach the rock band. We stopped there for water and the chance to appreciate the view. I took advantage of the time to adjust a crampon that had been slipping on the way up. Skip saw me working with it and offered to do it for me.

"No, thanks," I answered. "I really do want to get self-sufficient up here."

"Good for you," he said with a smile. "As strange as it seems, you may be on a mountain without me someday." We both laughed, but the image was important, and I embraced it. A concept that had been very frightening before didn't seem so now. I felt proud and grateful for the progress I'd made, and excited about what the future might hold.

It was playtime descending from the Rocks as we ran, used our boots as skis, and slid our way down. We laughed, hooted, and hollered, and tripped over our own feet whenever we got going too fast. Pure fun. I went to sleep that night exhausted and happy.

Our summit attempt was delayed for two days by a storm that kept everyone off the mountain. Finally, it seemed to have blown itself out, and I went to bed anticipating Skip's 1:00 A.M. wake-up call. The brightness of the rising, almost-full moon in the window by my head awakened me, and I was sure it must be time to get going, but I didn't hear any voices. Had Skip overslept? Was it too windy to go? What was going on? I checked my watch and, seeing it was only 11:00, laughed quietly at my eagerness. Nola slept soundly in the other bed. Knowing that we had a full day of climbing ahead of us, I turned away from the window and closed my eyes. I'd hear Skip's voice soon enough.

"Wake up, ladies. It's time." Skip's voice stirred my adrenaline through the sleep that had recaptured me.

I sat up and reached for the pile of clothes I'd laid out before I went to bed. Nola hadn't stirred, so I reached over and touched her shoulder. "Nola. Wake up. Time to go."

"Huh?" Sleep still enveloped her brain.

"Come on. We've got a mountain to climb."

"Mmmmhhhh." Nola rolled onto her back, arms stretching above her head. Again there was a mumbled "Mmmmhhhh." Then she blinked her eyes and sat up, her brain now reconnecting with her body. "Is it morning?"

"Well, sort of." I was pulling on my second pair of socks. "It's one o'clock. We leave in an hour."

As she groped in the semidarkness for her own pile of clothes, I heard, "Oh, God, where's the coffee?"

"Downstairs." I had to laugh at how focused I was on getting down to the dining room for a cup myself. I hadn't been a coffee drinker until I started climbing, and now I found it almost a necessity for an early-morning start. I finished dressing and grabbed my pack. "See ya down there."

I downed half a cup of steaming coffee laced with sweetener and milk, then ate some granola while I ran through my internal checklist of gear one more time: outer boots, ice axe, and crampons were waiting by the door. Gore-Tex expedition jacket, down jacket, extra gloves, two water bottles, snacks, first-aid supplies, camera, and film were in my pack. Should I check it again? No. I'd packed, unpacked, and repacked it a number of times the night before—the things were all there.

Our group gradually assembled in the common area: some arrived wide awake and eager to get climbing, some still rubbing the sleep from their eyes. The clump of boots, rustling of clothes, and clatter of cups, bowls, and silverware competed with the light bantering tinged with nervous expectation.

"Okay, gang, time to go." Skip and our Soviet guide, Dema, moved toward the stairs leading down to the first floor.

I put on my boots, picked my crampons and ice axe, and followed

Larry across the gangplank that bridged the trench eroded by snow-melt from around the building. He moved slowly, cautiously, tele-graphing his nervousness. As we bent over to put on our crampons, I wanted to offer some encouragement. I finished buckling my straps, put my hand on his shoulder, and asked, "How're ya doin'?"

He reached up, placed his gloved hand on top of my mittened one, and patted it as if to comfort me. "A little nervous, if the truth be known."

When he straightened, I hugged him. "Here's a morale hug for you." He returned it fiercely. We stepped apart, but my hands stayed on his waist, his on my shoulders, our hearts remaining connected for a few seconds.

"Thanks, Margo." Several people had started moving up the hill, following the tracks of those ahead in the moonlight "I guess it's time."

"All you gotta do is put one foot in front of the other." I moved out ahead of him, but stopped after only a couple of steps. Turning back to face him, I added, "And you know you don't have to do this. This isn't a punishment. I climb because I love it. That's true for Skip, as well. Are you climbing this mountain for Skip or for you?"

Larry paused and looked right into my eyes. "That's something to think about." Then he lowered his head and began climbing. I began my own ascent, soon becoming lost in the marvelous experience of following my own shadow up the mountain The snow had the consis-tency of Styrofoam, seemingly created for the express purpose of pro-viding the perfect surface for using on crampons. The night was warm, even with the light wind that was blowing. In spite of the bright moon, the cloudless sky sparkled with the thousands of stars I'd seen now on each of the seven continents.

We stopped at the Rocks of Pastukhov for water and a little nourish-ment. Larry sat by himself, obviously deep in thought. I walked over to him, asking once again, "How ya doin'?"

"I'm not enjoying this very much. I don't think mountain climbing is my thing. I want to turn around, but Skip's been trying to get me on a trip for so long, I don't want to disappoint him."

I smiled, understanding his dilemma. Larry was prepared to climb 5,000 vertical feet at high altitude, with little or no enjoyment for himself, to make a friend happy. I knew the feeling. I'd often done things I had no desire to do because someone else wanted me to, acted against my heart's instincts rather than disappoint someone, said "yes" when my insides screamed "no."

I said, "What would you do if this weren't Skip's trip. If he weren't here?"

"I'd go down." His response was immediate and clear. But I could see the doubt and turmoil in his eyes.

"Larry, this is about you. I love Skip dearly, but whether or not you climb this mountain is about you, not about him. I really encourage you to honor your heart here. It's okay for you to go down. The choice is yours, not anyone else's." I stood up to move back over to where I'd dropped my pack. "Listen to your heart."

Larry did go down. The rest of us continued on our way toward the saddle between the twin summits. At 17,160 feet, it was a welcome bit of semilevel ground leading to the last 1,000 vertical feet, the final push to our objective, the west summit. After six hours of climbing, my legs felt washed out. The sun had come out, heating our bodies and softening the snow's surface enough so that we broke through the crust and had to posthole our way across the traverse. That meant I'd take a step, sink in almost to my knee, pick my back foot up high enough to get it out of the hole it had made, step forward, and sink in again. Postholing was one of my least favorite things about climbing. It turned a one-foot-in-front-of-the-other, low-angle traverse into an ordeal, increasing exponentially the effort required for each step.

The traverse seemed to take forever. We rested from it at the saddle for close to an hour, refueling our bodies for the final push. As I forced down some nuts and raisins, I looked up the steep face and wondered how I was going to climb it. Martha wanted to turn around and go down. I said no.

Skip's insistent encouragement helped us overcome our lethargy and we followed cautiously as he and Dema took turns kicking steps into the snow. The storm that had kept us from climbing the past two days had created wind-blown slab conditions here, making the footing unsure. I wondered more than once if the surface might slide, and breathed a sigh of relief as my slow, steady progress brought me over the crest, in sight of the summit. It was still quite a distance away but only slightly uphill. I felt Jonathan's presence and God's strength as I kept my eyes glued to the summit and made my way across the snow.

My emotions surged toward the 18,510-foot summit as my body struggled upward, and when I finally stood on the top of all of Europe, tears and laughter mixed with the back-pounding hugs of others on the team. Skip and I stood, arms around each other, for the requisite summit photo, and he leaned over and said into my ear, "That's five."

I put my head on his shoulder and laughed out loud. Europe spread out below us in all directions. "Skip, do you realize we haven't had one bad summit day? They've all been clear and calm and sunny. It's true for every mountain I've been on. It's incredible."

Skip grinned at me. "You're right! I hadn't thought about it. Even more reason to have you on Everest."

My breath caught for an instant. What would it be like on Everest? Would my luck hold? Would the cold or the weather or my body keep me from its summit? And how was it that I, Margo Chisholm, was even able to wonder such things? Standing on top of the highest mountain in Europe, I envisioned myself on the summit of the highest mountain on Earth. The key to getting to Elbrus had been doing the simple footwork put in front of me. The distance from here to Everest would be covered the same way. My immediate task was to get down safely from this summit.

The descent was slow, harder than I'd expected. Skip and Dema placed a fixed rope on the steep face above the saddle, which provided a measure of security that helped us breathe more easily in the thin air. The ever-softening snow caused deeper postholes as we plodded down. When we reached the Rocks of Pastukhov, Ed and I recognized a track left by someone sliding down the slope on his or her backside. We glanced at each other and in almost the same movement, sat in the snow, shortened the length of our adjustable-length ski poles, and pushed off for a slide down toward Priut Hut on our Gore-Tex-covered butts. There were no hidden crevasses here, and laughter and screams of delight trailed behind us as we struggled to maintain some semblance of balance and control in our slide. When the slope leveled out, we picked ourselves up and walked to the warmth of the giant aluminum hut, laughing all the way. It was a delightfully fun finish to a successful day.

Larry was outside sunning himself when we arrived. "Hi, guys," he called. "How was it?"

"Great!" I said. "We missed you on the summit, but I'm glad you listened to your heart and came down."

"I'm glad I did. I truly enjoyed my hike back down. Dawn was breaking, the view breathtaking, and I just walked at my own pace and enjoyed myself immensely. There are other pleasures about climbing besides making the summit. I had a great day in the sun down here, talking with people and reading."

I smiled and nodded my head. We accepted the congratulations and friendly greetings of the members of the hiking club sharing Priut Hut with us, but were too tired to eat much of the dinner of soup and cabbage set out in the dining room and soon collapsed happily into our beds. The next morning we hiked down to the top of the chairlifts and rode them to the mountain's base.

Back at our hotel, the couple who were our hosts greeted us effusively and led us to tables they'd set up outside with flowers, fruit, and bottles of champagne. They were popping the corks off the bottles before we could even get the packs off our backs. It was a lovely welcome, and we were easily caught up in their excitement for our success as we made toasts all around.

Soon, we were able to take the long, hot showers I'd anticipated when we first arrived. Afterward, we shared a gracious lunch, during which our hosts told us they'd arranged a visit to a nearby dacha, or summer home, that had once belonged to Brezhnev's minister of health. In Moscow I'd heard about the dachas, the description of the beauty and elegance of these estates tinged with disgust at the opulent spending by the State on political bigwigs when the common people lived in such poverty. The strong opinions, spoken quietly by a hotel clerk, reflected what we found to be a widespread disillusionment with the traditional Communist rhetoric and support for the rapid changes taking place in opening up the closed Soviet society.

After lunch, everyone napped for a couple of hours before we followed a lovely path through the woods to the dacha. The exterior of the building was rather plain by Western standards, but the interior sparkled with the grandeur the clerk had derided: marble floors, carved cathedral ceilings, and a wide curving stairway, rich window coverings, a sauna, and a soaking pool. Nola and I were wandering through the rooms, admiring them, when we heard beautiful piano music echoing softly through the hallways. We followed the sound and found the rest of the group listening to Tod as he played selections ranging from Chopin to Joplin.

We took up lounging positions around the pleasant music room and could have listened for hours, but Tod had seen the sauna and ended the impromptu concert after only half an hour so he could indulge his tired muscles. Our disappointment passed quickly as we stripped off our clothes and alternated between the dry, hot air of the sauna and the cool water of the pool. Our conversation ranged from humor to politics to baseball, and I enjoyed the camaraderie and fun that continued to characterize this trip. Any remaining fatigue washed away in the carefree atmosphere. Looking around at my friends, new and old, relaxing in the very civilized luxury of that Russian estate, I had to smile and shake my head. I'd just climbed my nineteenth mountain in three years, the fifth of the Seven Summits, and I was sitting in a pool in an elegant house that used to belong to a Soviet political minister. It seemed too far-fetched for me to have gotten here from the depths of despair and incomprehensible demoralization in which I had been mired only five years before. Yet this was not a fantasy. I was here. I took a breath of deep joy and whispered a prayer of thanks.

We returned to the hotel for a feast of barbecued shish kabob, ribs, and chicken washed down with vodka, champagne, and cognac, with Russian Coke for me. A stream that seemed to sing its own song in celebration of our summit success flowed only a few feet from our picnic table. The evening continued with a tipsy, mellow frivolity and occasional outbreaks of laughter. Glasses clinked together until late into the night, as climbers toasted each other with drinking arms entwined.

Only once did Martha try to ruin it for me with her scathing words. "See, you're not like them. You'll never be like them." I excused myself from the table and went to stand alone by the stream, tossing pebbles into the current. "If you were really recovered you could have a glass of champagne, too. You'll always be damaged. What's wrong with you anyway?"

"Nothing, Martha." I knew my answer was the truth. "Nothing's wrong with me." I spoke the words with quiet but strong conviction and walked back up to the table to rejoin the laughter and fun.

We left for Moscow the next morning, reversing the four-hour bus journey and three-hour plane ride. It gave me time to replay the trip to Elbrus in my mind and heart. The mountain had lured me to the Soviet Union, but the trip had also been about the camaraderie of the people and visiting a foreign country. There'd always been more to my climbing than simply reaching the summit of a mountain, but on my previous trips I'd still been focused on the summit. I was more relaxed and confident on Elbrus, more willing to let go of the goal and participate in the process of getting there. Once again, in following this dream of mine, I'd received unexpected gifts and pleasure.

We shared a final dinner together in Moscow, and after hugs and farewells, most of the group left for the airport. Skip, Guy, and I were joined by new members Michael, David, and Claude to make up the team which would leave in a few hours for Pik Lenin. They arrived only minutes after the others left, and it was an abrupt shift from a comfortable group of friends to strangers just beginning to feel each other out. I was the only woman again, and as we left for the airport, I already missed the comfortable fellowship of the last twelve days, and Nola's company in particular.

*　　*　　*

At 23,405 feet, Pik Lenin is the third highest mountain in the Soviet Union. It is part of the Pamir Mountains, a section of the most north-western reaches of the Himalaya, extending from Nepal and Tibet, through India, Pakistan, Afghanistan, and China into Kyrgyzstan. The highest summit, Pik Kommunizma (24,590 feet), lies about 50 miles to the southwest, also in the Pamirs. Pik Pobeda (24,405 feet), the second tallest, stands more than 150 miles to the east in the Tian Shan Mountains. The Pamirs contain 105 peaks over 20,000 feet, most of which are rarely climbed: some are still waiting for their first ascent.

Lenin is one of the most commonly attempted 23,000-foot peaks in the world. It has a reputation as a high-altitude "walk-up" because of its long and relatively nontechnical approach via the Lenina Glacier and Razdelny Ridge, yet the success rate for summiting is far less than 50 percent. Dangers include its altitude, extremely changeable weather, and avalanches regularly released down its steep couloirs and faces. Only the year before, forty-three climbers had lost their lives in a single avalanche, and in 1974, all eight members of a Soviet women's team of climbers perished when they were caught in a violent storm high on the mountain. It was not the risks, but the excitement of the climb, however, that was foremost in our minds as we settled into our Base Camp in Lukovaya Polyana (Luke's Meadow) under clear skies and a moon waxing toward full.

The meadow served as a satellite area several hundred yards above the larger, more militaristic Base Camp established at Achik-Tash. Some of the expeditions arrived by helicopter from Osh. A few used helicopters to transport gear across Travelers' Pass to Camp I, the roar of their engines and throbbing of their rotors drowning out the quiet beating of the wings of the resident "little brown birds" and their musical chirping. Nondescript LBB's had been a surprisingly frequent presence on my climbs on high mountains, their range seemingly extending to most continents. Here, in contrast to the intrusive noise of the aircraft, they were particularly welcome.

The night before our carry to Camp I, sleep came only sporadically, as I was awakened by the sound of violent vomiting at least a half a dozen times. One of our teammates was clearly very ill.

Skip's tent was the closest to mine, and I thought I recognized his voice as the source of the groans behind the retching. I felt badly for him and wanted to help, but I knew Skip well enough to understand that he'd prefer to be alone. I couldn't help wondering, though, what this would mean for the climb. He was astoundingly strong, but if he was as sick as he sounded, even he wouldn't be able to make the trip to Camp I. Skip and the carry were both in God's hands. There wasn't anything I could do except send healing thoughts while his guts tried to turn themselves inside out.

Skip's absence when I arrived in the mess tent for coffee the next morning supported my suspicions. In all the trips we'd done together, it was a rare occasion that he wasn't up and moving before me. "Was that Skip last night?" I asked Jonathan Bobaljik, a young man half my age who was a liaison for an American group just coming off the mountain. Jonathan was pursuing a passion for linguistics, and when he wasn't studying and teaching he was either climbing on some remote mountain or in an even more remote village studying the language and culture of its people. We'd met him in Osh, and he'd asked if he could camp and climb with us for a few days until his group arrived back at Base Camp. I thoroughly enjoyed the addition he made to our group. We were kindred spirits, walking different paths, yet with a common intent: both living out dreams that touched our hearts deeply, going against the mainstream. This morning he held a cup of hot tea with both hands to keep them warm in the chill of the morning.

"I think so," he said. "Didn't sound too good."

"Sure didn't," Guy added.

"I felt so badly for him," I said. "I hope it's nothing serious."

As I took a sip of my coffee, a pale, slightly wobbly Skip appeared at the doorway and paused, as if not quite able to decide what to do next.

"Skip. Sit down." I motioned to one of the boxes we were using for stools. "How're you doing?"

"Not so well, Margo."

"Would you like some tea?"

"No, no tea, thanks. I was up sick all night and won't go with you today. Gena will take you to Camp One and then continue on by himself to Three. You guys can descend on your own, and I'll be fine by the time you get back. I think I must've eaten something that'd gone bad. I've stopped throwing up so I'm already getting better. I'm going to go back and lie down. You guys have a good day, and I'll see you later."

Gena was one of our Soviet guides and knew the mountain well. Although I was somewhat uneasy to be going without Skip, I turned my attention to finishing breakfast and being ready to leave by our planned departure time of 7:00 A.M. We wanted to be well up the glacier before its surface became too soft, so it was important to get an early start.

At 7:00, Jonathan, Gena, Guy, and I stood just outside the mess tent, waiting for Claude, Michael, and David. They had arrived late for breakfast and seemed in no hurry to finish. By 7:15 my patience was wearing thin.

"Come on, guys." I called through the canvas wall of the mess tent. "The weather won't wait for us." I attempted to keep my irritation out of my voice.

"Aw, don't worry, Margo. Fifteen minutes won't make that much difference." I wasn't sure whose voice it was, but all three men seemed to share a lack of concern for the four of us who were waiting. I shook my head at their inconsiderate attitude and looked to Jonathan and Guy for support. They simply shrugged. Finally, the threesome emerged and casually returned to their tents to get their packs. Another ten minutes passed before they came back to where we were still waiting.

"Ready?" Michael's sarcastic tone sharpened my irritation.

The degree of care required as we switchbacked up the steep slope leading to Travelers' Pass focused my attention away from the frustration simmering inside. It had been my understanding that the route to Camp I was a virtual stroll, and I was surprised by the uncertain footing on the switchbacks as they crossed and recrossed the dark red, dry, pebbly dirt.

A couple of times Gena offered to take some of the weight from my pack. When I refused, he shook his head in resignation at the heavy packs Americans carried. The Soviets had long preferred lightweight, high-speed climbing, frequently holding competitions for speed-climbing mountains. They are known around the world for their singular focus on reaching a summit. When Gena told me I was strong, I took it as a compliment. As much as Soviet men like speed on mountains, they dislike having women as climbing companions. I accepted his comment as an unusual indication of respect.

When we reached the glacier, we sent Gena on ahead so he could make Camp III as he'd planned. Despite Gena's limited command of English, Guy, Jonathan, and I understood his communication of where the route ran up the glacier. We'd been told there were many tents and climbers at Camp I and that we couldn't miss it. The six of us milled around, watching Gena almost run up the pock-marked ice, and as no one else seemed inclined, I assumed the role as leader. The slog up the glacier was no fun. It wasn't difficult climbing, but simply hard work with the surface softening in the midday sun. In my default role of leader, I felt somewhat obligated to be encouraging and keep the group together, not an easy task as Michael, David, and Claude lagged behind. Nearly six hours after leaving the meadow, we arrived at the loose assemblage of tents that made up Camp I, and Jonathan and I selected a place to set up the tent we'd brought to cache the gear we'd carried.

The weather began to close in as soon as we arrived, and I wanted to get the tent up, the gear stowed, and get back down to Base Camp as quickly as possible. "Who's got the tent?" I asked.

"I think Michael does." Jonathan had slipped his pack off his back and, like Guy, was pulling out the gear to be left here.

"Where is he?" I looked up from my own pack, realizing for the first time that none of our three companions was anywhere in sight. "Where are they?"

"I think they're in there." Guy pointed to a large white canvas tent that seemed to serve as a gathering place for the many expeditions inhabiting this desolate camp. "Some guy stuck his head out and offered tea as we walked by, and those guys peeled off."

"Damn," I muttered and closed my pack, glancing up at the sky, darkening by the minute. "Come on, guys, let's go get them."

As we walked toward the big tent, clouds rolled down the steep face that rose above Camp I. We'd soon be in them, making the descent more difficult and dangerous. I poked my head in through the flap that served as a door and looked around. Our team members were sitting comfortably, sipping tea and chatting with other climbers. "Guys, c'mon, let's get the tent up."

"Not until we've had our tea, Margo." Michael was casually straddling a camp stool. "A half hour doesn't matter that much."

"With the way the weather's closing in, Michael, it might. Will you guys come help us?"

He lifted his steaming cup toward me as a salute. "We'll be there in a minute."

"Bullshit!" I muttered under my breath. "Did you bring the tent up, Michael?"

"It's in my pack out there. Help yourself." He clearly had no intention of moving, and the others seemed to be following his lead.

Opening Michael's pack to remove the tent, I looked at Guy who was shaking his head. "Why don't you try?" I said to him. "Maybe they'll listen to you."

Jonathan and I carried the tent to its site while Guy entered the large tent. I couldn't hear what was said but he emerged shortly by himself.

Fifteen minutes later, our tent was up, and the gear that Jonathan, Guy, and I had carried was stowed. There was still no sign of the other three.

This time Jonathan volunteered to go into the big tent. He, too, emerged alone, shaking his head. He carried two of the three packs belonging to the tea drinkers over to us and returned for the third as Guy and I emptied the first two into the tent. Now I knew how Skip had felt that day on Denali when he returned from his carry to a higher camp only to find that those of us who'd stayed behind hadn't dealt with the kitchen or water. I felt the same anger and disappointment at the lack of team effort being shown by our companions. As we finished stowing the gear, the other three members of our team strolled up.

"Hey, you guys do great work," Michael said.

I could have slammed him in the face. "We've got to head back down. Now!" It was a challenge to keep my voice calm. I certainly didn't want to be the leader but no one else seemed to be taking the responsibility. "Weather's closing in, and I'm concerned about us losing our visibility. Get your packs on and let's go."

"Well, master, whatever you say." Michael was smiling. David and Claude smirked their appreciation of his ill-founded humor.

I didn't know what I wanted to do more, hit him or cry. I said, "Everybody ready?" I tried to persuade myself it was their inexperience on a big mountain that underlaid their blasé attitude. But my mind screamed, "Fine. Get yourselves down this damn mountain. I don't give a shit." I turned and headed out of camp, tears pricking my eyes. "No," I said to myself. "I will not cry. This is not about me, it's about them. It doesn't matter what they think of me. What matters is that we stay a team. If they don't realize how important it is to stay together, we'll just have to do everything we can to make sure they get down, like it or not." Jonathan followed close behind me while Guy gestured for the other three to go in front of him so he could be last and act as a sweep. I was grateful for their support.

The descent felt like a battle of wills. Not comfortable in the role of leader, despite the open support of Guy and Jonathan, I made conservative decisions about route choices. The three independents argued, sometimes choosing a different line of travel. We were clearly operating as two groups of three climbers rather than a team of six. I debated continuing to fight to keep us functioning as at least a modicum of a unit, perhaps keeping them from making a dangerous error, or simply letting them make their own choices and pay the consequences. My experience in the mountains was certainly limited, but their lack of attention to time and weather and consideration for their fellow climbers reflected an attitude that I believed could, too easily, lead to trouble.

When my decision to follow a circuitous route on moraine to avoid what I judged to be a too-risky crossing of a stream swollen by snow-melt resulted in our having to ascend a very steep, dry dirt couloir with a considerable risk of dangerous backsliding, the hostility from Michael and David was palpable. Claude was dehydrated and exhausted, and his feet were badly blistered, so he was moving extremely slowly. Michael and David wanted to go on ahead by themselves, but I was adamant that we stay together. They did wait but were very vocal in their disapproval. Once we reached the top of Travelers' Pass, I told them to go for it if they wanted to. Little danger remained of their losing the route or having an accident. Guy went on ahead, too. Jonathan and I stayed with Claude on his slow, painful walk to Base Camp.

I did a great deal of soul searching during the final hour's walk into camp. Was I overly cautious? Was I too authoritarian? Did I make the right decisions? Certainly they weren't popular with everyone. Had I acted inappropriately? What could I have done differently? I replayed the day in my head. The courses I'd taken on Rainier and Baker, and my experience on other expeditions had taught me that cooperation and consideration were lifelines when climbing, and that independent action could put the individual and the group equally at risk. After much thought, I still wasn't sure if my actions had been appropriate or not but I knew I wouldn't have done it any differently.

Twelve hours after we'd left that morning, Claude, Jonathan, and I straggled into Base Camp. The others had arrived half an hour earlier. I was physically tired and emotionally exhausted but also grateful for my willingness and strength to take the leadership role when necessary and to fill that role responsibly to the very best of my ability.

The next morning, we heard that a helicopter was making a run to Camp I and had room for more gear. Did we want it to take our remaining equipment and food? Given the experience of the day before, we were all in favor of this windfall. We assembled everything quickly, keeping only what we'd need for that night, and carried the loads down to Achik-Tash to stow on the chopper. After we watched the helicopter fly off toward the glacier, I took a shower and washed the grit out of my hair. My negative attitude toward my companions washed down the drain as well.

The next day we moved up to Camp I, carrying light packs that contained only our personal gear and sleeping bags. Following Skip on the long slog up the glacier, I'd broken through the crust of ice and slipped into a puddle of water up to my knee for the umpteenth time. Irritated by the uneven, arrhythmic pace required by the unfriendly ice, I vented my frustrations loudly. "I hate climbing on this glacier. It's a pain in the tail."

"That's really a neophyte attitude, Margo," Skip called over his shoulder. "This isn't a bad glacier at all."

I was taken aback by his response, but listened as he told stories of other glaciers he'd been on much more difficult than this one. As I listened, I was able to change my attitude to one of acceptance rather than irritation, and Skip noticed.

"I've got to hand it to you, Margo. You can turn your negative attitude around to a positive one faster than anyone I've ever known."

I was pleased and grateful, both for the lessons I'd learned in recovery that allowed me to make those changes and for Skip's noticing. I remembered what I'd told so many others, "If you could only see yourself through my eyes, you'd see what a miracle you are." I knew that I was catching an important reflection of myself through Skip's eyes.

The first night at Camp I, it snowed. I was using a new tent, my own mountaineering tent, and it was keeping me warm and dry in the wet, heavy snow that covered everything in camp. The Soviets' climbing and camping equipment was significantly inferior to that of the Europeans and Americans: They carried wooden ice axes, wore wool clothing, and their old canvas tents sagged under the weight of moisture and collapsed in a snowfall. I felt something I hadn't experienced on a mountain before. I loved the people, the beauty, and the reality of being here, but my heart wasn't really in the climb. I wasn't sure why I felt that way, but the day with Michael, David, and Claude had dampened my enthusiasm even further. Skip told me that having the summit would be good for my climbing résumé and I knew he was right. I decided to stay in the present and trust my intuition as we moved higher up the mountain.

This camp was a hodgepodge of tents and climbers and it was dirty. Garbage from past expeditions littered the whole area. It was something I'd noticed on Elbrus as well, but here the lack of concern with carrying out trash was appalling. The camp had a haphazard quality, as if for many of the expeditions summit fever overrode any concern for ecology, esthetics, or community.

A full day and second night of snow held us back. Last year's deadly avalanche had captured everyone's attention, and caution was the key word with the heavy snow we'd had for the past two days. We would have to wait in Camp I until the vast face above the route to Camp II released its heavy load. New snow covered everything, hiding the trash and enhancing the beauty of the rugged setting. In the evening, the tents, backlit by the moon, became dark spots in the film of falling snow. Climbers were silhouetted against the sides of their tents, the light of their headlamps glowing like fireflies caught in the storm.

The next morning I woke up to find that my ski poles had been stolen during the night. We'd heard rumors that other groups had experienced thefts and damage to equipment at Camp I and higher, but I never believed it would happen to me. When I began asking around about the poles, I heard stories about slashed tents and stolen food, fuel, and crampons. I began to have an eerie feeling about the mountain, sensing an unfriendly atmosphere on its slopes. I hoped it didn't portend disaster. As a reflection of a cultural assumption that "what's yours is mine" or even an impoverished or jealous desire to steal from the "wealthy Americans," I could rationalize the thefts, but there seemed to be an energy here that I couldn't put my finger on. I hoped it was all in my head.

A Soviet climber heading down loaned me his set of poles when he heard about my loss, his generosity partially making up for my sense of violation. I was grateful for my willingness to look for the lesson in every situation, and to accept whatever was happening as being perfect, no matter how it looked or felt. As difficult as it was sometimes, I learned I could get angry without letting it ruin my entire trip. I could feel the disappointment at this loss but not look at everyone as a potential thief.

That afternoon, Jonathan left for Base Camp to meet his companions. I missed him immediately, but we'd made plans to climb New Hampshire's Mount Washington during the winter as part of my Everest preparation, and I looked forward to seeing him there.

The face above the route didn't slide that day, so we didn't know if we'd be able to make a carry to Camp II the next morning or not. At dinner, we planned to carry anyway, but Skip and I agreed privately that neither of us liked the mountain and wouldn't be overly disappointed if it snowed for four or five more days and we just bolted. At the same time we both knew that we'd come to Pik Lenin to climb and really wanted a clear night and a clear route in the morning.

The face had not slid by the next morning, but we felt that the snow had settled enough to be safe, so we made our first carry to Camp II: 3,000 vertical feet onto the ridge that led to the summit. Once we moved there, we'd have only one more camp before the summit. We started out at 7:00 A.M., climbed for six hours, sometimes at a gentle angle, sometimes a steep one, and sometimes traversing exposed faces that sloped sharply away from us. It was the best of mountaineering: hard work, good snow, warm sun, loads not too heavy, friendly conversation, and steady, rhythmical climbing, a day when my feet took care of themselves, leaving my head to revel in the beauty of the scenery and the experience.

The site for Camp II was much smaller than Camp I, with little flat ground. Tents were set up on platforms dug out from the side of the slope. We created our platform, pitched a tent, stashed our gear, and headed back down. The warm sun had grown hot, and we all felt its effects as we down-climbed through snow that became ever softer, turning the smooth rhythm of our ascent into an awkward, sinking stagger.

When I arrived back at Camp I, I felt weak and teary and much more tired than the day's effort should have caused. I couldn't imagine making the trip to Camp II again the next day. I didn't understand it, and Martha grabbed the opportunity to launch her usual tirade of "What do you think you're doing here anyway? Don't you realize yet that you can't do this climbing stuff?"

I told her to shut up and walked behind a rock to pee. The dark orange color gave me the answer to my perplexity. I was dehydrated. I drank a liter of water quickly and noticed an immediate physical and emotional improvement. It was another reminder of how aware I needed to be about the effects of high altitude on my system. If I really wanted to climb Everest, I'd need to remember all of these lessons. I continued to force myself to drink water throughout the night.

We talked to another American expedition staying at Camp I and learned that gear they'd left at Camp II had been rifled. Their tents had been used while they'd been higher on the mountain, and Russian food and matches were left behind. The tent door had been left un-zipped, so the storm had blown snow inside, soaking everything that wasn't taken. My unease with the mountain deepened.

The next morning we were to move up to Camp II. I was still exhausted when I woke up and my emotions were on edge. As we packed up I noticed that my thinking was muddled. I had a hard time remembering what items went in what containers, where they belonged in my pack, and even how to stuff the tent after I'd taken it down. I had trouble finding any part of the positive attitude I'd experienced over the previous days. By the time we reached the top of the first bench on the face, I had fallen far behind everyone else. My pack felt extra heavy as did my legs. My brain was even more slow and dull.

We redistributed much of the gear from my pack among the other five climbers. I was embarrassed not to be able to pull my own weight, and in spite of less weight, I couldn't gain access to any additional strength. Roped up, we began to climb the steep section ahead.

Skip kept the pace slow to accommodate my weakness, and still I wasn't able to keep up. I called for rest stops every few minutes. I felt lightheaded and clammy. My arms and legs weren't working right. I had trouble keeping my balance. My body was like an engine whose timing was off. The spark plugs were firing, but they were off the cycle needed by the pistons so everything was working against itself.

Getting all the way to Camp II felt like an impossibility. Old thoughts of inventing or exacerbating physical symptoms as an excuse crept in but I ignored them. The truth was enough. "Skip," I called out weakly, stopping once again. "Skip. Something's wrong."

He turned around because of the pull on the rope from my lack of progress not because he'd heard me. I stood, unable to speak, unable to move, unable even to hold my head up, I only wanted to lie down.

"Margo, are you all right?" I heard Skip's question and couldn't even respond. "Margo, come on up to me. You can't stop there— you're on a snowbridge. Walk toward me, slowly. Now!" He reeled me in like a fish on a line, the others on the same rope moving cautiously behind. When I reached him, my legs could hardly hold me up. "What's up?" he asked.

"I'm not okay. Something's very wrong." My voice didn't sound like me. I sat down in the snow, no longer able to support my own weight. Skip conferred with the others but I was too out of it to care what they were talking about.

"Can you make it to Two?" Skip's voice came from a long way away. I could only shake my head sideways in response. Someone was removing my pack from my back and pulling out the two tents I was carrying.

"Guy, put one of the tents in your pack and the other one in Sasha's. Sasha, take Margo down to Camp One and have the doc check her out." Skip was giving orders, and people were moving around me, but it was as if I were in a fog, unable to respond or help in any way. "Margo." Skip's face was directly in front of mine. "Margo, look at me." I raised my head slightly. "Margo, you're going to be fine. All you have to do is put one foot in front of the other. Sasha will be right behind you. It's all downhill. You'll be fine." Dazed, I looked at Sasha, another of our Russian guides. He extended his hand in the direction of Camp I and said simply, "Come."

I could only nod weakly in response as Skip straightened up and led out toward Camp II, the four others following, roped behind him.

Weak, shaky, and uncoordinated, I lurched down the well-trodden track, ski poles often the only thing that kept me from falling. Sasha stayed close, carrying my pack as well as his. My brain felt like cotton.

When we made it to Camp I. Sasha took me directly to the Soviet doctor. My blood pressure was very high and my heart rate was low, the opposite of what was normal for me when I climbed at high altitude. When I didn't respond to oral medication and acupressure, the doctor injected a strong heart stimulant laced with niphedipine to lower my blood pressure. Gradually my vital signs approached normal. Sasha led me to the tent he'd set up for me. He was very solicitous, bringing me tea and biscuits, and I slept away the remainder of the day except for the times Sasha woke me to bring me more liquids and when the doctor came to examine me again that evening.

I was improved enough to ask him if I could ascend to Camp II the next morning to rejoin my teammates. The doctor looked at me in amazement, shook his head in what I can only imagine was astonishment at the obviously foolish ideas of this crazed American woman, and replied through a translator, "If it is okay to die for you, then you go up tomorrow. Otherwise, down is better. Your head is very sick. Better you go down."

I tried, through the translator, to wangle a different opinion out of him, but he was adamant about the danger of my going higher on the mountain. Finally resigned, I made plans with Sasha to descend to Base Camp the next morning. By the time I was once again cocooned in the warmth of my sleeping bag, I knew I was done with this mountain and wasn't sorry to be going down rather than up.

"This summit just wasn't meant to be mine," I thought. My heart and body were now both solidly behind my not going any higher. I trusted there was a reason for me to spend my days in the meadow rather than on the mountain.

Three men from the American expedition whose gear had been pilfered had also returned to Base Camp and the four of us formed a friendly quartet, going down to Achik-Tash for rejuvenating showers and sharing meals together with their wonderful Soviet cook, Lena. I called them the three J's. Jack was a delightful 6-foot 9-inch tall real estate developer from North Carolina with whom I spent much of this time at Base Camp. We made a Mutt and Jeff duo that invariably caused double-takes. Jerry and Jim were also from the South. Quieter and a nice balance to the silliness Jack and I often brought to Luke's Meadow. We all hitched a ride in a huge Russian helicopter on its way to Moscovina, the Base Camp for Pik Kommunizma. It flew to over 20,000 feet with the engine screaming in the rarefied air as we swooped across sharp-edged ridges, past huge rock faces and down the longest glacier in the Soviet Union. We opened the windows in the unpressurized aircraft, faces and hands freezing from sticking them out to shoot photos. Everyone onboard was hooting and hollering, Soviets and Americans alike, kids playing together in the incredible wonder of the Pamirs. We were even able to retrieve our extra gear from Camp I so Skip and the rest of the guys wouldn't have to carry it down when they made their descent from the summit.

My exhaustion persisted, and as my friends' teammates reached Base Camp with tales of the cold and extreme weather on the summit, it was clear that my choice not to continue the climb was the right one. I realized that in the last two-and-a-half months, I'd attempted three major peaks, successfully making the summits of two of them. The returning climbers reported that Skip and the others were in good condition and looked ready to go for the summit themselves. As thunder rolled across the face of Lenin, I prayed for their safety, for the weather to clear enough for a summit run.

August 16 dawned to a gloriously clear day, a classic sun-shining, birds-singing kind of day in the mountains. I visualized our team reaching the summit as it stood out against a cloudless sky. Late in the day, one of the Soviet climbers came by camp to let us know that our team had tried the summit the day before but had been turned back by the weather and were making another attempt that morning—my intuition had been right. From where I was sitting it looked as if they'd be successful.

That night a waning half moon played peek-a-boo with the clouds and bathed Lenin's summit ridge in a supernatural glow. The North Star hung just above the summit like a Christmas tree ornament. I took it as an affirmation that my being willing to believe in myself, to listen to my body and heart might keep me from what my mind says is the goal of my climbing, but letting go of the summit didn't mean letting go of my dream. I was learning about the truth of my passions and quiet power through what might easily have looked like failure. I could be disappointed without being disappointed in myself.

The guys returned to Base Camp on August 18, triumphant and tired. We were at the end of the climbing season here. Most of the tents had already disappeared from the meadow and all of the climbers were gone from Camp I. Even the local Kyrgyz shepherd was moving his flock out of the high ground. But we still had a few days to wait until our scheduled transportation would arrive.

*   *   *

On August 19, I celebrated my two thousandth day in recovery while preparing to leave the Pamirs after another incredible adventure of both body and heart. Almost five-and-a-half years since my last drink, drug, and bulimic behavior, I was completing five weeks of climbing in the Soviet Union, including the fifth of my seven summits. I was looking forward to six months of good, hard training to prepare for Mount Everest. I knew if I was supposed to, I'd climb it, too. A light breeze dried the laundry hanging on the lines of our tents and brought fresh hope. I felt the strong presence of Jonathan and his encouragement and love. Some of the other American climbers had known him, too, and their reminiscences warmed my heart.

We headed down to Achik-Tash for one last shower. Stopping at the monument erected along the path honoring those climbers who'd died on Lenin, we gave thanks for the success of our team. We found the Achik-Tash camp abandoned: the tent walls had all been removed, and only the wooden floors stood at silent attention around the frame that just days before was the bustling mess tent. There was a strange emptiness and sense of foreboding in the air. Sasha and another Soviet guide met us, gesturing and talking passionately with one another as they approached. They told us they'd heard on the radio that the KGB and military had attacked Gorbachev in Moscow, taken over the government, and were trying to end *Peristroyka*. Autonomy for the individual states that made up the Soviet Union was to have taken effect the next day, but the old guard had showed that it was more violently opposed than anyone had realized. Moscow was in chaos. We were deep in the Pamirs, backed up against Afghanistan and China, and a bus was scheduled to pick us up in two days. All we could do for now was wait to see what happened next.

I prayed for the people we'd met in Moscow, the Caucasus, and here: Their lives were now in turmoil. Nearly all of them had talked about the radical changes that were taking place and the great unknown that awaited them. Meanwhile, we six Americans and two Soviets were grateful for the cocoon we had created together there in the middle of the beautiful meadow called Lukovaya Polyana as storms swept the mountains and political upheaval raged in the cities. Lost in our individual thoughts, we passed time with cooking, crossword puzzles, and reading. Political winds blew around us but we stayed warm and dry inside.

The peace I felt was wonderful. Whatever happened to us over the next few days, my path when I got home was clear: training for Everest. I knew I could do it if I were willing to approach it one small step at a time.

The first step was to wait. I thought about the paradox of standing still to achieve my goal as one afternoon I climbed alone to rocks high on the slope overlooking the meadow. Dark storm clouds descended. Leaning into the wind, exposed to a drop of several hundred feet, I let the fierceness of the blowing gropple—snow pellets that often precede hail—sweep over me. I could feel my self-confidence and my passion holding me in place, protecting me, giving me strength.

Our bus arrived close to the time it had been scheduled to appear, the driver updated us on the latest news he'd been able to gather from the radio, newspapers, and travelers out of Moscow: Gorbachev was back in power, the Russian people were jubilant over what they felt to be a great victory, and Moscow was returning to normal. Still, it took us almost two full days to reach Moscow as airline flights had been canceled, then reinstated.

I took four days to sightsee in both Moscow and St. Petersburg, immersing myself in the beauty, cultural elegance, and magnificence of St. Basil's, the Kremlin, and Gum, then The Hermitage, St. Isaac's, and the Smolny Institute.

Of everything I experienced during those days, it was the wooden cross and flowers erected in Red Square, memorials to the three students killed facing the tanks of tyranny, that held my attention most closely. The date was carved into the cross: 21.08.1991. They had died while we were waiting in the meadow. While I was finding the depth of my own power, peace, and freedom, others were dying for theirs. I walked away from the hastily constructed shrine with a new and deeper sense of my own passion and purpose.

CHAPTER TEN
It Is Finally Happening

Monday, October 21, 1991, San Diego
I have a dream: to climb Mount Everest. Taking
a step in its direction on a daily basis is
being responsible to myself and to that dream. I
don't have to do it perfectly. Just take one
small step.

"M. C. Dreamers may I help you?" The receptionist for my office in the small complex of executive suites was friendly and professional. No matter that my "suite" was the size of a walk-in closet and didn't have any windows. It wasn't meant for show but function: a desk, a computer, and a map of the world. Colored pins marked where I'd climbed and been on treks and rivers, and where I was scheduled to climb next. On seven continents spread out in Mercator Projection, four blue pins identified rivers, seven green ones were for treks, each of the five yellow signified one of the Seven Summits, fifteen white pins located other mountains I had climbed, and the two red ones, representing Kosciusko and Everest, focused my attention on the major task at hand—preparing to climb Mount Everest.

"M. C. Dreamers," I heard the receptionist answer another call. I liked the name that was invented by a close friend: "M. C." my initials, and "Dreamers" signifying the passion both for following my own dreams and facilitating others in discovering and following theirs.

The logo on my business cards and letterhead showed a climber in snow with twelve footprints in front of an outline of mountain peaks, printed in purple ink on lavender stock. It conveyed a professional image while subtly communicating my spiritual path. Whenever I handed one to somebody I had a sense of pride as well as an opening to talk about my work—training, fund-raising, and organizing for Everest.

The office gave me a place to go in the morning, somewhere to "go home" from at night. Located in the heart of Pacific Beach, it was close to my gym, my running route, and my 12-Step support group meetings. At my regular Saturday morning meeting I discussed my priorities and finding balance between work and recreation. Afterward, a friend, who'd been sitting in those rooms with me for the past five years, gave me a big hug. "Remember when you came back from Nepal in 1989?" he reminded me. "You said you'd decided that you were a trekker, not a climber. How many mountains have you climbed since then? Six, eight, maybe more, and at least three of them were the highest on their continents. I think maybe you're a climber after all."

Yes, I thought, I am a climber. But beneath any label, I'm Margo: forty-three years old and a woman I respect. I always thought that the only way I could gain respect for myself was by being what others wanted me to be. Today I was living my life from my passion.

Martha continued to bring up every criticism she could think of to tell me why I wasn't doing anything right, why I'd never get up Everest, and why I would fail in my life. Finally, I got fed up, and on Becky's suggestion, wrote Martha a letter of resignation. "I quit trying to meet your impossible standards. I quit allowing you to call me lazy and stupid. I quit trying to make you happy." Martha's voice represented everyone I'd ever tried to please, and as I typed, I got more and more angry until I was afraid I'd break the keyboard with my furious fingers. I was angry at the people who had asked unreasonable, impossible things from me and angry with myself for believing they knew better than I. Angry at the people who had taught me that others' opinions were more important than mine and angry with myself for buying into that belief. Angry at Martha for demanding the impossible and angry at myself for listening to her. The words flowed, and the anger lessened and finally dissipated, leaving me with a stronger sense of the truth of Margo, a firmer conviction that life didn't have to be about pleasing everyone else, that I deserved to live from my own heart, and that by living from my own values and integrity, I had much more to offer to other people than when I was trying to give them what I thought they wanted.

Once I had fired Martha and the rest of the world as my supervisors and put myself in charge of my own life, I realized I didn't know how to do the job. I trusted God to be CEO but I had no idea how to manage my own department. So I wrote a "Help Wanted" ad:

PROJECT SUPERVISOR. *Woman to supervise single employee in diverse areas. Must be loving, honest, nonjudgmental, patient, encouraging, self-motivated. Must have a working knowledge of and an ability to live in a place of balance between work and recreation, and to guide employee in finding that balance. Requires skill in communication, exercise physiology, writing, organization, teaching, and the trait of managing from love rather than power, guilt, or shame. Must be process- rather than goal-oriented. Perfectionists need not apply.*

This was how I deserved to be treated.

Slowly I began to notice a change in my life. Even when I didn't do things perfectly, my respect for myself increased and was mirrored back to me by the respect others showed me.

I took care of myself physically by addressing the pain in my right foot, which had had an impact on my climbs on Vinson and Denali and had continued to be a problem after I returned from the Soviet Union. I could not go to Everest without doing something about it. A podiatrist's diagnosis was "Morton's Neuroma," an inflammation of an intersection of nerves between the third and fourth toes on my right foot. When a metatarsal arch inserted in my running shoe did not relieve the problem, I underwent surgery on October 3, was fully recovered within six weeks, and could train pain free for the first time in several months. I had been told that the surgery was not always successful, and I took my complete recovery as a good omen for Everest.

When I went home to Greenwich for Christmas, I was able to be with my parents, celebrating with them in their home in a way I'd never experienced before. It was as if I was no longer coming home as a little girl, trying to get their approval. I'd taken those strands out of the tapestry I was weaving. I came to my parents as a loving woman, independent and wanting to bring them joy. In return, they gave me acceptance and acknowledgment of their love for me in a way I'd never felt before. Even the misunderstandings and deep emotional wounds we'd created over the past few years seemed to be healed.

God was helping me in every area of my life. If He could do this, He could certainly get me to the summit of Everest.

It Is Finally Happening

Thursday, January 31, 1992, San Diego
People ask am I excited? Am I afraid? Am I
nervous? I'm all of those and more.

Jonathan Bobaljik and I had talked in Russia about the possibility of doing a winter ascent of Mount Washington in New Hampshire while I was back east for Christmas. The mountain has a harsh subarctic climate and winds that have been recorded as high as 231 mph. Its summit is in the clouds more than three-quarters of the time, and winter conditions are notoriously severe. Jonathan and I had continued our discussions by phone after returning home from Russia.

"Mount Washington is infamous for having the worst weather in the world, and it would be a great chance for you to climb in the kind of conditions you'll probably have on Everest." Jonathan's words, echoing slightly over the long-distance wires, reinforced a comment Skip had made to me after Pik Lenin. He'd recommended that I read a book on the history of Mount Everest and had marked a couple of sections for me to pay particular attention to so I could "see how bad it can get up there and start setting your mind to how you'll survive in conditions like that."

Both passages had been about climbers living through extreme conditions very high on Everest. They described the experience of being out in –40 degree temperatures accompanied by 70 mph winds with no tent to go to, no respite from the conditions, and no one to depend on except oneself. Could I do that? So far I'd been blessed with never having to deal with such severe conditions on a mountain. Although only 6,288 feet high, Mount Washington, I decided, would be a terrific training opportunity for me.

In the parking lot of the Pinkham Notch Camp on December 31, Jonathan and I hauled our packs out of the car and headed for the trail leading to the highest point in New England. The weather was astonishingly clear and calm with a temperature of 10 degrees, almost balmy for 7:00 A.M. on a New England winter morning. We'd spent the night of December 29 on the flanks of the mountain in an attempt to complete a three-day traverse of Mounts Washington, Adams, Jefferson, and Madison, but a blizzard nearly buried us and our equipment. We aborted the attempt and spent the following night in a motel drying enough gear and clothing to support a one-day summit run.

"Doesn't look like we'll be weathered off today," Jonathan said, searching the empty blue sky for clouds. "Let's do it."

We'd opted for a nontechnical route up the mountain because I didn't want to chance an injury so close to Everest. Two and a half hours on a hiking trail, highly traveled in the summer but virtually deserted on this crisp winter day, brought us to the tree line. It had led through a lush forest of evergreens, in some places gently meandering at a low angle and in others switchbacking steeply up the mountain's lower faces. We emerged onto a bleak, rock-strewn ridge that rose toward the summit. The snow had been deep in the trees, but here the effects of the strong wind were evident, the ground nearly swept clean of snow.

"I can't believe this," I said, wiping sweat from my face. "It's warm and clear. What is this? I came here to climb in rotten weather, and it's warm and clear!"

Jonathan laughed. "That's the first time I've ever heard someone complain about the weather being too good." He drank deeply from a water bottle and looked up toward the summit from which telltale plumes of snow extended. "Clear or not, there's some wind up there. We'd better get going."

I drank from my own water bottle and swallowed a handful of gorp before swinging my pack onto my back and moving upward once again.

We spent another two uneventful, one-foot-in-front-of-the-other hours and reached the summit with no sign of Mount Washington's infamous weather. It was blowing about 30 mph—virtually calm for this wind-torn spot—as we stood on the highest point in New England, presented with a clear view of Pinkham Notch, the White Mountains, and southern Maine. We didn't even need the down parkas we carried in our packs. "So much for training in awful weather," I said, "but it's hard to be disappointed. This is magnificent!"

"That it is," Jonathan responded, leaning against the wind. "This is the fifth time I've been up here, and I've never seen it this nice. Not even in the summer. Well, you can still tell people you've done a winter ascent of Mount Washington."

"And they'll have a vision of us freezing!" I laughed out loud, the hood of my Gore-Tex jacket snapping loudly in the brisk wind as if laughing with me.

The wind increased on the way down, but on the whole, Mount Washington was very kind to us. Once again, the Universe had blessed me with good weather on a summit day. And this time I hadn't even wanted it!

Three months remained before I'd leave for Mount Everest. Three months of training, thinking, anticipating, and projecting how it would be when I got to the mountain, how it would be on the summit. Skip had talked a great deal about the extreme conditions, especially the cold, and this turned into a constant fear. I found myself worrying about it while I went for my run around the bay. There wasn't any part of the climb that seemed quite as major to me as the cold. I even talked with Todd Burleson, the expedition leader, about it during one of our phone conversations.

He'd listened to me quietly as I explained how I'd never experienced extreme conditions before. "Yes, Margo, of course the weather can be very harsh. We never know what to expect on a mountain. That's why we prepare ourselves as best we can, take the best equipment we can, and then deal with whatever is presented to us. It's part of the adventure, and Everest is the biggest adventure of them all. You'll do fine."

Of course, he was right. I could let go of my fear, my projections, and feel the excitement of going for my dreams, or I could stay home. Staying home was not a viable option. I prepared myself the best way I knew how, showing up to train and accepting the offers of friends to run last-minute errands. I allowed the Universe to support me as each day, I did the simple footwork in front of me, trusting that it would all add up to my standing on the summit. Some people admired me, some said openly they couldn't understand why anyone would do what I was doing, but I knew I was following my heart and that a woman I could respect was emerging in the process. I didn't need anyone else to understand.

I sat in my room, surrounded by the litter of my preparations for two-and-a-half months of travel: clothes I'd decided not to take, wrappers for film, batteries and other odds and ends I'd purchased, and the duffel bags themselves. One carry-on bag held books, clothes, and layover essentials, the other my computer and camera. For the umpteenth time I checked my tickets and passport. Then the traveler's checks, the phone number for my friend Shirley in Australia, and my watch. She had moved from San Diego to Sydney several years earlier to work in the field of codependency. Since then she had published a book and established a successful therapy practice. I looked forward to seeing her both on a personal and a professional basis.

My ride to the airport was half an hour late. I was getting angry. It wasn't a good way to start my trip, but nothing could interfere with my leaving to complete my dream. I was only a fifteen-hour flight from Australia, a week away from my sixth summit, Kosciusko, and three weeks away from Everest Base Camp.

A phone conversation I'd had with Mum the day before had been more auspicious. It had been the one I'd always wanted to have with her: honest, warm, loving, no games. Simple truths plainly spoken. A gift on the eve of my trip. She was still scared about my climbing and didn't understand why I did it, but she acknowledged how important it was to me and said she'd be working on the weather on the mountain for us. Mum seemed to have a way with weather, as though she could communicate with the wind and rain. Whether that was true or not, it certainly did appear as if, when she put her mind to it, the weather responded, and I was going to need all the help I could get if I was going to make the summit of Everest.

During the twenty-four hours between the phone call and my sitting on the duffel bags in my bedroom, I'd examined my passion for completing the Seven Summits. I knew I had already won great triumphs getting to this point, but I wanted the summit of Everest as well. I wanted it more than I had even been willing to admit. I imagined it so many times, I could almost taste the sense of accomplishment of standing on the highest point on Earth. I wanted to hug Skip, cry, and celebrate my sobriety there. At lunch yesterday, Norton and his unbridled support had given me a marvelous sendoff. A true friend from the beginning of my climbing, he was one of my best cheerleaders. When at last I boarded the plane for Australia, I knew that I was leaving for this trip as physically, emotionally, and spiritually prepared as I could be.

Sightseeing and spending time with Shirley was fun, but after five days, I was anxious to begin climbing. My impatience to get through this part of my trip was distracting. Sitting on Shirley's balcony in Avalon, just outside Sydney, I watched waves break against a rock just offshore. It caught my attention when I saw it, duplicating within me the feeling of peace and serenity I'd received the first time I saw my "God Rock" along Hunter Creek in Aspen.

I decided to go for a run and ended up on the beach overlooking the rock. The sun was directly behind it, backlighting the waves that crashed on it from two directions. When they broke, they sent a ridge of seawater directly toward me as I sat quietly, my eyes closed. Slowly I breathed in the power of those waves. The image of the summit of Everest came into my mind's eye, surprising me. One moment I was present on the beach, the next, there it was. Another image followed, of Skip and me standing on the summit together. Yes! God seemed to know I needed to be reminded that He was in charge of my trip, including the timing. I could be at ease here with Shirley, while He held the summit open for me.

Meanwhile, the two days before I went to Kosciusko, Martha's negative voice dissected in minute detail my body image, training, and mountaineering skills. In spite of my having resigned from Martha's control, it took all the emotional energy I had to get in my rental car and drive to the grass park in Cooma where I was to meet Geof and Sarah. They'd been my guides in Bolivia and now we were going to climb my sixth summit together.

Mount Kosciusko is located in the Snowy Mountains of the Australian Alps, in southeastern New South Wales. P. E. Strzelecki was the first European to encounter the mountain in 1840, and he named it for a fellow Pole, Tadeusz Kosciuszko. At only 7,309 feet, it is an easy hike to the top. An increasing number of climbers consider it unworthy to be called one of the Seven Summits, so they substitute Puncik Jaya, more commonly known as Carstensz Pyramid, at 16,023 feet, the highest point in Indonesia and thus still within Australasia. My intention was to climb Kosciusko now and Carstensz next year, thus covering both bases.

I'd been very much looking forward to seeing Geof and Sarah. We'd kept in touch by letter over the years, and while I'd been fond of Sarah from the start, Geof's writing had shown a side of him that was very different from his guiding style. On a mountain he was focused and aloof; in his letters he'd been warm, philosophical, and open. The photograph they sent me showed a loving family, and Clare, their then eight-month-old daughter, had looked straight at the camera with blue eyes full of love and life, reflecting a wisdom far greater than her age. Without even meeting her, she instantly captured my heart. Geof and Sarah had sounded genuinely pleased when I called to ask if they would accompany me to the summit of Kosciusko, and we came together easily and comfortably. The three of us talked nonstop about mountains, politics, ecology, and babies as we set up our tents in a campground on the shore of Jindabye Lake only a few miles from Kosciusko.

"Margo, it's so good to see you," Sarah looked at me over the lantern we had placed on the blanket between us, a smile covering her entire face. Her Australian accent altered the sound of my name in a way I loved. Clare sucked happily at her breast.

"It is indeed," I answered and sipped my hot chocolate. "Sure doesn't seem like it's been three years."

Geof returned from the picnic table which served as our kitchen and sat down next to Sarah, watching adoringly as Clare nursed. His large, strong hand gently stroked her small head and fine blond hair. Sarah watched him watching their daughter and smiled. In Bolivia I couldn't have imagined that Geof would be this kind of a father. Here, I was filled with a sense of family in the best meaning of the word and felt a little envious of the openhearted way in which Geof and Sarah loved Clare. No limitations, no conditions, no expectations: just love and acceptance. As a result, Clare reacted to the world with wonderfully innocent abandon, openness, and joy—just as a baby ought to.

"Margo, it's wonderful, what you've done and what you're doing." Geof raised his eyes from Clare to me. "Both with your climbing and with your life. I'm glad we get to be a small part of it."

"It'll be great to climb your sixth summit with you tomorrow and then send you off to Everest," said Sarah.

"Thank you," I said, deeply touched by the validation and support of these two people. Geof was an experienced climber and had been to Everest. Sarah understood what it was like to be a solo woman among men on a mountain.

We hugged warmly when we said good-night.

Waking to the familiar pffft-pffft-pffft of the single-burner stove brought many memories and feelings with it: the simple pleasure of sleeping in the outdoors, reluctance to get out of a warm sleeping bag, anticipation of a hot cup of coffee, and strong, conflicting memories of the excitement of a summit day.

This morning there were also other, less familiar things to hear: crows cawing to one another, talking, it seemed, with intonations I hadn't realized they were capable of, and cooing, a gentle and happy sound that I recognized as Clare, a year old now.

The smell of coffee wafting through the partially open door of my tent proved irresistible. I sat up. Today I would climb the sixth of my Seven Summits. Tonight there'd be only one left. I felt grounded, centered, and confident. "I have a right to be climbing Everest. I have a right to be the first American woman to climb the Seven Summits. I have a right to call myself a mountaineer." The words echoed brazenly in my heart as if I'd spoken them aloud. I'd worked hard for those rights, and I thanked God for His part in them as well.

It was a glorious morning, sparklingly clear and warm. We ate breakfast, then drove to the base of the mountain and rode the chairlift, which serviced skiers in the winter, up to the beginning of the paved walkway that led to the summit. Sarah carried Clare in a backpack so she could take in all of the sights along the way. The branches of the snow gum trees swayed wildly in the gusty, fall wind, sweeping parabolic paths against the sky. Their leaves, beginning to change color, reflected the sunlight as they moved. At the top of the chairlift, however, the wind proved too much for Clare, and she and Sarah rode back down as Geof and I continued on the two-hour walk to the summit. Once again our conversation ranged widely, from climbing to politics, the environment to addiction. Our moods changed from reflective silence to silly laughter, then back again.

We talked about Everest quite a bit. Geof had been a member of the Australian Everest expedition in 1984, but had contracted cerebral edema on the Great Couloir route, eliminating any chance of his reaching the summit with the others. His experience provided additional evidence for what I already knew: strength and mountaineering experience did not guarantee a summit. Mountains are not conquered: They allow climbers to reach their peaks. Or not.

We stayed on the summit of Kosciusko for more than an hour, sitting in the wind, watching the large number of people who were truly there for a walk in the park. It was difficult to connect this tourist-filled hump with Aconcagua or Vinson or Denali, and the significance of the climb didn't settle in with me until Geof stopped on the metal-grated path as we walked back down to the chairlift. "Oh, by the way, congratulations on your sixth summit."

"God, that's right." Surprised by my own lack of recognition of my achievement at the top, I said, "I almost forgot. It's hard to realize this is one of the seven."

"But it is, and you've done it. Good on ya, Margo." I smiled at the phrase that was so very "down under." Gary Ball had used it on Vinson. "Good on ya, Maggot," had come over the radio when he heard I'd summited. That had been number three, now there were six. There was only one to go. The big one.

After a night at their home in South Durras, Geof and Sarah sent me off to Nepal with a gorgeous photo of Clare and heartfelt wishes and prayers. My visit with them had given me much more than just my sixth summit.

Getting to Lukla on our first try was a very auspicious beginning. Having safely landed on the dirt runway in the Twin Otter that brought us here, nineteen of us waited for the helicopter that was carrying our extra gear. Eleven of our group were climbers, including Todd Burleson, the expedition leader, and Skip. The other eight were trekkers who would accompany us to Base Camp, stay a couple of days, and head back. They were being led by Skip's wife Elizabeth. Two other climbing guides, Pete Athans and Vern Tejas, had walked in ahead of us and were already at Base Camp along with Karen and Liz, who would act as Base Camp Managers. Two of the climbers, Parry and Steve, would be arriving several days later to complete our full expedition complement of seventeen climbers, guides, and support staff.

The number did not include the Sherpas, without whom an expedition like this one was not possible. Ong Chu, the expedition cook, and Lakpa Rita, our sirdar, or head Sherpa, walked in with us, along with a kitchen staff of three and many porters and yak herders carrying duffel bags, food, and kitchen gear. Ten climbing Sherpas and a Base Camp staff of six were already at Base Camp working to establish the site that would be our home away from home for the next two months. In 1989, I learned to appreciate and respect these friendly people who are so very strong and eager to please. I welcomed the opportunity to spend more time with some of them.

After several hours, we finally began the two-hour walk to Phakding where we'd spend our first night in the Khumbu Valley. I remembered from 1989 that the walk was an easy one, downhill all the way, and looked forward to this pleasant reentry into this region I held close to my heart.

In the three years since I'd first walked toward Namche Bazaar, there'd been little change. There may have been a few more buildings, but the smiling, friendly Sherpas were the same, and the rhododendrons still grew as big as trees, mixing with birch and pine to give depth and color to the hillsides. I knew that as we climbed higher the trees would give way to shrubs and sparse grasses, and then finally to the rock and ice that protected the approach to Mount Everest. It was all very much the same, and yet it wasn't. What was different this time?

I walked with Ken, a hand surgeon from Long Island who seemed happy to listen to my prattling as my enthusiasm and nerves revealed themselves in my loquaciousness. It was an old habit, and at one point I said to Ken, "I know I'm rambling on but I'm just so excited to be here. Do you mind that I'm talking so much? Would you like me to shut up?"

A genuinely nice man, he responded with a smile. "No, I'm enjoying it. I'm more a listener than a talker anyway."

I asked him some questions about himself, then rambled on some more, energized by the reality of being in the Khumbu Valley on the way to Everest. "I gotta tell you, Ken, that even before I left home for this trip, every time someone asked me where I was going, and I told them I was going to climb Mount Everest, I wanted to cover my mouth with my hand and giggle like a six-year-old unable to contain her excitement. It just seems so unbelievable!"

Suddenly I knew what was different from 1989. I was here to climb Mount Everest. The passion, anticipation, and pride in my quest changed how I saw the environment around me and how I felt inside.

Although Ken didn't show the same childlike enthusiasm, he clearly understood and shared the depth of my feelings. "Margo, Skip told me that you were a great person to have on an expedition. I'm already seeing why."

My heart sang, and I smiled from the center of my being. It was true that he listened more than he talked, but Ken said enough for me to know that this was a gentle man with an open heart who wanted very badly to climb Mount Everest. His quiet determination and my effusive exhilaration fit well together. I knew I'd found an ally.

During our rest day in Namche Bazaar, the group took time to walk up to Khumjung, one of the villages that have benefited from Sir Edmund Hilary's generosity to the Sherpa people. Sir Edmund was being flown in by helicopter for a ceremony in Khumjung, and we welcomed the opportunity to see this legendary climber. In 1953 he had been the first man, along with Tenzing Norgay, to successfully climb Mount Everest. The anticipation of the people was palpable, the air almost crackled with it. His work on behalf of the Sherpas, through his Himalayan Trust, has so deeply affected their lives that they revere him almost as a god. Through his efforts, two hospitals and several schools have been built in the valley.

As soon as he climbed down from the chopper he was swarmed and led to a seat in front of a small stage, where songs, dances, and a variety of acts were performed in his honor. Afterward, round faces smiling, a continuous line of Sherpas filed past Hilary, as each presented him with a kata, a white ceremonial scarf, and bowed to the man whose unkempt hair and trademark bushy eyebrows shielded his eyes. The village was filled with laughter. It was a loving and noble afternoon for a man whose accomplishments were not subsumed by his ego but returned to the people whose mountain he climbed.

On the fourth day, our team climbed the long, steep hill leading up to the Thyangboche Monastery beside which we would spend the night. I was grateful for the ally I'd found in Ken. I felt physically strong but increasingly emotionally distanced from most of the climbers, more so than on any previous climb. Bob, who was part of the trekking group, and I had talked about it on the walk out of Namche that morning. This was our fourth trip together, and we'd become friends at home as well as in the wilderness.

"This is going to be a long climb if the climbers don't lighten up," I said loudly enough for him to hear as he walked in front of me. We'd eaten a leisurely breakfast and were a ways behind the others. "They're all so quiet and intense. I have a hard time talking to most of them and don't feel emotionally safe with anyone except Ken. Even

Skip feels more distant. I'm afraid that if I show any vulnerability at all, I'll get eaten up. It just doesn't feel emotionally safe. I'm having much more fun with you trekkers, and I worry about what it'll be like when you leave."

Bob's response was kind and also reflected his sensible, analytical way of being. "I wonder how much of that is about different styles of communication under pressure. You seem to deal with the stress of what's ahead by being more outgoing and talking a great deal. The others seem to draw into themselves more and get quiet. That's what I do when I'm nervous, and I know I'd find your chatter somewhat irritating. That may be part of the distance you're feeling. We trekkers aren't under any pressure, so we enjoy your extroverted nature."

"Ugh. I'll bet you're right." I didn't like having my character defects displayed so clearly in front of me, but it was always beneficial to see my behavior reflected through someone else's eyes. "Thanks, Bob. I don't much like hearing that, but it does explain some things that have happened. And it's something I can be aware of and change. It doesn't solve the dilemma of who I'm going to talk to when you and Elizabeth and the others turn around, though. You guys are my only emotional support." A tint of self-pity colored my appraisal of the situation.

"Reality check," Bob responded. "You brought your journal, right? And you said that Ken was easy to talk to, right? And Skip will be with you, right? And there are two more women at Base Camp, and all those kids you talk about who live inside you are here, right?"

"Okay, okay. I get it." Again the accuracy of Bob's perception cut through my self-pity to the place where I knew I was never alone. Not only were there some people on the trip with whom I felt at least somewhat comfortable, but my inner family and spiritual support team were always within reach. I needed only to get quiet inside to feel their presence. If it felt unsafe to express my feelings directly, I had tools to take care of myself emotionally even without feeling safe with other people. Remembering to use them would be the challenge, but I knew that God did not intend for me to be alone on this mountain.

"Thanks, Bob."

"Anytime," he answered, continuing to walk up the trail in the lumbering gait that so reminded me of a friendly Papa Bear. I was glad he was my friend.

As Ken and I crested the Thyangboche hill together that afternoon, my heart was warmed by the sight of an almost completed monastery. The burnt-out shell of the old monastery had jarred me in 1989, and I had not been able to feel Jonathan in the place I'd most expected

242

his energy to be. Now, I felt him right away, an almost physical presence standing beside me, joining his strength, faith, and energy with mine. I stopped and breathed it all in: the newly built monastery almost glowing in the setting sun, Jonathan's presence, yak bells clanking softly on grazing animals, Sherpas singing as they worked setting up trekkers' tents. I felt serene and strong, complete somehow. I suspected this trip was about much more than reaching the summit of Everest.

The Rinpoche, the highest lama in the Khumbu Valley, lives at Thyangboche and had agreed to bless our climb personally. He had been unwell lately, and we were fortunate that he was willing to perform this ceremony for us. We would have a Puja or blessing ceremony at Base Camp, but the Rinpoche's blessing was special. The morning after we arrived, we filed into a room similar to the teahouse dining areas we'd been in and were served strong tea. The Rinpoche entered a few minutes later, moving slowly in a hunched manner, easing slowly onto a carpeted bench at one end of the room. Lakpa, our sirdar, placed a bag of prayer flags and a bag of rice on the table in front of the Rinpoche, and both were blessed by him. They would be carried to Base Camp to use in our Puja there. Our entire Sherpa crew was clearly in awe to be in the presence of this reincarnated lama.

Lakpa had instructed us in the appropriate actions for the ritual, and we followed his lead, each approaching the Rinpoche one at a time and offering him a kata with a 100-rupee note carefully folded inside. He shook out the note and placed the kata over our head while chanting a blessing, then we backed away, head bowed, hands together in the traditional Buddhist manner. Jonathan was even more present than he'd been the previous afternoon, and I was touched to the core by honoring the simple yet deep regard the Sherpas have for the spirit of the mountains.

Two nights in Pheriche, and one in Lobuche brought us to Gorak Shep, the last camp before Base Camp. To call it a village was a complete misnomer as it consisted of only three teahouses, all smoky enough to convince us to set up our own tents. We had left Lobuche about 6:00 A.M. that morning to allow time to reach the summit of Kala Patar before the perennial wind started howling. Kala Patar, or "Black Hill," is named for the rock covering its upper slopes. It rises 2,000 feet above Gorak Shep to reach an altitude of 18,192 feet and is the classic site from which to view Everest. I'd climbed it in 1989, so this year it was familiar rather than frightening. I started up the steep trail with strength and confidence, remembering Ken's comment as we'd arrived in Lobuche the previous afternoon.

"Margo, you came up here really strong today. I'm impressed."

I smiled a "thank you" at him. "I really found my 'Go Mode' today."

"Whatever that is, it sure worked."

"Go Mode." I didn't remember exactly when I had named it that, but the method had been a part of me since the first climb in Africa. It was walking or climbing at a pace that allowed me to go forever, simply putting one foot in front of the other, adjusting my speed to the difficulty of the terrain, not pushing, not getting out of breath, not fighting. Simply going forward, slow and steady.

It was with me there again on Kala Patar as I moved up, strongly and evenly, not getting tired. It allowed me to enjoy my surroundings as well as the climb and brought together the physical, emotional, and spiritual pieces of being in the mountains.

"God's love. God's strength. God's will. I can." The words that provided the base for my "Go Mode" automatically entered my mind. Familiar from past mountains and many training runs, the mantra created a rhythm that accessed a deep place I couldn't touch without it. Over and over I repeated it in my head, and as always, it became a meditation that brought the strength of my body and the power of my soul together to get me up the hill. It stayed with me all the way to the top of Kala Patar and still echoed as I stood on a rock outcropping looking across the Khumbu glacier at Everest Base Camp, the Icefall, and the top of the world that was the summit of Mount Everest. The view was exquisite with mountains in all directions: Nuptse, Everest, the West Shoulder, Changste with the Lho La in front of it, Pumori, the Shangri peaks, Taweche. It was to the black pyramid of Everest that my eyes returned. "My God," I breathed to myself. "It's really happening. I'm going to climb that mountain." I'd stood in this same place in 1989 and could not, in my wildest fantasies, have imagined I would be returning two-and-a-half years later to climb it. But here I was. I spread my arms wide and hollered into the wind, "Yippee!"

Skip came up on one side of me, Ken on the other. "There she is," Skip said, his voice reverent in the face of such grandeur. The three of us stood shoulder to shoulder, just looking, for a full minute. Then we talked about the route for several minutes. The route on the final day of climbing would follow the southeast ridge so prevalent against the sky, and we could see the landmarks of the Hilary Step and the South Summit. I had to focus to breathe. It all seemed somehow unreal.

Elizabeth called Skip away, and Ken and I remained, still staring at the mountain.

"It's you and me, all the way to the top," Ken said.

I had grown fond of him and was pleased that he seemed to feel the same. I put my arm around his waist. "Absolutely," I replied, and we continued to study the mountain.

I caught up with Elizabeth on the way down. She had stopped to take in the majesty of our surroundings yet again. We had not spent much time together on this trip, and I relished the opportunity to have a few minutes. "Incredible, isn't it?" I asked.

"It's unbelievable," she said, her voice catching in her throat. "Skip has wanted to climb this mountain for twenty years, and he's finally got the chance." She turned to me, and I saw the tears in her eyes. "I just know you're going to get up there. I want you and Skip to summit so badly that I can't make room to care about anyone else."

I smiled, and through my own tears I said, "Me, too." We hugged for a long time.

That night, the Big Dipper, North Star, and Orion were almost lost in the swarm of stars overhead. The endless black sky seemed to make the stars even brighter, and the late-rising moon hadn't begun to diffuse their light. A loud boom signaled an avalanche off Nuptse as I was drifting off to sleep. Some time later, I dreamed of standing on the summit.

We were the eleventh expedition to arrive in Base Camp. The countries of India, New Zealand, Spain, The Netherlands, Great Britain, Russia, and now the United States were all represented in the international village created on the Khumbu Glacier at the base of the Khumbu Icefall. The glacier starts at the foot of the Western Cwm where it is called the Icefall and follows the floor of the valley down to just two miles above Pheriche. From Gorak Shep to Base Camp, we walked on its surface, split with crevasses, littered with debris carried down from the mountain over the centuries, and studded with spikes of ice. Protected by rocks or other debris from the melting that lowers the area around them, the spikes rise out of the surface like thorns and make walking by any direct route almost impossible.

Our Sherpas and two guides who preceded us had established an area that would serve as our Base Camp. Surrounded by the other expeditions, our site was filled with the cacophony of languages and bright colors of international climbing. Buddhist prayer flags snapped in the wind. They were strung from the poles that were raised as part of the traditional Puja by the Sherpa for each expedition. The Puja ceremony was a colorful and impressive ritual, the centerpiece of which was a lama who had traveled from Pangboche to perform the ceremony, sitting on the rocks of the glacier chanting from old, hand-printed copies of sacred Tibetan Buddhist books, rocking in time with his chanting. Rice and barley flour called *tsampa* were thrown to the winds as offerings for the gods and juniper was burned in a fragrant offering of a different form. No Sherpa would enter the Icefall until the Puja had been performed. Sagarmatha, Mother Goddess of the Universe, must be honored, recognized, and given offerings for the protection of the climbers.

On the first morning at Base Camp, I was awakened by a voice. "Margo. Are you awake?"

"Sort of. Is that you, Bob?" I'd been in a deep sleep, exhausted from the hike in and the altitude.

"Yeah, it's me. We're leaving early because it's snowing and we want to get back to Pheriche. We're already pretty well packed, and it won't be long before we go." This was an unwelcome surprise. The trekkers had planned to leave today but several hours later. "I wanted to have a chance to say good-bye."

"I'll be right out. Don't go before I get there." I scrambled to put on the layers of clothes required for the 20-degree temperature and snow outside.

I found Bob and Elizabeth near the large tent that served as a dining and community room for our expedition. They were drinking their last cup of coffee before leaving, nursing it as slowly as possible. Neither of them wanted to leave.

"Thanks for getting me up, Bob. I'd have hated not to be able to say good-bye." But I also hated to be saying it. A quick hug, and they were gone, disappearing into the quietly falling snow. I felt as if my whole support system had left with them. Bob and Elizabeth were two of my best allies, and I'd come to rely on them during the trip to Base Camp. I was thankful for Bob's reminder about all of the resources I had at my disposal and went directly to my journal after they headed back across the glacier toward Gorak Shep.

During the next few days, while we acclimatized and finished setting up camp, I worked hard to find my place on the expedition. I'd always figured that if I mentioned some shortcoming of mine before anyone else, then it wouldn't hurt so much when they noticed it and maybe they'd accept me a little bit. That theory was behind my commenting to Vern Tejas about how slow I'd be. I respected Vern greatly for his climbing abilities and his attitude on mountains, and I'd enjoyed the brief time we'd talked while on McKinley. His skill and his capacity for fun made him a desirable climbing partner. I was certainly glad he was here and wanted him to accept me.

"Margo," he said, "don't paint yourself into a corner about your strength."

Vern's reminder was an important one. I watched my behavior more closely. I caught myself talking about my cramps when I started my period, wanting the guys to know how hard I was working to be there, but was able to gather up my inner family and go inside for support rather than look outside for sympathy. The old fears about having screwed up on McKinley and not deserving to be here percolated hotly at the back of my mind. I observed myself compensate by trying to win Skip's approval, hoping he'd notice the chores I did around camp and tell me what a good job I was doing. I felt more separate from him than I had on any of our other climbs. It had not been true on the trek in but since he had returned to Base Camp from spending a night in Pheriche with Elizabeth and the trekkers on their way out, the connection had felt different. There were many factors. Certainly one of them was Everest itself, which increased the pressure for both of us: Skip had dreamed of standing on the top of this mountain for twenty years; I wanted this summit more than I had wanted any single thing in my life. It was the first time I had done a climb with Skip on which he was not the leader. His philosophical approach to both climbing and guiding suited me, but here, working for someone else, he was having to do some things differently. Whatever the reasons, I missed our connection.

I realized I'd forgotten to acknowledge God and Jonathan for their help and presence. The more I separated myself from their strength, the more I had to justify my existence, and the louder Martha's voice became. My emotions went up and down almost hourly. The climbers maintained emotional distance from each other, but I was able to connect with some who had fears similar to mine. Mike and Hugh, for instance, were also concerned about their ability to keep up the sustained effort required to make it to the summit. It helped to know that I wasn't alone, yet there really wasn't any way to share the experience. The others weren't talking about it, didn't want to talk about it. I found myself going frequently to my tent or for short walks to let my tears flow, to feel the fear and the loneliness this climb's intensity presented.

Yet I had moments of great joy and appreciation, too. One day I sat in the sun outside my tent in a makeshift chair made up of my Therm-a-Rest mattress placed into a special nylon cover, doing needlepoint. My legs were wrapped in my sleeping bag. The sun warmed my face. I pulled the colored yarn through the design laid out in little squares and had to laugh. Here I was, doing what I so often did on my couch at home, but at 17,500 feet at the Base Camp for Mount Everest!

Gratitude became my safety line linking mornings to afternoons and one day to the next. As I had suspected, the value of this trip was proving to be much more than the mountain climbing. It was training for difficult, noncommunicative relationships, days of boredom and being uncomfortably cold, mornings filled with malaise when I didn't want to get up, and the quiet anticipation of standing on the summit. I soon discovered that I could choose to focus on the problems that arose almost hourly and the attitudes that flared up between team members, or I could focus on my gratitude for being there on the Khumbu Glacier.

A sack of mail arrived bringing with it five letters for me. Each one gave words of encouragement. The most important letter came from Mum. I got tears in my eyes when I saw her scrawled handwriting. Her near blindness made writing even a few words a difficult task, and she had made the effort to write me a two-page letter. The gesture touched me deeply, as did the letter itself. She said she respected and supported me and that I was an inspiration. The shift that had taken place in her support for me over the past few months was incredible, and I wondered how much of that change was a reflection of my new attitude and way of living. All I knew was that I was, at last, receiving the support and love from her I'd always wanted, always hoped I could be good enough to get.

As we waited to advance to Camp I, the Sherpas and some of the guides began to move up through the Icefall, stockpiling equipment and supplies for Camps I and II in preparation for us. The rest of us familiarized ourselves with the oxygen masks and bottles we would use climbing above Camp III and practiced crossing aluminum ladders like those that spanned the crevasses in the Icefall, a somewhat awkward task in rigid plastic climbing boots and crampons. The degree of comfort with which we were able to walk across and climb these ladders would affect the difficulty of the trip up to Camp I. I had to remind myself constantly to hydrate. Drinking and eating enough would be two keys for my having the strength and spirit to get to the summit.

The next day we moved into the Icefall itself to practice on the lower portion of the route. While we took turns clipping and unclipping ourselves from the safety ropes and gingerly walking out over the void of a crevasse, I commented to Pete Athans, one of the guides, about the fears that kept coming up for me. "I've had really strong visions of seeing myself on the summit, Pete, but there's part of me that's scared of everything from falling into a crevasse to freezing to death to being blown off the mountain."

"Margo, I'd be worried about you if you weren't afraid. This is Everest we're climbing, not just any mountain."

In my heart I knew he was right, but my head still told me that I shouldn't be so emotional. Then I got it. What I was feeling was simply the enormity of the undertaking I was facing. I was preparing to climb the seventh of my Seven Summits, to be the first American woman to accomplish that feat. I was preparing to stand on the summit of the highest mountain on Earth. I, Margo Chisholm, recovering alcoholic, drug addict, and bulimic, was getting ready to do that—I had a right to feel afraid.

Our move through the Icefall to Camp I was incredible. The climb was awesome, powerful, mysterious, glorious, beautiful, difficult, and scary. The sun reflected brightly off the ice, some of it so blue it looked like the ocean off La Jolla. Mum was doing good work with the weather. Although it had been snowing when we got up at 4:00 A.M., by the time we left at 5:00, it was clear and stayed that way all day. Seracs leaned against one another in haphazard arrangements. Crevasses opened up 10, 20, sometimes 30 feet across, some as deep as they were wide, some seemingly without a bottom. Even with the trail worn by the Sherpas and other climbers who'd gone ahead of us, and the fixed ropes giving some sense of protection, the climbing required all of my concentration. This wasn't like any climbing I'd encountered before. This was Everest, the Mother Goddess of the Universe, and I was moving up onto her back.

I stood at the base of a serac waiting with Mike and Pete while Ken made his way slowly up the second, then the third section of aluminum ladders to reach the top. It felt good to be in queue like this once in a while, having a chance to breathe deeply and look at the magnificent shapes and colors all around us. The bright yellows, reds, purples, and blues of our climbing suits contrasted with the white snow, blue ice, and gray rock. It was like climbing through a bombed-out city of ice. We couldn't see our objective, but surmounting one obstacle after another, we trusted we'd arrive at our destination.

About two-thirds of the way through the Icefall I stopped for a rest. When I lifted my pack onto my back and began walking again, my legs felt as though all of the strength had been drained out of them. They ached with each step and I couldn't find a rhythm to my climbing. The route was so irregular that none of my mantras seemed to work. The final climb into camp felt like one of the longest walks of my life.

Camp I sat just above the Icefall at the beginning of the Western Cwm. Crevasses cut the surface, leaving jagged gaps. Footsteps followed the line of least resistance around them, forming a maze pattern in the snow.

After some snacks and water, enough of my energy returned to help Skip fill water bottles and set up one of the tents. The day had been scary and exciting, and I was filled with big doubts and huge hopes. A headache, brought on by the altitude, started at the top of my spine and wrapped around to my temples. It was bearable, and some Ibuprofen helped me sleep that night, but as I began to move around the next morning, it worsened dramatically, I wanted to die. Diamox, the standard treatment for mild acute mountain sickness, and the increased oxygen intake from purposefully hyperventilating, lessened the pain although the headache remained throughout the day.

In the afternoon when I climbed with some of my companions up to the first ladder on the way to Camp II for acclimatization, I was still very fatigued and couldn't imagine how I'd get up that pitch the next day. I returned to Camp I, planning to drink more fluids, climb into my sleeping bag, and acclimatize some more. Within two hours my head was being torn apart once again. More Diamox, more hyperventilating, more feeling as if I'd throw up any minute, then it subsided, and I drifted off to sleep saying the Serenity Prayer. God would certainly have to help me if I was going to get higher on the mountain.

The next day I was up at 7:00 A.M. and off by 8:00, headache free. Such is the nature of the effects of altitude. Sometimes it works to stay put to let the body adjust to it, sometimes the climber has to descend. I was fortunate: the fluids, Diamox, and time had worked, and I felt strong as we climbed for five hours, up and over and around obstacles into the long valley known as the Western Cwm. Huge rock and ice faces rose thousands of feet on either side, Nuptse, Lhotse, and Everest forming a horseshoe whose floor was the Western Cwm. The headache at Camp I and the effort of moving through my fears in the Icefall had been discouraging, but as I made the long slog across the ice of the Cwm, the wonder of being on Everest took precedence, and my excitement rose to match the magnificence of the raw power of the mountains that embraced me.

The first two days at Camp II were spent acclimatizing to the 21,500-foot altitude. We had to keep activity to a minimum until our bodies could continue to adapt to the thin air. My headache didn't return, but on the morning of the third day, as I climbed a short ways up a slope with Hugh and Mike, the feelings of separation and being alone swept in. Each climber on my team was lost in his own thoughts.

They weren't going to climb for me; they were each on their own quest for the summit. This expedition was not about climbing together, even though we were dependent on one another for safety. The higher we got on the mountain, the more each climbing team would depend on the strength of its individual members to achieve success. Individual effort seemed to be the key, but because I couldn't talk about my fears of failure, they felt bigger to me than anyone else's. I had to accept that climbing this mountain was my job alone; no one else could help me do it.

At Camp II we had a sweeping view of the Cwm laid out from the top of the Icefall to the foot of the Lhotse face. Mike, Hugh, and I had walked a little above our camp to get some perspective on our position. "This is so incredible. I can't believe I'm finally here," I said. Tents at Camp III on the face were nearly invisible dots of color; climbers were specks of pepper on the ice. "But I don't have a clue how I'm ever going to get up that face, let alone to the summit. Sometimes I get so scared I can hardly breathe." The words were out of my mouth before I could stop them. I didn't know whether it was safe to be vulnerable with these men or not, but now it was too late.

"I know what you mean," Mike said. His strong exterior had hidden what lay just below the surface. "When I thought about climbing Mount Everest, even when I imagined it on the trek in or down in Base Camp, it seemed too big to do. But somehow standing here, I can break it down to getting to the face, then up the fixed ropes, then up to Camp Four, then each step from there to the summit, and it feels do-able."

Hugh shook his head and smiled. "I was just thinking the same thing. I didn't think anyone else worried about it. God, it's good to know I'm not the only one."

The response of these men gave me not only the knowledge that I wasn't alone in my fear, but a way of climbing this mountain. It was back to one step at a time. I could do that. I knew how to do it at home, and I'd done it on a lot of mountains to get here. I could do it here, too. It would be hard—for all of us—but I only had to show up one day at a time. I could have my tears and fatigue; my strength would grow as I acclimatized.

The next couple of days, my emotions were all over the face of the mountain. I worked hard not to get caught up in their swirling, changeable movements. I looked for the strength that I'd touched in Base Camp, that I'd had on other mountains. One minute I'd think I'd found it, only to be swept away again into fear. I kept showing up, helping out around camp, talking with other climbers, taking short excursions out into the Cwm or up the slopes above camp. Mum kept doing her thing with the weather. Sometimes I hoped secretly that we'd get a storm so I wouldn't have to climb, then I'd recognize the fear behind the thought and let it go. The wind did blow much of the time, sometimes in gusts up to 50 mph, but most of the time it was bearable and the skies were clear. The summit was waiting.

We climbed partway to Camp III to become familiar with both the altitude and climbing on the Lhotse Face. I moved well in my "Go Mode" up the fairly low-angle slope of the Cwm to the base of the fixed ropes. Once the pitch steepened, however, I slowed way down. The Lhotse face was formidable, and even with the fixed lines, I was not comfortable on it. My calves got very tight as I struggled to find a way of placing my feet on the steep ice that allowed enough flex in my ankles to keep all my crampon points on the surface. Much of the ice was water ice: clear and hard. It took concentration to prevent my crampons from skating off it, and although my technique was fine, I had no confidence in it. We climbed only a short way up the ropes, not far enough for me to become more comfortable on the steep ice, and when we turned around, I was more afraid than when I had been at the bottom. How would I ever be able to make it to Camp III when I felt so awkward?

After five days of living at 21,500 feet, I had adapted well and answered each "soup ready" call when it came, forcing myself to drink fluids in between meals as well as at them. Physically I felt stronger each day, but emotionally I seemed to be fighting some vague sense of unease, of separateness, as if something was missing.

On the sixth day, I developed a fever and began coughing badly. Skip's arrival that afternoon bolstered my morale, but the next four days were a physical and emotional roller coaster. The seventh day was worse, and it was difficult to hold on to any hope of ever climbing above Camp II again, but on the eighth day I felt better and walked up to the foot of the ropes with Skip, Hugh, and Louis. On the way down I was delighted and honored to be walking in the Western Cwm with Skip. It had been he who had first suggested I come on this expedition and who had taught me many of the skills I needed for it. He had been at Base Camp for much of the time I had been at Camp II, and I had missed his tangible support and was grateful to have it now. I shared a few of my concerns about the Face with him, and he responded reassuringly, mirroring his vision of the strength I could not see in myself.

"I know you, Margo. You'll do great." He looked out over the Cwm toward Pumori and added, "It is just incredible to be here. And it's great to see you here."

"Thanks," I replied. "I feel the same way." My spirit soared even as my body deteriorated once again.

The next day I stayed in my tent, coughing, while the rest of my companions climbed up to Camp III. Then I struggled down through the Icefall to Base Camp, only to be sent down to Pheriche with nearly all of the other climbers on the expedition. We had a variety of ailments—bronchitis, pneumonia, and HAPE—but only three of us had to stay close to the HRA medical facility while we recuperated.

Vern, Parry, and I spent three weeks in Pheriche and Deboche before we were well enough to go back up on the mountain. When we returned to Base Camp we were immediately assigned to summit teams.

I got up at 5:30 A.M. Friday morning to see Vern, Skip, and the rest of the first team of climbers off as they made their way through the Icefall on their way to Camp II, and then to the summit. My friend and my mentor walked off together, leaving me with only my inner resources as I visualized my own imminent summit attempt. My team would leave the day after the next. After the guys left, I puttered around for the rest of the day, keeping myself busy, feeling fit and strong and confident. I wanted to focus on the summit, not on the tightness growing in my chest. I wanted to believe my coughing was just the standard high-altitude hack, not the return of my pneumonia. I didn't want to put energy into anything that might keep me off the mountain. I even ignored the heavy yellow phlegm I was coughing up.

Saturday I woke up feeling odd, sort of off balance and weak, shaking inside as if I'd had too much caffeine. I wrote it off first as my body complaining about spending such a long time at debilitating altitudes and later as the effect of the strong Australian coffee I'd enjoyed at breakfast, a welcome change from the instant Nescafe that was our usual fare.

Standing alone, just outside the door of my tent, I was looking up at the Icefall and fighting hard to maintain the denial of my physical symptoms when Pete stopped by.

"Didn't get much sleep, huh, Margo." Pete's words were a statement rather than a question.

"A fair amount," I responded, still watching the climbers in the Icefall, who looked like ants on an iceberg.

"You coughed quite a bit during the night, and I didn't much like the sound of it. I was down in the Kiwi camp earlier this morning so I asked Jan to come up and listen to your lungs. Okay with you?"

"Sure," I said offhandedly, rejecting vehemently the possibility that she would find anything wrong. I had coughed during the night, but with the amount of time we'd all spent at Camp II and the amount of respiratory illness that had run through the expedition, almost everyone was coughing: the dry, high-altitude hack that became so familiar on big mountains. Mine didn't seem worse than anyone else's, but apparently Pete thought differently. "I'm fine," I said, "but if you need to have her look at me, that's okay."

"Great." He turned toward the mess tent.

I stopped him with a question. "Why Jan rather than Ken?" Ken, our own doc, was on the same summit team as I was. If there was something going on with my lungs, I thought I might have a better chance of talking him out of saying anything than I did with Jan. Right then, my only concern was getting back on the mountain. I didn't care how I felt. I just wanted to get back on the mountain.

"He's busy getting ready to go up tomorrow, and Jan said she had plenty of time. She's had a lot of experience up here." I nodded, and he headed toward the mess tent. "See ya later."

"Okay." I took a deep breath. I didn't want to think about what Jan might find and was turning toward my tent to find something to do that would quiet my mind when Parry called from the door of his tent.

"Margo, we're going for a walk in the Icefall. Wanna come?"

"Sure," I called back. The perfect solution. Parry, Ken, Hugh, and I headed up to the ice with a man who was filming a video about Nepal. He asked many questions and stopped frequently to film, so we moved very slowly. Nevertheless by the time we got to the foot of the first ladder, I was tired and coughing badly. Not a dry hack at all, but a phlegmy cough that sounded way too much like the one I had had at Camp II three weeks before. The cough continued as I walked, discouraged, back to camp, falling far behind the others. My chest was tightening, and I walked with my head down, afraid of what was happening.

Pete caught me as I walked by the door of the mess tent. "Did you see Jan yet?"

I fought to keep from coughing as I shook my head, "No."

"I don't want to seem like I'm pushing, Margo, but you're beginning to sound like Vern when he had such bad double pneumonia, and I'm concerned."

"Margo, I'll check you out in the medical tent." Ken's voice came from inside the mess tent, and I could no longer put off the examination. He listened to my lungs as I took deep breaths that irritated my chest and made me cough. "Are you coughing up any phlegm?"

"Some," I answered reluctantly.

"What color?"

"Kind of a greenish yellow."

He listened to both sides once again, spending more time on the right, where the earlier pneumonia had been. "I don't like what I'm hearing, Margo. You've got something going on in there." His voice told me he didn't like giving me this bad news, and he couldn't look at me. "It's certainly not like it was at Pheriche, and there's nothing conclusive, but there are definitely noises, and the air flow is decreased on the right side. I'm not sure what to tell you."

"Ken, if I were your wife, what would you tell me?"

He let out a deep sigh, and his eyes finally rose to meet mine. "I'd tell you to wait for twenty-four hours. It's too borderline to call right now, but you shouldn't go up in the morning."

I felt how hard this was for him and kept my own emotions tightly reined. I didn't want him to see the depth of my own disappointment. "Okay. Thanks. I think I'll get a second opinion from Jan."

"That's a good idea. I'll tell Pete what I just told you. Let me know what Jan says. It's not over yet."

My stomach had dropped to the ground, and I had a difficult time hearing anything in Ken's voice that gave me much hope.

The New Zealand camp was no more than five minutes from ours, but I was aware of my breathing with every step. I felt my chest tighten, holding back a cough, and could feel the wheezing in my lungs. I tried to breathe less deeply. I was winded when I arrived.

The Kiwi expedition was also a commercial one, led by Jan's husband Rob Hall and his partner Gary Ball. They were the same pair who had brightened my Vinson climb, and I'd enjoyed spending time in their camp, getting to know them better here. There was a light-hearted camaraderie in the Kiwi camp that was missing in ours, and I felt a closeness with and debt to both Gary and Rob for coming back to help us with our injuries on Mount Vinson. A special connection with Rob existed for me ever since our talk during dinner in Punta Arenas. All of that and more flashed through my mind as I walked into their camp. Jan was in the communications tent working on the radio that linked the climbers above to Base Camp.

"Hi, Jan." I tried to sound as cheerful as I could.

"Hi, Margo, how's it going?" Suddenly she grimaced. "Oh, God, I was supposed to come up and give your lungs a listen, wasn't I? I forgot all about it. Here, have a seat. I'll do it now."

"No problem," I said, taking a seat on the equipment barrel in front of her. "Ken listened to them this afternoon but I'd like your opinion as well."

"You bet." She breathed on her stethoscope to warm it up and said, "Pull up your shirt, and let's find out what's happening in there." I really missed having another woman on our expedition. I could feel myself relax in Jan's presence, even though what she found might keep me off the mountain.

Jan's evaluation was the same as Ken's: bronchitis and tracheitis. There was something going on, but it wasn't distinct enough to make a call. Waiting for twenty-four hours was the best option. We'd find out by tomorrow whether or not my lungs would support my going back on the mountain.

It was hard to hear, and I struggled with the not knowing. As much as I wanted to climb this mountain, in some ways it was harder to be told to wait than to be told I couldn't go back up.

At dinner that night, I put on a cheerful attitude I didn't feel. My mind obsessively played with the question of what to do, bouncing back and forth with equal vehemence from, "Go anyway, regardless of what they say," to "Okay, I'm done. I don't have it in me to fight this and still climb." I didn't sleep well that night.

I got up early the next morning to see what was meant to be my team of climbers off and felt no better. There were hugs and well wishes all around. "We'll see you at Two tomorrow," Ken said into my ear as I hugged him tightly. They were spending two nights there to increase their chances for the summit, and I could catch up with them tomorrow if I was able to climb. I couldn't stop the tears as I watched "my" team leave Base Camp in the dark, circles of light from their headlamps growing smaller as they moved toward the Icefall across the rubble of rock that had been brought down over eons by the movement of the glacier and covered the ice at this level. Although my mind could not put the words together, my heart knew then that I was done: I simply did not have the strength to fight the illness in my body and climb, too. It would have been foolish and dangerous.

So, it was done for me. My heart knew but my mind continued to argue. Ken, Parry, Frank, and Pete left this morning, climbing up through the Icefall on their way to the summit. I was supposed to be with them, but instead, I was back in my little tent, too disappointed even to cry. I hadn't told anyone that I'd decided I didn't have the strength to go back up. I still believed I could go up anyway, that I'd be stronger tomorrow, that I'd power through the illness, that it was only a matter of willpower. My heart knew better.

I was eating breakfast with Todd a few hours later. We were the only climbers from our group remaining at Base Camp. "You coughed hard last night," he said. "Did you get any sleep?"

"Not much," I replied, and in a flash, my head accepted the decision my heart had already made. Haltingly, I told Todd, "I've decided not to go up tomorrow. I just don't have the strength." I couldn't stop the tears any longer, and they flowed freely down my cheeks. "I'm sorry," I said in the voice of a little girl.

"No need to be sorry, Margo. It's the right choice. And until you got sick at Camp Two, you were right in the pack."

I knew he was right, knew I'd made the right choice. I hadn't wanted it to end this way. Not by being sick. I didn't know if I could have made the summit but I believed I could have given it a good run. Despite the acute disappointment, I was willing to believe there was a reason for this, a lesson for me to learn. Later that day I wrote in my journal, "Dear God, I don't like this, I didn't ask for it, and I hate that it's happening. BUT, I'm willing to believe that you know something that I don't know and I'm willing to say thank you for this obnoxious opportunity to grow." It was a prayer I'd been taught early in my recovery, and it had always helped to release the intense anger and disappointment that came when my life didn't work the way I wanted it to. It worked this time too.

Martha tried in vain to make me wrong, to make me responsible, to make me a failure for choosing not to go back on the mountain, for the bronchitis in my lungs. But I didn't buy it. I knew I wasn't a quitter or a wimp or a failure. I'd been through the Khumbu Icefall, lived in the Western Cwm, climbed partway up the Lhotse Face, stood directly under the summit of Everest. No, I wouldn't stand on the summit. I'd worked hard emotionally, too. I'd made some new friends: even when most of the climbers protected their emotions so carefully, a couple were openly antagonistic, and one had ignored me completely. Yes, I longed for someone to hold me while I felt the weight of the reality that I would not get back on the mountain. But I had walked a path I was proud of to get there, and not one step of it could be taken away from me, not by Martha, not by anyone.

I settled into my choice, surrendering to the reality that my body was not well, that it would not support my being on the mountain again. Waves of disappointment washed over me, followed by a deep gratitude for being able to live out my dream of climbing, of having spent so much time at Camp II on Mount Everest. No, I wouldn't complete my quest for the Seven Summits—at least not this year. Already a couple of people had asked me if I'd return. Return? The possibility began to weave through my awareness as I found ways to be useful while our teams of climbers were making their way toward the summit. Pete tried Everest five times before he made it to the summit. Maybe I had one more try in me. I didn't have the money at the moment and wasn't sure how I'd find it, but I didn't have to make any decisions that day, not even the next. I could hold the possibility open, feel the excitement deep down inside when I allowed it to be present, and be content at Base Camp while Skip, Vern, Parry, Rob, and all of the other climbers on the mountain were working so hard up there.

Like us, the Kiwis had direct radio contact with their team and reported that Skip, Vern, and Louis were about 40 minutes from the South Summit at 9:10 A.M. The weather on the summit was nearly perfect. John Helenek stayed at the col, snow blind because he'd climbed yesterday without his glacier glasses. They had kept icing up, and he couldn't see and decided the overcast sky would protect his eyes without them. His carelessness would cost him a shot at the summit.

We waited for each subsequent radio transmission, setting up the solar panels that charged the batteries on the rock outside the dining tent.

"Base Camp, Base Camp, do you read?" The radio crackled with static but it was clearly Vern's voice.

"We read you. Is that you, Vern? Where are you?" Karen spoke into the radio as we all looked up at the mountain as if we might be able to see them somehow. We had last heard from them at the foot of the Hilary Step, approximately an hour to an hour and a half below the summit.

"Base Camp, Base Camp, we are all on the summit." Despite the breathlessness caused by the removal of his oxygen mask, we heard the pride in Vern's voice. It was 11:55 A.M. on May 12, 1992.

"Yes!" Karen exclaimed loudly, raising her fist in victory. The large group of Sherpas and westerners that had gathered around the radio broke into pairs and trios, hugging and patting each others' backs, jumping up and down like children, smiles revealing white teeth in faces burned brown by the sun. "That's great. How is everyone?"

"We're all fine and happy to be here. The weather's great and the view even better."

I thought, "Bravo, Mother," as I looked at Karen and asked, "May I?" She smiled and handed the radio to me. "All right, Vernon! Congratulations!"

"Thanks, Margo," Vern replied, breathing heavily.

"Is Skip nearby?" I asked.

There was a pause, and then a quiet, familiar voice said, "Margita."

I answered, "El Cuernador," using the nicknames we had given each other in Patagonia three years earlier. "You made it," I said, my grin threatening to split my face apart. I moved away from the others, wanting to be alone to share this victory with Skip.

"I did," he replied. "I'm sorry you're not here with me."

"You're there. That's almost as good. Take care of yourself on the way down." I'd run out of words and handed the radio back to Karen as Skip replied, "We will."

I didn't listen to the rest of the conversation. My heart was overflowing. I had said all along that it was 95 percent as important to me that Skip summit as it was that I did. His twenty-year dream of standing on the top of Mount Everest had come true. He was the first man to guide the Seven Summits successfully, and I'd shared five of those summits with him. He'd played an enormously important role in my living my dreams, and now I was able to be a part of his realizing his own. Still, I could not deny the intense disappointment I felt at the same time. I'd wanted to stand on the top of this mountain as badly as I'd ever wanted anything. And it was not to be. The feelings of joy and disappointment mingled inside me, moving around each other like two birds in a courtship ritual.

The air in Base Camp was almost electric. More than thirty climbers made the summit that day: Kiwis, Americans, British, Indian, Dutch, Russians, and Sherpas. We could follow the progress of the climbers above by the shouts from each camp as their group radioed in from the summit. It was a happy day, one to be remembered.

A week later, I stood on the large rock that had protected my tent the last two months and looked over Base Camp. Platforms that supported expedition tents a couple of days ago were empty now. A full moon rose from behind the Lho La, bathing the camp and the mountains in a stark brightness. My expedition had put two teams on the summit: four guides, three clients, and five Sherpas altogether. I was not the only one who didn't make it, not the failure in the group, although from time to time Martha still tried to pull that picture up.

The last few days in Base Camp had been filled with packing up, saying good-bye as some climbers left to meet their own schedules, and private periods of reflection about coming back. I had received another letter from Mum, telling me they were proud of me no matter how high I climbed. I believed her, and it touched me deeply that she'd taken the time to tell me so.

The walk out from Base Camp was particularly nice. Ken and I had a perfect day going from Deboche to Namche Bazaar. The valley was especially beautiful, with the rhododendron blossoms ranging from pale pink to magenta and many different shades of green on the hillsides. Across the river, it appeared as though an artist had brushed a single stroke of red along the foliage. Ken's walking pace and manner made for a comfortable time of decompression after two months on the mountain.

As I tightened my seatbelt in the small twin-engine workhorse of Royal Nepal Airlines sitting at the end of the runway at Lukla, I thought back to the waiting and the walking I'd done over the past weeks. I anticipated the waiting I had ahead of me before I arrived home in San Diego, the flights from Kathmandu to Bangkok, then to the Los Angeles Airport where Ray had taken me to begin this trip and where he would meet me at its end. The propellers whined in the 9,403-foot altitude and we began to roll downhill toward the precipice that signaled the end of this dirt runway. In a moment we were airborne. As we flew above the silt-clouded waters of the Dudh Kosi toward Kathmandu, we left behind the Himal, the Khumbu Valley, and the majesty of Everest.

I didn't want to be seventy and wonder what might have happened if I'd given Everest another try. All the time I told others: Go for your dream. Don't let anything get in your way. That's the truth I needed to live, too. I knew, at the core of my being, that I still wanted to stand on the summit of Everest. I had to find a way to come back.

CHAPTER ELEVEN

There Are Higher Mountains Than Mount Everest

Saturday, June 13, 1992, San Diego
I wish I knew how to be more proud of where
I am in my life. Others are. Why is it so
hard for me? Because I still don't know that it's
okay to not be a doer.

"When I put my head down at night, I feel like I'm scared of something, Ray." My friend had watched me return from many climbs and sometimes understood my process better than I did. "I'm scared to go to sleep and don't know why. I've felt off ever since I got home. This feels like something more than my usual reentry stuff. I feel like there's something really wrong."

"Margo, cut yourself some slack." I could count on him to be direct and to the point. "If I had a dream and put myself out there with people the way you have, especially a dream as big as climbing Mount Everest, and then I came home and had to tell those same people I'd done my best and still hadn't climbed it, and that now I was going back to try it again, I'd be scared shitless."

"But I don't get it. Everyone has been so supportive and gracious to me. They're telling me they think what I'm doing is incredible."

261

My friends and others had been wonderful, even when I told them I hadn't made it to the summit. "And I still feel like a fraud."

"Well, how do *you* feel about not getting to the top of Everest? What did your folks say? What's Martha telling you?"

"Martha says I'm a failure, that I didn't have any business being on Mount Everest in the first place." I began to feel uncomfortable as his questions probed the feelings that lay beneath my vague sense of fear and unease. "Mum and Dad were supportive, but they wanted to talk about what I was going to do now. And Mum mentioned that someone had asked why they hadn't received a thank you for their donation toward my climb. I told her I'd get them out as soon as I could. What'd they expect, that I'd send postcards from Camp Two?" My guilt and sense of failure were growing as I put words to them.

Ray sat across from me at the table in the little café on the beach, his hand wrapped around his mug of coffee. My stomach began to feel as if he were stirring it as he slowly swirled his half-filled cup, listening, weighing my response. "Yes, and . . ." He always had a way of leading me into my feelings, especially the ones I didn't want to feel.

"Dammit, Ray, I'm disappointed, and I feel like a failure and a fake. I'm afraid they're just being nice so they won't hurt my feelings. That they really feel sorry for me but are afraid to say it to my face. That they think I'm crazy for even thinking about going back."

"Well, are you?"

"Am I what?"

"Disappointed, a failure, a fake, and crazy?"

"Disappointed? Yes. You're damn right I am. I don't feel like I had a good shot at the mountain. My body gave out before I even had a chance. A failure? No. It might look that way if finishing the Seven Summits was my only goal. But it wasn't. You know that. Being there was much more important than standing on the summit. It was such a privilege to just be on the mountain. And I'm not a fake. I've climbed six of the Seven Summits and almost twenty others besides." Ray was smiling, his coffee cup empty, resting in its saucer. I could feel energy flowing through my body, sitting me up straight in my chair. "And I'm certainly not crazy for going back. Some climbers have made four, five, even more attempts. This is my passion. I am a climber, and standing on the summit of Mount Everest is my dream. The only failure would be not to try again."

"So, what is it you're afraid of? Why are you having trouble sleeping? What is it you're not letting yourself feel?"

Now it was my turn to pick up my coffee mug and rotate it, cupped in my hands. I set it down and looked into his eyes. "That I might be wrong about my passion, that I might really be crazy, that maybe I really am a failure. I'm scared that Martha may be right. Hell, I'm having trouble getting back into doing the daily stuff of life: bills, returning phone calls, writing the thank-you notes. Maybe this is just another obsession. I'd rather be back on the mountain than be here. Maybe my wanting to go back is a way to avoid moving on with my life."

"Maybe your life *is* about your going back." Ray had this way of turning phrases around so they hit home, hard. "If your life was about being an accountant or stockbroker, maybe going back to Everest would be avoiding something. But your career is about adventure travel, and telling others that if you can go for your dreams, they can go for theirs, too. Margo, you're probably living out the truth of your life with more integrity than most of the people in this café. You're human. Where's God in all of this?"

"I haven't been talking with Him much."

"Jonathan?"

"Haven't been checking in with him, either. In fact, that was one of the things I noticed on the mountain, too. I pretty much tried this one on my own." Ray'd nailed me once more. "Damn. I've been doing it again. It's no wonder I'm so scared. I've been doing it alone. I can never feel my power when I'm doing that. Thanks, Ray, at least now I know where to start to change things."

I returned to the basics I'd been taught in early recovery to re-connect with my spiritual energy. I prayed, meditated, talked with others, worked with my inner family, and opened my heart to Jona-than, but when the result I wanted—freedom from my growing sense of melancholy—wasn't quickly forthcoming, it was all too easy to forget to do the work. I continued to struggle, and my eating addiction spoke loudly, "It's all right to eat more. It'll make you feel better to eat a big, junky meal. It won't matter this time." I chose not to use the tools I knew would fight it. I knew at a heart level that each time I chose to bring my eating addiction to the table, there would be conse-quences, yet I continued to do it. I played with my disease and pushed against every boundary I set. My morning resolve to eat healthy food would be broken by noon. I'd set a plan for dinner and then add on a dessert. I gained weight in spite of an aggressive training schedule.

Becky began to ask about my behavior. I was training to work with her, facilitating some of her groups, and she had noticed some subtle changes in my attitude. "Margo, as long as there's a part of you that believes it's still an option to add on to a meal or to always eat larger portions than you need or junky food, you're at risk for relapse. It means there's still a voice inside that doesn't believe you're powerless over your eating. That attitude will communicate itself to the groups, and that's not okay. Who is it inside you who thinks she's still got some power over your eating?"

"It's my eight-year-old, Beck. I know that," I answered, knowing her words were true, yet resisting their meaning. "I'll do some writing about it tonight." But I didn't. The sadness at not having the chance to go for the summit, the anger at my body for betraying me by getting sick, my envy of Vern and Skip that hid behind my joy at their success all stayed masked behind the veil of junk food. I resisted every tool I'd ever used to break out of this place before, every tool I suggested to women I talked to on the phone.

I watched the Olympic trials on television. Men and women were pushing themselves to their limit for the opportunity to participate in the Olympics. No promises, no guarantees, just them and their dreams. I felt as if it was a reflection of my dream of Everest and the process that was in front of me. Martha told me I didn't have the discipline necessary to do the work to get to Everest much less get to its summit. I cried with the athletes who stood on the winners' platforms and with those who didn't, feeling the depth of their commitment. I knew in my heart I wanted to stand on top of the world, knew that I could, but I continued to play with my disease. Martha's negative chatter grew louder as the summer progressed. It became increasingly difficult for me to challenge her.

My fears wrapped themselves around everything I tried to do. Training, paying my bills, setting up meetings with friends who offered to help with PR and fund-raising for my return expedition, each step felt laborious. My moods fluctuated from one extreme to the other like a mechanical swing on overdrive. One minute I'd be excited, looking forward to completing a task. The next I'd be mired down in some detail or in tears, unable to do the next thing on my list. A physical and psychological haze began to obscure everything, settling around me like dust blown across a drought-plagued field. Then the mood swings were joined by hot flashes, signaling the onset of menopause. At least they offered a plausible explanation for my out-of-control emotions. Maybe I was too old to be climbing.

Even as the haze grew more dense, I gave workshops and presentations at Canyon Ranch. The participants, women and men alike, commented on how they found hope for their own lives from my sharing the principles I used to overcome my addictions and follow my dreams. It was a wonderful experience to show my slides and talk with a roomful of people, have conversations with them the next day about their dreams, and watch them find a new vision for themselves because of my willingness to talk about mine.

The Universe seemed to be supporting my going back to Everest despite my fears and doubts. Even Mum was finding ways to help finance my participation in the new expedition. In a phone conversation she said, "I was talking to your father last week, and I said, 'How can we send Miggie to the top of Mount Everest?' " She was willing to support this even when it made her nuts, simply because she knew it was what I really wanted. It was what I'd always wanted—them loving and supporting me because I was me, regardless of how they felt about what I was doing. She offered to sell one of her favorite paintings to raise money for my return. Her eyesight had deteriorated to the point where she could no longer appreciate the painting visually but I knew selling it was still a sacrifice for her. The money was important, yet more meaningful was her willingness to support me in following my dream. It was an offering of love from an unconditional place, requiring enormous courage on her part. It touched me more deeply than I could tell her. It was the most eloquent evidence that by living my life from my truth, I could bring miracles into my own life and that of others.

Support didn't always come so easily. One Sunday in July, after our weekly volleyball game on the beach, my friend Peter sat down next to me.

"Margo, I hear you're going back to Everest." His tanned and fit fifty-something body reflected his healthy passion for surfing and long-term sobriety. "Are you sure about your motives?"

"What do you mean, Peter? My motive is simple. I want to climb Everest. I want my dream of climbing the Seven Summits to come true."

"I've just wondered whether maybe you switched addictions, that's all. You've been so focused on climbing, and you already tried Everest once, now you're pushing yourself so hard to go back. I wondered whether your passion has become an obsession, that's all."

"You're not the first one to wonder, Peter. There've been a couple of times I've wondered myself. The best I can do is listen to my insides and stay willing to hear if it's not God's will for me to go back. It really feels like a heart decision. Isn't that the way you feel about your surfing?"

"That's different. It's something I love to do. It gives me a spiritual high just to be out on the water. Riding the wave is a bonus. Besides, it's been part of my life since I was a kid. And I don't have to train three hours a day to do it."

"Climbing may require more training, but the bottom line is I love it. Being on a mountain gives me a connection with my soul I don't get anywhere else. The summit's a goal, probably like a good wave for you. Just because I've got to work to prepare myself to get there doesn't take the joy away. Sure I'm focused. I have a deep passion for climbing big mountains, and it requires hard work every day to get ready. That part's like a job. I want my career to come from living my dream and helping others live theirs. The preparation for Everest—fund-raising, training, selling T-shirts—is the office work that supports all that. So in a way what I'm doing is showing up for work."

Peter watched the waves and the group of surfers riding the swells, looking for just the right one. "I guess I can understand that. I can't imagine having to put in the kind of time and effort you do. It must be a really big passion. Just keep checkin' it out with your insides."

For a minute or two, I embraced the passion I'd just been talking about: the knowledge that I was meant to go back to Everest. Then, as the first surfer began to dig into the approaching swell, letting it carry him toward shore, a wave began to swell inside me. It grew taller with sadness, cresting in a heaviness and foreboding that washed over my passion. Suddenly, I wished I was home in my bedroom. I didn't want to be out here with people who expected me to laugh and play. I didn't feel like playing or like keeping up a front. I didn't feel strong or passionate, either. Maybe Peter was right, maybe climbing had become an obsession I was using to keep my feelings at a distance. And yet the spark that was my own truth, that burned deep inside me, knew that that was a lie and fought against the darkness to stay alive. I walked down to the water, away from the people, where my tears wouldn't be noticed.

Weeks of training passed with increasingly deep emotional troughs. My trainer was having me push my muscles to failure to build up their endurance, and I was carrying increasingly heavy loads on my back as I climbed for hours on the Stairmaster. While training gave me pleasure, the rest of my life seemed to take place in a dark cellar, cut off from my heart. Despite the people who were helping me do the office work to support my climb, I felt increasingly alone.

By August, training and life in general had become a huge effort. I went to a pulmonary specialist to have my lungs checked out and to get advice about how to avoid the bronchitis that plagued me so frequently. He told me I had exercise-induced asthma. I tried an inhaler, which didn't seem to help at all. I worried that the physical manifestation had some emotional or psychological basis. Everyone I talked to about what I was experiencing had a different opinion about what was going on for me. The cellar grew darker.

At a meeting with my friend Keren about fund-raising ideas, I burst into tears at her suggestion that I do another mailing. "I can't do it. I can't deal with one more thing on my plate. It's just too damn much," I said, sobbing into my hands. "God, Keren, I'm sorry. This isn't about you. It's about me. I don't know what's going on."

Leery of how I might react, she gently but firmly responded, "Margo, it's just one of those times we all go through. You need to work the Steps on this stuff. Go to more meetings. Do some service. You're way too focused on yourself." Her words probably made sense, but all I could hear was that I was doing something else wrong. I felt as if I was doing my whole life wrong, and here was one more piece of evidence.

Later, over coffee one morning, a physician friend watched my face flush and my entire body run with sweat as I experienced one of the dozen or more hot flashes that plagued me daily. "It's only natural for you to be feeling and acting the way you are, Margo," she said. "You're going through menopause. You need to look into estrogen replacement therapy. That'll solve the hot flashes and all the emotional stuff as well. Go see your gynecologist." I had avoided taking that step, unwilling to acknowledge the reality that I was menopausal, was truly a middle-age woman. I couldn't avoid it any longer.

I met Jan for lunch at the end of September. A psychotherapist and my good friend, she listened as I shared openly my feelings about being more and more out of control and disconnected. As was happening frequently, I could not prevent my tears. "Margo, you've been talking about this for a couple of months now, and it just seems to be getting worse. I've watched you struggle so hard without getting anywhere, working much harder than you need to in order to keep functioning. This isn't like you."

"I know that, Jan. I've been saying that all along. There's something wrong, and I can't seem to figure out what it is. I've done everything I know to move through this, and I just seem to get sucked into it more and more. People tell me, 'Trust the process, Margo. This, too, shall pass,' and I just want to scream. I'm having a really hard time hanging on to that place inside that trusts that this will all be okay. I'm willing to get whatever the Universe is trying to tell me, even if it's that I'm not supposed to go back to Everest. I don't have any sense that that's what this feeling is about, but I don't have a clue about what is going on, either." As I spoke, I grew more and more upset.

Jan finally interrupted me. "Margo, stop. Stop. Take a breath." She waited while I followed her direction. "Good. Look, whatever's up is more than you can deal with by yourself or just with the program or even just with hormones. Have you called Diana yet?" Diana's name reached through my tears. Jan knew Diana had been my therapist for the first three years of my recovery and that I'd seen her for a couple of short-term issues since then. Jan had been encouraging me for several weeks to call her. I shook my head. "Well, in my opinion, you need to, and if you don't, I will. You don't have to feel like this."

I went to more meetings. I saw my gynecologist and my therapist. I went on an estrogen patch and made an appointment with a psychiatrist to be evaluated for medication to treat what Diana had diagnosed as agitated depression. I kept showing up, no matter how I felt. Even when it seemed as if I were dragging an anchor around with me. I wanted to be strong and willing and energetic, and most of the time I felt vulnerable and weak and emotionally out of control instead. I worked out, made contacts for presentations, called people back, then fell apart. I felt as though I were going through some major shifts that had much deeper implications than menopause or clinical depression. Something told me that what I was experiencing on the surface was a reflection of spiritual work being done inside, that the depression was a blessing, leading me toward a major shift in myself. Before I sought out further professional help or medications I decided to follow the advice of a spiritual counselor and spend a few days camping outside Sedona, Arizona, just being with myself and letting the desert climate and its deep spiritual energy work on me. I packed my sleeping bag, tent, and stove and headed for the low mountains of western Arizona.

Rest, sit still, relax, and let whatever is inside come out without forcing it. This became a new mantra for me as I drove toward Sedona from the old mining town of Jerome. I became aware of an expectant energy building in my chest. It seemed as though something inside was anticipating the energy of the rock formations that greeted me as I entered the small town filled with artists' galleries and metaphysical bookstores. The wind- and rain-carved sandstone was deep red: vibrant in places where it was touched by the sun, warming in others, shadows allowing the subtleties to reveal themselves.

I drove through town to the campground in Oak Creek Canyon where I had made reservations for the next six nights. As I set up the only tent in a campground filled with RVs, I felt that there was more going on than just menopause and depression. Several hours later I sat on my Therm-A-Lounger in front of a cozy fire, reading Dan Millman's *Sacred Journey of the Peaceful Warrior*. I felt as if I, too, was on a sacred journey, almost as if there was a new, undiscovered part of Margo waiting inside me to be born. I put down my book and stared into the fire.

Driving toward Boynton Canyon the next morning, I had to pull my car off the road just to give myself the space to breathe. The raw beauty of the cliffs and carved rocks had an energy in them that was almost palpable. A shift had taken place inside me the night before. A fullness pushed itself toward the surface. Sadness? Gratitude? I wasn't sure. I knew I didn't have to force it. Whatever it was I'd come here for was taking place.

I remembered the birth I'd attended just a few weeks before. My good friend Maggie had invited me to be present when her son Cody was born. I saw his head present itself, crown, then emerge from his mother's body, and I was swept away with the wonder of birth. As I sat with them later, holding the newborn infant in my arms, the reality that I'd never have my own child moved through my body, touching my uterus and my heart. The twinge of sadness was replaced by the deep knowing that living my dream was somehow bringing a new life into the world.

During the days in Sedona, I gave birth to a new spiritual awareness. Cody had appeared within hours of Maggie's first labor pain, but my newborn truth took days to emerge. Hiking comfortably along well-worn trails, lying in the sun, quietly breathing in the ancient wisdom of this land, I was introduced to spirit guides within me who loved me, held my kids, and showed us all the truth of who I was: fallible, yet absolutely perfect in my imperfections. Jonathan reappeared one night, present at a near-physical level, lying with his head in my lap. Martha was absent, as were her judgments and criticism and negativity. When I took down my tent at the end of my stay, I knew I was different from what I had been when I arrived. I looked forward to going home. I no longer feared my life.

Returning to San Diego, I found that many of the symptoms I'd been experiencing had disappeared. Life was somehow easier, and my energy was increasingly focused on my climb. I refinanced my home to raise the rest of the money I needed for the trip and began organizing myself to spend the winter in Aspen.

Leelee had suggested it during a week I spent with her and her family there in August. We had hiked up Hunter Creek one morning, and talking about the irony of my training, I said, "It's always made me laugh that I prepare on the beach in Southern California to go to the ice and snow at 20,000 feet. I'm sure that's at least part of why I have developed such an affinity for Stairmasters!" I was infamous to all who knew me for spending hours on a Stairmaster with a heavy pack on my back. It was how I trained for the mountains with no mountains around.

Leelee walked up the trail that followed Hunter Creek in silence for several minutes. We reached the Benedict Bridge, and Leelee stopped in the middle, looking down at the water. It had been a dry summer, and the water was low. It sang a soothing song of serenity as it made its way over and around the rocks on its way down to its meeting with the Roaring Fork River. "Why don't you train here this winter?"

"Hmmm . . . I don't know. I've never thought about it," I stammered. "It's a nice idea but I don't know how I'd work out the logistics."

"You could stay with us. You'd have your own room downstairs just like you do now. The boys would love it, I'd love it, and I'm sure J.B. wouldn't mind."

"Oh, Looloo, it's an incredibly appealing idea." My mind was jumping ahead, already solving the problems Martha brought up.

The idea excited me. "How long were you thinking?"

"The whole winter."

"But you'd better talk to J.B. before we go any further. I don't want to step on his toes."

"You're right. I'll do that tonight. I'd love to have you with us for the whole winter."

"Would it be okay to be here for Christmas? I'd love to spend the holidays with you and your boys—all three of them." Their close-knit family had long been known to me as "Leelee and the boys." I enjoyed her husband's dry humor and adored her two sons. Michael, ten, and Matt, eight, were beautiful skiers and terrific kids.

We continued up the trail in silence. As we reached the first meadow in Hunter Valley and I caught the first glimpse of my God Rock, I knew Aspen was where I was supposed to be. I'd left a chunk of my heart there when I moved to New York in 1978. It was time to reclaim it. Spending the winter and staying with Leelee while training in the snow and altitude would be a perfect opportunity to prepare for Everest while I explored an intuitive sense that Aspen was my real home. The pieces fell into place with little effort: I would leave for Aspen in early December and stay through early March.

Wednesday, November 14, 1992, San Diego
I want to do this trip to Everest totally differently
from last year. I think that's what this
second chance is about. My stomach just got real
excited. That feeling that says, "Yeah, that's
it." I want to take my spirituality to Everest. I
want to do the climb my way not their way.

During preparations for my stay in Aspen, I received an expedition roster from Todd that shook me badly. There were four guides and fourteen climbers listed, five of whom were returning from last year. Once more I'd be the only woman. I'd need every ounce of my energy and focus to get to the top of Everest. I wasn't willing to use any of it to deal with men who didn't want me in camp and who would, in all likelihood, make no great effort to hide that fact. Believing I would be a detriment to the overall expedition if I knowingly joined a team with preexisting personality conflicts, I called Skip to discuss the situation.

"I know Rob and Gary are running a trip, and I really liked the energy of their group. Even before I left Base Camp last year I thought about going back with them instead of Todd. But I figured it would be too awkward. This roster changes everything, though. I'm not willing to put myself into that kind of situation again. Maybe I should call the Kiwis and find out if they still have room. Is there some standard protocol to follow about this?"

"Nope. You're the client." Skip had been leading his own expeditions for twenty years, and I knew he'd tell me if there was a "right" way to do things. "As a guide, I do the best I can to put together a group that's compatible. But each client has his or her own right to choose whom to go with."

"My heart wants to go with Rob and Gary but I don't know if it's okay to switch trips like that. What do you think?"

"Margo, I can't tell you who to go with." I'd never heard Skip make a disparaging remark about anyone. He had always demonstrated a strong sense of ethics, and I was not surprised that he wouldn't tell me what to do. "I will say again that it's your choice. And remind you that you're the one who talks so much about following your heart."

I had my answer. "Thanks. I'll let you know what happens."

Late that night I called Rob Hall in New Zealand, allowing for the eighteen-hour time difference.

"Adventure Consultants, Rob Hall here."

I smiled at the warm memories brought back by the familiar voice. "Hi, Rob, this is Margo Chisholm calling from the States."

"Hello, Margo." I smiled again at the Kiwi pronunciation of my name. "How're you going?"

"Well, thanks. I'm calling to see if you still have room on your Everest trip next spring."

"Absolutely. Is this for you? I thought you were going with Todd."

"I was, but he's got several people returning from last year, and I had trouble with a couple of them. I don't want to have to waste any energy having to deal with problem people. I figure I'll need all I have to get up the mountain, so I'm checking out some options. Do you know who else will be on your trip?"

"Good plan, Margo. So far we have six clients, three of whom are women."

"No kidding! That's incredible."

"It's unusual, all right. Gary and I will be guiding along with a mate of ours named Guy Cotter. We have a couple from Australia who are your age, a Kiwi dairy farmer a bit younger, a British woman, also your age, who lives in the Middle East, a hot-shot French woman who's climbing without oxygen, and a strong young buck from Finland. Jan will be back as the doc and a woman named Helen Wilton will be Base Camp Manager. I think that's the lot."

"It sounds real good. I love the idea of climbing with that many women. I'll probably do it but I want to sit with it overnight. Will you save me a spot until tomorrow?"

"You bet. We'd love to have you along."

"Thanks. Say 'Hi' to Jan and Gary. I'll call you tomorrow."

I hung up the phone already knowing what I wanted to do. Martha immediately told me I couldn't make the change. "You can't afford to give up the deposit you've already paid Todd. You screwed up again. You just have to live with your mistake. Call Rob back."

"No," I retorted, hoping to drown out the thoughts with my spoken words. "There's nothing wrong with making a mistake. I'm not a bad person because I change my mind. This choice is about taking care of me, giving myself the best possible shot at the summit. You can come along if you want, I can't stop you, but I won't put up with any more of your bullshit." She didn't answer.

I called Rob the next day and told him I was in.

Before leaving for Colorado, I spent five days in November hiking by myself in Yosemite National Park. I'd climbed twenty-one mountains on seven continents but had never spent a night in the wilderness on my own. It was time. I planned to hike 50 miles with a 50-pound pack in five days. During the day I hiked through stands of pines so thick I was cold in their shade and watched the glasslike surface of a high mountain lake that rippled from the wake of a duck migrating south. At night, the Big Dipper pointed to the North Star as the moon turned the peaks above my tent into silver sculptures. When I had told my friends in San Diego what I was going to do, their reaction, without exception was, "Aren't you concerned about being out there all by yourself? What if something happens?" Yet, it was time. I was comfortable with the idea of backpacking on my own. I was well-equipped, strong, and had given a friend instructions about what to do if I did not call him by a certain time. There was only one thing that concerned me: the bears.

Yosemite's bears were black bears and quite timid by nature. Under normal circumstances they were easily scared away by loud noises, but recently they'd become accustomed to backpackers and could be fairly aggressive in their search for food. All backpackers were given guide-lines about handling food in bear country, and I was careful about hanging my food and all my kitchen gear from a tree limb high enough and far enough away from the tree trunk that it could not be reached by a bear.

November being well past the season when the park was filled with people, I didn't see anyone after my first couple of hours of hiking. The solitude was part of what I had come here for but it also left me alone to deal with any bears that might appear. I had a way-beyond-average fear of hearing a snuffling sound against my tent wall in the middle of the night. I established a ritual at which my common sense laughed and that my kids inside followed without fail. Every night before I went to sleep, I walked all the way around my tent saying "Go away bears. Go away bears." The potential embarrassment of anyone seeing me engaged in such foolishness was far outweighed by my little-girl belief that this would certainly keep the bears at bay. It must have worked, I didn't see a single bear.

I returned to Yosemite Valley at the end of the fifth day with a deep sense of satisfaction in my strength and self-sufficiency and a pleasure in knowing I didn't have to travel to other continents to find contentment in the wilderness. Another piece of my internal jigsaw puzzle fell into place as I learned that I could be alone in the wilds of nature without being lonely.

Making preparations to leave San Diego for the mountains of Colorado, I felt as if I were done there and that my time in Southern California was drawing to a close. I was in the middle of a passage, between two expeditions to Mount Everest, but even more important,

273

between two different parts of my life. I just didn't know yet what was ahead of me.

Leelee and her "boys" embraced me as a member of their family, and I welcomed the chance to be a part of a nuclear family in a way I'd never experienced: family dinners, each member talking about what they had done during the day, and disagreements about watching television before homework was finished. All these were pieces of a life I had not lived since my own childhood. I'd come here to train and reconnect with a community I'd left fifteen years earlier and had been given an unexpected gift. I cherished it.

I began to establish a connection with Aspen. I attended 12-Step recovery meetings and Leelee reintroduced me to acquaintances still living in the area. I was given a three-month membership at a club with excellent facilities and worked with a personal trainer to keep me on my weight training program. I substituted runs around Mission Bay with hikes up a local ski mountain on snowshoes with a heavy pack on my back, and soon I had settled into a demanding daily routine of one-and-a-half hours of weight training and between one and four hours of aerobic activity. The asthma—or whatever was going on with my lungs—was a problem in various situations. I was used to doing interval work, which entailed running or climbing at a maximum level for anywhere from thirty seconds to several minutes, recovering for a minute or so, then repeating the sequence several times. It had been an effective way to improve my aerobic capacity in the past, but now I found that rather than increasing my fitness, it created pain in my chest and coughing, which hampered further training. I altered the level at which I trained, staying within a moderate range of intensity. I alternated skiing, hiking up Buttermilk Mountain on snowshoes, running, stationary biking, and my old standby of working on a Stairmaster with a pack on my back. The first few weeks were better than I could have imagined with the exception of my right ankle, which was weak and susceptible to sprains. I had sprained it with moderate severity in Yosemite and hadn't given it a chance to heal completely. I continued to push through several minor twists of it, refusing to acknowledge that what it needed was rest.

The Christmas holidays came and went, heaped with the joy of the season and the exuberance of two boys, although a miserable sinus infection put a damper on my appreciation of what was usually a magical time. Shortly following the arrival of the new year, my father came to visit me and my niece, who was also living in Aspen. Meg was Barb's daughter and my parents' only grandchild, the deserving apple of our familial eye. We'd always been close and greatly enjoyed each other's company. Our busy schedules had kept us from spending as much time together as we'd planned since I arrived in Aspen, and we took the occasion of Pop's visit to snowshoe up Buttermilk together before picking him up for breakfast.

I was still feeling the effects of the infection I'd been fighting, so when my head began to pound fiercely 10 minutes up the hill, I wrote it off as a result of remaining congestion and continued to climb. The pain worsened swiftly, however, and I had to stop. I felt sick to my stomach and my temples were pounding in rhythm with my pulse as if some expert in medieval torture were driving nails into my brain. My knees gave way, and I slumped to the snow.

"Miggie, what's wrong?" Meg asked, concern in her voice.

"I'm not sure," I answered shakily, holding my head in my hands. "I've got a horrendous headache all of a sudden. Let me just sit here for a minute."

"Do you want to go home?" she asked.

"Just give me a minute." The brightness of the sun seemed to pierce my eyes as my head continued to pound in an unimaginable fashion. I knew I needed to get down from the hill. "Yeah I think we'd better go." I struggled to stand up and vomited suddenly, violently into the snow.

"Should I get the ski patrol?" Meg, trained as an Emergency Medical Technician knew this wasn't just any headache.

"No, I don't think so." I was moving down the hill, slowly, but moving. "I can make it."

"I'm going ahead. I'll meet you at the bottom with the car." I appreciated her suggestion.

I climbed into the car, and Meg drove me home and helped me into the house. "What sounds good to you?" It was wonderful to have someone taking care of me.

I could hardly open my eyes against the pain in my head. "Nothing sounds good but maybe a bath will help. Call Shirley Carnel and tell her what's happening, would you? I gotta do something about this headache." Dr. Carnel was the ear, nose, and throat specialist who'd been treating my sinus infection. The only thing I could figure was that this was somehow related to it.

"Miggie." Meg had been gone for only a couple of minutes. "Dr. Carnel wants to see you right away. Can you move?" I was sitting in the tub, head in my hands, rocking in rhythm with the horrific pounding in my temples. Meg's calm voice belied the fear in her eyes.

"I've got to, Meg. There's something very wrong going on here." I got out of the tub, the effort triggering another series of vomiting, now only dry heaves, but strong and sustained. I was very frightened.

Fifteen minutes later I was at the Aspen Valley Hospital, sent there immediately after Dr. Carnel took my blood pressure. They took it again in the emergency room. It was dangerously high and combined with the vascular nature of my headache, created concern among the staff that I had had a cerebral hemorrhage. They began an IV and moved me immediately into ICU where they could monitor me more closely. I had never experienced this kind of pain intensity before, and I just wanted it to stop. They gave me Demerol with no results, then morphine. Still no change. I was now pleading with the nurses to make it stop. Finally they gave me enough Seconal to knock me out. I spent two nights in the ICU undergoing tests and being observed carefully. It wasn't until the second evening that I was told the extent of the staff's concern about me when I was admitted. "You're real lucky you didn't stroke out," was how one of the nurses put it.

All the tests came back negative. My doctor believed I'd had a reaction to the estrogen patch I was using, so I took it off immediately and resigned myself to hot flashes and mood swings. The residual dull headache passed within a week, and as soon as it was gone, I returned to my training schedule. I didn't have any time to waste. My body would just have to heal while I trained. But it didn't. I was run down from the incident, and my sinus infection returned.

I walked into Dr. Carnel's office limping from the ankle I'd twisted yet again that morning and sniffing from my draining sinuses. "Margo, what are you doing to yourself?" she asked after I had told her the history of my ankle. She cautioned me about pushing myself too hard. "If you really want to go to Everest, you're going to have to listen to your body and give it time to heal. If you continue the way you're going, you won't get there at all." I knew she was right, but I needed to train. She suggested a month of no aerobic exercise. I countered with two weeks. "Just promise me you'll listen to your body, Margo. You'll never get to Everest otherwise."

Leelee was home when I got there and she held me. "I'm scared. I don't get it. The ankle, the sinuses, the blood pressure, I can't seem to stay healthy. I certainly can't train if I'm not healthy, and I can't climb Everest if I don't train, and now Shirley says if I train too hard I won't get to Everest. I just don't get it!" I collapsed into her lap and cried on her shoulder, frustrated and fearful, feeling lost and confused.

It had taken one doctor, one psychologist, and two physical therapists to make me hear, but I had finally understood. I had unexpected quiet time during the next two weeks as I honored my promise to listen to my body. I walked around the golf course instead of carrying a pack up Buttermilk. I pedaled comfortably on a stationary bike instead of climbing miles on a Stairmaster. I did a moderate number of reps at low weight instead of pushing hard to lift heavy weights. An odd thing happened. I didn't get weak. I had been worried about how much fitness I would lose, and what happened was just the opposite. I felt better than I had all winter, and when I felt 100 percent again, I increased my intensity level in small increments. I listened to my body, and it responded. I was deriving more benefit from training at a less intense level that was within my body's limits than from forcing myself continuously against them.

The message was clear: It wasn't just about being strong. It had been my will to get as strong as I possibly could for Everest, and I'd pushed my body too hard. It had been my will, not God's will, and I'd paid the price for acting it with a blind stubbornness that almost resulted in my not being able to go. For my last weeks in Aspen, I paid attention to what I had been told and to how I felt inside, training in a reasonable way that exercised my body without overtaxing it, that honored both its strengths and the places where it was not so strong. I listened, and my serenity returned.

On March 5, 1993, I made my final trip up Buttermilk. It was the last time that winter I would walk up this mountain, snowshoes on my feet, ski poles in my hands, following the line of the chairlift. Actually, I made three round trips: a total of 5,400 vertical feet with 30 pounds on my back, moving slowly and steadily. People riding the lift called down to the short woman in purple tights with a big red pack on her back: "Are you crazy?" or "Aren't you going the wrong way?" or "What're ya doing?" "Go Mode." It was how I would need to climb when I got to Everest: moving at my own pace, not trying to keep up or do it someone else's way. I felt strong. My body was healthy. I was ready: ready to leave for another attempt at realizing my dream.

It was almost 5:00 P.M. when I reached the top for the third time, and I was alone. The ski lifts had closed, and the patrol had left to sweep the mountain. The sun hung low in the sky, creating long shadows in the roaring Fork Valley below. I knew I was home. This was where I belonged and where I would return after Everest. I'd have to pack up my things in San Diego and make arrangements to sell my house, but this was where I would really be coming home to. It was quiet and beautiful, and my heart filled with the realization of why I worked so hard. Increasing the chances at reaching the summit of Everest was only part of it. Just as it was the process of being on a mountain that filled me rather than just reaching the summit, so it was the process of training that filled me rather than simply the result. I had the satisfaction of putting one foot in front of the other, the exhilaration and beauty of the view and the mountains, the presence of God and Jonathan and my inner family there in the afternoon light; I felt intensely alive. Tears began to flow, of course, and I smiled at them. I was proud and strong and grateful.

Shortly after I returned to San Diego, my body seemed to be, once again, getting in the way of my return to Everest. I was scheduled to leave in only four days when bronchitis set in—again. Antibiotics, inhalers, cortisone, Prednisone. Again. Three days on medication brought no improvement. My lung specialist told me I'd better cancel my trip. "You're wasting your time and money," he said. I felt as if I was starting exactly where I had ended last year. How could I get up Everest if I was sick before I even got there? It had been the story of the winter: ill health in the face of knowing that Everest was to be my path. When I got home from the doctor's office, I collapsed into a puddle of tears on my bedroom floor, then sat looking out the window at the view of San Diego I loved so much. A quiet, calm message came from deep inside my heart. Go.

Martha said, "What's the point? What are you going to do? Go and not climb? Go and try to climb even if you're sick? We know how well that works! Go and . . ." My heart stopped her words with its knowledge that going was about experiencing the journey and being present for whatever happened. I needed to have completion somehow. If I did not go, there would always be a blank wall where there should have been a story. A huge crevasse in the road of my life where there needed to be a bridge.

It would be different this year. I would allow my spirit to experience the mountain. Last year I had fought it and often denied the fear and feelings that Martha so easily labeled weak. This year I would allow my yin and my yang to work together on the mountain, to achieve a new level of empowerment that I knew was formed by the joining of strength and honest vulnerability. The two were neither incompatible nor mutually exclusive. Their joining was necessary for my spirit to be whole. Completion would come from experiencing the mountain fully rather than from reaching the summit.

As the time for my departure for Nepal grew nearer, I became more excited. I'd had nine months of climbing mountains higher than Everest: the mountains of personal growth. Now, the truth that I was really okay, even with all of my imperfections, filled the black hole that had always been inside me, the one I'd learned to avoid with faked injuries, then with alcohol, drugs, and food. The hole that had held such terror for me most of my life seemed to have been filled. I felt excited physically, emotionally, and spiritually. God, Jonathan, and all of my inner family and guides had walked me through my injuries and illness and had been with me in my training, too.

I knew they'd be with me on the mountain. I felt strong in every area of my life, and on my last day in the gym, as I lifted 250 pounds in three reps of squats, my pride rose from the soles of my feet. My "YES!" rang out through the gym. Other people working out hardly took notice of me, but I knew where I was going and what it meant to me.

CHAPTER TWELVE

The Summit Is Only the Excuse for Being Here

Friday, March 19, 1993, Los Angeles
I'm getting to live this dream again. It's mine and
mine alone. I'm going in order to climb to the
top of Mount Everest. I'm ready to do that. And
by being, being present and experiencing myself
and my surroundings, I will get as high as I'm
supposed to. Breathe, Margo, and stay aware.

I gave my two duffel bags to the woman behind the airline counter and felt the first real twinges of excitement when she handed me my tickets saying, "They're checked through to Kathmandu for you, Ms. Chisholm. Have a nice flight."

The flights through Bangkok and into Kathmandu's Tribhuvan Airport were uneventful, and as I waited for my luggage, I giggled to myself. How was it that I had come from not being able to leave my house to thinking a flight to Nepal was uneventful? It was a delightful example of what happened when I simply showed up for my life and put one foot in front of the other.

That simple process also got me past the young Nepali boys who stood just outside the exit of the airport, clamoring to carry my bags to a taxi. The sign bearing my name carried by a small woman with bright eyes and a ponytail was a welcome sight. "Jan," I called happily. "What a lovely surprise." The Nepali man with her loaded my bags on various parts of his body, and we followed him to a small van that would take us to the Garuda Hotel.

Jan and I talked nonstop on the twenty-minute ride, and she accompanied me to the desk at the hotel. "They'll get you settled," she said. "Rob and Gary and I have a lot of errands to do so I'll leave you on your own. We're all meeting at Hem's for dinner tonight at six."

She gave me a hug and headed toward the door.

The trip roster Rob had faxed to me had confirmed the names and home addresses of the other participants, and I was looking forward to meeting them all. The list was unchanged from the one he had described on the phone back in October: Rob Hall and Gary Ball were joined by Guy Cotter, a fellow New Zealander, as the third guide; Jan returned as the team physician and Helen, also from New Zealand, was the Base Camp manager. The climbers, including me, provided a truly international blend: John Gluckman was a forty-two-year-old Kiwi dairy farmer from the North Island; Ken, fifty, and his wife Christine, forty-six, were from Australia; Rosalind, forty-five, was a British expatriate living in the United Arab Emirates; Chantal, twenty-nine, was a French physical therapist but spent most of her time climbing and was the only woman to have climbed K2 without oxygen; and Veikka was a twenty-five-year-old Finn. When the time came for dinner, we all met in the lobby for the short walk to our destination.

The balcony of Hem's restaurant overlooked a street jammed with small cars bullying their way through the mopeds, rickshaws, and pedestrians that flowed from curb to curb. The horns and bicycle bells were no match for our laughter, though. I'd just taken the last bite of a surprisingly good Nepali version of an American hamburger when John told the punch line of the latest in a string of cow jokes. I had to struggle not to spew my mouthful over my neighbor. We all laughed out loud at John's farm humor. I was delightfully surprised at the light and friendly atmosphere we'd already established. There wasn't a Type-A personality in the group, and it was clear that each of us wanted to stand on the top of the world, but we were also committed to enjoying the process.

Between my bursts of laughter, I managed to swallow the food that had thankfully remained in my mouth and announced, "There's been more conversation at this table tonight than there was during the whole first week of our walk to Base Camp last year."

"God, how did you survive?" asked Christine.

"I don't mean to make it sound awful. It wasn't. It was just a much more intense group: more focused on the climb and the summit, more closed—and they were all men. There were two other women at Base Camp but all the climbers were men. I can't tell you what a treat it is to be doing this trip with three other women climbers!"

As I chatted with Helen on the way back to the Garuda, I wondered aloud if the ease happening almost immediately among us all was due to our being evenly split between men and women.

"I don't know," she said, "but it sure is a good group." Helen was a housewife with a husband and four children in New Zealand. She'd entered a radio contest two years earlier and won a trek to Base Camp with Rob and Gary's expedition. It had opened a whole new world to her, and managing Base Camp for this expedition was her first step toward a shift of her life focus to adventure travel and climbing.

"I just can't believe this is happening to me!" Helen's smile supported the truth of her words. "It's a dream come true."

"I know what that's like," I said, nodding my head.

"I know you do, Margo. I already feel a real kinship with you. This is going to be such a good trip!"

I was drawn to Helen's enthusiasm for this great adventure, and looked forward to our opportunity to share it.

During the flight from Kathmandu into the sloped, still-unimproved airfield at Lukla, I was drawn into the magic of the Himalaya and the wonder of my being here at all. Jonathan walked with me a ways on the trail to Namche Bazaar, and he reminded me that I was doing this trip differently from either of the other two times I'd been in the Khumbu, that there were new lessons for me to learn. I was still wondering what they would be when we arrived at the Khumbu Lodge, the teahouse where we'd be staying.

When Jan had taken my vitals before we left Kathmandu I was nervous and felt like a bad girl because I was having trouble with my lungs from bronchitis. Jan believed it was mostly from the enormous amount of pollution in Kathmandu and predicted they'd be clear before we got to Pheriche. My conviction that I was supposed to be there allowed me to trust in the process and deal with issues as they came up without the emotional trauma or inner confrontations I'd experienced on earlier trips. When I felt tired on the trail, when my legs and knees hurt and it seemed as if my lungs were working harder than they should have been to draw in the air I needed, God's voice told me everything was okay and I'd let out a sigh of relief, relax a little bit, and keep on hiking up the trail. Even Martha's voice wasn't overwhelming, simply irritating.

The first morning in Namche we awoke to new snow. It covered everything, creating a fairy-tale atmosphere outside and increasing the welcoming warmth of the interior of the teahouse and its yak-dung-burning stove. Time passed quickly with good conversation, crossword puzzles, and reading. During the afternoon, Roz, Helen, Jan, and I walked up to Shyangboche. Six inches of snow covered the tops of the stone walls lining the terraced plots, leaving their vertical faces uncovered to cut gray swaths in the white landscape. The trail was slippery, and we told tales and laughed out loud during our "Women's International Epic Traverse" up the south side of the 1,000-foot hill behind Namche and back down its north slope.

Climbers from Todd's expedition began to filter into Namche, and I wondered how it would be to see them and reminded myself that I wasn't wrong for choosing another group, it was only a choice. I already knew I'd made the right one.

We awoke the second day to an incredible storm, the snow and wind delaying a planned walk to Kunde and Khumjung. During a break in the weather, we decided to walk up anyway. The snow along the trail and on the mani walls highlighted the Buddhist prayer carved into the stones and added a special serenity to the setting. Yet as the wind blew the snow into our faces and as I became increasingly cold and tired, my inner voices wanted to focus on how miserable I would be feeling in a little while. I passed a chorten and prayer flags placed by pilgrims along the trail, however, and was reminded of my focus for this trip. My misery flew away along with the prayers of the believers as the flags waved in the wind. An easy joy and deep gratitude wrapped me in their warmth as I talked with Chris and Ken about the magnificence and power of the Icefall. We paused for a rest, and John passed me some iron tablets with the comment, "These will help you to the summit. We all want to help each other to the summit." The laughter, sensitivity, and camaraderie fed my soul and demonstrated our mutual support.

The next morning dawned bright and sunny. John began the day with the comment, "It's a great day to be alive." And it was. I walked to Thame and back alone, giving my spirit guides the space to connect with me in the Khumbu Valley. The new snow added a softness to the trees, and the surrounding mountains rose, majestic and powerful, in their mantel of soft white powder. Hawks soared overhead and images of my guides and Jonathan accompanied me. Even Skip's energy showed up. Gratitude and a strong image of being on the summit were with me throughout the day. When I returned to Namche, I ran into one of the climbers from Todd's group and had a good conversation about this year's climb. Last year we'd had some tension between us, but we both seemed different now, and I enjoyed reconnecting with him.

After the two-day weather delay, our team left early the next morning for Thyangboche. This walk had become one of my favorites. The trail rose steeply out of Namche, following a number of paths widely used by Sherpas, tourists, and yaks. Normally dry and dusty, today the paths were covered in melting snow, creating a combination of slush and mud that made walking more challenging than usual. Only an occasional pine tree rose above the low scrub that grew alongside the trail as it leveled out 500 feet above the town and wound in and out, traversing the slopes high above the Dudh Kosi river. I quickened my pace as I approached the left-hand bend in the trail, which I knew would reveal the first clear view of Everest and Ama Dablam. As I rounded that bend, their classic forms appeared and all I could do was stand in the middle of the trail with tears rolling down my cheeks as the raw beauty fed my passion. Sagarmatha seemed to be welcoming me. There was none of the sense of being overwhelmed I had felt last year, only the warm conviction that I was meant to be standing on her summit.

I walked for a while with Kami, the Sherpa who was to be our cook at Camp II. He'd been a part of many American expeditions and had spent some time in the States. His English was very good, and we talked about places he'd been, including New York and Los Angeles.

"I have a good friend who lives in Los Angeles," Kami said, as he followed me along the trail on the plateau above the Dudh Kosi River. "Do you know Rick Ridgeway?"

I was startled by the familiar name. Rick had been on Minya Konka in 1980 and had held Jonathan in his arms as he died. I'd met Rick at Jonathan's memorial service. His clear description of the peace in Jonathan's eyes when he died helped me walk through my grief at my friend's death.

"I do," I answered and told Kami about Minya Konka and about the good friend who'd died there.

"You mean Jonathan?"

I stopped in my tracks, stunned, and turned to face Kami. "You knew Jonathan?"

"I knew him pretty well. I worked with him a few times and he showed me some of his slides. He took beautiful pictures."

I smiled, deeply touched by our connection. "Yes, he did. I have several of them on my walls at home. He was a very special man in my life. It's a great treat for me that there is someone on this trip who knew him."

Kami reached out to me with his right hand. I took it, and we shook hands warmly. "For me, too." One by one, threads of coincidence and attitude were being added to the intricately woven tapestry of this trip, confirming for me that there were no mistakes about my returning.

Up to this point, Veikka, our Finnish team member, had been the most reticent one of our group. Clearly bright and good-humored, I was not sure if his quietness came from shyness or defense or simply being more of a listener than a talker. Whatever the reason, I was surprised when he passed Kami and me on the trail only a few minutes later and put a hand on my shoulder and said, "This is too good to be true." His words were more accurate for me than he knew.

We arrived in Pheriche the following day, and the tiny collection of teahouses brought back mixed memories for me. The HRA clinic had an uncomfortably familiar air about it as we sat in on the mandatory briefing on altitude sickness. The Gamow Bag sat ominously along one wall, pregnant with the image of Parry inside it last year. The "beach" where Parry, Vern, and I spent so many hours, Vern playing his fiddle and me writing on my computer, brought back a smile. Under the best of circumstances Pheriche was a windy, drab place. Weakened as I had been by illness last year, it had become a near prison for me, and I was not comfortable being here now. I was the first one on the trail when we left for Lobuche two days later.

Soon after arriving at Base Camp, I was in my roomy tent unpacking my gear, separating what I'd need in Base Camp from the things I'd take with me up on the mountain, thinking to myself "What a joy to be here!" I spread out my sleeping bag and arranged my books, Walkman, and journal so they were close at hand, then stuck my head out into the bright sunshine just as Veikka walked by.

He stopped, looked up at the Icefall, and said, "It is something, isn't it?" His warm heart shone through his somewhat formal English and Scandinavian reserve in a smile that lit up his eyes as I pulled myself out of my tent and stood next to him. The reticence he'd exhibited during the walk to Base Camp seemed to have eased since we arrived.

"That it is." I put an arm around his waist, following his gaze at the imposing jumble of ice. We stood for several minutes, quietly, gazing at the mountain and taking in its strength. Then Veikka turned toward me, gave me a quick hug, and abruptly turned away, heading toward the dining tent.

"I'm glad you're part of the team," I called after him.

"I'm glad you're here, too," drifted back as he continued walking.

Our team represented only a small part of the nearly 400 people residing in the temporary town known as Everest Base Camp during the spring climbing season. Nearly half of them would be moving up on the mountain as climbers and Sherpas supporting the climbers. There were fourteen expeditions, neighborhoods within the town, arranged in clusters of tents of varying sizes, shapes, and colors. Each had a large community tent at its center and its own stone altar supporting a tall pole with strings of Buddhist prayer flags extending from it, each string anchored by rocks, allowing the flags to carry their prayers on the wind. The altars and poles had been erected during the Puja, a Buddhist ceremony held by each expedition before any of its members or Sherpas set foot on the mountain. On each altar was a fire, fed almost continually with small pieces from juniper trees, giving prayers yet another way to travel to the spirit of the mountain. The distinctive odor wound its way throughout camp and up into the Icefall, tied permanently in my memory with images of climbers heading off into the dark for the top of the world.

Like any other town, sometimes the site bustled with activity and sometimes it seemed nearly empty, its residents making themselves known only as they moved from one tent to another. Bright, wind-free mornings brought everyone outside, airing sleeping bags, doing laundry, or simply sitting in the warmth of the sun. Cold, snow-shrouded afternoons sent climbers and Sherpas alike to the comfort of their tents. Warming waves of laughter would sometimes burst through the sides of the expedition cook tents where the Sherpas tended to gather, their voices drowning out the steady whoosh of the stoves.

Shortwave radios crackled with the daily BBC news for the international community, sharing the same airspace with Nepalese music. Random rings, beeps, and chirps emanated from communications tents as modern technology allowed connection with friends and family back home via satellite. Buddhist prayers being hummed softly as juniper was placed on the slow-burning altar fires sometimes filled the spaces between the voices, radio broadcasts, and sounds of fax machines and computers.

Every sound, sight, and odor of Everest Base Camp was familiar and comforting in my second climbing season there. It seemed incredible that such a remote and magical place was familiar to me—known—a place I'd been before. I'd spent so many years feeling as if I didn't belong anywhere. Belonging here filled me with awe as frequently as my name came floating across the glacier.

"Hello, Margo!" This time it was Lobsang Tenzing, the nephew of Tenzing Norgay who had accompanied Sir Edmund Hilary to the summit on the first ascent of Everest. No matter how I was feeling physically or emotionally, Lobsang's large grin and friendly wave always made me smile. He was part of an Australian expedition honoring the fortieth anniversary of the first ascent of Everest, and their camp backed up to the Kiwis', our tents only a few yards apart. A mountaineer with many ascents to his credit, Lobsang was one of the most skilled climbers in camp, and despite my limited experience he treated me with an honest and open warmth that added to my conviction that this was exactly where I was supposed to be.

Life in Base Camp, the view of the Icefall out the back door of my tent, and the work of helping to organize the kitchen tent and sort out food and equipment for higher camps kept me occupied for a couple of days, but by the time we left on our first trip to Camp I, I was ready. I'd done all of the preparation I could, was acclimated, hydrated, and rested and felt connected to my companions and to the mountain. Some of those first nights in camp felt just plain luxurious when I used a hot water bottle to keep my feet warm in my sleeping bag.

The first trip from Base Camp to Camp I took me seven-and-a-half hours with Rob following closely behind most of the way, teasing, encouraging, supportive—very much like Skip in ways that I greatly appreciated.

"I'm taking too long," I mumbled.

"Too long." Martha agreed as I struggled up yet another vertical ladder, breathing hard, chest tight and sore. "You might as well turn around now. You'll never get to the top. You must be crazy coming back here. Are you totally out of your mind? What possessed you to say you'd do this again? You're not strong enough, thin enough, fit enough, anything enough to do this. You're going to fall off this ladder and kill yourself. Turn around now and go home! You'll never make it."

I paused, frightened and tired, at the next of the seemingly endless number of ladders. How many were there? I'd lost count at forty. Martha's doubts became my own, and I thought, "Maybe I really can't do this."

"Yes, you can, Margo." Jonathan's spirit was once again stronger than my fear and fatigue.

I'd cried my fear into Ray's chest before I left San Diego, and he'd reminded me that Jonathan would be with me. "Just remember to keep your heart open, Margo. He'll be there." And he had been—was now, as I struggled through the upper reaches of the Icefall.

"You deserve to be here. It's all right to acknowledge your fear. It will lead you to your strength." Jonathan's words comforted me. "Trust the process and take a step."

"I don't know if I can." These words were not Martha's. They were mine: my own honest fear, clearly voiced.

"Yes, you can," Jonathan answered. "You only have to put one foot in front of the other—in your heart as well as your body. Breathe, Margo. Allow the fear and doubt to be present and take the next step."

"Like life," I thought and clipped the carabiner attached to my harness into the fixed line that served as a safeguard against a fall into the seemingly bottomless crevasse. Jonathan and I carefully stepped onto the first rung of the ladder crossing the empty space below.

Nearly two hours later I slowly, wearily trudged up the low-angle approach to Camp I, already established at the head of the Icefall.

"Yo, Maggot. Good on ya!" I looked up to see Guy Cotter, one of our guides, waving energetically from in front of the three tents that made up this acclimatization stop. His enthusiasm tapped a final, hidden reservoir of strength in my legs. I returned his wave and picked up the pace into camp.

Guy met me with a bear hug that took away much of my weariness. He was fifteen years younger than I and happily married, but his grinning good looks, cheeky sense of humor, and sensitivity, which lay closer to the surface than he would have liked, touched my inner kids. They developed a lighthearted crush on him and flirted outrageously. He and I had begun a good-humored, teasing friendship that I enjoyed a great deal.

We stayed at Camp I only long enough for a snack. We'd met our objective in climbing through the Icefall: it wouldn't be the unknown obstacle to us anymore on this trip. On the way down, Guy placed himself between Christine and Ken, and me. Like Rob on the ascent, Guy used his humor and sensitivity to support us all the way to the foot of the Icefall where we were met by Ang Tsering, our sirdar, and several of the Sherpas, armed with hot drinks and welcoming handshakes.

That evening the entire team gathered in the large blue dining tent after dinner to celebrate Gary Ball's fortieth birthday, and Chhongba, our very talented Sherpa cook, slipped through the flap from the kitchen tent holding a beautiful layer cake decorated with "Happy Birthday Gary." As many of the Sherpa crew as could squeezed in around the edges, and we all sang "Happy Birthday" and toasted this man who had led us to Camp I and back and now was being a gracious, entertaining host.

Gary nodded his head modestly saying, "Thank you one and all," as he grabbed for a bottle of bourbon. Twisting off the cap, he hurled it into a far corner of the tent. "Oops, I dropped the top. I guess we'll have to drink it all."

The Sherpas uncovered previously hidden bottles of Nepali beer and rum, setting them on the level pile of flat rocks covered in blue plastic that served as our dining table. Someone snapped a cassette tape of rock music into the Walkman that had been plugged into speakers hanging from the tent's metal frame, and the music began to blare. It was clear that we were having a party.

An hour later I pushed the flap of the tent aside and headed for the artfully constructed rock platform in the far corner of our camp that served as the toilet. Crosby, Stills, and Nash's voices singing "Suite Judy Blue Eyes" were filtered through the blue walls, serenading me on my errand. The black sky was a loosely woven fabric of shimmering stars. There was no moon, yet the Icefall seemed to glow with its own eerie light. Was it possible that only six hours earlier I had been descending through the maze of fixed lines and ladders and giant seracs? Not only possible, but true.

Giggles came from the dining tent, and Chantal's distinctive laughter echoed between the mountain walls, bringing me back to the cold night air. I continued on my mission, eager to return to the celebration. As I approached the tent once again, I heard a rhythmic stomping inside, and when I entered, I was greeted by Chantal, surrounded by three Sherpas, all dancing on the table! Chantal's great strength in the mountains was balanced by a strong spiritual base from which she lived exuberantly. "Margo, come on. Come dance with me."

Her enthusiasm was irresistible. I joined her, as did most of the expedition. The party lasted well into the night, certainly the first disco to be seen at Base Camp. At one point Jan, Helen, Chantal, and I danced and lip-synched the words to the song "I Need a Man," accompanied by hoots and hollers from the men. It was after midnight when I finally crawled wearily and happily into my sleeping bag. The lighthearted energy of the Kiwis blended well with their dedication on the mountain and underlined their stated desire to have everyone reach the summit of Everest and enjoy the process.

After three more days of rest and acclimatization in Base Camp, including a day spent waiting as a snowstorm blew across the glacier, my second climb to Camp I took me eight hours, even longer than the first trip. I was constantly distracted by a flash of blue ice over to my right or a fascinating formation off to my left. Even the process of crossing a 10-foot wide crevasse on a ladder intrigued me, and the way the bright sunlight was absorbed in the darkness of its depths gave me a sense of awe. Martha's voice became a litany. "Too long. It's taking you far too long. You'll never get to the top. You might as well turn around now."

The voices of Jonathan and Ray and my inner guides encouraged me on. "You're doing great, Margo. Be present. This is all a gift for you. Enjoy it."

The next day I lay on my side in the warmth of the sun just behind the tents at Camp I, curled around a water bottle struggling to keep drinking and not throw up. Like last year in this same place, my head pounded from altitude sickness, I was dehydrated from the resulting nausea, and I'd been vomiting at regular intervals. My teammates teased me mercilessly, many of them themselves having experienced the same misery at one time or another in the mountains, knowing that laughter was often the best way to take the mind off how badly the body felt.

Jan, relaxing on her Therm-A-Rest next to me, worked a crossword puzzle and tried to distract me from my misery by reading the definitions aloud. "What's a four-letter word for 'Japanese aborigine?' " she asked, chewing on her pencil.

"I have no idea," I groaned.

From inside his tent Gary called out, "I'll bet you know this one, Maggot. What's a five-letter word for acclimatization?"

"I give up, Gary," not even wanting to hear his answer.

"Vomit," he answered with a laugh.

"Damn," I replied and rolled over, obeying his instruction.

My headache was gone the second morning as we prepared to walk up the Western Cwm to 21,500 feet and Camp II, but my stomach was still unsettled, and I was weak from lack of food and fluids. Despite my love for the Cwm, I didn't look forward to the trip. The first hour of the route wove around and across the crevasses in the transition between the Cwm and the Icefall. The angle of the glacier increases there, and the ice begins to tumble like a very slow motion waterfall ending at Base Camp. Some of the wider crevasses required ladders, but we jumped across the smaller ones as if they were small streams swollen by spring runoff.

Clouds had closed in as we left Camp I, surrounding us with white. The air was filled with swirling snow, and my sense of space became altered, tilted, ungrounded as we moved toward Camp II. In the whiteout I could only determine the way by the footsteps of others in front of me. The resulting vertigo and my memories of being lost on Vinson increased the uneasiness in my stomach. My feet became lead weights and the muscles seemed to be missing from my legs. Though not roped, five of us followed closely behind one another so we wouldn't lose our way in the soft blanket that effectively closed out the rest of the world. I was moving very slowly, but despite my protestations, Rob insisted that I lead. Although he didn't say it, Martha was sure it was so I didn't get left behind.

After the first hour, the route eased into a low-angle, easy meander with crampons up the left side of the Western Cwm. When I had walked it in 1992, I had moved well and was strengthened by the awe I felt at being in this incredible valley surrounded by the walls of some of the highest mountains in the world. On this day the mountains were concealed by the smothering whiteness, and the route seemed endless. The four-and-a-half hours it took to reach Camp II were some of the most difficult physical times I've ever had in the mountains.

The mildly increased angle of ascent just below Camp II required my stopping every few minutes. "Hold it," I mumbled yet another time and stopped, leaning on my ski poles for support. "I'm sorry, Rob," I said, shaking my head in embarrassment and fighting back tears.

"No problem, Margo. We're making good time and there's no rush. Camp isn't going anywhere." He had taken back the lead and now stepped down to me, the end of a climbing rope in his hands. "Let's help you out a little." He tied me into the rope and then attached it, only a few feet away, to his own harness. When he turned and continued up the hill, the rope pulled me forward. Short-roping he called it. I was being hauled up the mountain. And right then, I was too tired even to care. I felt as if I'd been transported to another world, where my body weighed three times as much as I was used to, where time was warped, each moment seeming to drag on for an hour. I wanted only to go to bed. How could I possibly make it to the summit if I felt like this below Camp II? I was mentally and physically exhausted.

Still totally spent at dinnertime, I wanted to stay in my sleeping bag but knew I needed food and drink. I was done in and spoke to no one. I couldn't get warm and fought tears as I forced down a bowl of soup. I couldn't find the place inside that believed I could climb this mountain. Head aching, stomach lurching, I was devoid of hope of getting any higher and just wanted to go to Base Camp. "You don't have to go down tonight, Margo. Just eat and sleep. We'll decide tomorrow." The words held little comfort for me, and I could not imagine feeling any differently in the morning.

After twelve hours of nearly comatose sleep, I awoke feeling like my own body had been returned to me, able once again to touch the place of hope where my dream of climbing this mountain lived. I dressed and walked out of my tent into the growing heat of a sunny day in the Western Cwm. The sun's rays bouncing off the ice of the valley floor and walls created nature's own reflector oven. The tents would soon become too hot to stay in.

It was a day of rest and acclimatization, one of several before we moved any higher on the mountain. During the afternoon Jan and I sat on our air mattresses in the sun, once again testing our altitude-impaired brains with crossword puzzles. Jan, officially the expedition doctor, was also on the climbing permit. Although her initial plan was to remain at Camp II, she was exceptionally strong and had climbed very quickly through the Icefall. The idea of going higher on the mountain, perhaps even to the summit, was clearly in her mind as we tossed crossword clues back and forth to one another, laughing at the sluggish manner in which our minds worked at over 21,000 feet, and talked about what it would be like even closer to the summit.

"You seem much better, Margo. I felt so badly for you last night." Jan had a warm and caring heart, and we were fast becoming friends on this climb, able to talk about life and love and things that were important to us back home. She and Rob adored each other. They were two people who clearly were meant to be together, and it was a joy to be around them. She continued with her encouragement. "It's so awful to have to climb when you feel shitty. You managed very well."

"Thanks. I appreciate that. I felt hopeless last night. Exhausted and ashamed Rob had to short-rope me. I don't know how I would have gotten to camp any other way." The memory of the previous afternoon was still fresh, and it was easy to touch the feeling of exhaustion and shame.

"You'd been sick, Margo. Anyway, it doesn't matter what yesterday looked like. You got here. And this is today. A different day. And look how you've bounced back! I admire your gumption. So what's a ten-letter word for 'personification'?" I looked at her blankly, and we laughed again at how slowly our minds were working.

As I had anticipated, the women on this climb, particularly Jan and Helen, were making an enormous difference for me. I could share my fears and doubts with them as well as my hopes and dreams. I didn't have to keep my feelings hidden away as if they were somehow wrong. By bringing my fears into the light, they dissipated; the dreams seemed possible.

*   *   *

I hit an emotional wall the day before we were to climb to Camp III. It looked a lot like the Lhotse Face, which rose 27,923 feet and stood like a bridesmaid dramatically at the head of the Cwm next to Mount Everest, providing a natural access to Sagarmatha's summit. Days before succumbing to my illness last year, I'd climbed a few pitches up the fixed ropes secured by ice screws and pickets. I had found the climbing intimidating, and my memory of its difficulty had been magnified by not going back up. Unresolved feelings of intimidation had grown into fear during the last ten months.

Sitting in my tent at Camp II, feeling my body struggle to adjust to the 21,500-foot altitude, my fear showed its many faces, each one a different question colored with self-doubt. Would I get sick again before I had a chance to go higher? Should I go down to Base Camp with Veikka today? Would I be able to handle the constant cold and exhaustion climbing at Camp III and above? Was I too slow to make the sustained effort needed for summit day? I talked about some of my fears with Gary as we sat in the community tent that evening.

He looked up from the cup of cocoa he was holding in his hands for warmth, "Maggot, sometimes you just have to pick your commitment level and go for it." His brown eyes looked deeply into mine, speaking the strength of his own commitment to climbing and to life.

It sounded so easy when he said it. I didn't know what mine was. That didn't seem to be my way. I could only put one foot in front of the other until I couldn't do it anymore. What if Gary's way was the right one, the one that would get me up the mountain? Slowly, my truth emerged from the cloud created by my fear. Radical trust. My spiritual guides and my own heart were what I could rely on. Not my mind's ability to figure out what was right or wrong, not by following someone else's way. I'd tried that last year and failed. I'd know what I was supposed to do when I was supposed to do it—not before. Being on Mount Everest for a second time and preparing to climb the Lhotse Face was already a miracle, an incredible victory in itself. My task was to show up and find out what the Universe had in store for me.

The next morning I walked strongly up the Cwm to the foot of the Lhotse Face, following Rob's long-legged stride. The plan for the day was for us to make the two-hour hike to the bottom of the Lhotse Face, then spend a couple of hours climbing the fixed lines that protected climbers from falls down the ice of the Face. Rob and I started two hours behind the others. I'd been up all night with severe menstrual cramps and had asked for a couple of hours of extra time for the medication I'd taken to begin working. Was it as a sign of God's perverse sense of humor that I once again started my period on a day requiring sustained effort on a mountain?

Within an hour of leaving camp, the pain was gone, and I felt strong and healthy in the startling beauty of this magical valley. I was in my "Go Mode," walking and breathing rhythmically, my mantra singing in my head: God's love, God's strength, God's will, I can. I could and I was.

When we reached the beginning of the fixed lines, Rob and I took a water break. We were standing above 22,000 feet, looking down the length of the Western Cwm, across the Khumbu Glacier to 23,442 foot-high Pumori, its summit rising only slightly above us. Jonathan's spirit felt very close.

"Rob, this is truly magnificent." My words were inadequate.

"That it is, Margo, that it is."

He, too, studied the view as if to memorize it. He had been there several times before, both as a climber and a guide and had already stood on the top of Everest three times. His reverence for it had not faded with familiarity. It was that depth of feeling, as much a part of him as his strength and leadership ability, which had drawn me to him, even in Antarctica.

Rob broke my reverie as he placed a hand on my shoulder and nodded at the bottom of the fixed ropes. "Let's head up, pal."

"You got it." I smiled, reminded once again of Skip. The two men were alike in many ways, including their guiding styles: supportive rather than autocratic teachers who placed importance on the process of the expedition as well as on reaching the summit. I attached my ascender onto the first rope, dug the points of my crampons into the ice and began to climb the Lhotse Face.

Less than two hours later, we met the rest of the team as they were heading down.

"Maggot, you're moving well today," Gary called to me from the top of the section of line I was ascending. I tilted my head back to look up at him and waved my thanks for his encouragement. There was a fairly flat section of ice at the top of this length of fixed line, and once there I unclipped my ascender and moved aside to greet the others waiting there. "We only turned around a wee while ago," Gary said. "You've made good time coming up here."

In four hours of climbing, I'd made up one and a half of the two-hour time deficit I'd started with. My "Go Mode" had stayed with me while I climbed the ropes, a first time I'd felt it on terrain this steep. I felt strong and knew I could have made it to Camp III if it had been on the agenda. It wasn't, and Rob decided that we would return with the others.

I looked out once again over the Western Cwm. From the shelf where we stopped I could see all the way to the top of the Icefall. "Gary, how high do you think we are? Looks like we're even or above Pumori."

"We're certainly above seven thousand meters, Maggot. Maybe closer to seventy-one hundred. Higher than last year, yes?" Gary remembered that my first goal was to get higher on the mountain than I had last year. Rob and I had moved up the 35-degree pitch for close to an hour and a half, much longer than last year. Clearly it was a new personal high altitude for me. I felt proud: I knew I could get to the summit.

I turned to head down, then stopped. "Hey, Rob. Just in case I don't get back up here, I'd better take a picture. Do you mind?"

"Glad to, my friend." He took off his gloves and reached out for my camera. "But you'll be back."

"I believe that." I felt the same conviction his voice had projected across the Cwm. "But I'd hate to have something happen and not have a photo."

"Smile," he commanded. And I did. The next time I was here, it would be on my way to Camp III. I'd faced my fears and walked through them once again. I had no doubts about being able to reach Camp III when the time came.

The climb down was uneventful, bright sunshine heating our bodies, allowing us to move in lightweight Capilene layers. From time to time, I'd realize that I was climbing down the Lhotse Face on Mount Everest into the Western Cwm. Sometimes I'd allow myself a glimpse between Nuptse and the west shoulder of Everest to Pumori standing proudly across the valley. As I walked down the Cwm, my crampons creaked with each step in the ice and snow. I laughed, filled with the awe of my being there and thought to myself, "Ho hum. Just another uneventful climb back to Camp II on Mount Everest."

We left on our planned descent to Base Camp early the next morning to avoid moving through the Icefall in the heat of the day. Continual freezing, melting, and refreezing made the ice unstable, increasing the chances of injury and death as the sun softened the ice. The light was miraculously clear, crystallizing the beauty and magic of the Western Cwm in my memory. I walked by myself, accompanied only by the squeaking of my crampons on the snow, moving quickly to get the circulation going in my cold toes, feeling strong and confident. I could almost feel the spirits of Jonathan and Skip walking beside me.

I first saw the Cwm in one of Jonathan's photographs from the 1976 Bicentennial Expedition. Since then it had hung on the wall in my living room wherever I lived, through all the misery and joy, addiction and recovery, despair and dreams, serving as a banner of possibility, a glimmer of hope in the darkness, a whispered voice that said, "Margo, you can." Jonathan's voice through his photograph, believing in me when I had no faith left. Being in the Cwm the previous year had been a dream come true all by itself, and the memory of Skip and me standing side by side on its ice, surrounded by the horseshoe of giant Himalayan walls, reveling in being in this place that both of us had dreamed about for so long was one I'd carried with me throughout my preparation to return. The words Skip spoke just before he left Base Camp last year, "It makes sense for you to come back next year. You have a reasonable shot at the summit," had become a mantra for me, giving me access to energy and hope when I became discouraged. As I moved down the ice, I smiled and raised my right hand to my forehead in a salute to the two men who had played such a huge part in bringing me to this place of my dreams.

Two hours later, the salute and the wonder were forgotten as I struggled through the icy maze. My strength decreased with each step as I descended. My chest was gripped in an unseen vise, and my lungs began to complain. I fought to hold in coughs that threatened to pitch me off the unstable ladders and left searing pain in their wake.

I had felt so great when I left Camp II. What happened? It seemed that my body was once again betraying me when I needed it most. "Dear God, what is this about?" I asked silently. It all felt too familiar. Why was this happening again?

Martha was the only voice that answered. "I told you so. I told you that you couldn't do it. I told you that you should have stayed home." Racked by another coughing spasm as I made my way to my tent, I wondered whether she was right after all.

I walked slowly to the dining tent to bolster myself with a cup of hot chocolate before Jan examined me. Her diagnosis? Bronchitis. Again.

Three days later I sat in the sun in front of my tent, tired, unwell, discouraged. I had been awake coughing for most of the night, and that morning I felt beaten. I couldn't imagine going back up the Icefall for any reason. Thoughts of being done, of just not wanting to continue putting out the effort anymore filled my mind. And yet during the night, even in the midst of the coughing, I had a clear positive image of getting to Camp III. My body was mired in a bog of physical and emotional exhaustion, but my spirit didn't seem to recognize those limits.

Base Camp was filled with climbing energy as people prepared to head back.

It was a year to the day since we'd come down from the many

nights at Camp II last year. I was ill then, too. There appeared to be many similarities between this year and last, yet I knew that was only how it looked on the surface. Guy stopped by my tent to check on me.

"How're ya going, Maggot? Any better?" He crouched down next to me.

I let my book drop into my lap. "I'm getting there." I hoped the words would make it true.

"I thought it might help you to know that last night Gary and Rob and I were talking about the trip and climbers we've been with. We all commented about how much courage and dignity you show under tough conditions. We really like having your determination and positive attitude around."

"Thanks." I had tears in my eyes and didn't have to hide them as he wrapped me in a heart-soothing bear hug. I wished I could see myself through his eyes. All I could do was take care of myself the best I knew how and keep listening to my heart and my body.

I looked up at the jumble of ice leading to Camp I and reminded myself, "This is my climb and my choice. There will be no disgrace or failure in not going back up. Martha is wrong. I am a real climber. I'm not superhuman or obsessively driven or able to shut down my feelings anymore. I *am* strong and determined and whole. I may not be a world-class climber but I am a real one. And, more important, I'm a real person." The truth was that I'd already reached a summit higher than I could have imagined just by showing up. I had no idea what would happen next. One day at a time I could accept what was presented to me and allow my heart to enjoy the beauty, camaraderie, and fun of being there in that place at that time.

The entire team had been in Pheriche, resting, for three days. It had been almost two weeks since I descended to Base Camp, where I remained while the rest of the climbers went back up the mountain to climb to Camp III before returning to Base Camp. Although I was free of infection, my lungs were still greatly impaired. One morning while I was in Base Camp, I'd awakened feeling strong and hope had returned, only to be dashed the next day, when Helen and I climbed to the top of Kala Patar and I fought for air during three coughing and wheezing attacks that brought me close to the point of passing out. Clearly something was still wrong.

The previous day I'd walked by myself over the ridge to Dingboche. The trail was steep, switchbacking to a point almost 500 feet above Pheriche. Long before I reached the top it became clear that going back on the mountain would be dangerous. My lungs simply weren't working well.

With medication and the lower altitude, I wasn't really sick anymore. Martha kept saying it was all in my head and I was only taking the easy way out. My heart knew better. We'd finished breakfast and Rob was heading out of the teahouse where we were staying to radio Base Camp when I called out to him.

"Rob, can I talk to you for a minute?"

He stopped and smiled. "Sure, friend Margo, what can I do for you?"

His friendly face made it a little easier to say the words I'd been dreading. "I'm not going back on the mountain. I don't know what's going on but I'm not getting any better, and it's clear I don't have the strength or lung power to function up there. It's just not going to happen." Tears rolled down my cheeks. I couldn't look at Rob. "I'm done," I said.

He put an arm around my shoulders and pulled me close beside him. "It's a smart decision. I'm sorry to hear it but I believe it's the right one. You could put yourself in real jeopardy if you tried to go back up. You're smart to listen to your body." He gave me a squeeze that telegraphed his support and understanding. "Are you going to want to go down?"

I leaned back so I could look up into his face. My tears mixed with a smile as I said, "Are you kidding? I wouldn't miss your summit attempt for anything. Especially not with Jan making a go at it. I'm the best cheerleader you'll ever have."

Rob smiled broadly, "That you are, Margo, that you are."

I watched Rob walk away to the slight rise across from the teahouse from where radio reception was the best and was aware once again of how different my experience was from last year's. The results might look the same but the experience had been totally different. This year the three guides had been supportive of the importance of listening to and expressing one's heart, and it had changed the whole atmosphere of the trip for me. As word spread among the rest of the climbers and crew that I wouldn't be climbing anymore, many sought me out to offer their encouragement and support. I felt as if the truth of who I was had been seen and was being acknowledged by everyone, climbers and Sherpas alike.

My choice was physically determined but my heart and my spirit were in total agreement. I knew that my own experience of the next three weeks would depend on my attitude. It could be a fight filled with regrets, recriminations, and self-judgment or a celebration of my spirit, of getting as high as I had, of being in this incredible place, and of supporting others in their quest for the summit. I chose the latter.

It was 6:00 A.M. in Base Camp and the prayer flags hung absolutely still. We were enshrouded in low clouds. A light snow fell, creating a quiet that was almost mystical, raising havoc with the generator and prohibiting radio contact with our summit team as they made their way from the South Col toward the summit ridge. Even the Goraks were exceptionally quiet, as if they, too, awaited news from above.

I was in the dining tent slowly drinking my second cup of coffee, watching Helen sleep on the bumpy stone bench across from me. She'd chosen an uncompromising bed that required near-death exhaustion on which to sleep. I smiled fondly, hoping that her rest could be uninterrupted. She'd had little sleep in the last three days as our team moved from Camp II to III and yesterday to the Col on their way to the summit.

I had grown close to both Jan and Helen during the time following my return from Camp II. They both listened to my frustration and self-doubt while affirming my faith in my choice not to climb. I, in turn, listened to Helen's frustration, self-doubt, and pride in maintaining the high level of logistical functioning in Base Camp, really a small village requiring planning and diplomacy. Her giving heart was as open to the world as mine, and we both felt things deeply, crying easily, whether in joy or sadness.

Our team was one of several expeditions that had left the South Col between midnight and 1:00 A.M. Rob had called on the radio before they left and reported that the weather was perfect: a temperature of 10 degrees below zero, virtually no wind, and bright stars beneath a half moon. He said he wouldn't check in again until it was light but we monitored the radio all night anyway. So far there'd been nothing but static. Helen finally succumbed to sleep about 4:30, still within earshot of the radio.

The clouds began to clear about 10:00 A.M., and at 11:00 we finally heard Rob's voice, intermittently through the static and dead air spots, "Base Camp, Base Camp."

Helen, awake since 8:00, ran to the radio. "Hello, Rob, we read you. Over."

Rob's voice repeated, "Base Camp, Base Camp, this is Rob. Over." Obviously he couldn't hear us. "We're on the South Summit. Over."

"Yes!" Helen and I cheered in unison, excited at the news.

"Weather is good. Gary, Guy, and Chantal have turned around but are all right. The rest of us are here and going well. Will call again from the summit. Rob, out."

Rosalind, Ang Tsering, and several of the crew were in the mess tent and heard the message as well. We all chattered away at once. Helen and I hugged and immediately wondered aloud what had happened with Chantal and Gary and Guy.

"Well, Rob said they were okay so we'll find out later what happened." Helen was able to set the question aside pragmatically, but the implications of the rest of what Rob said touched her deeply. "God, Margo, Jan's on the South Summit!"

We couldn't help but be especially excited for Jan. She'd moved so well and strongly on the lower mountain that it just seemed appropriate for her to keep going. She was lean, compact, and incredibly fit, and her determination fueled a strength that never buried her sensitivity. The prize of the summit would be a fit reward for the support she gave so freely to everyone else.

I'd stopped by her tent the night before she left for the summit and given her the guardian angel pin that had been given to me by a friend in San Diego. "This will keep you safe. Climb from your heart and think of me on the summit." Jan talked openly about her fears and the certainty of only being able to go one camp at a time. She said that thinking about the totality of the climb was too overwhelming even to consider. I knew exactly what she meant.

Cheers rose from other camps around noon as various teams reached the summit. Helen and I paced in the communications tent, unable to sit still, unwilling to leave the radio. Rosalind sat quietly, head down, as she had ever since she was told that she, too, was ill and not going back on the mountain. And we waited.

It was almost 1:00 P.M. when the radio crackled to life, injecting us with adrenaline. "Hello Base Camp. This is Everest summit." The tent erupted in cheers, drowning out the rest of Rob's words.

Helen shouted into the radio, "Rob, that's terrific. We read you loud and clear. Congratulations. Is Jan with you?"

There was a pause, and then we heard, "Hello, Helen. I'm here." Jan's voice was soft and breathless as her words came to us from the top of the world.

"Oh, Jan, that's terrific." Helen's overwhelming joy coming out as a classic understatement.

I leaned over the microphone and added, "Bravo, Jan. We're all delighted for you."

"Thanks, Margo, we'll see you soon."

Another pause, then Rob's voice replaced Jan's with logistical tasks for Helen. Jan, Rob, Veikka, and John had reached the summit with Ang Dorje, Chhumbe, and Nuru. Helen and I hugged each other fiercely, rejoicing in their success while Rosalind smiled, then Helen turned to the satellite system to establish a telephone link between Veikka and a Finnish radio station. He was the first Finn to climb Everest and the station wanted a live interview. Such technology could not have been envisioned forty years earlier when Sir Edmund Hilary first stood on the summit.

I walked outside and sat on a rock looking up at the Icefall, the bright sunlight now revealing its rugged mass. "Keep them safe on the way down, God," I asked silently. My strong delight in our team's success collided with my own intense disappointment at not being with them. I had reached the end of my dream of standing on the highest point on Earth. I knew at a heart level that I would not return a third time. My quest for the Seven Summits was over. I wept, wanting to be held and rocked and comforted, sensing that inside I was doing just that for myself.

Word reached us that evening that everyone from our team had returned safely to the Col. More than thirty people had reached the summit that day, among them climbers and Sherpas from the British team, the Aussies including Lobsang, climbers from Todd's team, some Korean women, and climbers from the American Sagarmatha expedition whose summit team included Dolly Lefever. I remembered Dolly fondly from Denali and had been pleased to discover she was here. I had gone to the American Sagarmatha camp to find her, and we had chatted for quite a while: about the difficulty she was experiencing being the only woman on her expedition, about my dream of climbing the Seven Summits, about it specifically not being a goal of hers, although this was the fifth of the seven for her, and about the presence on Todd's team of Sandy Hill Pittman who was, like me, trying for her seventh summit. Sandy and I had spoken several times but had never discussed our being in competition with one another to be the first American woman to complete all seven. Dolly's success that day was almost as great a cause for rejoicing for me as was Jan's. It was a day of success and celebration.

The next morning, Gary called from the Col with bad news. A miscommunication between exhausted climbers the night before had resulted in the report that all climbers were safe there. In fact, Lobsang had not returned from the summit the previous day. He'd talked with an American about an hour below the summit on the way down but no one remembered seeing him after that. Gary said there was hope that Lobsang was still alive somewhere above the Col, and although any search above 8,000 meters is both difficult and dangerous, several climbers had made the supreme effort to head back up toward the summit to assist him if they could.

His body was found two days later, 300 meters above the Col. He'd apparently fallen down a rock gully and been killed instantly. We'd pretty much given up hope of finding him alive by that time but the confirmation was still devastating. Helen and I had both grown very fond of the Australian team and dealt with our own grief by supporting them. I hadn't known Lobsang well but his death touched me deeply. It was the first time an acquaintance of mine had been killed on a mountain while I was present. It was the second time on this expedition that our team had been touched by death.

Two weeks earlier, the Nepali women's team had sent Pasang Lamu and three Sherpas to the summit in what many considered an attempt made too early in the season to be safe weatherwise. The extreme weather created by Everest provides for very narrow and somewhat predictable windows of opportunity to reach the summit. Their expedition's timing seemed to be motivated by the drive for her to be the first Nepali woman to reach the summit, ahead of another expedition in Base Camp containing both Nepali and Indian women. The four did reach the summit in strong winds but Pasang was exhausted on the descent and stopped just below the South Summit in deteriorating weather, refusing to continue. Her sirdar, Sonam Tsering, stayed with her and sent the other two Sherpas down to the Col to get more oxygen. They had no radios. The two Sherpas were exhausted when they reached the Col, and were too weak to return immediately. Pasang and Sonam Tsering were never seen alive again. It was thought that Pasang did not survive the night and when Sonam tried to descend on his own the next day in poor visibility, he walked off the edge of the 7,000-foot Kangshung Face.

Sonam had been Rob and Gary's climbing sirdar the year before, and they were deeply affected by his death. They lost a friend under circumstances that seemed preventable.

Three deaths already on the mountain. There had been four the year before, but none of them had touched me personally. Now I experienced my own sadness and that of my friends like a heavy shroud surrounding the beauty and mystique of the mountain.

I spent the afternoon at the foot of the Icefall, welcoming our team back down and celebrating with those who'd reached the summit. Jan and Rob were the last to arrive, and it was a joyous time. The dark veil of death was not forgotten but was lightened by the joy of their accomplishment. I walked back to camp with the two of them, listening to Jan's tales of summit day, carried by mixed-up swirls of shared joy, sadness, and disappointment.

That evening, our communications tent became the center for dealing with the logistics of Lobsang's death. We doled out tea and biscuits to the many people who had been close to him and who now grieved. It got to be too much for me, and I went outside to the large rock that had become my refuge. The Icefall was gorgeous in the dark of the evening. Lobsang's tent, not far in front of me, was silhouetted against it. I cried hard, tired tears. Jonathan's energy was palpably present and then, as my tears subsided, was joined by Lobsang's, bringing a comforting sense of calm. I stood up and turned toward the mess tent. I was ready to go home.

Over the next two days we broke camp and began the walk to Lukla.

Gary and I talked about climbing as I rubbed his shoulders in a teahouse along the way. "Ya know, Maggot, the summit is only the excuse for being here."

It was as if he'd looked into my heart. Of course I felt disappointed at not reaching the summit, disappointed that my dream was at an end. But I'd also experienced challenge, beauty, spiritual peace, new friends, and the incredible satisfaction of knowing I did the very best I could. I'd had the women on the trip to share my heart with, the whole group to laugh with, and the encouragement of all even after my role changed to one of support rather than active climbing. And with the disappointment had come relief when I heard about the terror Jan felt on the summit ridge and the stories of the winds on the Col. A part of me was glad I had a legitimate reason not to climb high mountains again. I felt embarrassed briefly, then let it go.

After three days of sightseeing and good-byes in Kathmandu, I boarded my plane at Tribhuvan Airport, still struggling to keep from coughing. It seemed as if I'd been coughing forever, though in reality it had only been a little over a month. I was beaten up physically, my voice was mostly gone, and I hadn't gotten to the summit. It sounded pretty terrible. It wasn't. My sense that I was supposed to go back had been right. It was worth it all: the money, the training, the mental effort, the fear, the discomfort—all of it.

As the plane lifted off the runway, I closed my eyes and watched the images in my head slowly dissolve from the rocks and ice and Kiwi accents of Everest to the warmth and beaches and friends of San Diego. Soon the beaches would be replaced by the mountains of Aspen and my God Rock. "Thank you God for bringing me back. Thank you for taking me home."

CHAPTER THIRTEEN
Walking Alone...
Together

Friday, February 17, 1995, Aspen
My head and my heart are full of the Khumbu.
It's like an old friend that calls to me with
open arms. The chance to be there with people I
enjoy is jump-up-and-down exciting.

"Hello?" I'd answered the ringing phone and tucked it under my chin, continuing to stir the pot of midwinter spaghetti sauce I was preparing for dinner in my kitchen in Aspen. I had finally found a place to call my own in the mountains of Colorado and was making it my own.

"Margo, is that you?"

"Helen? Hi! This is a surprise." Hearing Helen's Kiwi accent always triggered warm memories of Everest Base Camp in 1993. She'd called a couple of weeks earlier telling me she'd once again be acting as Base Camp Manager. Now, my voice immediately became animated with excitement. "What's up?"

"I'm just working on the trip list and was so excited about who's going to be in Base Camp I had to call and let you know."

"Helen, I'm not sure I ought to hear this. It's going to make me want to be there even more." I knew there were ulterior motives behind her excitement. During the first phone call we'd talked about the possibility of my joining them for a week or so at Base Camp.

Money was tight. I didn't even know if I could get a ticket on a flight. Still, during the two weeks since we had talked about it, I'd fantasized often about going. I'd just finally made the decision the day before not to go. I really didn't want to hear what I'd be missing, but the kids continued to jump up and down. They wanted badly to know who would be there. "Okay, who?"

"Well, Rob and Jan and me, of course, and . . ." She paused for effect, like a kid holding on to a secret just as long as she could, her excitement very present, even on this transpacific call. When she couldn't keep it to herself any longer she added, "Chantal!"

"You're kidding!" I responded, laughing.

"No," she said, "I'm not. And there's more. Guy's working for Rob again, and Mike Groome and Veikka will be there climbing Lhotse. Ken and Frank will be back with Todd, along with Pete. Keith is going to be there doing Lhotse with Brent Bishop, and of course Ang Tsering and Chhongba will be there. Margo, it's going to be incredible! You've just got to come." Then, like an expert salesperson she dropped her heavy close. "Jan says so, too."

A reunion at Everest Base Camp! I immediately loved the concept, yet Martha was running through her own list in my head, "It's expensive. You don't have time. It's a frivolous thing to do."

"Oh, hush," I told her under my breath.

"What?" Helen hadn't heard me clearly.

"Nothing." I moved back quickly to our conversation. "Oh, Helen, I'd love to come! But I need to think about it. There just isn't anything practical about it at all."

"Margo, you're the one who's always telling me to listen to my heart. Well, listen to your heart."

I smiled. Hearing the words I spoke so often to others now repeated to me gave them a different perspective. "Good point. Let me sit with this for a couple of days, and I'll call you back."

"Okay. Don't wait too long. Oh, Margo, I so want you to come."

I was touched by her friendship and genuine desire to have me be a part of Base Camp. "Me, too, Helen." My mind was already racing with possibilities. "We'll see. I'll call you in a couple of days. I love you lots."

"Me, too." Her voice was still filled with excitement and expectation. "Call me soon! Bye."

"Bye." My mind ticked through the details I'd have to attend to, the pieces that would have to fall into place.

The next evening I was relaxing on my couch doing needlepoint, watching the end of a documentary about elephants on television.

For twenty-four hours my mind had been preoccupied with images of returning to Nepal. Was it possible? Could it happen? Over the credits, a voice announced that the next program was about a climb of Mount Everest. My eyebrows lifted in surprise, and I smiled at this "coincidence." Elephants and Everest back to back—what a treat. For the next hour I watched the photographs shot from the summit, listened to climbers describing what it was like to be there, and was buried by an immense wave of sadness.

I felt for the first time in the eighteen months since I'd returned from Everest that I was truly grieving for not having reached the summit. I'd wanted to stand on the top of Mount Everest more than I'd ever wanted anything in my life. More, even, than I'd admitted to myself. I'd wanted it from the depth of my passion for living. And I hadn't made it. Now I would never see the view from the top of the world, nor would I walk the knife edge of the summit ridge. I would never endure the hardship required to be there again, but neither would I experience the fulfillment achieved by those who did. The dream was over, and I felt it deeply, my sadness enveloping me. My dream of being on the summit of Everest was over finally, indisputably and irretrievably finished. Tears flowed freely as acceptance slowly opened my heart.

"It's time to say good-bye, Margo. Go to the mountain and say good-bye." The voice was clear. It was my own truth speaking. I picked up the phone and dialed New Zealand.

"Hello, Helen? I'm coming."

I had to go back to Everest one more time: to connect there with my spirit one more time; to heal the losses I'd experienced in two short years; to set my heart's desire free. I had to go back and now was the time. After my phone call to Helen, after the television programs were over, I sat on my couch and reviewed the last twenty-four months.

Wednesday, June 9, 1993, San Diego
Little steps. That's how I climbed the mountains,
that's how I'll move forward in life.

During the first months after I returned from Mount Everest in 1993, my emotions had been distracted by other events in my life. The excitement of moving to Aspen and taking care of the details involved in selling my home in San Diego; packing my household goods and finding a place to live in my new hometown kept me from having to think about the fact that I'd been to Everest again and hadn't made it to the summit.

On August 5, I'd been pricing items for the moving sale I was going to hold over the weekend. I'd been wandering around the house for a couple of hours making decisions about my belongings. Did I really want to sell that CD? How many books did I want to keep? The insistent ringing of the cordless phone gave me a welcome break, "Hello?"

"Hi, Mig." Dad used the nickname I'd given up fifteen years earlier. My heart skipped a beat. My hand stopped in midair, halfway through the tag I was writing. Even though I'd expected this call all summer, I wasn't really ready for it.

"Is it Mum?" I already knew the answer.

"She died just after five P.M. here in her bed. Quietly." His voice was calm, controlled.

I glanced at the clock. It was almost 3:00 P.M. Pacific time; she hadn't been dead an hour. "Were you with her?"

"No, it seemed like she waited until I wasn't in the house. Chris was with her." It was so typical for Mother not to want to "burden" Dad with his being there when she died. And fitting that Chris had been by her bedside. Their friendship had been held together by a deep love for each other, and Chris was one of only two women with whom Mum had been able to let down her carefully constructed defenses more than a little. Dad said that Mum's other friend Audrey had been with her only an hour earlier.

"Oh, Popeye." My own control was turned up to high, taking its cue from my dad. "We've been expecting it for such a long time, and it's still a shock."

"I know, Mig."

"Are you doing okay?"

"I'm fine." His voice was even, convincing to those who were willing to accept the surface response. "Chris is still here, and we're waiting for the ambulance."

"Okay." I was running out of words and control. "I'll call the airlines and get back to you as soon as I know when I can get there."

"Good. Just let us know, and I'll pick you up."

"Okay, Popeye. I love you."

"I love you, too. I'll see you when you get here." He broke off the connection.

I stood in the middle of my living room, the receiver frozen in my hand for more than a long time. Mum had been ill for such a long time. Even in my very early recovery, I'd wished she could let go. I remembered a conversation we'd had more than ten years earlier. Mother had felt particularly lousy that day, and her eyesight was deteriorating rapidly. No energy, almost no vision, joints swollen and aching, allergic to almost anything synthetic and to most foods, blood sugar volatile, she'd broken down in my arms, a rarity for this woman who'd been so strong.

"Mig, I just don't want to do this anymore. I feel so rotten all the time, and I can't do anything but sit around the house. I can't see to do needlepoint or to play golf, and I don't have the energy even if I could. I can't do anything I want to do. What's the point of living?" I held her as she cried, being a mother to my mother, aware even in the midst of my addictions of how our roles had shifted, aware of how much she hated to lose the tight control she kept on her emotions and fall apart like this, aware of how much I loved her.

"Oh, Mum, I wish I had an answer. I wish I could fix it. But I can't." It was true. There weren't any solutions. All I could do was love her and hold her when she'd let me.

"I know you can't." She reached for a tissue to blow her nose, her back straightening, pulling away from my embrace. "I'm all right now. I'm sorry you had to see that."

"I'm not." For a moment I'd felt closer, more connected to her than ever before. "You have a right to cry and get mad. I wish you'd do it more often."

"It doesn't serve any purpose." Her voice was tightly controlled once again, but I could feel the incredible effort it took to keep her despair hidden.

"It's okay to cry, Mum." We were so different, she and I. "I really do wish you could do it more often." My emotions had been right out on the table since the day I was born while she kept hers tightly under wraps.

The electronic beeps on the phone finally brought me back to the present. I depressed a button, then released it, automatically dialing my travel agent's number.

I called Barb and Meg, then Judy and Ray. Friends came by simply to be with me, letting me run through all the emotions I needed to, sometimes holding me and stroking my head, sometimes helping me put price tags on items for the sale. They didn't expect anything, didn't try to fix anything, just let me be and feel. One minute I'd be rational and calm, attending to some detail, making a phone call, or moving a piece of furniture, the next, I'd crumble into a ball on the floor, sobbing, or stomp my feet in anger. They stayed until I'd cried all the tears and screamed out all the anger I had in me, then let me settle into some quiet time by myself, reminding me they were only a phone call away. I took a hot bath and sat on my bed, writing in my journal:

I love you, Mum. I wish you a joyous freedom from the body that has been such a burden for you. Thank you for being my mom. Thank you for rubbing my head in circles when I was little and for letting me sit in your lap when I needed to cry. Thank you for your generosity. And for your love. I welcome your spirit into my heart to visit anytime. I hope you're not afraid. I think you are. It's OK to be afraid, Mum. I hope you know that now. I love you. Good-bye.

Tears flowed openly and easily as I wrote. Tears of grief for the loss of my mother, tears of a little girl wanting her mother, and tears to fill the hole in my life that would never be filled again.

The flight to New York seemed especially long. I read, watched the movie, chatted with my seatmate, anything to keep my feelings at bay. I thought I'd prepared for this. I'd persuaded myself that I looked forward to the release it would give Mum. But there was no way to prepare for the enormity of the hole I felt inside: My mother was dead. Inside, I rocked and wept, while outside I held myself together, behaving in a way my mother would have been proud of.

When I arrived in Greenwich I noticed a hibiscus plant on a small table in the kitchen of my parents' house, next to the chair from which Mum had lived so much of the last years of her life. The leaves were healthy and green when I arrived in Greenwich but there was no sign of color, not even a bud was visible. Two mornings later, the day of my mother's funeral, that plant wore a magnificent blossom whose dark red center was surrounded by a layer of white, then deepened into the soft yellow of the outer petals. It came, seemingly, from no-where, and I welcomed it as a reflection of my mother's spirit, shining clearly from that bright bloom.

Less than a month after my mother's death, I stood in front of the huge window in my bedroom looking out at the view of the city of San Diego, its lights twinkling, a half moon shining brightly in the sky over Mission Bay. My going away party was in progress downstairs, and my friends had just finished a round of toasts to me, sharing about what I'd meant in their lives. My heart was filled with their love, almost too full, and I needed to be by myself for a little bit.

Leaving San Diego felt bittersweet. I'd allowed people into my life at a level of intimacy I had never known before: Becky, Ray, Maggie, Judy. So much had happened in my seven years in that house: growth, adventure, achievement, fear, grief, joy, love, tears, laughter, healing, change, friendship. My season there was done, and it was time to move on. I turned away from the window and rejoined the people downstairs.

The move to the teeny "doll house" in Aspen went more perfectly than I could have imagined. Its 780 square feet of rustic wood was about a third the size of my town house in San Diego, but it had my required three bedrooms—a master bedroom, guest room, and office—and fit me perfectly. It even had a yard with a small creek running along one edge, creating an atmosphere of peace that called gently to me saying, "This is where you belong, Margo."

In Aspen, I renewed the friendships I'd made while there to train for Everest. I enjoyed spending neighborly time with Leelee and her family. Our homes even shared a back fence! I busied myself with fall chores at 8,000 feet in the Rockies, buying cold-weather clothes and snow tires for my car. I began to run and work out some, but a bout with pneumonia laid me low for five days with a temperature of 102 degrees. The day my fever broke was the first time I'd felt like even answering the phone when it rang.

"Hello?" My voice was weak, my mouth still dry from the fever.

"Margo, is that you?" It sounded like Helen on the other end, but the voice was so quiet I could hardly hear it.

"Helen? This is Margo. Is that you? What a nice surprise." A call from my friend in New Zealand always cheered me up. "Your timing is perfect."

"Margo, I have some bad news." Her nearly inaudible voice presaged the seriousness of what she was about to tell me. "Gary has died on Dhauligiri. I'm sorry to have to be the one to tell you."

I'd answered the phone in the kitchen, and now I had to lean on the counter to hold myself up. "How? What happened? Is Rob okay? Oh, God." I ran out of words.

"I know." Helen's voice was compassionate. "I couldn't believe it either." She went on to tell me the details but I only half heard them. Something about pulmonary edema at Camp IV, not being able to descend in the dark, going down to Camp III the next day and Gary seeming better, then his dying two hours later. Rob didn't even have a chance to say good-bye because he thought Gary was getting better. Rob convinced Veikka to go to the summit in Gary's honor. Oh, God.

"Margo, are you all right?"

I answered her dully. "I'm okay, Helen. Just stunned. Thank you for letting me know. I think I'll go now."

"Yeah. Okay. Look, I'll talk to you in a few days, okay? Margo? Okay?"

I couldn't even answer her for a moment, then I said, "Yeah, okay. Bye," and hung up the phone.

"No!" I yelled at the top of my lungs, grabbing the edge of the kitchen counter for support. "No, god damn it. It's too damn much." I sank to the floor and cried primal sobs that rocked back and forth over huge, dark waves of grief. "Not Gary, too. Not Gary." The ferocity of the sobs was not just for Gary. They were for Lobsang and Mother; Mark and Julie, acquaintances who'd also recently died climbing; and now Gary. Too many people to lose in so short a time. Too many memories to leave behind. Too many empty spaces left inside my heart. Rationally I understood about death and letting go and moving on. But I was feeling the grief of being left behind, so much grief mixing together in my heart. Weakened by the pneumonia, I was still angry and so hurt I wanted to throw things, to curse at God. I had never felt so alone.

"Breathe, Margo. Breathe and hang on. This, too, shall pass." I said the things I had been taught to use in difficult times over the last eight years, but as I made my way down the hall to my bedroom I mumbled, "The hell with all that recovery stuff. It's just too damn much right now."

But I did breathe and I did hang on and it did pass. As it always did—whatever "it" might be. I called Skip to give him the news, then settled into bed with my journal and my memories of Gary. So there was no more Hall and Ball; no more Gary and Rob. My heart reached out to Rob. It was impossible to think of Rob on a mountain without Gary. They fit together like jigsaw puzzle pieces, each with strengths that complemented the other. I'd laughed with Gary and shared my heart with Rob, but they both had given me wholehearted support and concern.

I looked up at the photograph of Gary that held a place of honor on my mantle. It was taken on his fortieth birthday at Everest Base Camp last spring. He was cutting a birthday cake and grinning widely. I smiled at his image and said, "Farewell, my friend. Go safely and well."

The weather turned colder and Aspen traded in yellow-leafed aspen trees and camera-carrying tourists for a winter-long blanket of snow and one-piece-suited skiers. I flew to Greenwich for Christmas but the holiday was subdued. The house there seemed strange without Mum. Barb and I tried in vain to create her traditional, always-perfect crème brulé, only to have it curdle at the last minute. She wouldn't let us forget her, and yet we had a feeling of gratitude and ease, too. A tension had been released in Mum's death, and we all felt it, glad that she was finally at peace.

That January, a long-standing soreness in my shoulders began to interfere with my sleep. My shoulders had first hurt in the summer of 1990 after I had returned from Aconcagua. The pain had simply become a part of my life, and it had been easy to ignore the slow, subtle escalation even while climbing. Finally, it began waking me up at night. The disruption of my sleep patterns sent me to an orthopedic surgeon who sent me to a physical therapist with no improvement. The surgeon then ordered arthrograms, X-rays of dye injected into the joints, and I had just seen him to discuss the results.

When I returned home, I picked up the phone and called Becky. She was waiting to hear my news.

"Hi, Beck. It's me." I was glad she was there to take my call. "Well, there's good news and there's bad news."

"So, what's the good news?"

"That I haven't been making the pain up or exaggerating it."

"And the bad news?"

"The problem is much worse than I thought." I had to laugh at the irony of what I'd found out. "Both rotator cuffs have grade III tears and need full surgery. I'll have surgery on the right one first and spend six weeks in a sling. As soon as I can steer a car with that one, we'll do the left. It'll be almost a year before I'm a hundred percent again. I've scheduled the first one for next week."

"Wow." Becky sounded stunned. "Margo, I'm sorry."

"At least I finally have an answer to the weirdness I've had in my shoulders for all these years. Both the surgeon and the physical therapist were amazed that I've been as functional as I've been with shoulders that look like this." My voice caught briefly as my bravado began to crack.

"Are you okay?" she asked.

"No, I'm not. I'm scared and ashamed. And Martha's telling me, 'Here you go again, dealing with life by having a physical problem. You're just like your mother. If you were really getting better you'd be healthy all the time.'" I was crying now, feeling the fear and shame of the little girl as I stammered into the phone, "Becky, I don't want to have to be sick anymore. I don't want to be like my mom."

"Margo, you are not your mother. Torn rotator cuffs do not mean you'll end up housebound. Come back to the present. We all have different ways in which we manifest our 'stuff.' One of yours is about physical problems. It's one of the ways God has chosen to give you the lessons of your life, and you're learning that. I've watched it change since I've known you. Let go of the shame, Margo." Becky's words were comforting but the shame was still a dark weight.

"I'm tired of whatever is behind this need to be unhealthy, this need to have an excuse to overcome, Beck." I could feel how emotionally spent I was having carried it around for so long. "I want to be able to let it go."

"And what I see is that's what you're doing." Becky mirrored reality to me without distortion. "You're doing the work, and the results are up to God. It's like anything else. Let go of the belief that says it should be fixed. Maybe God will continue to give you lessons through your body. There isn't any shame in that. The shame's been put on you by other people. You can give it back and be gentle with your body. You're doing great."

"Thanks, Beck. I know I'm doing the best I can." As much physical strength and emotional healing as I'd gained in eight years of recovery, I knew that my path was still about progress, not perfection. I was grateful for those around me who loved me enough to share their perspectives and experiences with me. I knew I'd need it as I went through the months of healing ahead.

The surgery on my right shoulder was performed on March 2, 1994, and the left one seven weeks later. The intensive five-day-a-week physical therapy following the surgeries was painful and exhausting and seemed to require most of my available energy. Returning home from an especially difficult two-and-a-half-hour session one afternoon in April, my heart was lightened by my father's voice on the answering machine.

"Hi Mig, it's Dad. I have some news for you. Call us when you get in." Us? Call us? Pop had been dating the woman who had been his executive assistant and good friend for more than thirty years since the beginning of the year. Our whole family had known Peggy for many years, and I was delighted that they were finding so much pleasure in each other's company.

Hoping his news was about a wedding, I dialed the phone. "Hi, Popeye. Is the news what I think it is?"

"Well, now, that depends what you think it is," he answered with a teasing sense of fun in his voice.

"Are you two getting married? Is that it?" I kept my voice calm in case I was wrong.

"You got it," Pop responded, his voice projecting a smile. "August thirteenth."

"Yippee!" I hollered. "I will be there with bells on. Oh, Dad, I'm so pleased for you. I send you a big hug over the phone." We spoke some more, and I talked with Peggy, congratulating her as well and then hung up the phone and sat with my pleasure. My seventy-nine-year-old father was marrying his seventy-one-year-old secretary of thirty-seven years who had never been married. It was a late-blooming love that shimmered in their voices. He had already given her a white Mustang convertible as a wedding present, and they were sailing on the *QEII* to Europe for their honeymoon, returning on the Concorde and then going down to Disney World. I smiled broadly, inside and out and was reminded, once again, of what a wonderful man my father was. We shared many values, although some of mine were dressed in slightly different clothes, and he modeled them well for me. As I continued to grow in my recovery, the similarities became much more apparent than the differences. I looked forward to celebrating his second marriage.

During the summer, my shoulders were healing well and I was itching to get out on the road. Barbara had relapsed a number of times since that first Family Week I'd attended in Tucson when my life had changed. But, she'd finally surrendered to her disease, too, and was living her dream in Montrose, Colorado, on a small ranch of her own. Ever since she'd been a little girl she'd wanted to live where she could be surrounded by dogs, cats, and horses. Now, I could drive to see her place. She took me on a tour of her pastures: one alive with seven mares and their new foals; another with half a dozen handsome ponies, and a third with a number of quarter horses, quietly grazing in the warm afternoon.

"Tweedles, who could have imagined that these two Greenwich debutantes would have ended up as recovering alcoholics living our dreams in Colorado?" We'd used our nicknames ever since I could remember, it was part of the bond we shared.

"Miggie, no one would have believed it." We were both laughing.

Our lives were about miracles that could never have been foreseen. Recovery from our diseases had given us not only our dreams, but so much more besides. And, in a few weeks, our father was going to be realizing some dreams of his own, too.

A little over a year after my mother died, I sat in my chair in the kitchen in Greenwich on the morning of Peg and Pop's wedding. I gazed out at the view that had always had an extraordinarily calming effect on me. It was hazy and still that morning. The pond, green with algae, perfectly reflected the upside-down image of the willow trees beside it. I could hear the cicadas humming, even through the glass door. I looked to my left at the empty chair that I still thought of as my mother's place. I was full of joy for Pop and Peg, but that view would always be my mother's view, as if God had given it to her to soothe her spirit in those tough times. "I love you, Mum. You'll always be my Muvver." The nickname I had used so fondly for so many years pricked my eyes with tears. "I hope you can be happy for Popeye."

As Dad and his new bride left for Europe, my niece Meg and I joined a group led by Skip and Elizabeth for a trip through the Grand Canyon. It was an opportunity for me to return to the canyon. The last trip I'd taken on the Colorado River I was loaded most of the time and didn't remember much about it. It was also a chance for me to share the company of three of my favorite people in the incredible beauty of one of the natural wonders of the world.

On our fourth day on the river, we walked up to the granaries that had been carved out of the rock wall by the Anasazi before Christ was born. I'd visited the same spot in 1985, tired and winded from struggling up the steep switchbacking path leading a thousand feet up from the river. Back then, I'd looked out at the magnificence of the canyon and had to fight back tears as I thought about the chaos of my life: I was fat and couldn't stop eating; I was dehydrated all the time but couldn't stop doing laxatives; I was unable to show up for life much of the time but couldn't stop drinking or taking drugs; I hated who I was when I looked at the mirror and couldn't find any direction for changing. It swept over me in a smothering wave as I stood on the ledge in front of the granaries in 1985.

Nine years later, I sat, slightly separate from the rest of the group, in almost exactly the same spot. The contrasts were striking. The ease with which I hiked up the path was a clear analogy for how far my life had come. This time the spectacular view was a reflection of the wonder that was my life, and my tears were from joy rather than despair. I closed my eyes and breathed in the heat of the sun, relaxed and content.

In my mind's eye I was transported to a stage, my whole support team spread through the audience of thousands of people in front of me: the kids, God, all my guides, and my family and friends were interspersed among all the people I'd touched with my story, all the people known and unknown to me, who carried dreams in their hearts and had given up hope of ever being able to live them. As one, they all stood up and applauded: applauded my courage, my determination, my willingness to walk through fear, to continue to put one foot in front of the other when it felt too hard, to live from the truth of who I am—applauded me, Margo. The image took my breath away, and I put my hand to my chest to remind myself to breathe as I experienced my own value in a way I never had. I looked around, wondering whether anyone else had seen the vision. They were all engaged in their own conversations and reverie, undisturbed by what I'd experienced. The gift had been mine alone.

I returned to Aspen strong, ready for whatever God had in store for me next. I was in transition from macho Margo, very fit mountain climber, to the Margo whom I fondly described as middle-age, menopausal, and marshmallow-bodied. I was becoming a woman who could allow her femininity and vulnerability to coexist with strength and courage.

I had to be vulnerable to let people in, and had learned that vulnerability didn't negate my strength. I could feel my strength in my heart and soul; people didn't need to always see it physically to have it be true. But if I was not doing something extraordinary why would anyone want to be around me? The old question, Martha's question, my mother's question, was still present. The answer came from deep inside. "Because I am Margo: a giving, loving, strong, feminine woman who dares to live from her truth." I believed it more each day.

It was February 27, 1995, my ninth sobriety birthday, and as I got out of my car to celebrate at my regular 7:45 A.M. 12-Step meeting, I waved to my friend Bobby who was walking up the sidewalk toward the redbrick church where the meeting was held. He walked slowly, head down, and didn't see me until I called to him.

"Hey, Bobby, what's up. Are you okay?" He didn't answer, didn't even look at me. I went toward him. "Bobby, what's going on?" He stopped walking and looked at me through eyes that were blank. "Bobby, what is it?"

"Kathy Daily's dead." My knees gave way, and Bobby reached out to grab my elbow and keep me from falling. "And the boys, too."

I felt like someone had driven a pole into my gut. I couldn't breathe. "What're you talking about?"

"Art was driving them home from a hockey tournament in Vail yesterday. They were in Glenwood Canyon and a boulder fell on the car. Art walked away untouched. Kathy, Tanner, and Shea were killed." Tears streamed down Bobby's cheeks. They'd been friends for a long time. She'd been the one who said the words that made him realize he was killing himself with drugs and alcohol. She had inspired him to seek help. He'd often said he was alive because of Kathy Daily. His grief was immeasurable. I'd known Kathy and the boys for only two years but she'd touched my life deeply, too.

Bobby and I walked hand in hand into the meeting. There was no safer place to take our intense feelings that morning than to the people in that room. I could share with them both the joy of my sobriety anniversary and the grief about these new deaths.

Two days later, a crowd packed Harris Hall in Aspen for the memorial service. Mourners overflowed outside and stood in the snow listening to the service on loudspeakers. Art Daily stood on the stage and spoke about his wife and two young sons who had been taken from him so abruptly. He read a poem written by ten-year-old son Tanner, aptly titled "Me, Tanner." In the poem, Tanner expressed his desire to go to Nepal. I was leaving for Everest Base Camp in six weeks.

At the reception following the service, I joined the long receiving line waiting to speak with Art. The line moved forward slowly until I faced the handsome, white-haired man who was wearing his grief with dignity. I hugged him and looked up into his blue eyes, red rimmed from tears. "My prayers are with you. Kathy was a special one, and I hold her and the boys closely in my heart." I paused for a moment, then continued. "Art, I'm going to Nepal in six weeks, into the Khumbu Valley. It's a place that's very special to me, and I would love to take Tanner to the country he so wanted to visit. If you have a photograph of him I could take with me, I'd be honored to find a special place for it there."

Tears came to his clear, blue eyes. He looked down for a moment, then found my gaze. "Thank you. That would be wonderful," he said softly and hugged me close.

As I organized my gear for my return to the Khumbu Valley, I carefully tucked several photographs of Kathy, Tanner, and Shea into the pages of my journal. My spiritual journey back to Everest Base Camp would fulfill dreams beyond my own. On the now-familiar flight from LAX to Bangkok to Kathmandu, my heart was especially open to the journey ahead. For the first time I would be traveling through the Khumbu without the support of a group. A porter took most of my gear from Namche to Base Camp: I didn't want to reinjure my freshly healed shoulders in some fit of unnecessary independence. I had nothing to prove.

A week later I sat on the terrace of the teahouse in Namche Bazaar that still made the best cinnamon rolls in the world. Trekkers filled the narrow streets of Namche buying artifacts from the many shops and vendors. Watching them, absorbing the energy and scenery that was so foreign to most of them, I was struck by how familiar it was to me. I loved having so much history with that exotic place. It was my seventh time in Namche Bazaar. I'd traveled the path between Pheriche and Base Camp ten times and been through the Khumbu

Icefall six. I shook my head in near disbelief at the miracle of my life during the past nine years and took another bite of a cinnamon roll.

Early the next afternoon, I sat on a rock just off the track to Thame, watching a herd of yaks carry supplies bought at the market in Namche that morning back to the Thame monastery. The walk to Thame from Namche was one of my favorites, and I'd chosen it that morning as a way to acclimatize during the layover day in Namche. Jonathan had been with me when I awakened that morning and his spirit walked closely beside me as I meandered in and out of the shadows of an evergreen forest.

As I walked, I became aware of another presence, as well. This one was inside me rather than outside, invited by Jonathan to join us. It was the spirit of me when I was twenty-five: the Margo who chose not to accompany him to Nepal, who chose drugs and eating over following her heart's desire. I felt her awe and gratitude at being here as well as the guilt she still carried about her choices of so many years ago. I stopped walking and welcomed her. Jonathan wrapped his energy around her, as did I, hoping to heal the shame that engulfed her. The part of me that died when I said "no" to Jonathan all those years ago came to life once again. She deserved to be there.

In the dining room of the Ama Dablam Gardens in Deboche, I watched Kaji, my porter, warm his hands in front of the wood stove in the kitchen. It was hot when we left Namche that morning, and now it was snowing. I took a sip of the hot chocolate Kaji had brought me, and memories of the three days I spent here with Vern and Parry in 1993 swirled around me. It was the place where we completed our recuperation, where our health and strength had been restored enough to return to the mountain. It felt good to be back. I had already received many gifts on this trip, the best of which had happened on the hill up to the Thyangboche Monastery earlier that morning.

I was on the lower part of the hill, a long series of steep switchbacks, in my "Go Mode," climbing easily on the internal energy made accessible by my mantra: God's love, God's strength, God's will, I can. Familiar, comfortable, energizing, almost hypnotic.

"Margo, may I walk with you?" I was tempted to look around but I knew the words were not spoken. I felt my mother's presence and welcomed her into this experience I'd wanted so often to share with her. Her fear about my climbing had prevented her from even hearing about the places I'd been and from understanding the deep passion that drove me. Now, rid of the limits her body had put upon her for so long, her spirit joined me and celebrated the beauty of this valley, the strength with which I walked, and the determination and passion with which I lived my life.

"I understand now, Margo, why you came, and I salute you. I'm sorry for putting my own fears and limits on you. Sorry I couldn't have been more supportive of the dream that was so important to you." Her presence was almost physical, walking beside me, drawing on my strength to get up the hill. I believed she did finally understand, and a new bond formed between her spirit and me. We became friends in a way that had never been possible before. It was healing at a soul level—a miraculous gift.

I took another sip of hot chocolate and felt, once again, a level of love and respect between my mother and me that had never been available for us while she was alive.

Two days later, on my way to Chukkung, I rested at the base of the chorten above Dingboche where Jonathan's spirit had been so strongly present in 1989. The wind blew in my face as I breathed deeply, grief filling my heart as if a floodgate had opened, balanced just as powerfully by a deep sense of unconditional love. I'd known the first time I looked at the photographs Art had given me that this was where I would leave the image of Tanner and him.

As I walked here from Pheriche, a small brown hawk appeared over my head, soaring on the wind, playing in its currents, staying directly above me. I was listening to John Denver singing about "the freedom I feel when I fly," and felt Tanner's spirit very strong in the presence wheeling overhead. When I reached the chorten it began circling, rising on the updrafts, and as I placed the photograph under a small rock, the hawk called out, a shrill cry, loud and clear.

I heard a young voice saying, "Tell Dad that I love him. Tell him I'm okay." I turned slowly around, a full 360 degrees, cradled by the surrounding giants: Lhotse, Lhotse Shar, Island Peak, Ama Dablam, Kangtega, Thamserku, Taweche. I hoped that Art could feel Tanner's spirit in Aspen the way I felt it there. It was a marvelous place for him to be playing.

As I walked away, I turned, watching the hawk still playing in the wind. "Enjoy, Tanner," I said. It dipped its wings and disappeared into the Himal.

I grieved as I walked back down the trail. For Kathy and the boys. For Gary, whose spirit was strong there, his smiling face shaded by his ever-present brown trekking hat. For Mother, who was so awed by being there. And Jonathan. I would always think of that as Jonathan's chorten. Yes, there was grief, and so much life as well. I felt the presence of all the people I'd known who had died before their time.

They were all there together. It took my breath away. So much love. And freedom. And peace.

Walking strongly up the Chukkung Valley I was aware of how much I liked the way people I met on the trail responded when they found out that I was going to stay at Base Camp and that I'd been on Everest myself. Being a climber was a large part of who I was, and I liked how people reacted to it. At the same time, I felt the difference between this trip and that of two years ago. Now I knew and liked who I was beyond the climbing and the training. I was okay with being a middle-age, averagely fit woman, content and excited about my life. I could take great pride and joy in what I'd done as a climber without being embarrassed that I was not one now, that I was not climbing anymore. I'd completed a major transition in how I saw myself since I moved to Aspen. It shone with bright clarity there in the place where I had been a climber and was one no longer.

Helen and I sat cross-legged on our respective wooden beds in the little room we were sharing in the Himalayan Lodge in Pheriche. She'd been waiting for me when I returned from Chukkung that afternoon, and we'd been talking and laughing nonstop ever since. Our friendship had been forged on the anvil of time spent under difficult conditions, and we reunited after two years as if it had been only two days. Her presence was a delightful surprise for me, and I enjoyed the prospect of sharing my joy with her as we made the two-day walk through the upper valley to Base Camp. I was also grateful for the opportunity to talk about Gary finally and grieve with someone who knew him. She told me about the memorial service and how the people he loved felt and dealt with his death. It gave me a closure that I'd wanted and needed badly.

Two days later, we reached the large rock that served as a memorial to climbers who had died on Everest, just below where the trail crossed onto the Khumbu Glacier itself. Names and dates had been carved into the rock over the years, covering its surface with the love felt for these climbers whose spirits had been set free on Everest. Although Gary had died on Dhauligiri, he, too, was remembered in this place. A Sherpa friend had carved his name into a stone with the Buddhist chant "Om Mani Padme Hum" and placed the stone on the rock with a kata draped over it as if to give comfort.

I placed a photograph of Tanner and Shea Daily in front of Gary's stone and had a clear image of Gary walking away with the boys on either side of him holding his hands. I couldn't think of anyone better to teach their spirits about the mountains. I walked on with a warm feeling in my heart.

A couple of hours later, Helen and I caught our first sight of Base Camp. "Home," I thought. "I'm on my way home." The climber part of my soul would always think of it that way.

I'd arrived too late for the Kiwi expedition's Puja. But I was able to participate in a personal ceremony Gyeljin was holding to bless particular items for two other members of the expedition: a photograph of the Dalai Lama that Chantal would take to the summit and a Z-stone necklace Doug had bought in Namche Bazaar. Gyeljin, who had once been a lama at a monastery, presented me with a *tsundi*—a piece of orange string to be worn around my neck—into which he tied a pack of barley seeds blessed by the Dalai Lama. It was a special gift, which honored me greatly. Jonathan and Gary were with me during the ceremony, which included Gyeljin's reading of prayers from the Tibetan sacred book written by hand on old parchment, a ritual of chanted prayers, thrown rice and tsampa, and burning incense and juniper. I felt hugely welcomed. I was included and welcomed because of who I was, not what I'd done.

A week later, I stood alone and watched the lovely, almost ghostly images of the climbers throwing rice and breathing the juniper smoke from the fire Ang Tsering kept fed at the Puja place, before they headed up the Icefall for the push to the summit. It was 3:30 A.M., and the darkness of the night sky was lit only by the almost unimaginable brightness of the stars and planets.

Hours later, I sat on a rock above the mess tent, cup of coffee in hand, staring up at climbers moving slowly through the Icefall. I loved looking up and knowing I didn't have to go through the icy, intimidatingly magical maze. It was absolute confirmation that I was done with big mountains. I watched the climbers and fingered the tsundi that hung around my neck, feeling pride, gratitude, pleasure, and fulfillment in what I had done, with no regrets at all.

Jan, Helen, and I followed the progress of our climbers by radio. Over the next four days as they moved ever farther up the mountain, finally leaving the South Col early the morning of May 7 and arriving on the South Summit at 12:10 P.M. They were another one-and-a-half hours from the summit itself and it was a little late, but we were still encouraged.

At 12:45, the American team led by Bob Hoffman radioed that our team was still on the South Summit and that Chantal was not doing well. At 1:00 we heard Guy's voice on the radio calling, "Rob. Rob? Robo. Rob?" Apparently Rob couldn't hear him. Kami called Guy from his radio at Camp II, asking what was happening. There was only silence.

We could only speculate and worry about what was going on.

Half an hour later, we heard that all of our climbers were okay and turning around. It had taken too long to fix the ropes, the wind was picking up, and it was just too late to keep going and be safe. Our radio contact once again disintegrated, and we sat in the mess tent waiting to hear that they had returned to the Col. Word came up in pieces from the Hoffman team that Chantal was very weak on the South Summit, that she collapsed, became incoherent, and was being carried down. We couldn't reach our team by radio, and the fear at Base Camp that Chantal was dead or dying was tangible. No one spoke those words, but we traveled back and forth between our camp and the Hoffman area, anxiously moving from our radio to theirs in search of more information.

Finally, Rob's voice came through saying Chantal was coherent and speaking, though still not able to walk unassisted. We breathed a little easier, trusting that our friend would not die that day. Two hours later, when all were safely in their tents at the Col and we'd heard Chantal's voice on the radio, exhausted but making sense, we allowed our fear to melt into the disappointment of an expedition that didn't reach the summit. It was well after dark. The climbers had been out for almost eighteen hours, and we at Base Camp had run a marathon of emotions, from bright cerulean hope and excitement through dark indigo fear and tension to dull gray relief and disappointment.

The energy level was low the next day, both in Base Camp and on the mountain. No one from the Hoffman team had reached the summit yesterday as some of them were caught in their own life-threatening difficulties, and only one of our Sherpas, Lobsang Zhangbu, a young, long-haired Sherpa of enormous strength, had made it to the top of the world. Our team was making their way down from the Col to Camp II, slowly, carefully, wearily. The events of yesterday had brought home to me with a vengeance how much the mountains and God had smiled on my climbing. Now I felt the validation that I was done.

I had come to Base Camp partly to have fun and partly to bring a closure to my circle of climbing. I was looking for a gentle, spiritual closure, many pieces of which I had experienced. Yesterday, however, the door had been slammed shut and the lock turned. I'd known I was done with climbing before I had come here. That knowledge had simply been driven to a deeper level in a harsh way, I was grateful it was no harsher. The climbers were coming down, and we would leave soon after.

Three days later it was farewell for real. For one final time I sat on a rock looking at the Icefall: majestic, deadly, magical, frightening. This was my final good-bye to an important stage of my life. I left it behind willingly and yet with some sadness as well. I felt at home there at the foot of this tallest of all mountains. Jonathan, Gary, Kathy, even Mother shared this farewell with me. They understood. They knew my heart.

"Oh, Jonathan, how do I thank you for opening my heart to all of this so long ago? I know it isn't ending, only changing, and I still feel sad. I'm almost loathe to leave. And it's time. I'll say my good-byes, take a final photo, and walk away from this place, this part of my life that has been so special to me and for me. It's changed my life in ways I couldn't have imagined. My gratitude and appreciation are boundless." I stood up and, with a final smile, turned away from the mountain, and headed down the glacier. Each step brought me closer to the miracles awaiting me in the future. I was done with climbing high mountains, but so many other adventures beckoned. The adventure of life was the biggest one of all, and I knew I'd be present for it on all levels: one step at a time.

ACKNOWLEDGMENTS

It was clear from the start that this book was meant to be. I tried hard not to write it but too many people said it was a story that needed to be told. The three years that we have been actively involved in the process of creating it have been three of the hardest and most rewarding of my life. There would have been no book without the assistance and support of many people.

I offer unbounded gratitude to Peter Ginsberg, who has been much more than an agent for us. His continual support, enthusiasm, faith, and teaching kept me going when our fears told us to quit. He directed the transformation of two people with a story to tell into authors.

Thanks to Trish Lande Grader, our editor, who pushed us in a way that allowed us to perform at a level we had thought impossible.

Loving gratitude to family: Pop, who supported even from a place of doubting; Barb, who supported from a place of absolute belief; Meg, who supported from a place of love.

And to friends: Becky, whose ten-year friendship sustains me in both the dark and the light times; Kelly, whose journey to becoming a professional writer gave me hope; both for sharing their hearts and lives with me; Joan, Joanne, and Mia, who listen and mirror the truth to me when I am unable to see it; Madeleine, whose support during the final push protected my sanity.

Acknowledgment to all who share my passion for the mountains and for climbing and special thanks to the climbers who, by example as well as words, validated my belief that climbing is about much more than summits. Skip Horner believed when I could not. Rob Hall, Gary Ball, Jan Arnold, and Helen Wilton brought joy to what could so easily have felt only like failure.

To all who walk their own path of recovery and have supported me in mine, thanks for teaching me it is possible to live life from my Truth.

And to Ray: friend, soulmate, co-author. He was a choice from my heart rather than my head; he walked me through the oceans of fear that some days threatened to drown me; because of him, this is the book I envisioned it might be; because of him I am more the person I envision I can be. Thank you from my soul, Ray. Namaste.

—Margo Chisholm
September 21, 1996

ACKNOWLEDGMENTS

I had never thought much about being a writer, let alone writing someone else's story. Then, in the middle of my middle-aged, middle-class life I faced the reality that I was living out someone else's dream, not my own. Crisis, disappointment, and pain became the firm bedrock on which I began to build a new life, from the inside out—a life based on my own truth and passion. As I trudged along my road, I met others living from their new-found courage, too. Ordinary men and women who were living extraordinary lives, some in traditional forms, some by pushing themselves outside of familiar boundaries. Margo Chisholm was one of these.

As a friend and fellow traveler, I watched Margo live out her truth and saw in hers a reflection of my own. She climbed mountains; I began to write. She had a story worth telling, and I began to help her find someone who could write it for her. Then, one day in 1993 she asked me to help put her life into words and that's what I've done. Margo, thank you for trusting me with your soul, for inviting me into the cauldron of the process of co-creation, and, most of all, for continuing to live a life filled with the arduous work of living from a place of truth and dreams.

A wide circle of friends and others have been a part of midwifing my voice as a teller of truth. Judy Reeves' love, grace, and personal courage in including me in her own dreams gave me the place of nurturing and freedom to begin this path. The community of writers who are The Writing Center gave me a place to be born. Jim Gahen, Louis Simpson, and the men of the Masculine Soul taught me how to go within to bring out my truth. Rick and Ashley Geist selflessly shared their craft and passion for the written word. Peter Ginsberg and Patricia

Acknowledgments

Lande Grader brought their personal commitment to telling a story well, and their professional experience, perspective, and resources. And, there were a thousand more. Each word, face, and hug is an integral part of this book.

—Ray Bruce
Aspen, 1996